INCREDIBLE HULKS: DARK SON. Contains material originally published in magazine form as INCREDIBLE HULKS #612-617. First printing 2011. Hardcover ISBN# 978-0-7851-5299-6. Softcover ISBN# 978-0-7851-5001-5. Published by MARVEL WORLDWIDE, INC., a subsidiary of MARVEL ENTERTAINMENT, LLC. OFFICE OF PUBLICATION: 135 West 50th Street, New York, NY 10020. Copyright © 2010 and 2011 Marvel Characters, Inc. All rights reserved. Hardcover: $24.99 per copy in the U.S. and $27.99 in Canada (GST #R127032852). Softcover: $19.99 per copy in the U.S. and $22.50 in Canada (GST #R127032852). Canadian Agreement #40668537. All characters featured in this issue and the distinctive names and likenesses thereof, and all related indicia are trademarks of Marvel Characters, Inc. No similarity between any of the names, characters, persons, and/or institutions in this magazine with those of any living or dead person or institution is intended, and any such similarity which may exist is purely coincidental. **Printed in the U.S.A.** ALAN FINE, EVP - Office of the President, Marvel Worldwide, Inc. and EVP & CMO Marvel Characters B.V.; DAN BUCKLEY, Chief Executive Officer and Publisher - Print, Animation & Digital Media; JIM SOKOLOWSKI, Chief Operating Officer; DAVID GABRIEL, SVP of Publishing Sales & Circulation; DAVID BOGART, SVP of Business Affairs & Talent Management; MICHAEL PASCIULLO, VP Merchandising & Communications; JIM O'KEEFE, VP of Operations & Logistics; DAN CARR, Executive Director of Publishing Technology; JUSTIN F. GABRIE, Director of Publishing & Editorial Operations; SUSAN CRESPI, Editorial Operations Manager; ALEX MORALES, Publishing Operations Manager; STAN LEE, Chairman Emeritus. For information regarding advertising in Marvel Comics or on Marvel.com, please contact Ron Stern, VP of Business Development, at rstern@marvel.com. For Marvel subscription inquiries, please call 800-217-9158. **Manufactured between 12/6/10 and 1/10/11 (hardcover), and 12/11/10 and 7/11/11 (softcover), by R.R. DONNELLEY, INC., SALEM, VA, USA.**

10 9 8 7 6 5 4 3 2 1

THE INCREDIBLE HULKS
DARK SON

CHAPTERS 1 & 4
WRITER: GREG PAK

PENCILS: TOM RANEY

INKS: SCOTT HANNA

COLORS: JOHN RAUCH

CHAPTERS 2-3
WRITERS: GREG PAK & SCOTT REED

PENCILS: BRIAN CHING

INKS: VICTOR OLAZABA

COLORS: JORGE MAESE

CHAPTERS 5-8
WRITER: GREG PAK

PENCILS/BREAKDOWNS: BARRY KITSON

INKS/FINISHES: BARRY KITSON & SCOTT HANNA
WITH JAY LEISTEN

COLORS: MATT MILLA

LETTERS: SIMON BOWLAND

COVER ARTISTS: CARLO PAGULAYAN &
M. JASON PAZ WITH JASON KEITH, GURU EFX,
LAURA MARTIN & BETH SOTELO

ASSISTANT EDITOR: JORDAN D. WHITE

EDITOR: MARK PANICCIA

COLLECTION EDITOR: ALEX STARBUCK

EDITORIAL ASSISTANTS: JAMES EMMETT & JOE HOCHSTEIN

ASSISTANT EDITOR: NELSON RIBEIRO

EDITORS, SPECIAL PROJECTS: JENNIFER GRÜNWALD & MARK D. BEAZLEY

SENIOR EDITOR, SPECIAL PROJECTS: JEFF YOUNGQUIST

BOOK DESIGN: SPRING HOTELING

PRODUCTION: JERRY KALINOWSKI

SENIOR VICE PRESIDENT OF SALES: DAVID GABRIEL

EDITOR IN CHIEF: JOE QUESADA

PUBLISHER: DAN BUCKLEY

EXECUTIVE PRODUCER: ALAN FINE

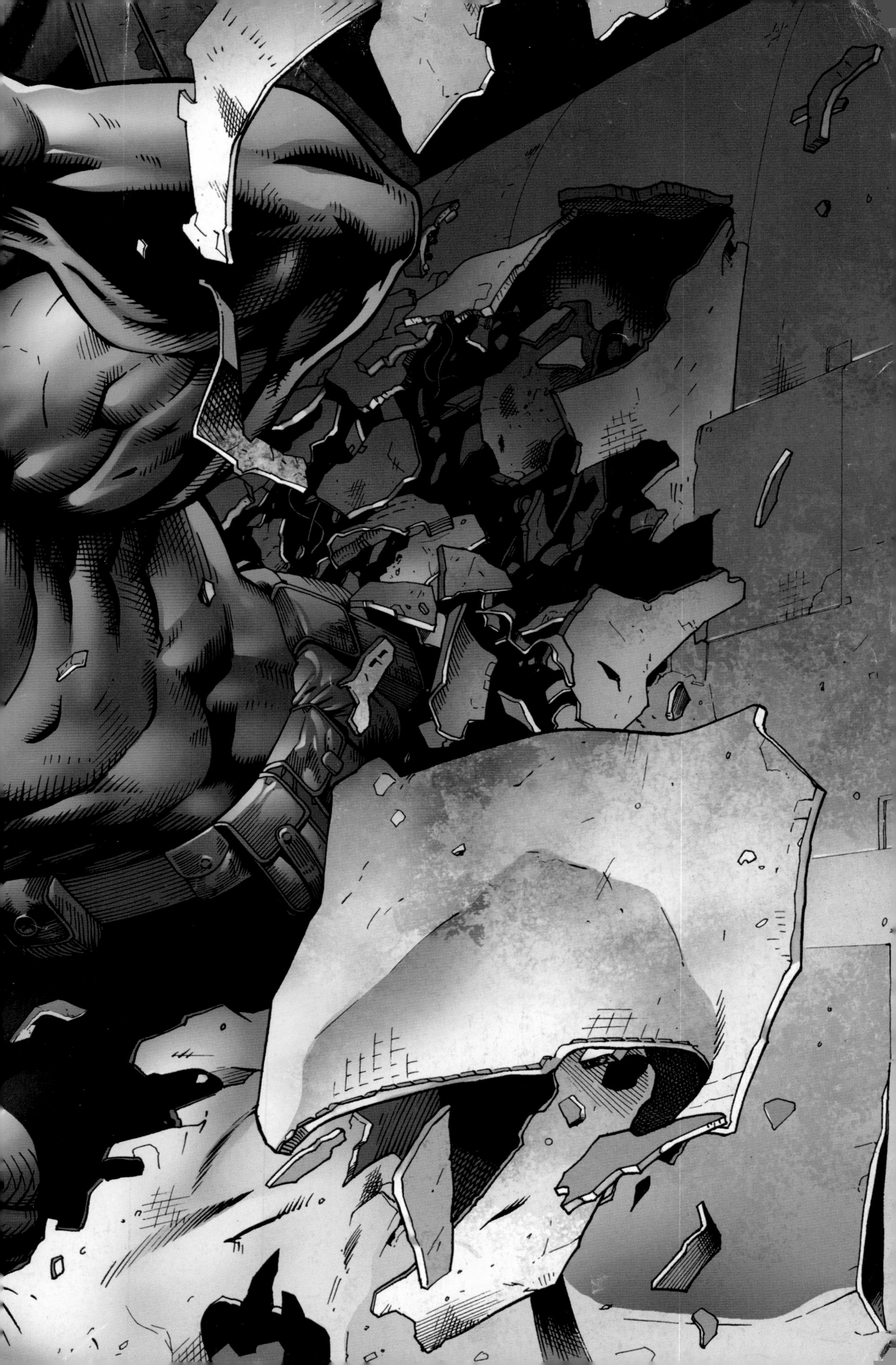

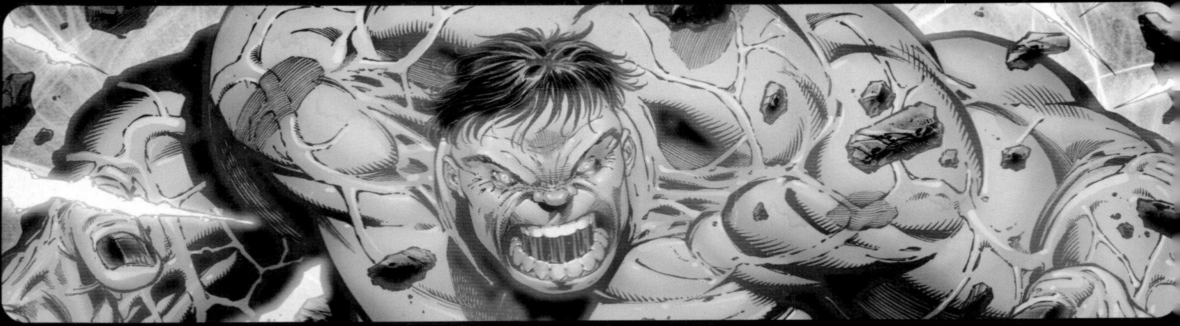

THE HULK (Bruce Banner) Irradiated by the very gamma bomb he helped to create, Bruce Banner now changes in times of stress into the super-strong raging behemoth known as the Hulk. For years, all the Hulk wanted was to be left alone. Now, he finds himself surrounded by a full family of Gamma-charged outcasts like himself.

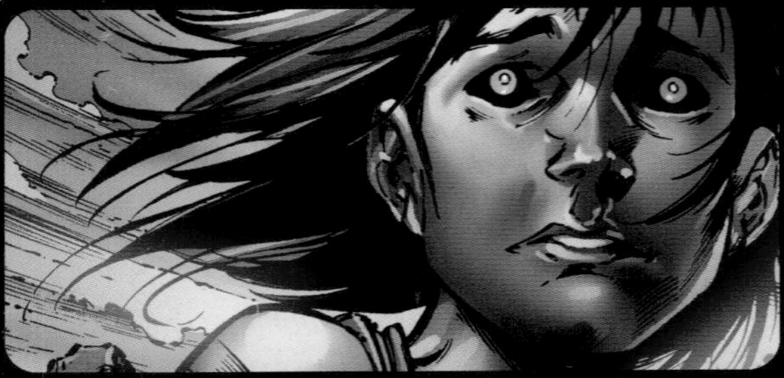

SKAAR The son of Hulk and the now-dead alien queen of Sakaar, Calera, young Skaar has inherited both his father's Hulk abilities and his mother's tectonic-based Old Power.

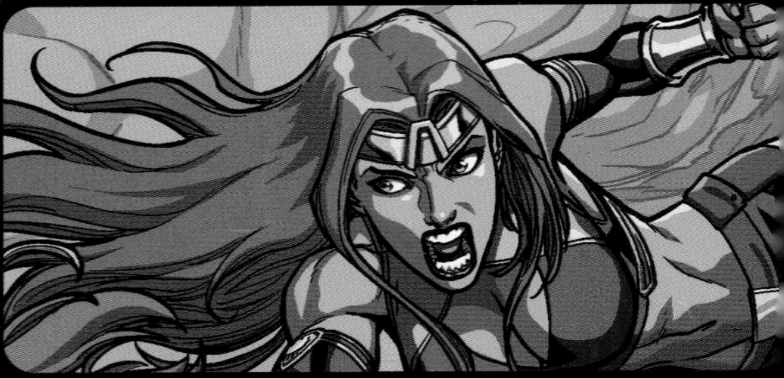

SAVAGE SHE-HULK (Lyra) Lyra is Hulk's biologica daughter from an alternate future, created through genetic manipulation by Thundra. Lyrta now resides in the present under the care of Jen Walters.

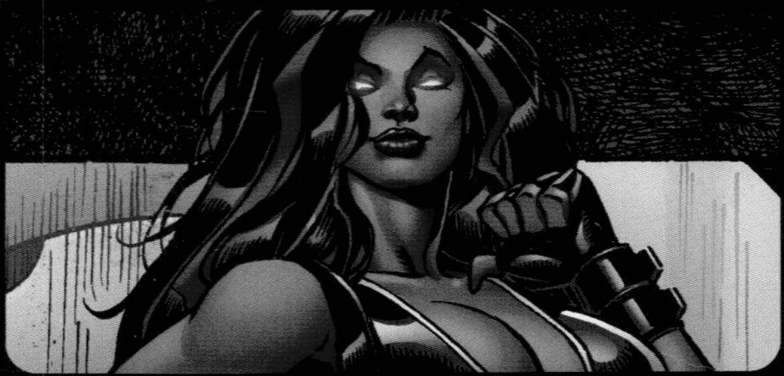

RED SHE-HULK (Betty Banner) Bruce Banner's first wife and long time love, Betty seemingly died of gamma radiation poisoning...but was revived by the Leader, who transformed her into a Red She-Hulk.

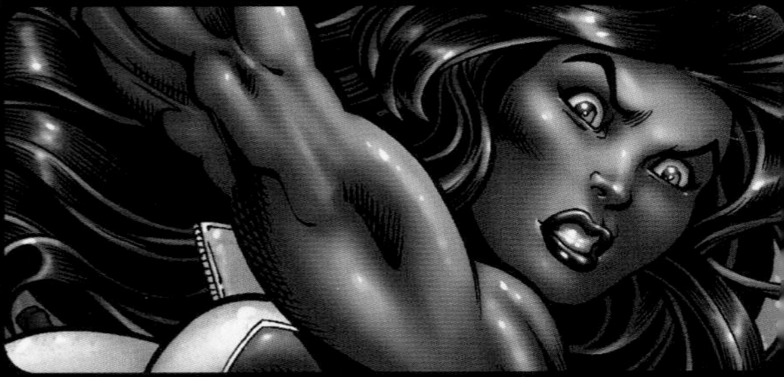

SHE-HULK (Jen Walters) The first member of Hulk's extended family, Bruce Banner's cousin Jennifer was changed into a female Hulk when Bruce gave her a life-saving blood transfusion.

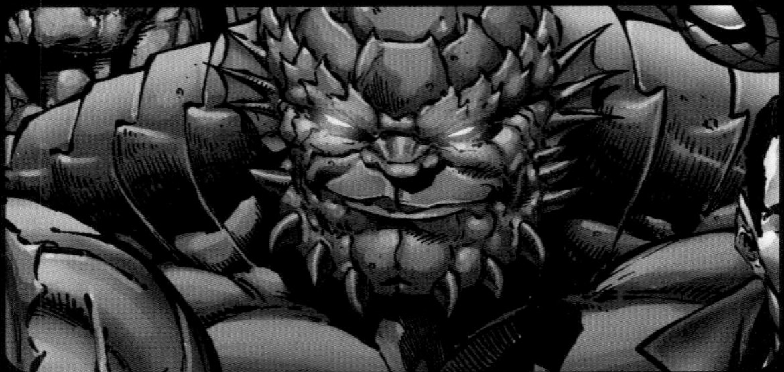

A-BOMB (Rick Jones) Hulk's oldest friend, Bruce was saving Rick from the gamma bomb blast when the Hulk was born. Now, Gamma-charged himself by the evil Intelligencia, Rick fights by his side as A-Bomb.

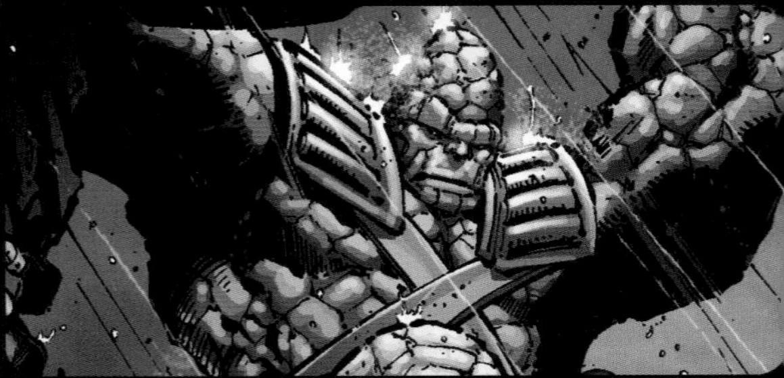

KORG The only non-gamma powered member of Hulk's clan, Korg is a stone-man from the planet Krona, and became Hulk's warbound brother on the vicious planet Sakaar.

Now, HULK and his team of monsters protect a world that fears their strength and rage as...

THE INCREDIBLE HULKS!

HIRO-KALA

SON OF HULK

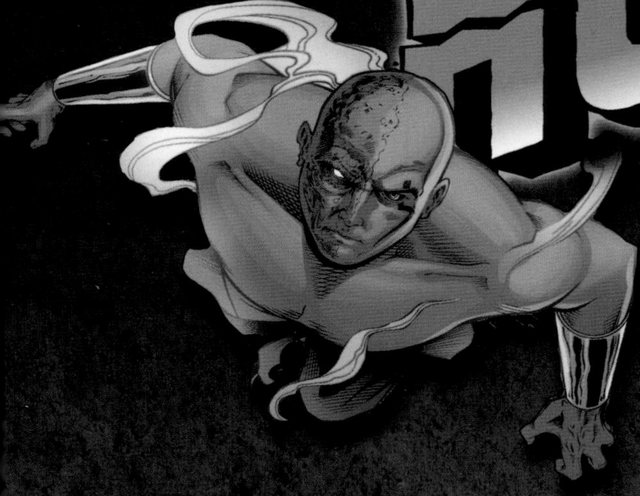

TWIN BROTHER OF SKAAR, UNBEKNOWNST THUS FAR TO EITHER FATHER OR BROTHER, HIRO-KALA WAS GRANTED THE TECTONIC OLD POWER OF HIS MOTHER, BUT DID NOT RECEIVE HIS FATHER'S GAMMA AUGEMENTED ABILITIES. CONVINCED THAT THE OLD POWER IS A BLIGHT UPON THE UNIVERSE, HIRO-KALA HAS PLEDGED TO DESTROY IT...

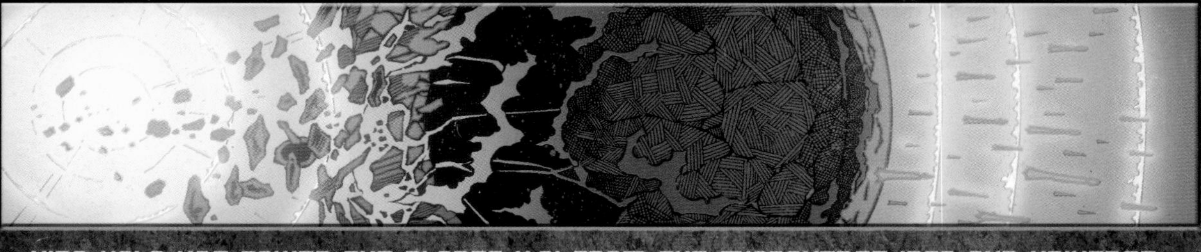

HIRO-KALA HAS TOWED THE PLANET K'AI FROM THE MICROVERSE INTO OUR UNIVERSE IN AN ATTEMPT TO ESCAPE FROM A RECENT BATTLE. THE PLANET DID NOT FARE THE JOURNEY WELL.

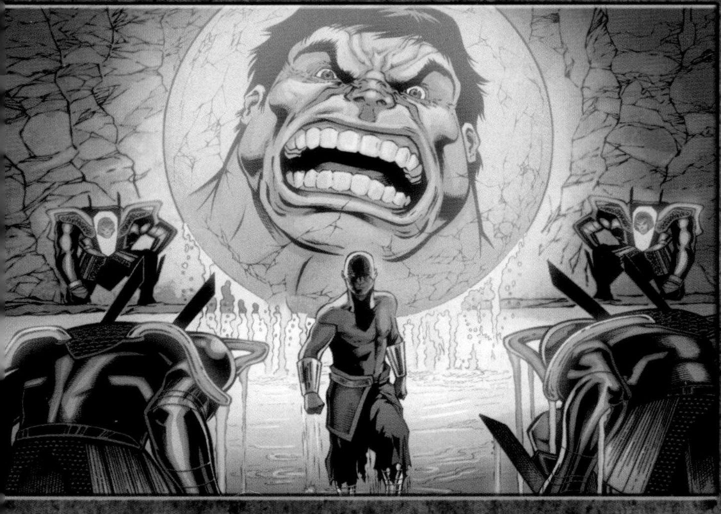

HIRO FOUND AND TAPPED INTO K'AI'S WORLDMIND, THE MYSTICAL POWERSOURCE IN THE PLANET'S CORE.

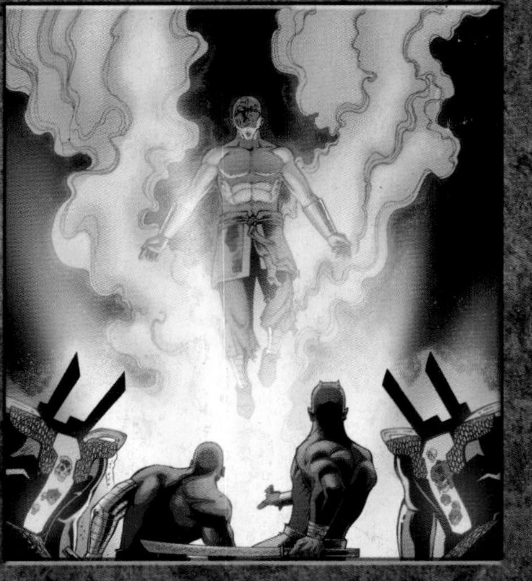

WITH THE WORLDMIND'S ENERGY, HIRO HEALED THE PLANET K'AI...BUT STILL, IT HURTLES THROUGH SPACE, IT'S DESTINATION UNKNOWN...

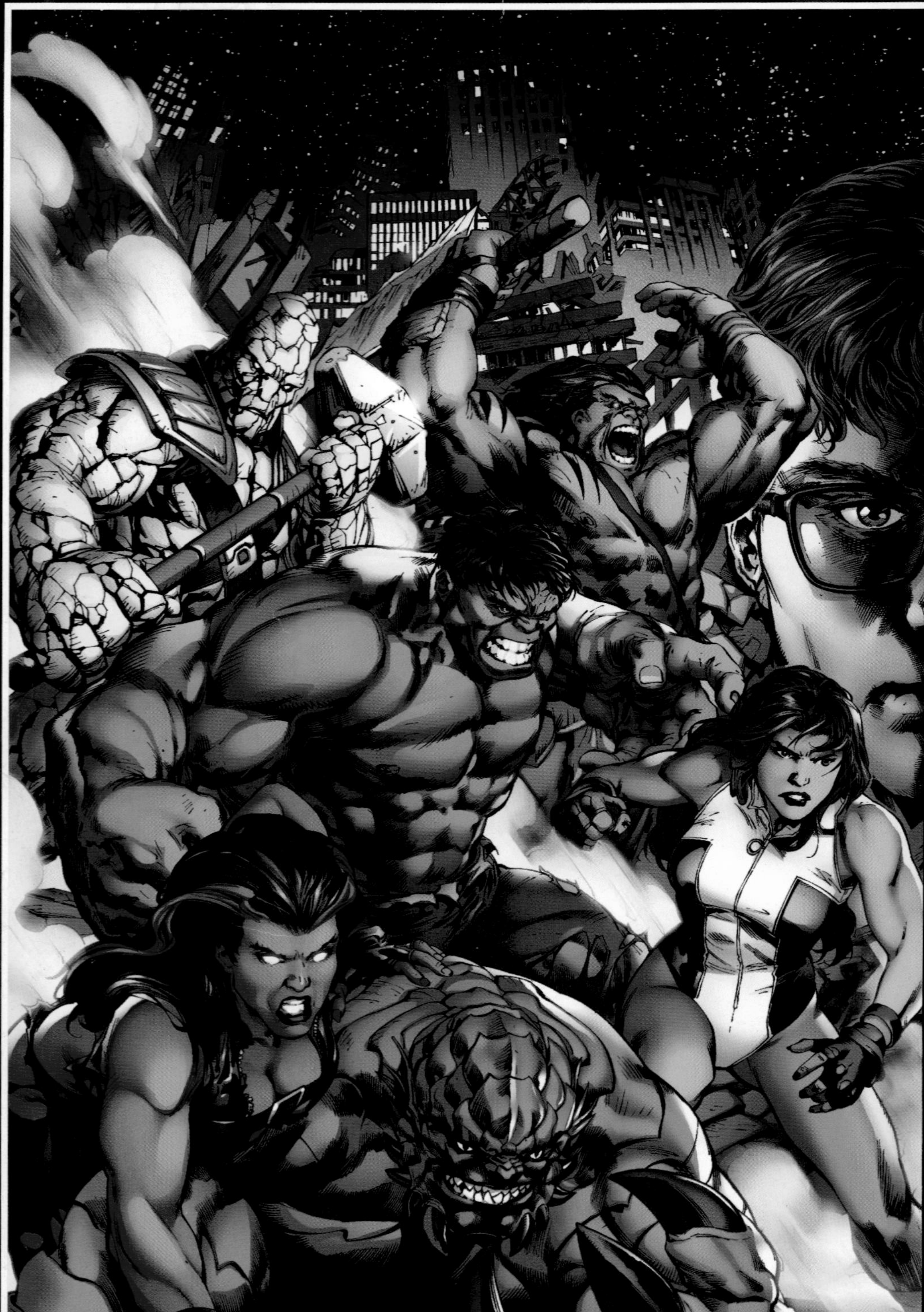

(612-613)

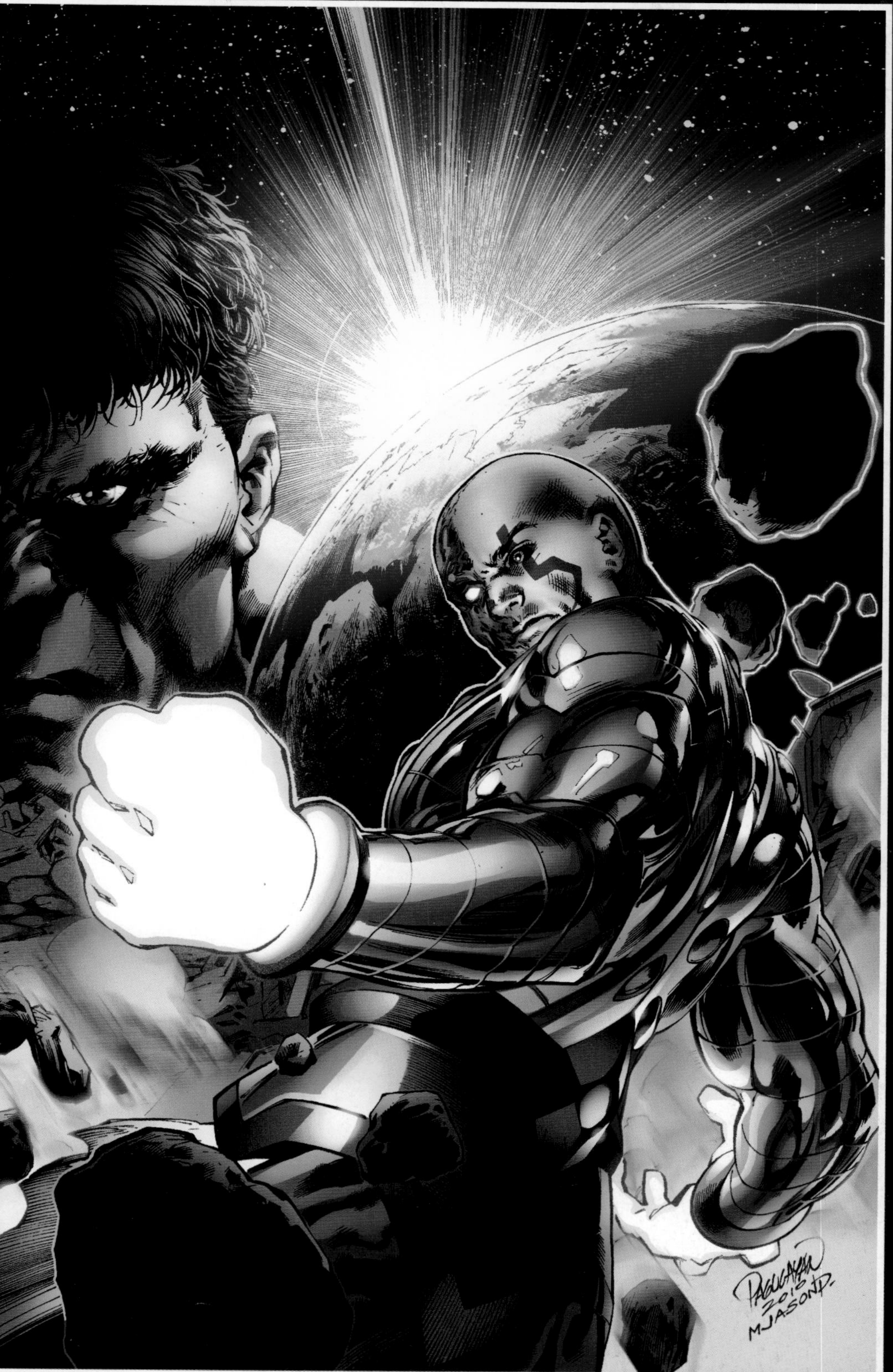
PAGULAYAN
2010
MJASON D.

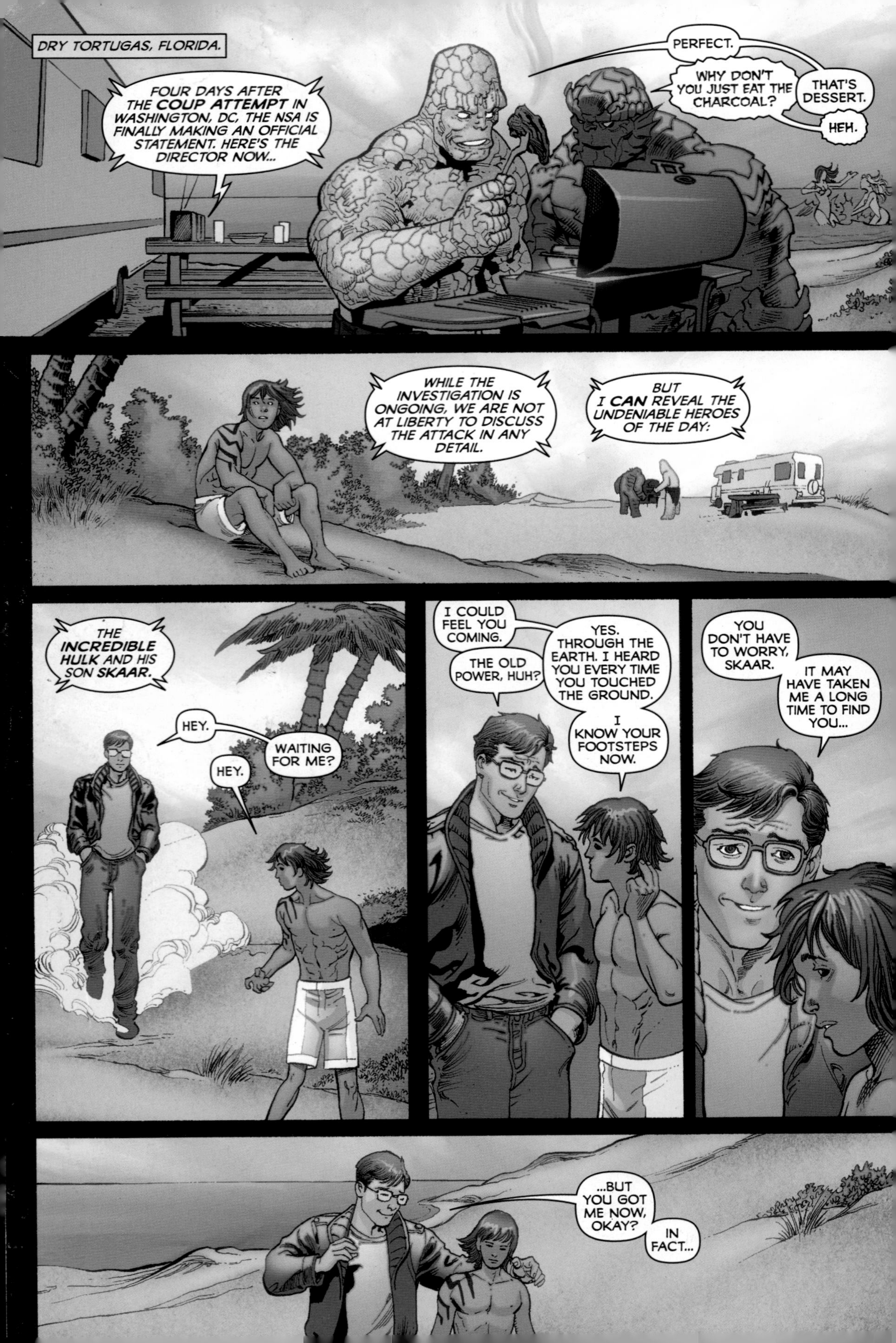
DRY TORTUGAS, FLORIDA.
FOUR DAYS AFTER THE COUP ATTEMPT IN WASHINGTON, DC, THE NSA IS FINALLY MAKING AN OFFICIAL STATEMENT. HERE'S THE DIRECTOR NOW...
PERFECT.
WHY DON'T YOU JUST EAT THE CHARCOAL?
THAT'S DESSERT.
HEH.
WHILE THE INVESTIGATION IS ONGOING, WE ARE NOT AT LIBERTY TO DISCUSS THE ATTACK IN ANY DETAIL.
BUT I CAN REVEAL THE UNDENIABLE HEROES OF THE DAY:
THE INCREDIBLE HULK AND HIS SON SKAAR.
HEY.
WAITING FOR ME?
HEY.
I COULD FEEL YOU COMING.
THE OLD POWER, HUH?
YES. THROUGH THE EARTH. I HEARD YOU EVERY TIME YOU TOUCHED THE GROUND.
I KNOW YOUR FOOTSTEPS NOW.
YOU DON'T HAVE TO WORRY, SKAAR.
IT MAY HAVE TAKEN ME A LONG TIME TO FIND YOU...
...BUT YOU GOT ME NOW, OKAY?
IN FACT...

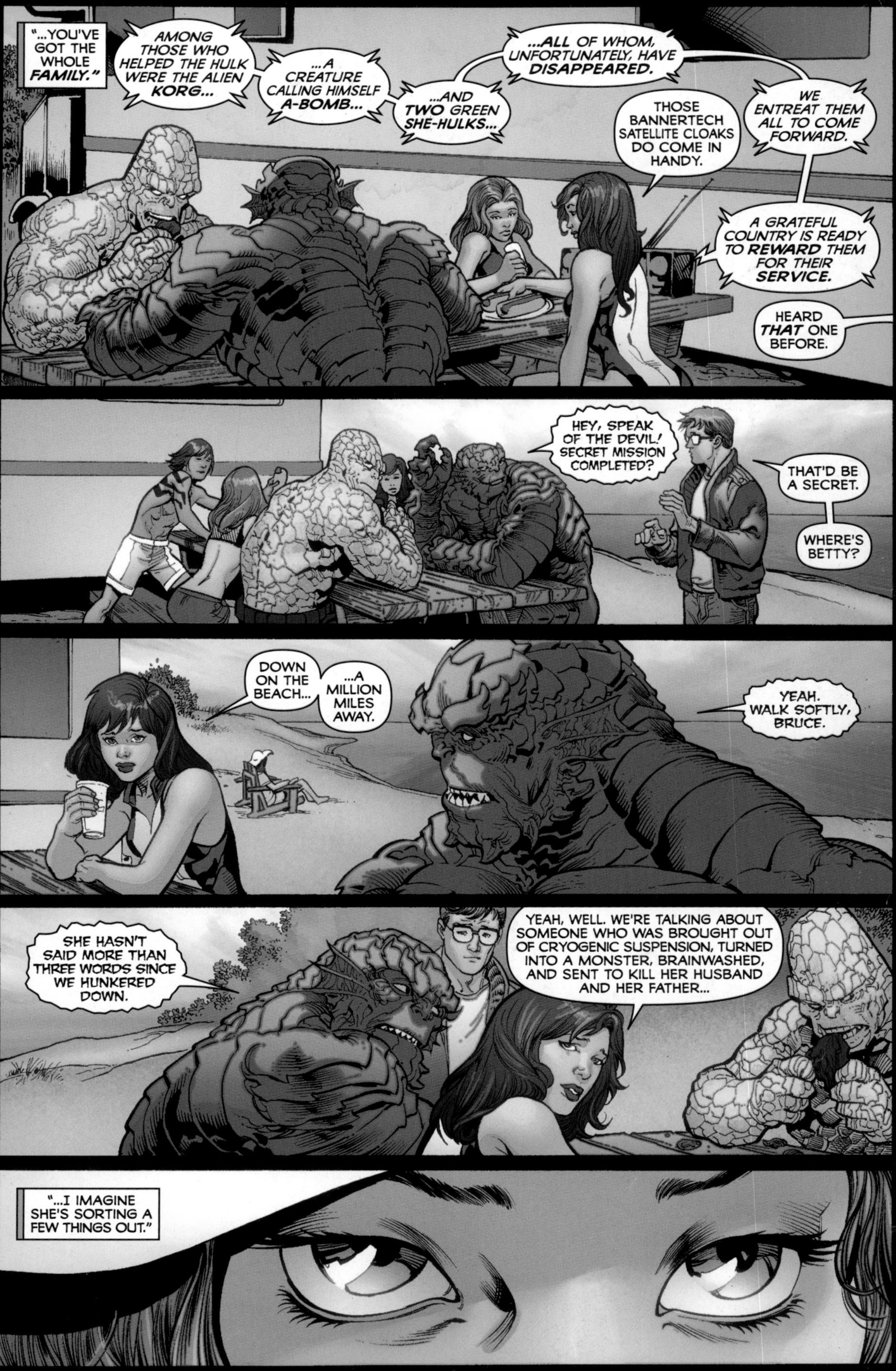
"...YOU'VE GOT THE WHOLE FAMILY."
AMONG THOSE WHO HELPED THE HULK WERE THE ALIEN KORG...
...A CREATURE CALLING HIMSELF A-BOMB...
...AND TWO GREEN SHE-HULKS...
...ALL OF WHOM, UNFORTUNATELY, HAVE DISAPPEARED.
THOSE BANNERTECH SATELLITE CLOAKS DO COME IN HANDY.
WE ENTREAT THEM ALL TO COME FORWARD.
A GRATEFUL COUNTRY IS READY TO REWARD THEM FOR THEIR SERVICE.
HEARD THAT ONE BEFORE.
HEY, SPEAK OF THE DEVIL! SECRET MISSION COMPLETED?
THAT'D BE A SECRET.
WHERE'S BETTY?
DOWN ON THE BEACH...
...A MILLION MILES AWAY.
YEAH. WALK SOFTLY, BRUCE.
SHE HASN'T SAID MORE THAN THREE WORDS SINCE WE HUNKERED DOWN.
YEAH, WELL. WE'RE TALKING ABOUT SOMEONE WHO WAS BROUGHT OUT OF CRYOGENIC SUSPENSION, TURNED INTO A MONSTER, BRAINWASHED, AND SENT TO KILL HER HUSBAND AND HER FATHER...
"...I IMAGINE SHE'S SORTING A FEW THINGS OUT."

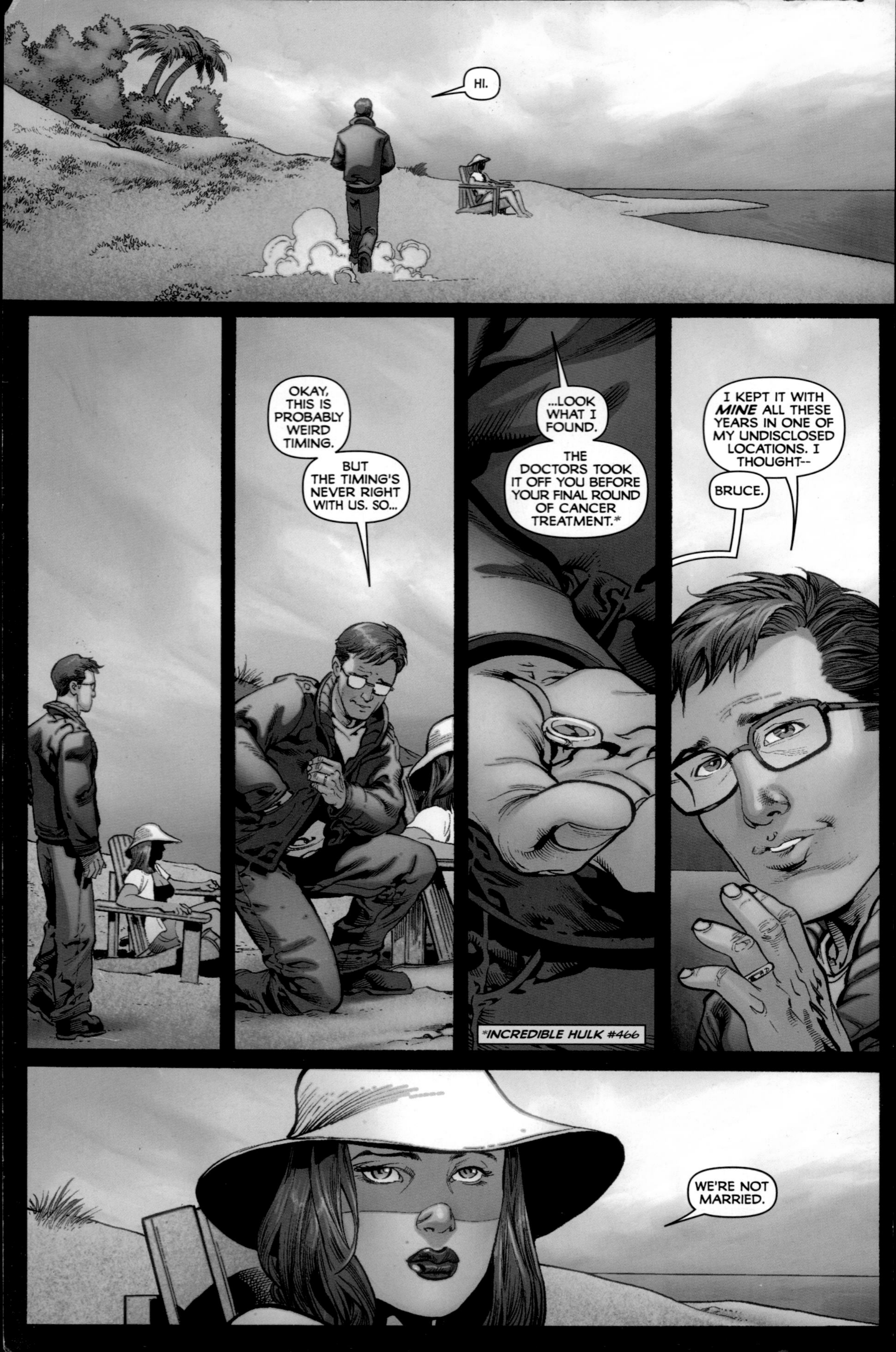
HI.
OKAY, THIS IS PROBABLY WEIRD TIMING.
BUT THE TIMING'S NEVER RIGHT WITH US. SO...
...LOOK WHAT I FOUND.
THE DOCTORS TOOK IT OFF YOU BEFORE YOUR FINAL ROUND OF CANCER TREATMENT.*
*INCREDIBLE HULK #466
I KEPT IT WITH MINE ALL THESE YEARS IN ONE OF MY UNDISCLOSED LOCATIONS. I THOUGHT--
BRUCE.
WE'RE NOT MARRIED.

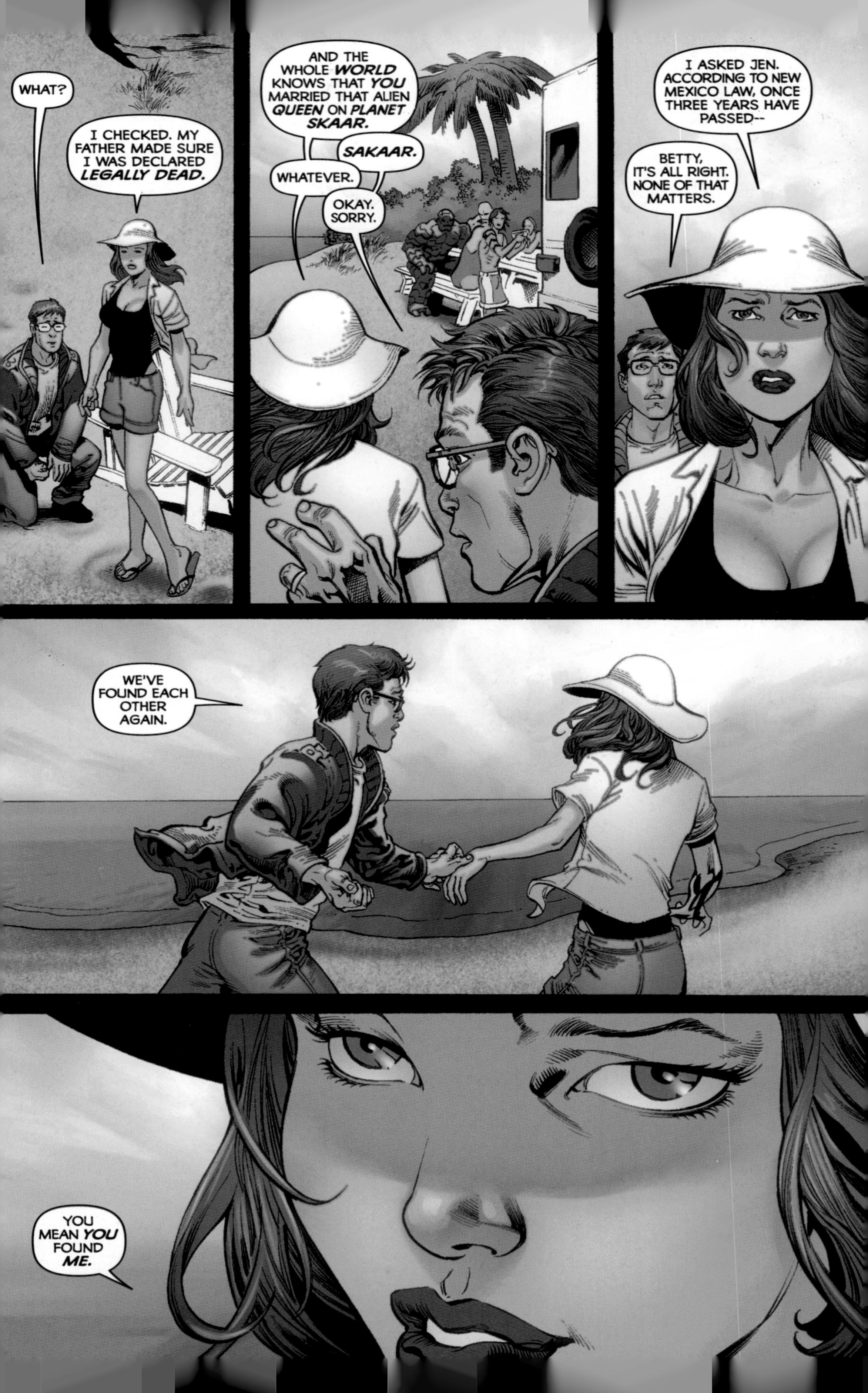
WHAT?
I CHECKED. MY FATHER MADE SURE I WAS DECLARED LEGALLY DEAD.
AND THE WHOLE WORLD KNOWS THAT YOU MARRIED THAT ALIEN QUEEN ON PLANET SKAAR.
SAKAAR.
WHATEVER.
OKAY. SORRY.
I ASKED JEN. ACCORDING TO NEW MEXICO LAW, ONCE THREE YEARS HAVE PASSED--
BETTY, IT'S ALL RIGHT. NONE OF THAT MATTERS.
WE'VE FOUND EACH OTHER AGAIN.
YOU MEAN YOU FOUND ME.

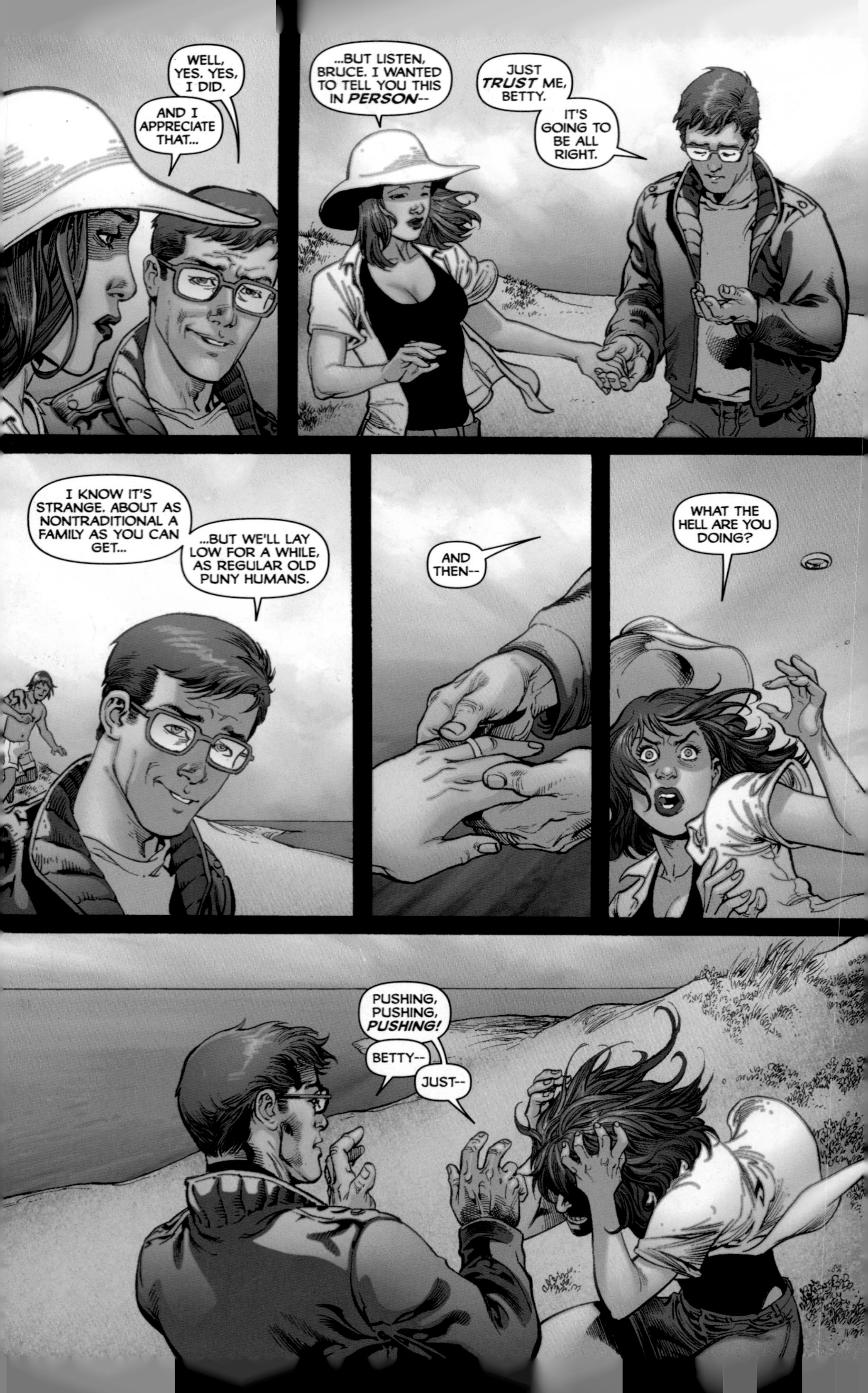
WELL, YES. YES, I DID.
AND I APPRECIATE THAT...
...BUT LISTEN, BRUCE. I WANTED TO TELL YOU THIS IN *PERSON*--
JUST *TRUST* ME, BETTY.
IT'S GOING TO BE ALL RIGHT.
I KNOW IT'S STRANGE. ABOUT AS NONTRADITIONAL A FAMILY AS YOU CAN GET...
...BUT WE'LL LAY LOW FOR A WHILE, AS REGULAR OLD PUNY HUMANS.
AND THEN--
WHAT THE HELL ARE YOU DOING?
PUSHING, PUSHING, *PUSHING!*
BETTY--
JUST--

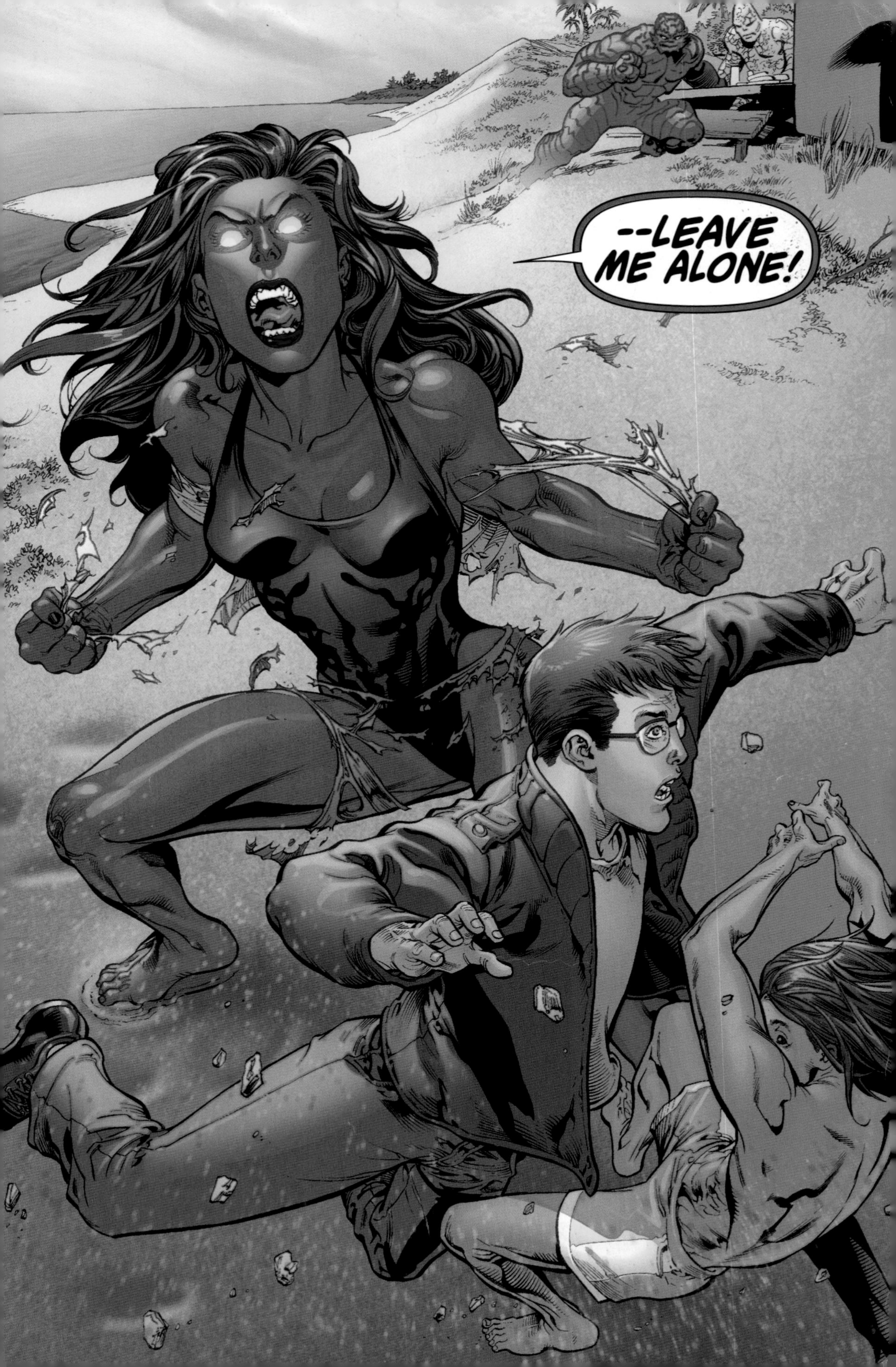
--LEAVE ME ALONE!

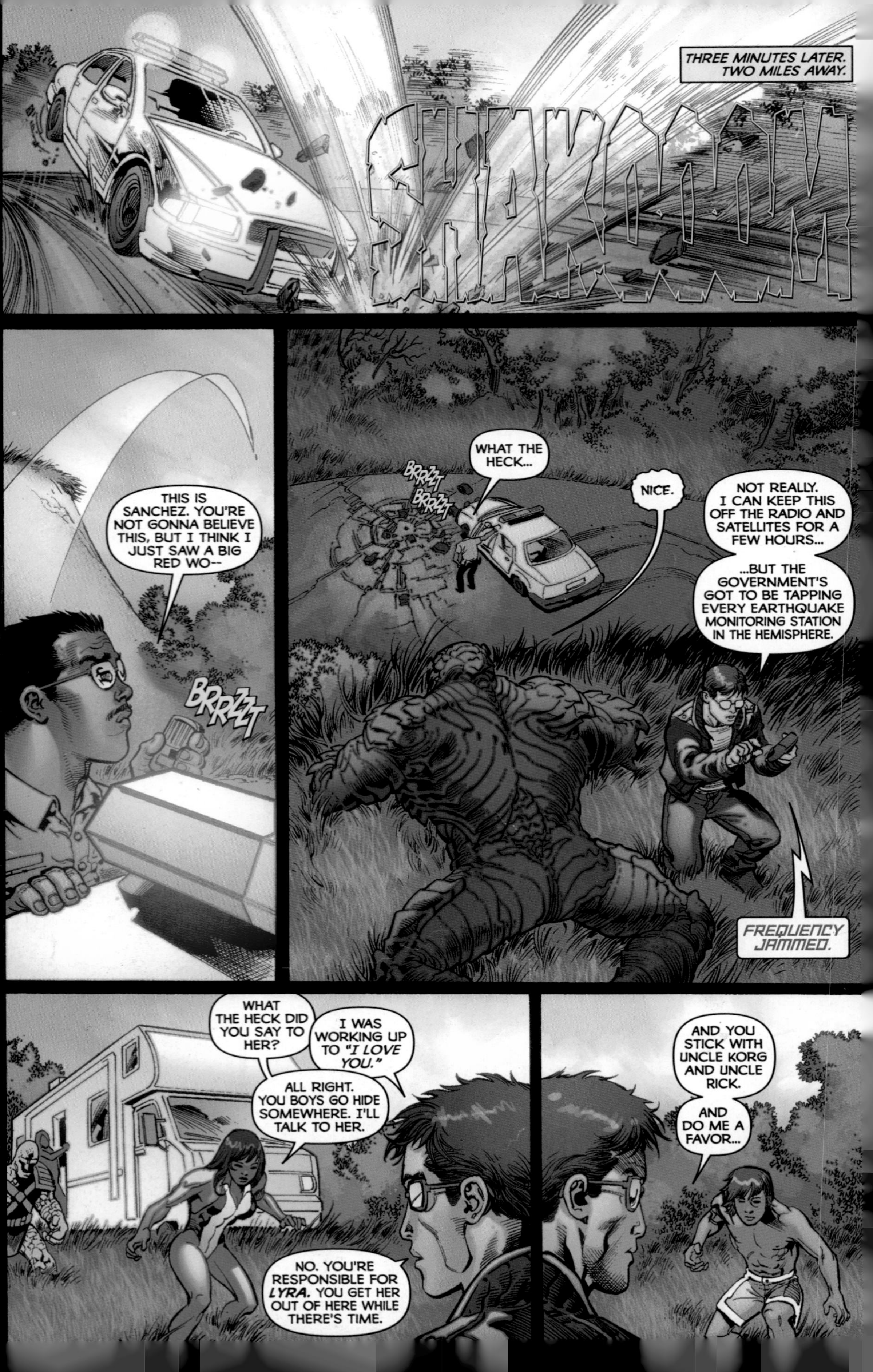
THREE MINUTES LATER. TWO MILES AWAY.
THIS IS SANCHEZ. YOU'RE NOT GONNA BELIEVE THIS, BUT I THINK I JUST SAW A BIG RED WO--
BRRZZZT
WHAT THE HECK...
BRRZZZT
BRRZZZT
NICE.
NOT REALLY. I CAN KEEP THIS OFF THE RADIO AND SATELLITES FOR A FEW HOURS...
...BUT THE GOVERNMENT'S GOT TO BE TAPPING EVERY EARTHQUAKE MONITORING STATION IN THE HEMISPHERE.
FREQUENCY JAMMED.
WHAT THE HECK DID YOU SAY TO HER?
I WAS WORKING UP TO "I LOVE YOU."
ALL RIGHT. YOU BOYS GO HIDE SOMEWHERE. I'LL TALK TO HER.
NO. YOU'RE RESPONSIBLE FOR LYRA. YOU GET HER OUT OF HERE WHILE THERE'S TIME.
AND YOU STICK WITH UNCLE KORG AND UNCLE RICK.
AND DO ME A FAVOR...

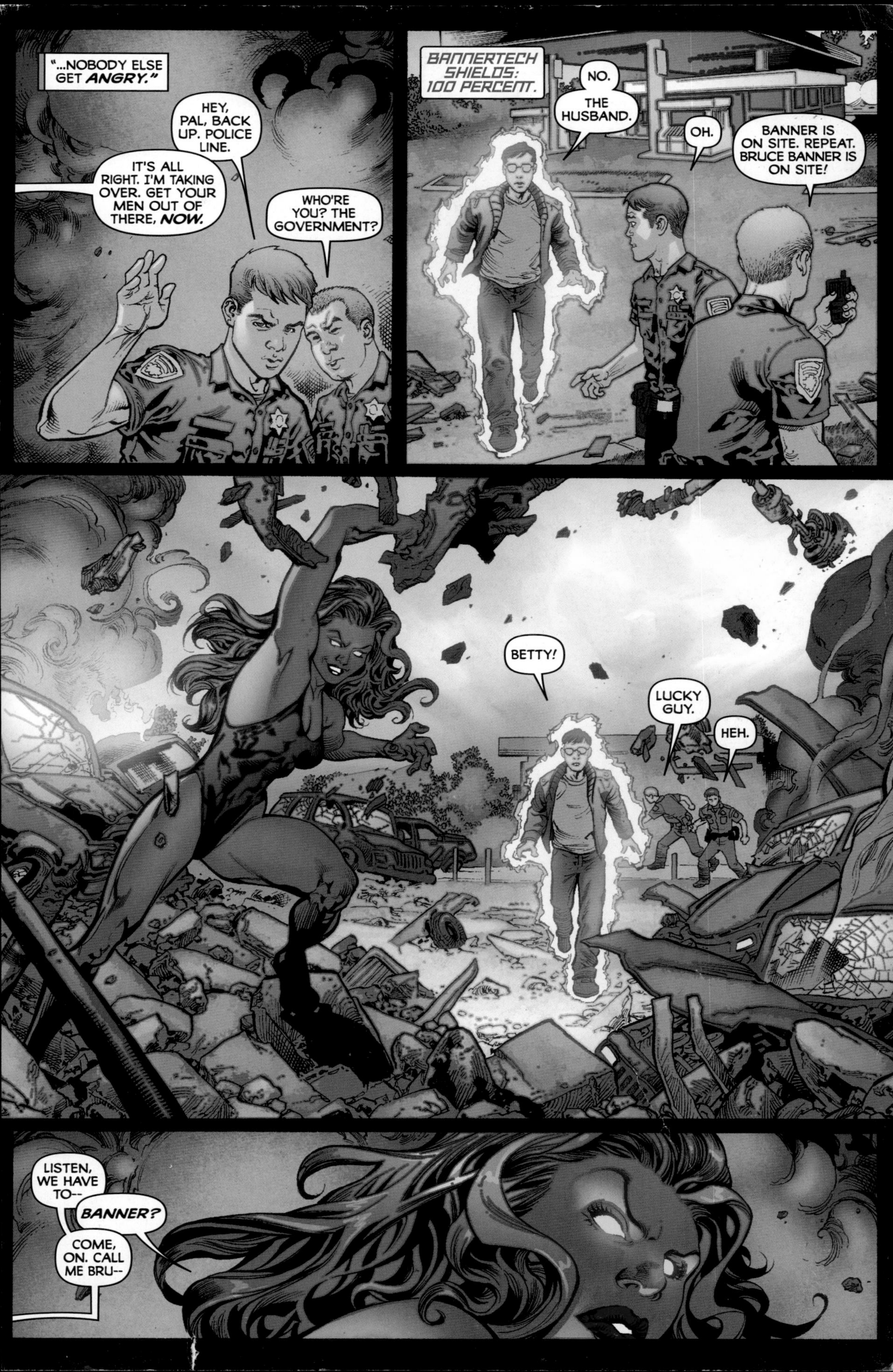
"...NOBODY ELSE GET *ANGRY*."
HEY, PAL, BACK UP. POLICE LINE.
IT'S ALL RIGHT. I'M TAKING OVER. GET YOUR MEN OUT OF THERE, *NOW*.
WHO'RE YOU? THE GOVERNMENT?
BANNERTECH SHIELDS: 100 PERCENT.
NO.
THE HUSBAND.
OH.
BANNER IS ON SITE. REPEAT. BRUCE BANNER IS ON SITE!
BETTY!
LUCKY GUY.
HEH.
LISTEN, WE HAVE TO--
BANNER?
COME, ON. CALL ME BRU--

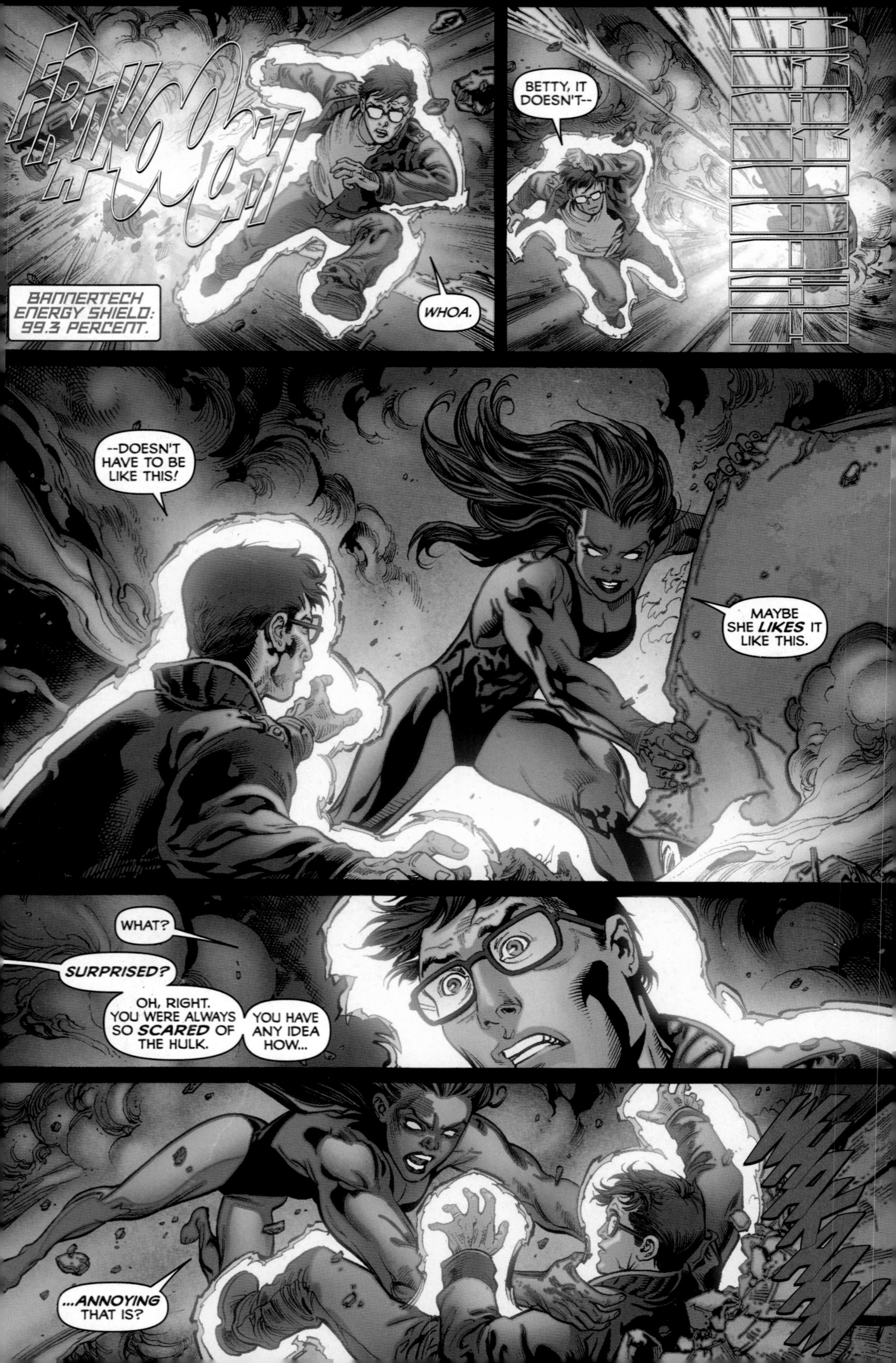
BANNERTECH ENERGY SHIELD: 99.3 PERCENT.
WHOA.
BETTY, IT DOESN'T--
--DOESN'T HAVE TO BE LIKE THIS!
MAYBE SHE LIKES IT LIKE THIS.
WHAT?
SURPRISED?
OH, RIGHT. YOU WERE ALWAYS SO SCARED OF THE HULK.
YOU HAVE ANY IDEA HOW...
...ANNOYING THAT IS?

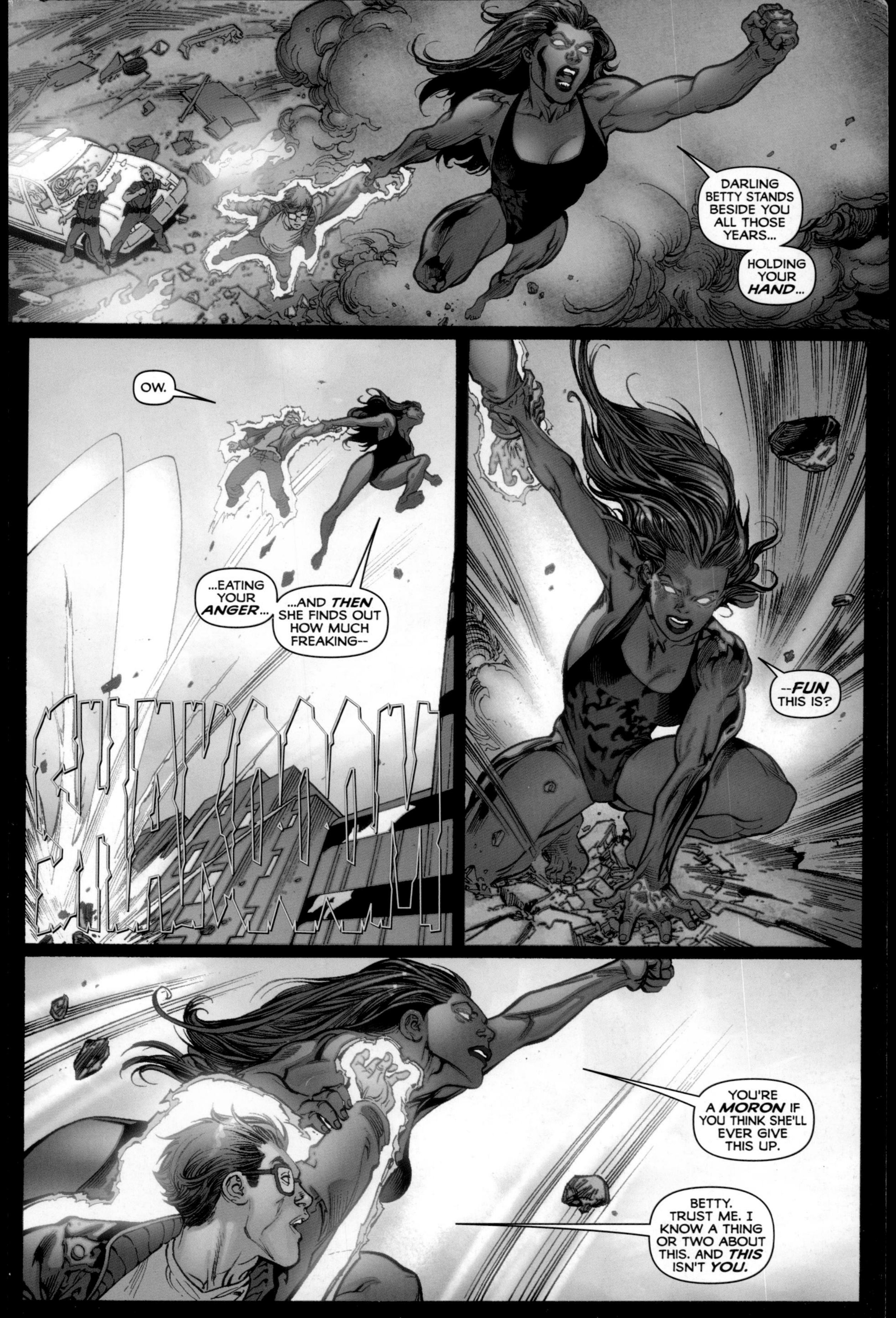
DARLING BETTY STANDS BESIDE YOU ALL THOSE YEARS...
HOLDING YOUR *HAND*...
OW.
...EATING YOUR *ANGER*...
...AND *THEN* SHE FINDS OUT HOW MUCH FREAKING--
--*FUN* THIS IS?
YOU'RE A *MORON* IF YOU THINK SHE'LL EVER GIVE THIS UP.
BETTY. TRUST ME. I KNOW A THING OR TWO ABOUT THIS. AND *THIS* ISN'T *YOU.*

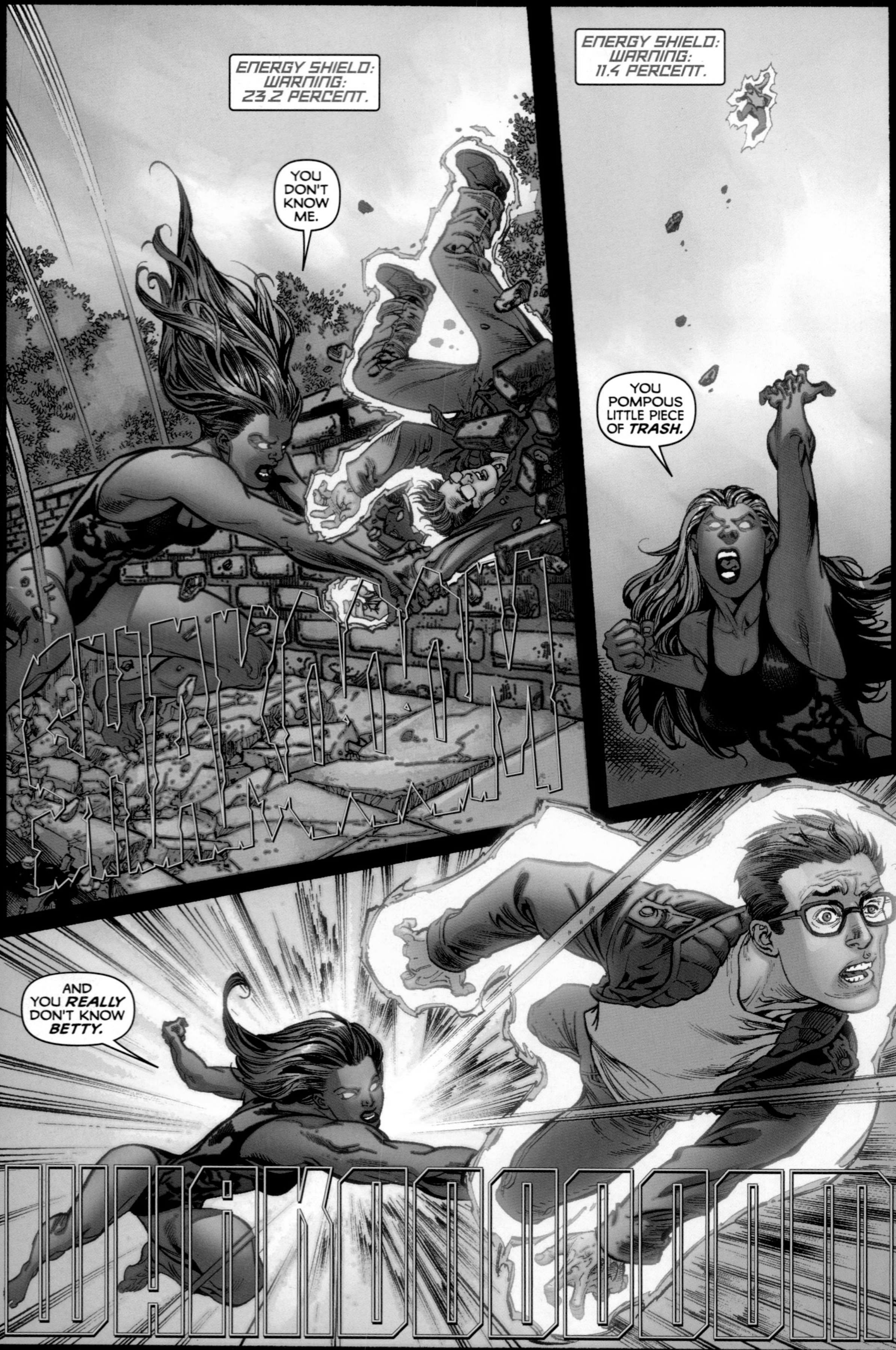
ENERGY SHIELD: WARNING: 23.2 PERCENT.
YOU DON'T KNOW ME.
ENERGY SHIELD: WARNING: 11.4 PERCENT.
YOU POMPOUS LITTLE PIECE OF *TRASH.*
AND YOU *REALLY* DON'T KNOW *BETTY.*

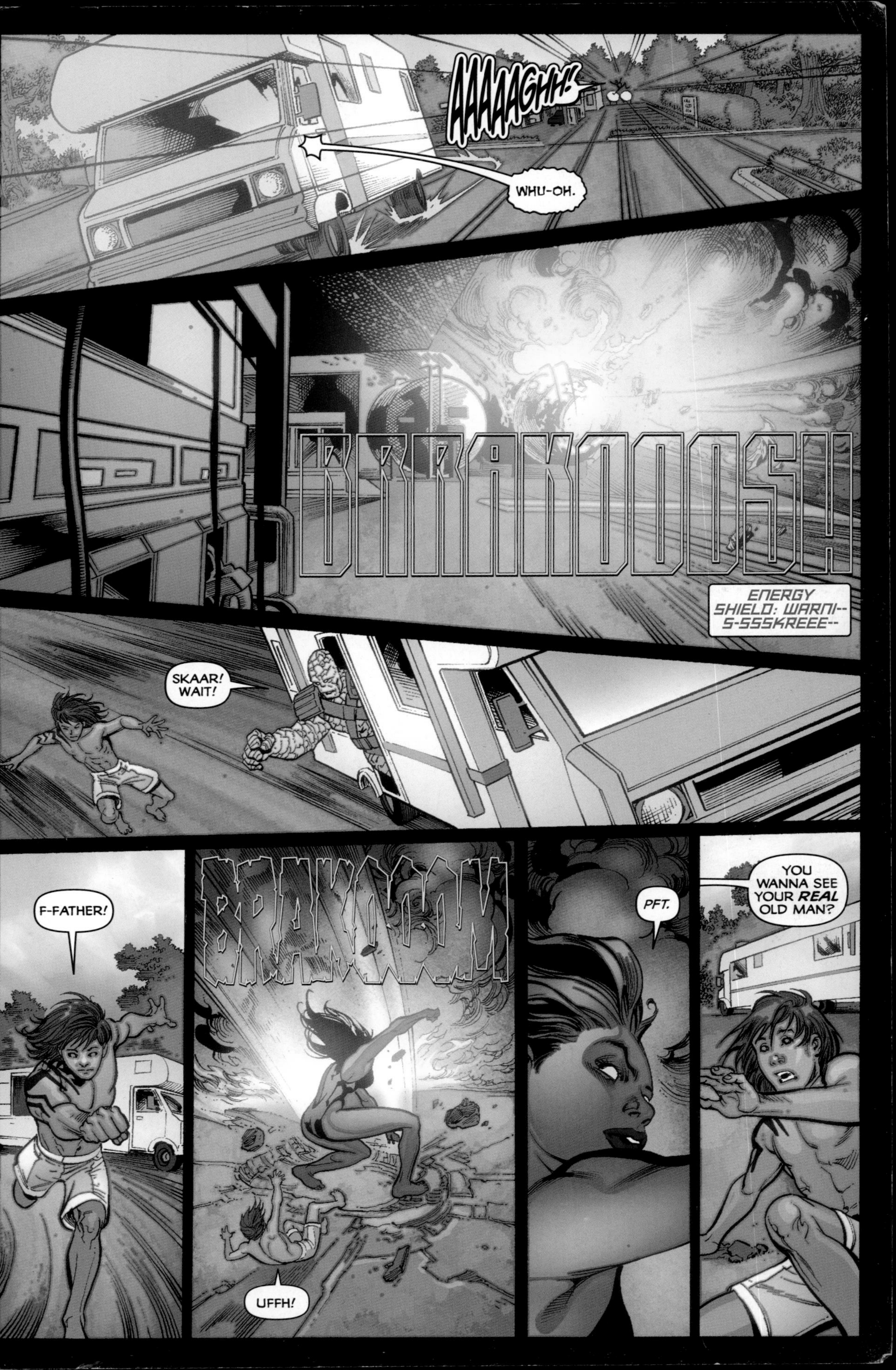
AAAAAGHH!
WHU-OH.
ENERGY SHIELD: WARNI-- S-SSSKREEE--
SKAAR! WAIT!
F-FATHER!
UFFH!
PFT.
YOU WANNA SEE YOUR *REAL* OLD MAN?

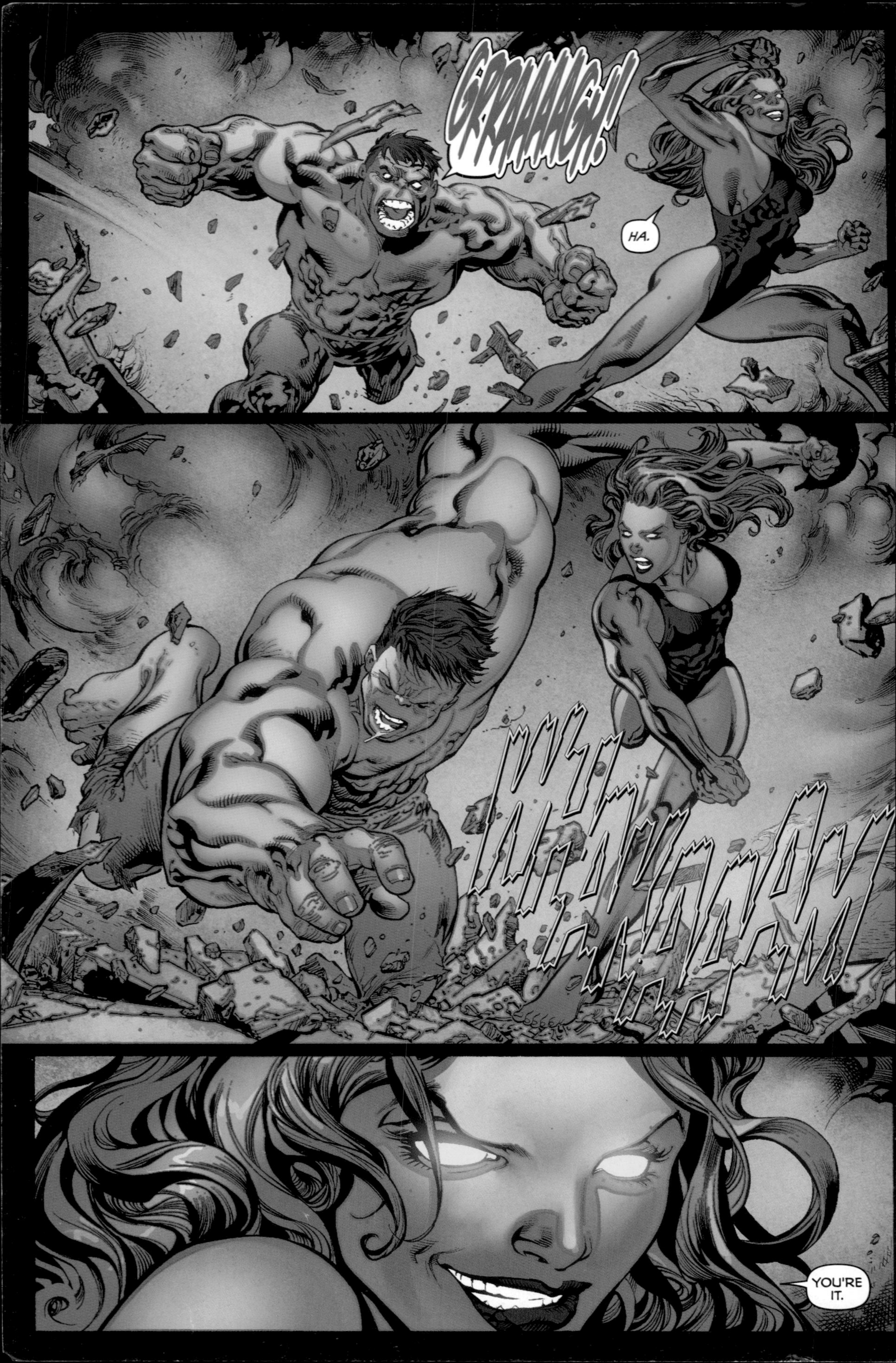
GRRAAAAGH!!
HA.
YOU'RE IT.

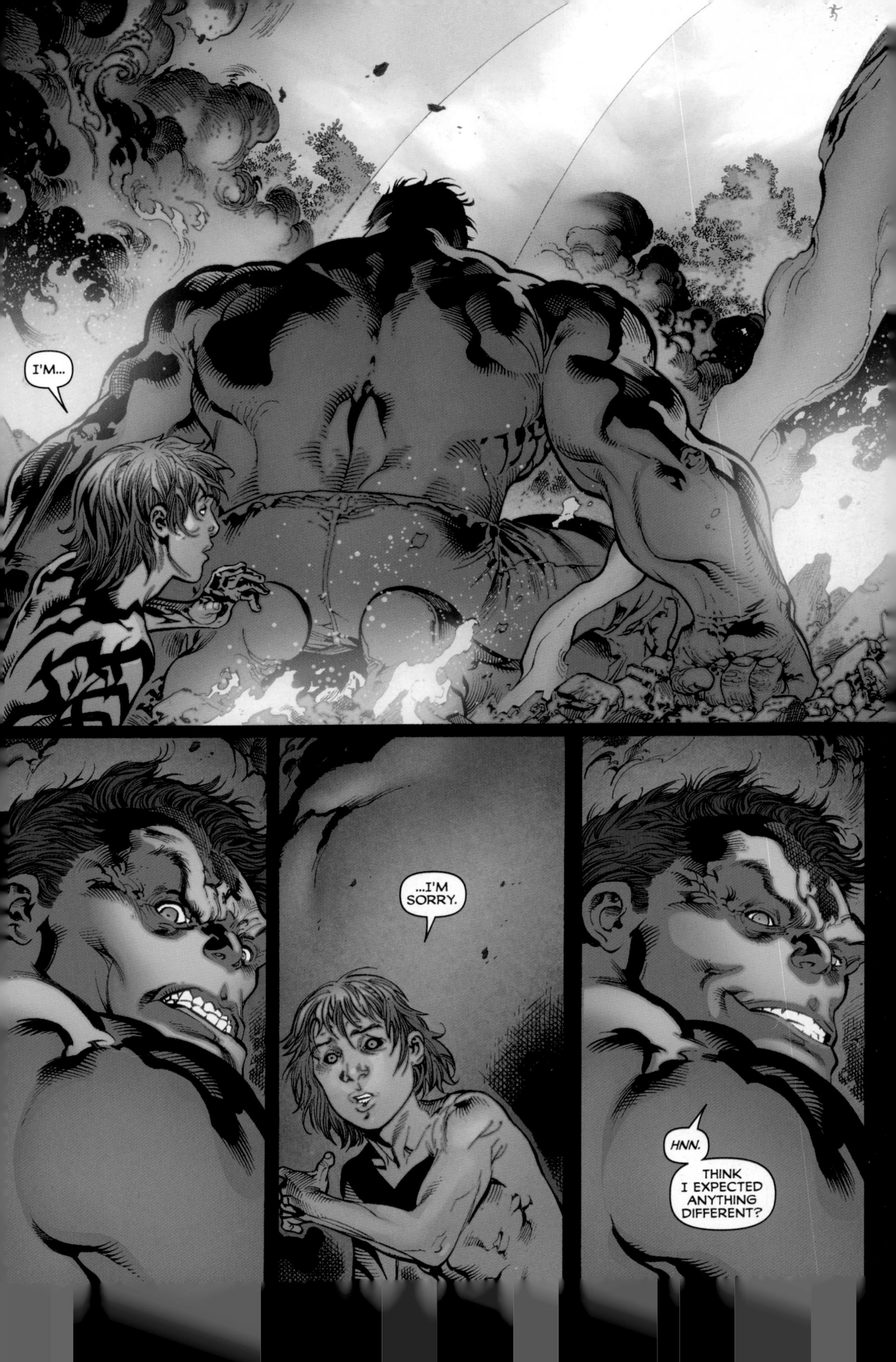
I'M...
...I'M SORRY.
HNN.
THINK I EXPECTED ANYTHING DIFFERENT?

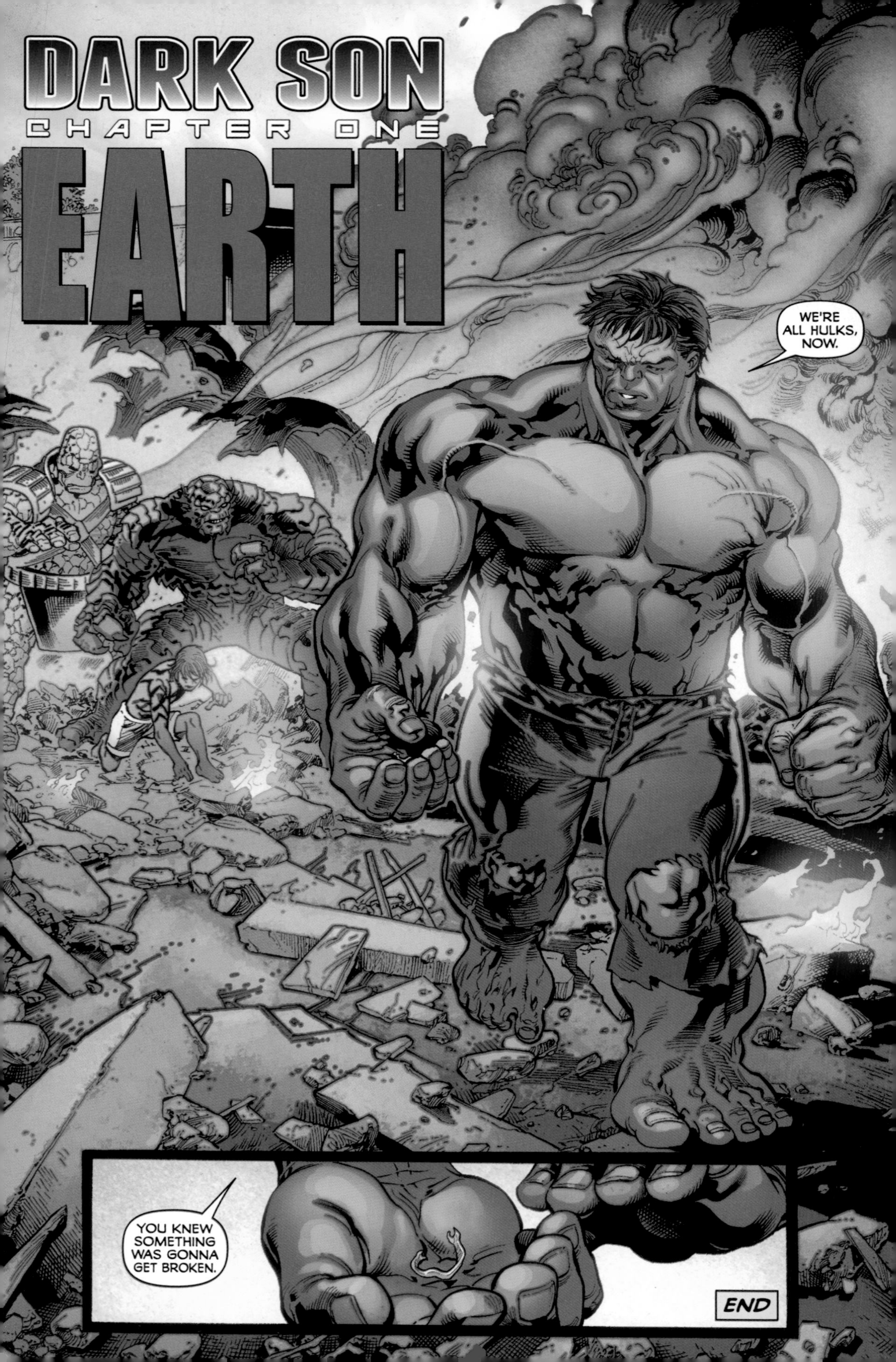

DARK SON
CHAPTER ONE
EARTH
WE'RE ALL HULKS, NOW.
YOU KNEW SOMETHING WAS GONNA GET BROKEN.
END

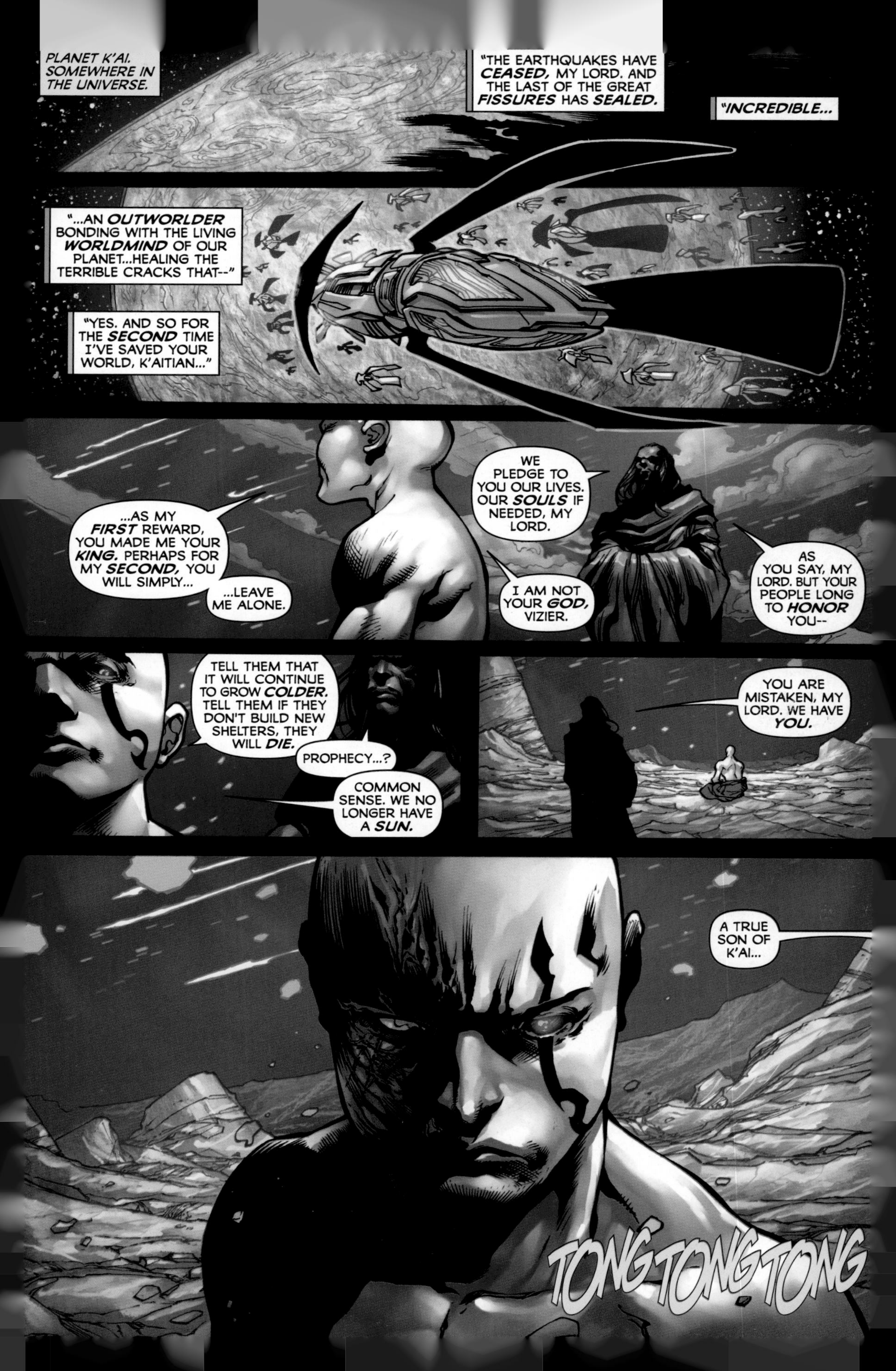
PLANET K'AI. SOMEWHERE IN THE UNIVERSE.
"THE EARTHQUAKES HAVE CEASED, MY LORD. AND THE LAST OF THE GREAT FISSURES HAS SEALED.
"INCREDIBLE...
"...AN OUTWORLDER BONDING WITH THE LIVING WORLDMIND OF OUR PLANET...HEALING THE TERRIBLE CRACKS THAT--"
"YES. AND SO FOR THE SECOND TIME I'VE SAVED YOUR WORLD, K'AITIAN..."
WE PLEDGE TO YOU OUR LIVES. OUR SOULS IF NEEDED, MY LORD.
...AS MY FIRST REWARD, YOU MADE ME YOUR KING. PERHAPS FOR MY SECOND, YOU WILL SIMPLY...
...LEAVE ME ALONE.
I AM NOT YOUR GOD, VIZIER.
AS YOU SAY, MY LORD. BUT YOUR PEOPLE LONG TO HONOR YOU--
TELL THEM THAT IT WILL CONTINUE TO GROW COLDER. TELL THEM IF THEY DON'T BUILD NEW SHELTERS, THEY WILL DIE.
PROPHECY...?
COMMON SENSE. WE NO LONGER HAVE A SUN.
YOU ARE MISTAKEN, MY LORD. WE HAVE YOU.
A TRUE SON OF K'AI...
TONG TONG TONG

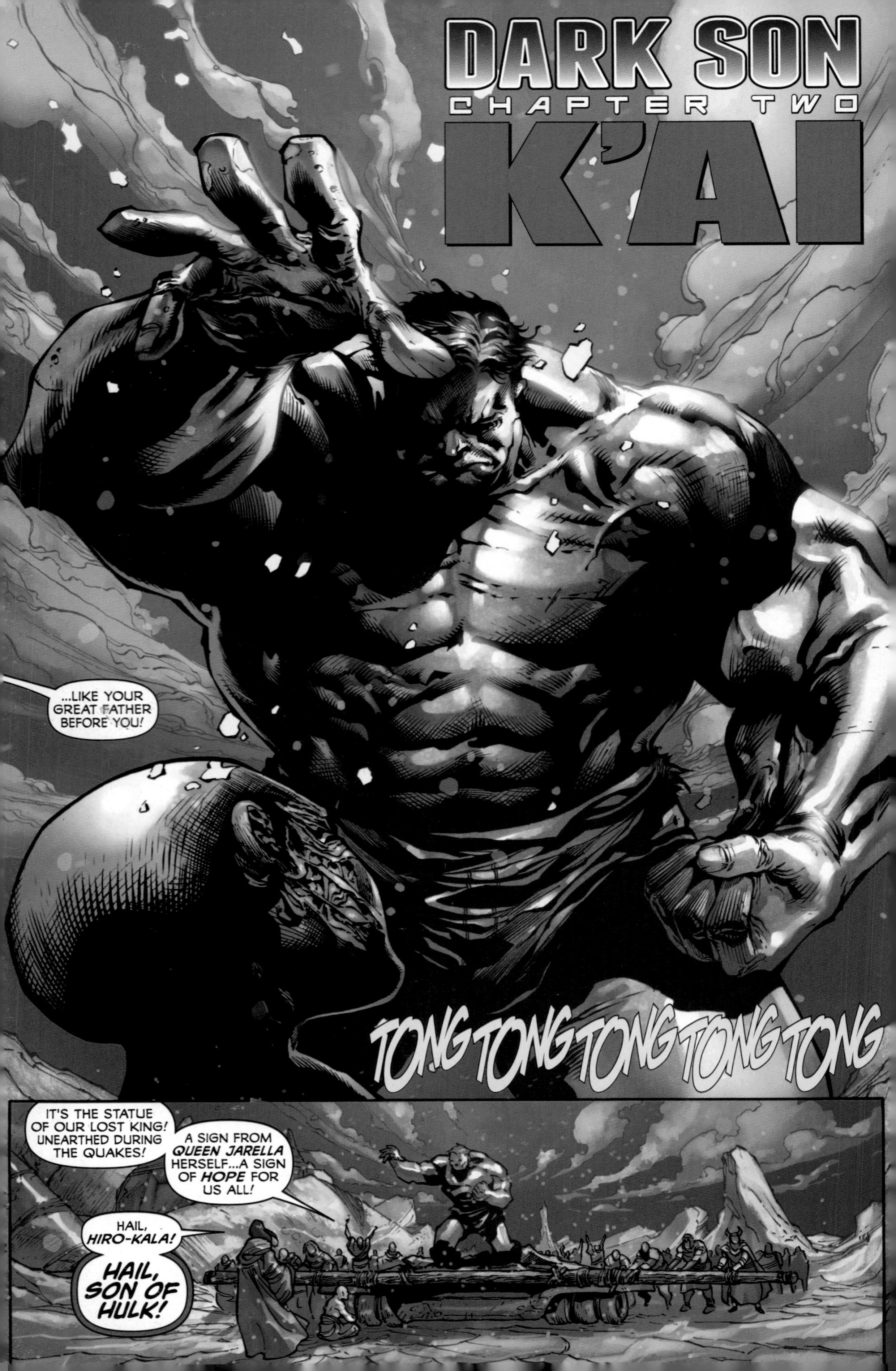
DARK SON
CHAPTER TWO
K'AI
...LIKE YOUR GREAT FATHER BEFORE YOU!
TONG TONG TONG TONG TONG TONG
IT'S THE STATUE OF OUR LOST KING! UNEARTHED DURING THE QUAKES!
A SIGN FROM QUEEN JARELLA HERSELF...A SIGN OF HOPE FOR US ALL!
HAIL, HIRO-KALA!
HAIL, SON OF HULK!

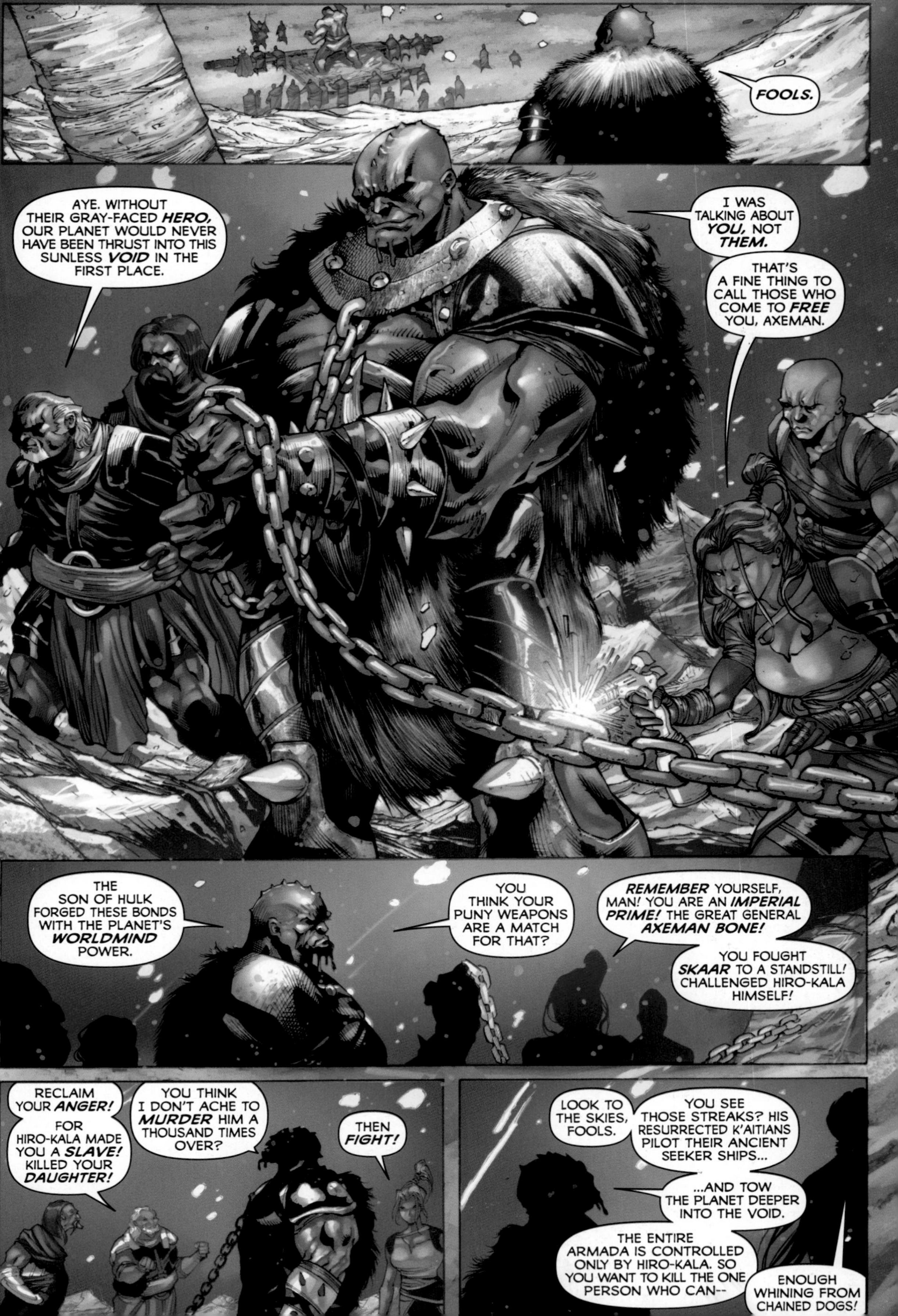
FOOLS.
AYE. WITHOUT THEIR GRAY-FACED HERO, OUR PLANET WOULD NEVER HAVE BEEN THRUST INTO THIS SUNLESS VOID IN THE FIRST PLACE.
I WAS TALKING ABOUT YOU, NOT THEM.
THAT'S A FINE THING TO CALL THOSE WHO COME TO FREE YOU, AXEMAN.
THE SON OF HULK FORGED THESE BONDS WITH THE PLANET'S WORLDMIND POWER.
YOU THINK YOUR PUNY WEAPONS ARE A MATCH FOR THAT?
REMEMBER YOURSELF, MAN! YOU ARE AN IMPERIAL PRIME! THE GREAT GENERAL AXEMAN BONE!
YOU FOUGHT SKAAR TO A STANDSTILL! CHALLENGED HIRO-KALA HIMSELF!
RECLAIM YOUR ANGER!
FOR HIRO-KALA MADE YOU A SLAVE! KILLED YOUR DAUGHTER!
YOU THINK I DON'T ACHE TO MURDER HIM A THOUSAND TIMES OVER?
THEN FIGHT!
LOOK TO THE SKIES, FOOLS.
YOU SEE THOSE STREAKS? HIS RESURRECTED K'AITIANS PILOT THEIR ANCIENT SEEKER SHIPS...
...AND TOW THE PLANET DEEPER INTO THE VOID.
THE ENTIRE ARMADA IS CONTROLLED ONLY BY HIRO-KALA. SO YOU WANT TO KILL THE ONE PERSON WHO CAN--
ENOUGH WHINING FROM CHAINED DOGS!

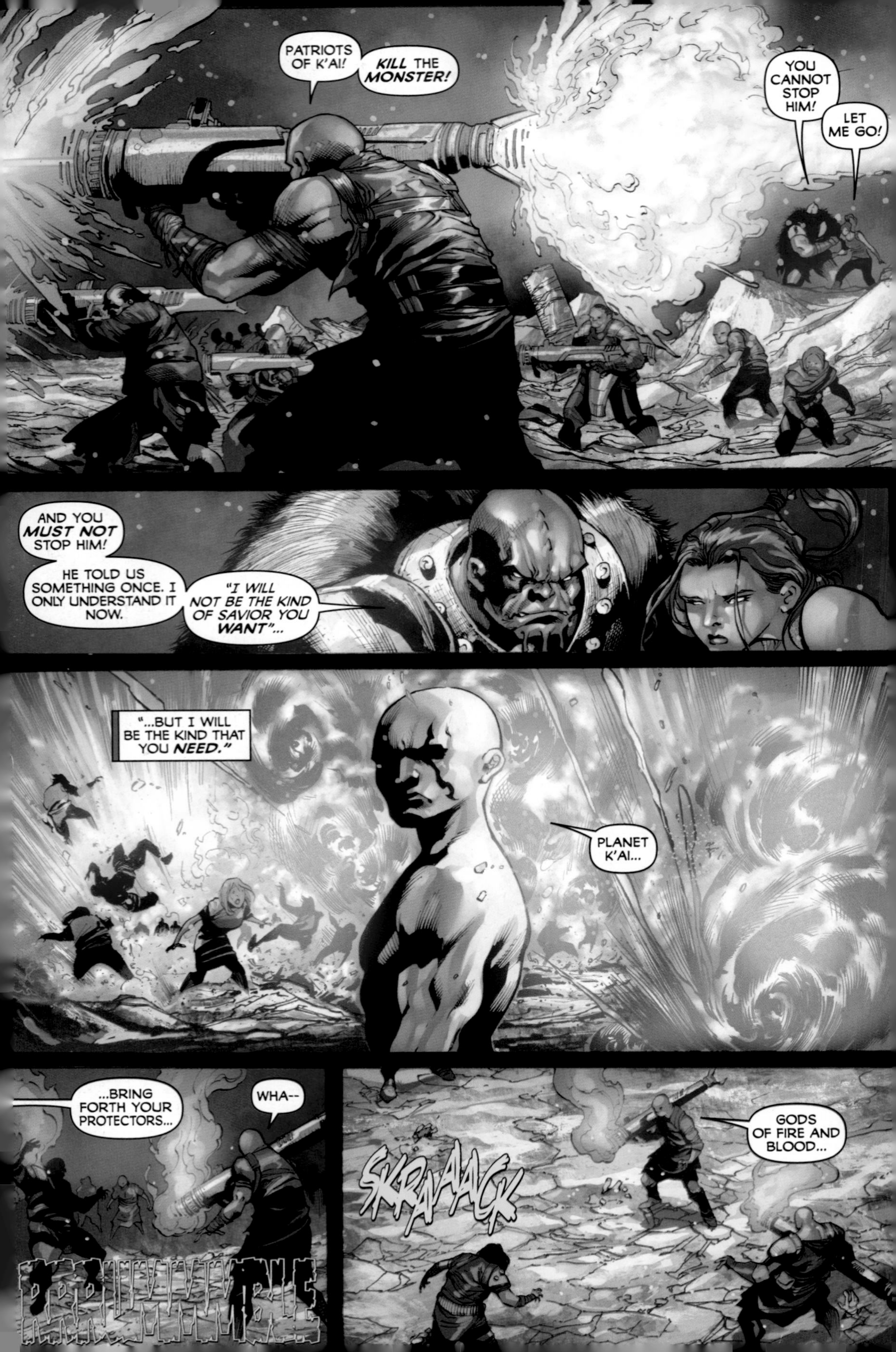
PATRIOTS OF K'AI! *KILL* THE *MONSTER!*
YOU CANNOT STOP HIM!
LET ME GO!
AND YOU *MUST NOT* STOP HIM!
HE TOLD US SOMETHING ONCE. I ONLY UNDERSTAND IT NOW.
"I WILL NOT BE THE KIND OF SAVIOR YOU WANT"...
"...BUT I WILL BE THE KIND THAT YOU *NEED.*"
PLANET K'AI...
...BRING FORTH YOUR PROTECTORS...
WHA--
SKRAAACK
GODS OF FIRE AND BLOOD...

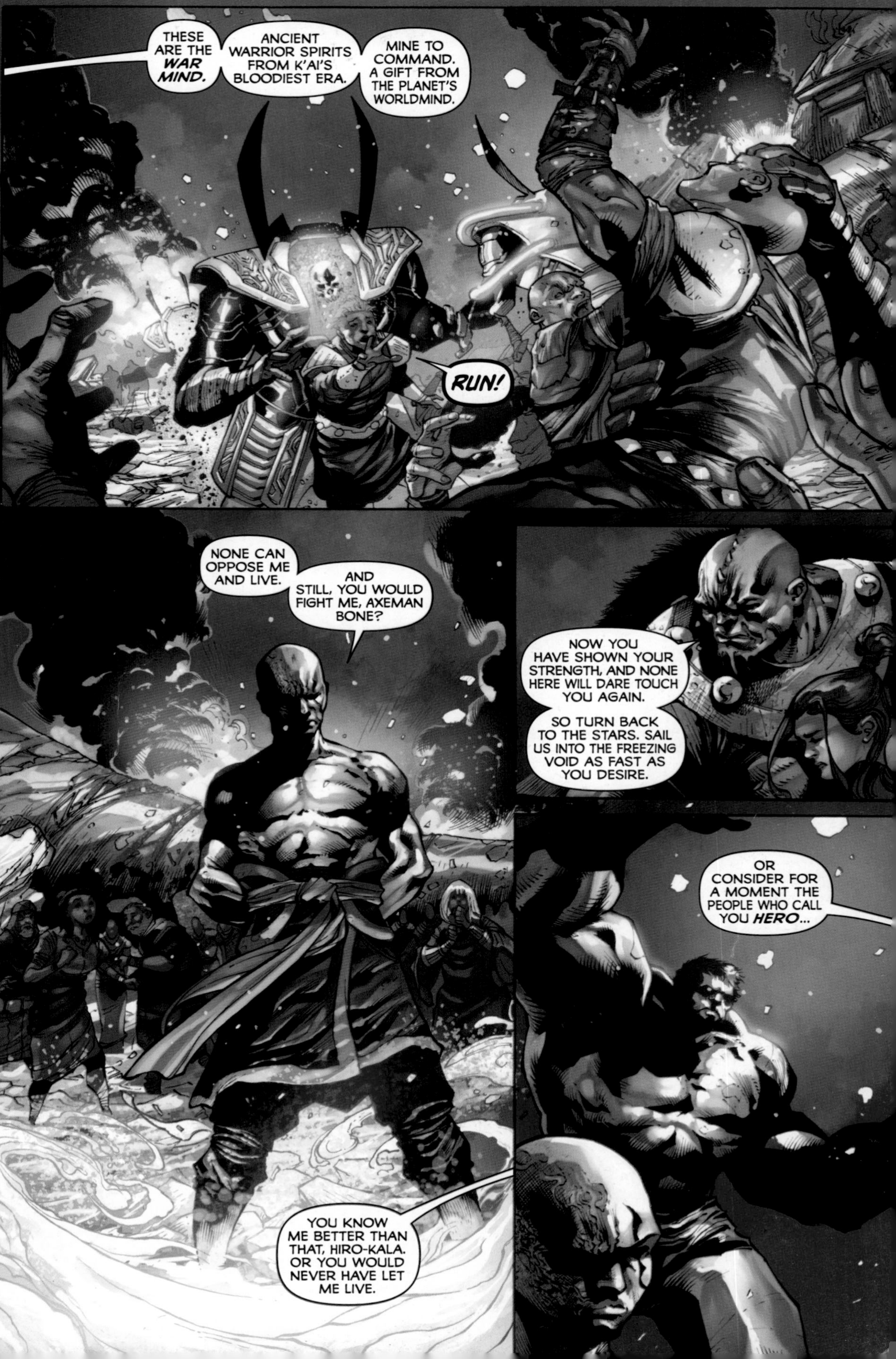
THESE ARE THE WAR MIND.
ANCIENT WARRIOR SPIRITS FROM K'AI'S BLOODIEST ERA.
MINE TO COMMAND. A GIFT FROM THE PLANET'S WORLDMIND.
RUN!
NONE CAN OPPOSE ME AND LIVE.
AND STILL, YOU WOULD FIGHT ME, AXEMAN BONE?
YOU KNOW ME BETTER THAN THAT, HIRO-KALA. OR YOU WOULD NEVER HAVE LET ME LIVE.
NOW YOU HAVE SHOWN YOUR STRENGTH, AND NONE HERE WILL DARE TOUCH YOU AGAIN.
SO TURN BACK TO THE STARS. SAIL US INTO THE FREEZING VOID AS FAST AS YOU DESIRE.
OR CONSIDER FOR A MOMENT THE PEOPLE WHO CALL YOU HERO...

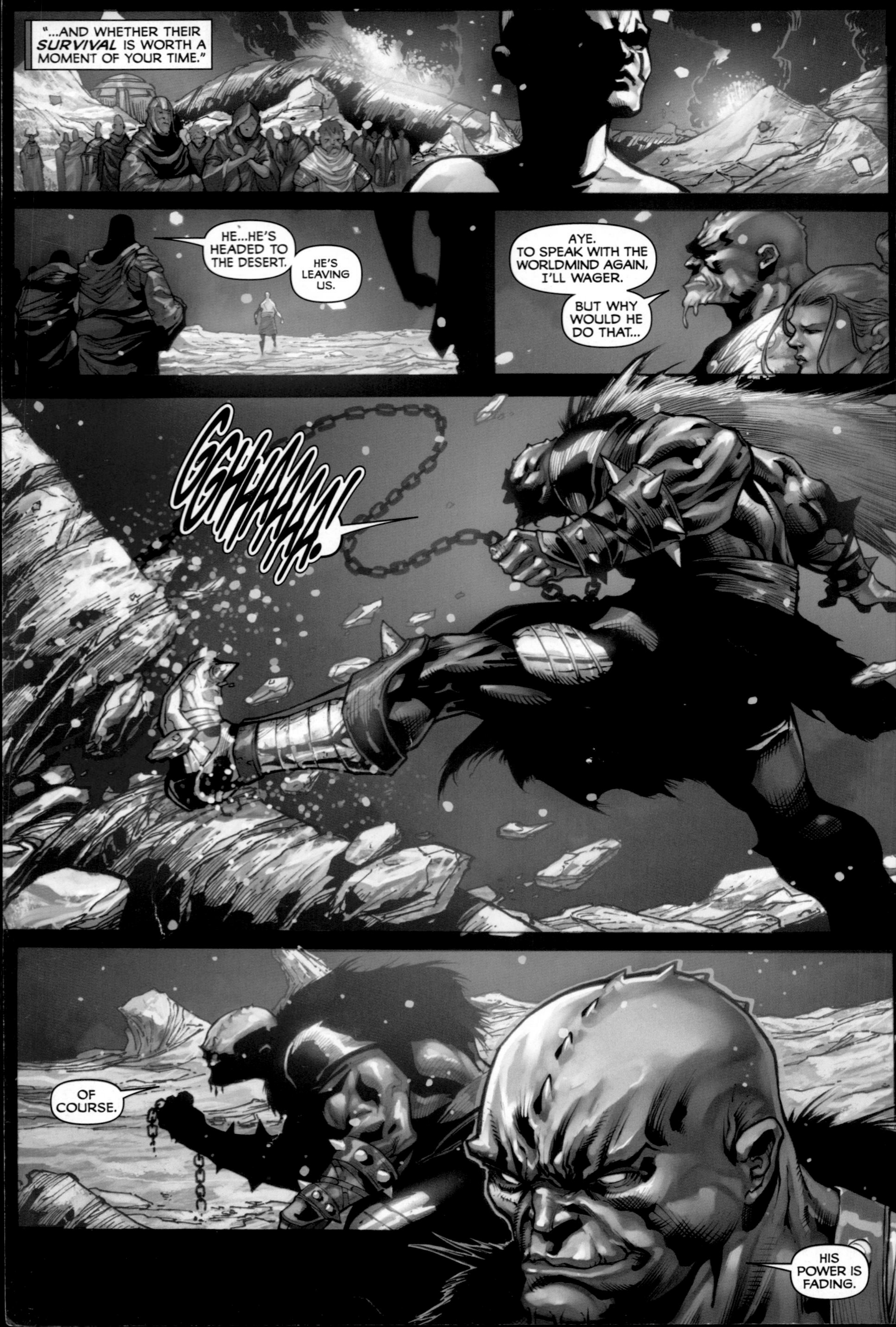
"...AND WHETHER THEIR *SURVIVAL* IS WORTH A MOMENT OF YOUR TIME."
HE...HE'S HEADED TO THE DESERT.
HE'S LEAVING US.
AYE. TO SPEAK WITH THE WORLDMIND AGAIN, I'LL WAGER.
BUT WHY WOULD HE DO THAT...
GGHAAAA!
OF COURSE.
HIS POWER IS FADING.

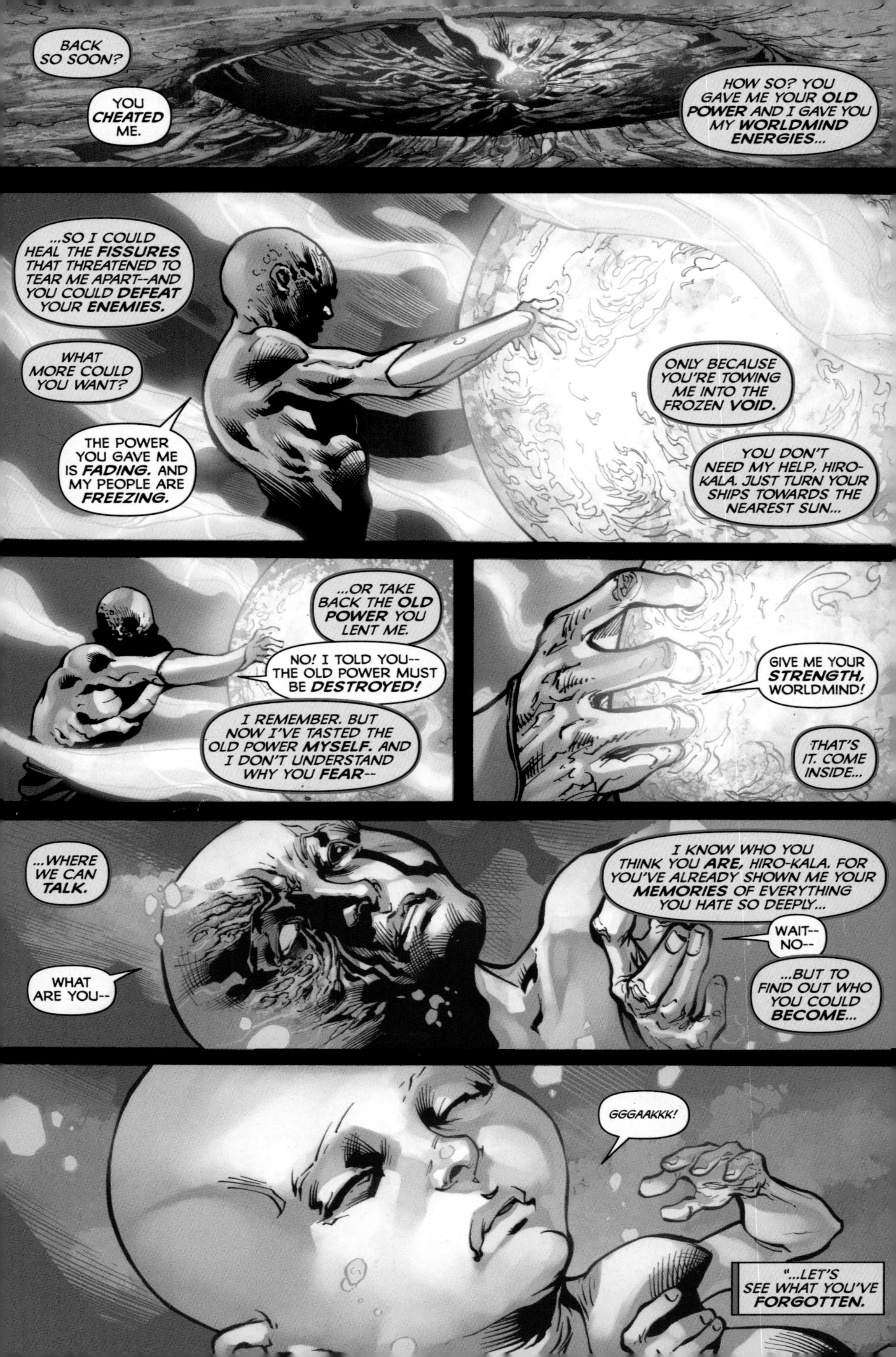
BACK SO SOON?
YOU CHEATED ME.
HOW SO? YOU GAVE ME YOUR OLD POWER AND I GAVE YOU MY WORLDMIND ENERGIES...
...SO I COULD HEAL THE FISSURES THAT THREATENED TO TEAR ME APART--AND YOU COULD DEFEAT YOUR ENEMIES.
WHAT MORE COULD YOU WANT?
THE POWER YOU GAVE ME IS FADING. AND MY PEOPLE ARE FREEZING.
ONLY BECAUSE YOU'RE TOWING ME INTO THE FROZEN VOID.
YOU DON'T NEED MY HELP, HIRO-KALA. JUST TURN YOUR SHIPS TOWARDS THE NEAREST SUN...
...OR TAKE BACK THE OLD POWER YOU LENT ME.
NO! I TOLD YOU-- THE OLD POWER MUST BE DESTROYED!
I REMEMBER. BUT NOW I'VE TASTED THE OLD POWER MYSELF. AND I DON'T UNDERSTAND WHY YOU FEAR--
GIVE ME YOUR STRENGTH, WORLDMIND!
THAT'S IT. COME INSIDE...
...WHERE WE CAN TALK.
I KNOW WHO YOU THINK YOU ARE, HIRO-KALA. FOR YOU'VE ALREADY SHOWN ME YOUR MEMORIES OF EVERYTHING YOU HATE SO DEEPLY...
WAIT-- NO--
WHAT ARE YOU--
...BUT TO FIND OUT WHO YOU COULD BECOME...
GGGAAKKK!
"...LET'S SEE WHAT YOU'VE FORGOTTEN.

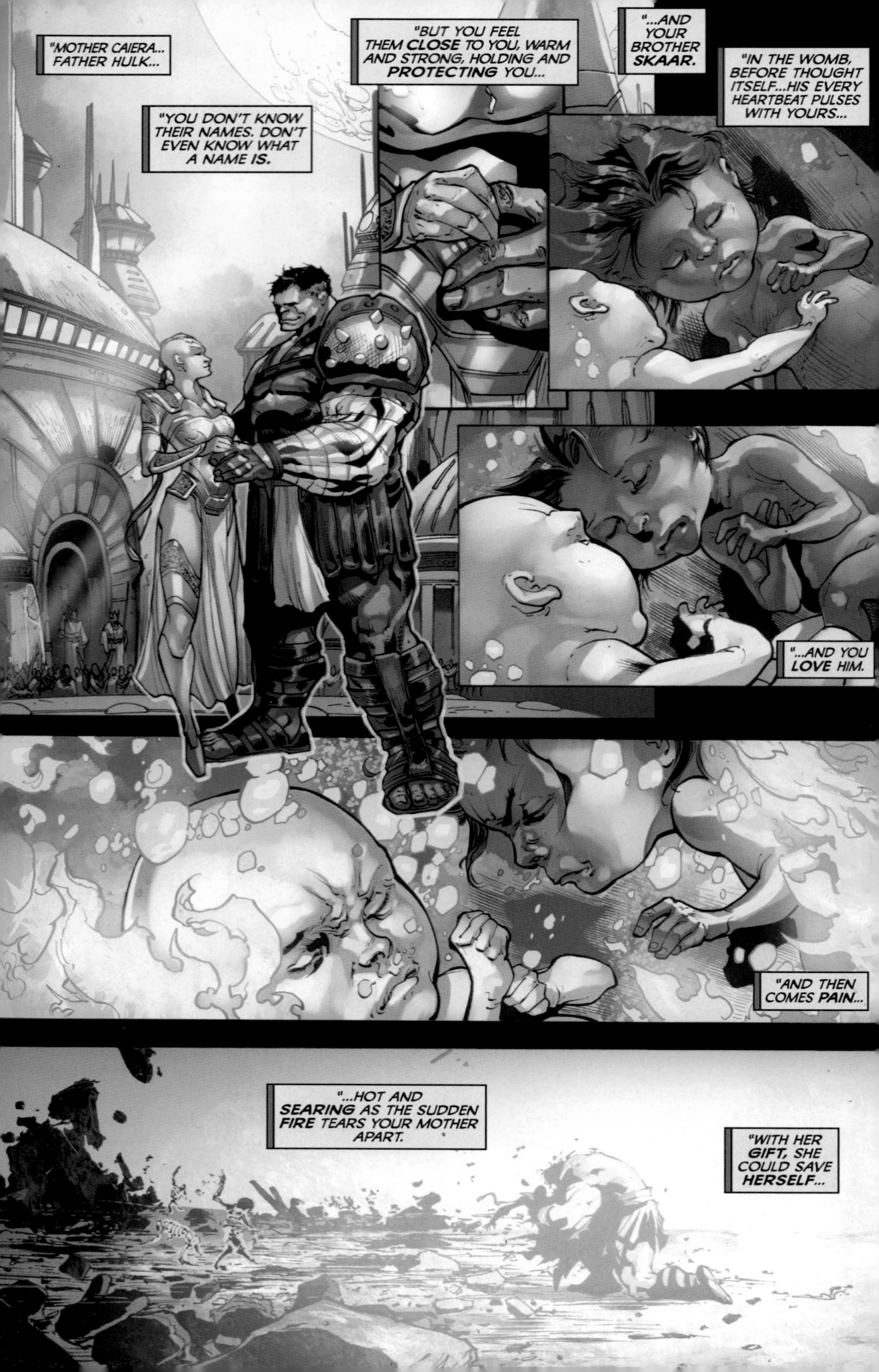
"MOTHER CAIERA... FATHER HULK...
"YOU DON'T KNOW THEIR NAMES. DON'T EVEN KNOW WHAT A NAME IS.
"BUT YOU FEEL THEM CLOSE TO YOU, WARM AND STRONG, HOLDING AND PROTECTING YOU...
"...AND YOUR BROTHER SKAAR.
"IN THE WOMB, BEFORE THOUGHT ITSELF...HIS EVERY HEARTBEAT PULSES WITH YOURS...
"...AND YOU LOVE HIM.
"AND THEN COMES PAIN...
"...HOT AND SEARING AS THE SUDDEN FIRE TEARS YOUR MOTHER APART.
"WITH HER GIFT, SHE COULD SAVE HERSELF...

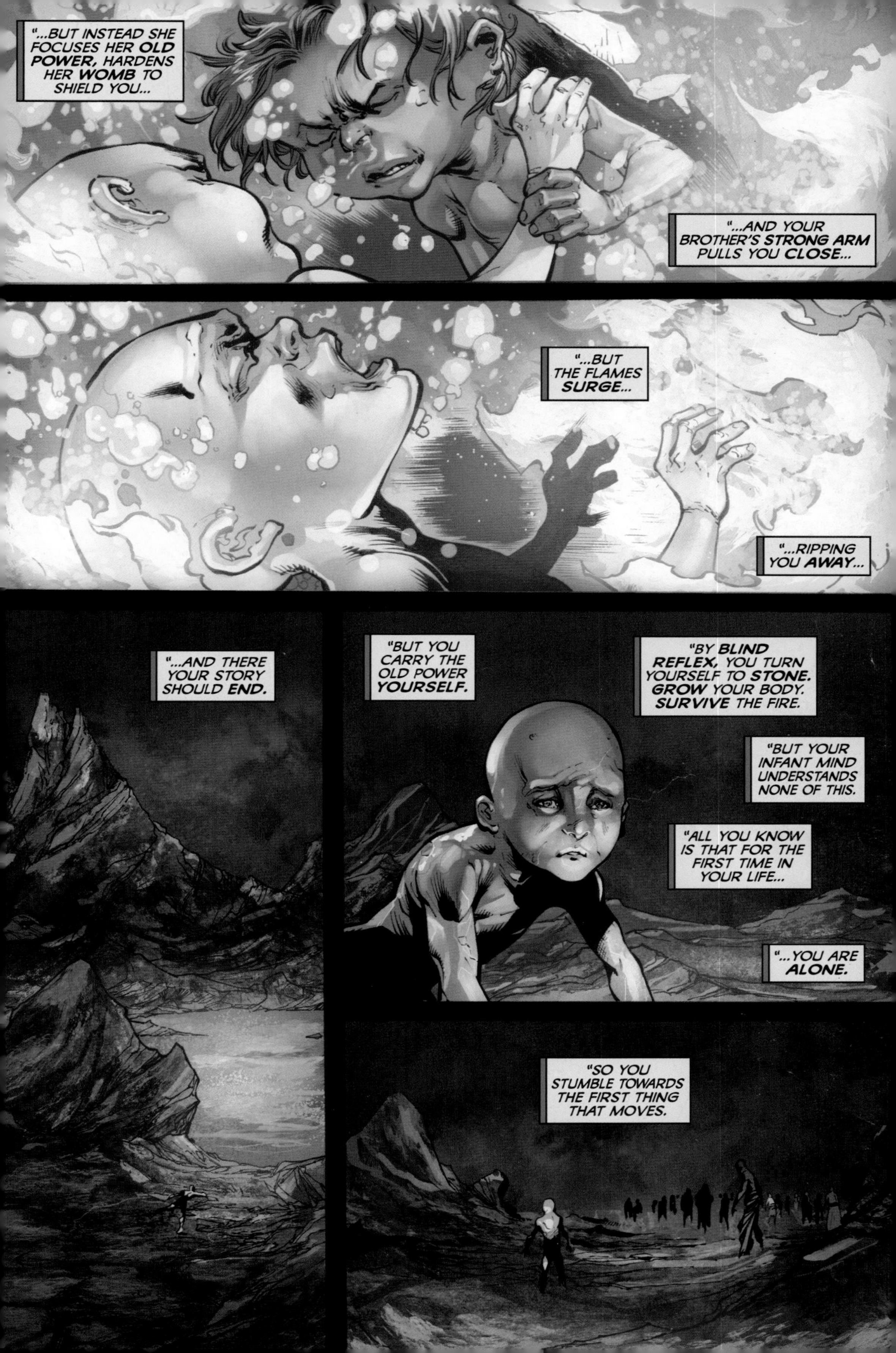
"...BUT INSTEAD SHE FOCUSES HER OLD POWER, HARDENS HER WOMB TO SHIELD YOU...
"...AND YOUR BROTHER'S STRONG ARM PULLS YOU CLOSE...
"...BUT THE FLAMES SURGE...
"...RIPPING YOU AWAY...
"...AND THERE YOUR STORY SHOULD END.
"BUT YOU CARRY THE OLD POWER YOURSELF.
"BY BLIND REFLEX, YOU TURN YOURSELF TO STONE. GROW YOUR BODY. SURVIVE THE FIRE.
"BUT YOUR INFANT MIND UNDERSTANDS NONE OF THIS.
"ALL YOU KNOW IS THAT FOR THE FIRST TIME IN YOUR LIFE...
"...YOU ARE ALONE.
"SO YOU STUMBLE TOWARDS THE FIRST THING THAT MOVES.

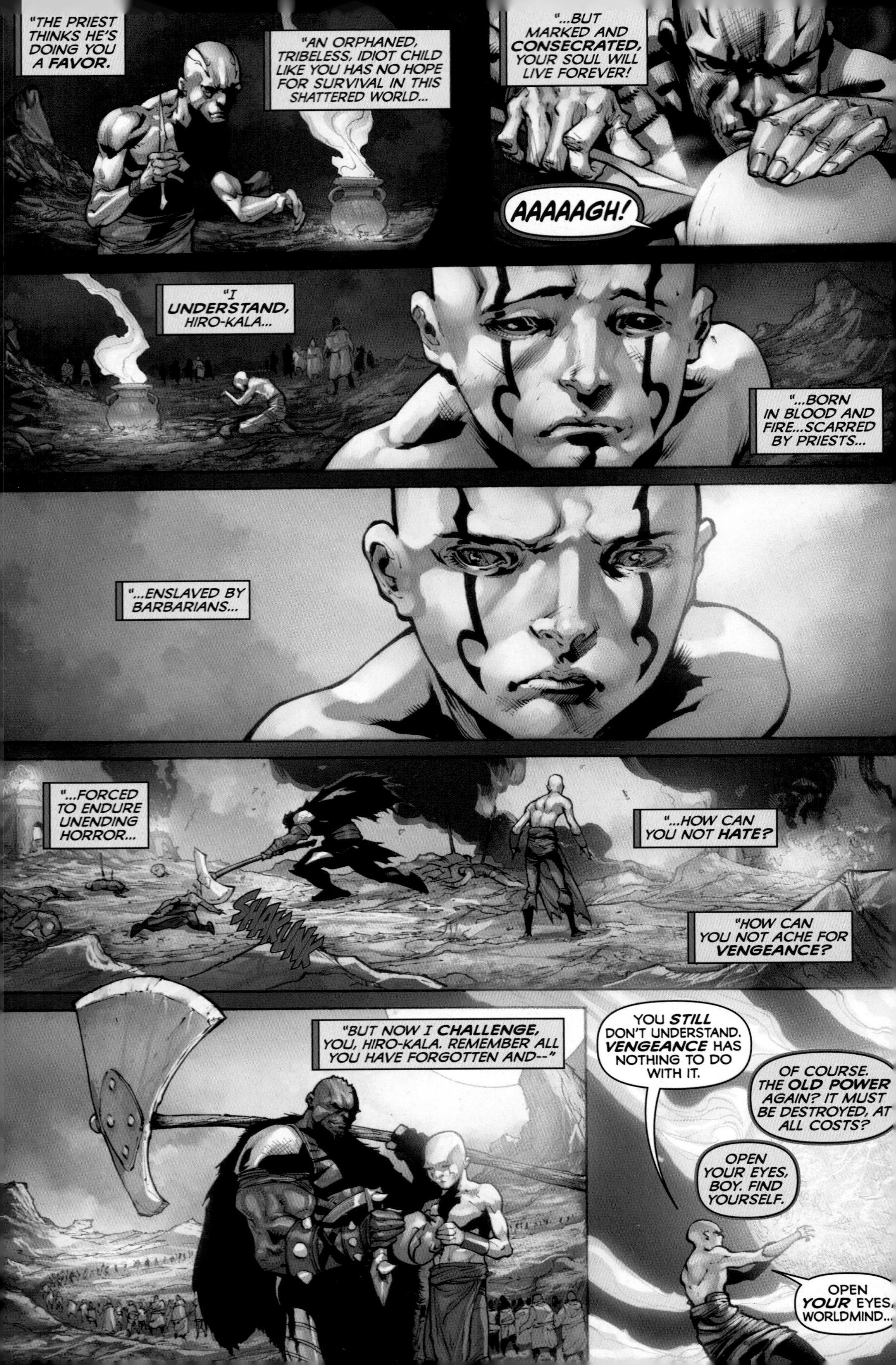

"THE PRIEST THINKS HE'S DOING YOU A FAVOR.
"AN ORPHANED, TRIBELESS, IDIOT CHILD LIKE YOU HAS NO HOPE FOR SURVIVAL IN THIS SHATTERED WORLD...
"...BUT MARKED AND CONSECRATED, YOUR SOUL WILL LIVE FOREVER!
AAAAAGH!
"I UNDERSTAND, HIRO-KALA...
"...BORN IN BLOOD AND FIRE...SCARRED BY PRIESTS...
"...ENSLAVED BY BARBARIANS...
"...FORCED TO ENDURE UNENDING HORROR...
"...HOW CAN YOU NOT HATE?
SHAKUNK
"HOW CAN YOU NOT ACHE FOR VENGEANCE?
"BUT NOW I CHALLENGE, YOU, HIRO-KALA. REMEMBER ALL YOU HAVE FORGOTTEN AND--"
YOU STILL DON'T UNDERSTAND. VENGEANCE HAS NOTHING TO DO WITH IT.
OF COURSE. THE OLD POWER AGAIN? IT MUST BE DESTROYED, AT ALL COSTS?
OPEN YOUR EYES, BOY. FIND YOURSELF.
OPEN YOUR EYES, WORLDMIND...

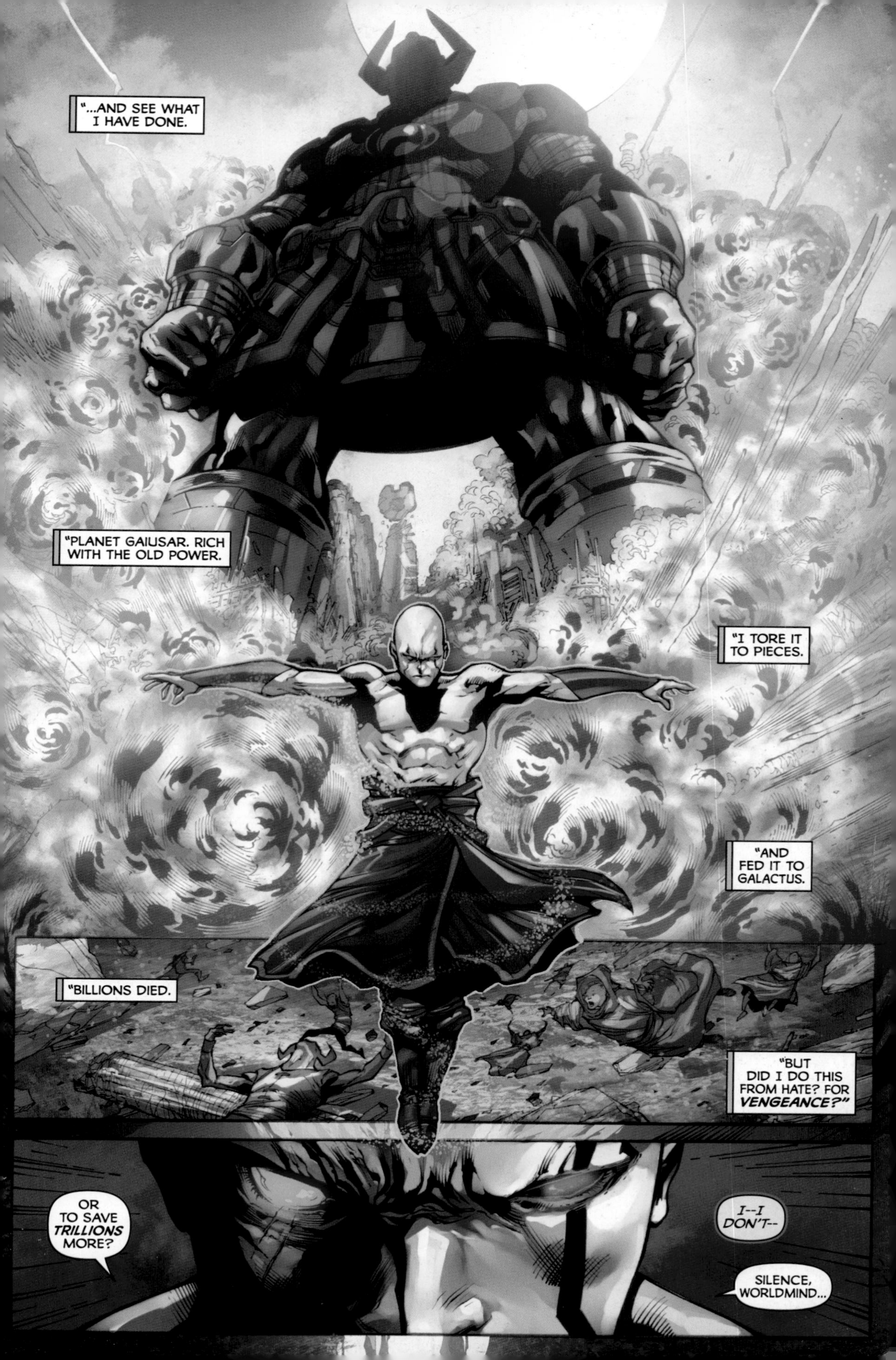
"...AND SEE WHAT I HAVE DONE.
"PLANET GAIUSAR. RICH WITH THE OLD POWER.
"I TORE IT TO PIECES.
"AND FED IT TO GALACTUS.
"BILLIONS DIED.
"BUT DID I DO THIS FROM HATE? FOR VENGEANCE?"
OR TO SAVE TRILLIONS MORE?
I--I DON'T--
SILENCE, WORLDMIND...

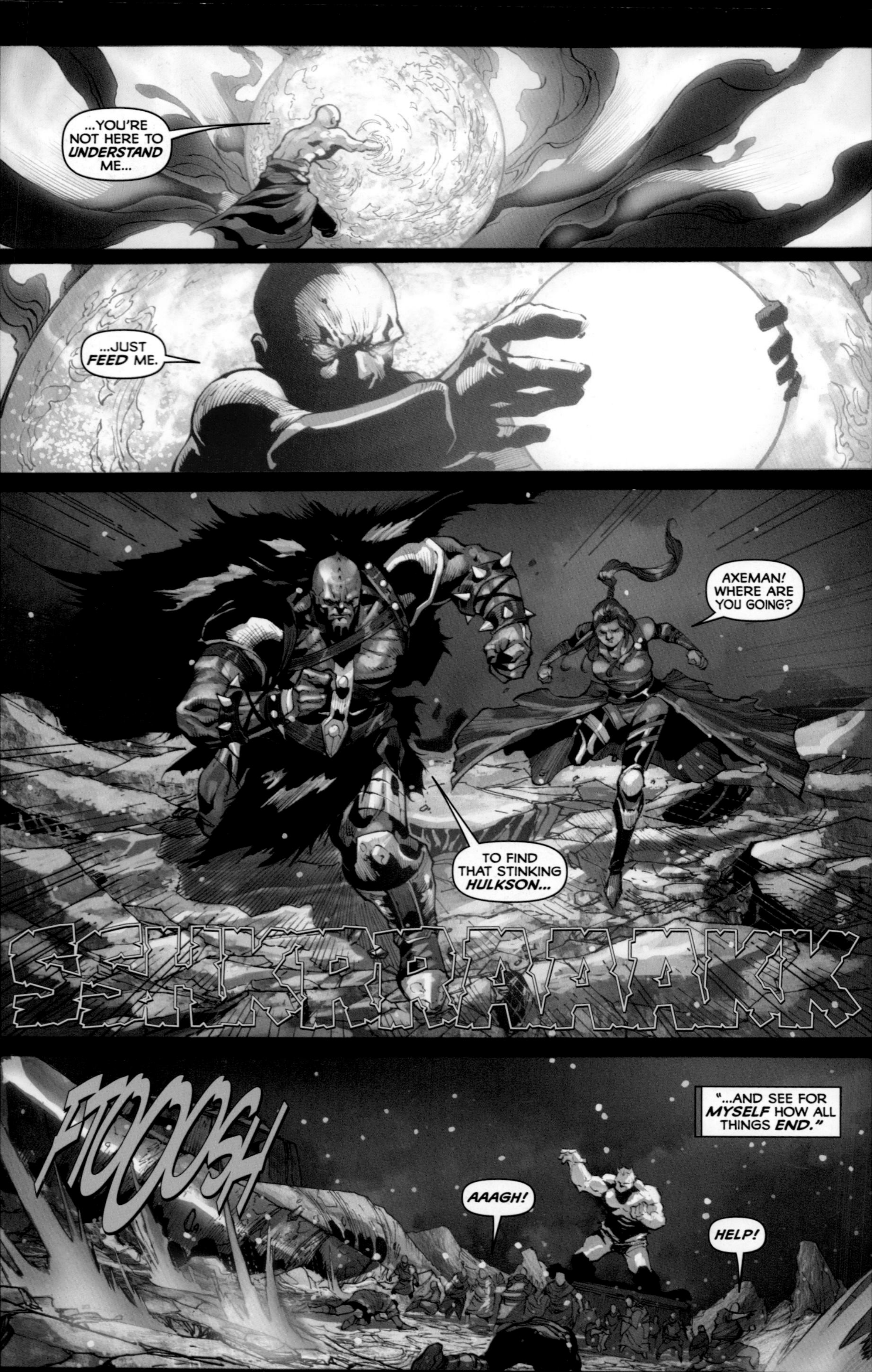
...YOU'RE NOT HERE TO *UNDERSTAND* ME...
...JUST *FEED* ME.
AXEMAN! WHERE ARE YOU GOING?
TO FIND THAT STINKING *HULKSON*...
SKRRRAAKK
FTOOOSH
"...AND SEE FOR *MYSELF* HOW ALL THINGS *END*."
AAAGH!
HELP!

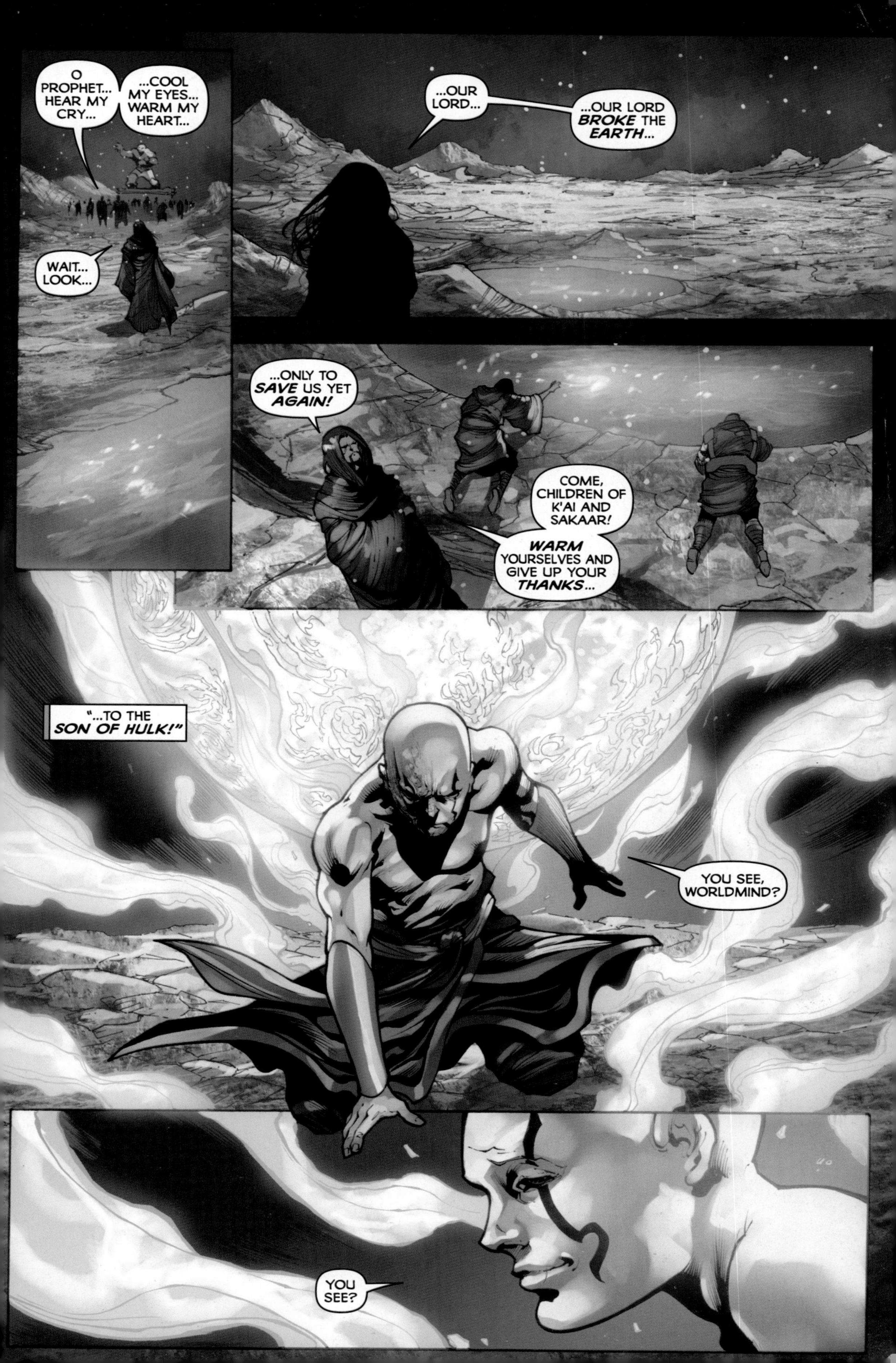
O PROPHET... HEAR MY CRY...
...COOL MY EYES... WARM MY HEART...
WAIT... LOOK...
...OUR LORD...
...OUR LORD BROKE THE EARTH...
...ONLY TO SAVE US YET AGAIN!
COME, CHILDREN OF K'AI AND SAKAAR!
WARM YOURSELVES AND GIVE UP YOUR THANKS...
"...TO THE SON OF HULK!"
YOU SEE, WORLDMIND?
YOU SEE?

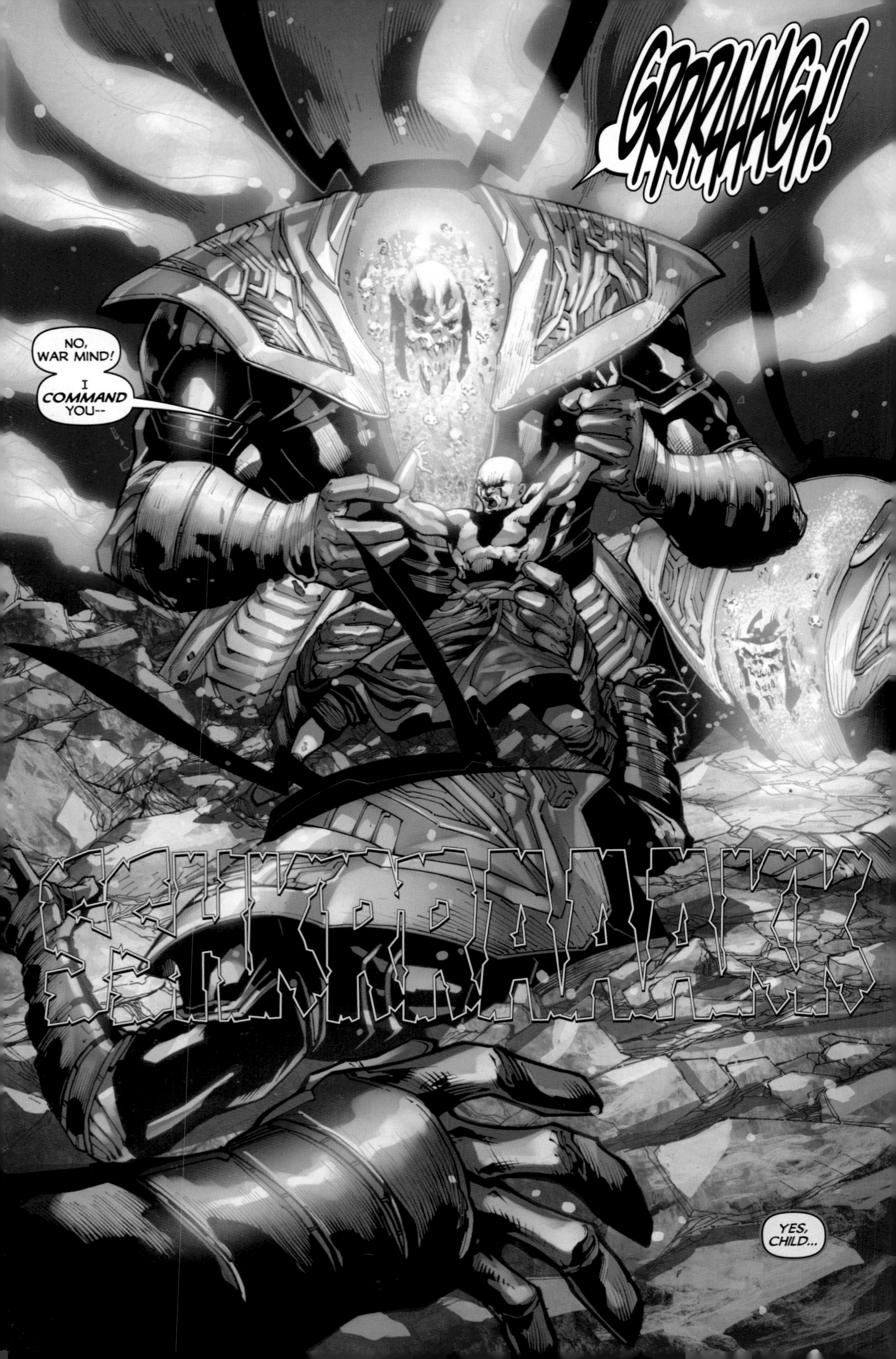
GRRAAGH!
NO, WAR MIND! I COMMAND YOU--
SKKRRAAAKK
YES, CHILD...

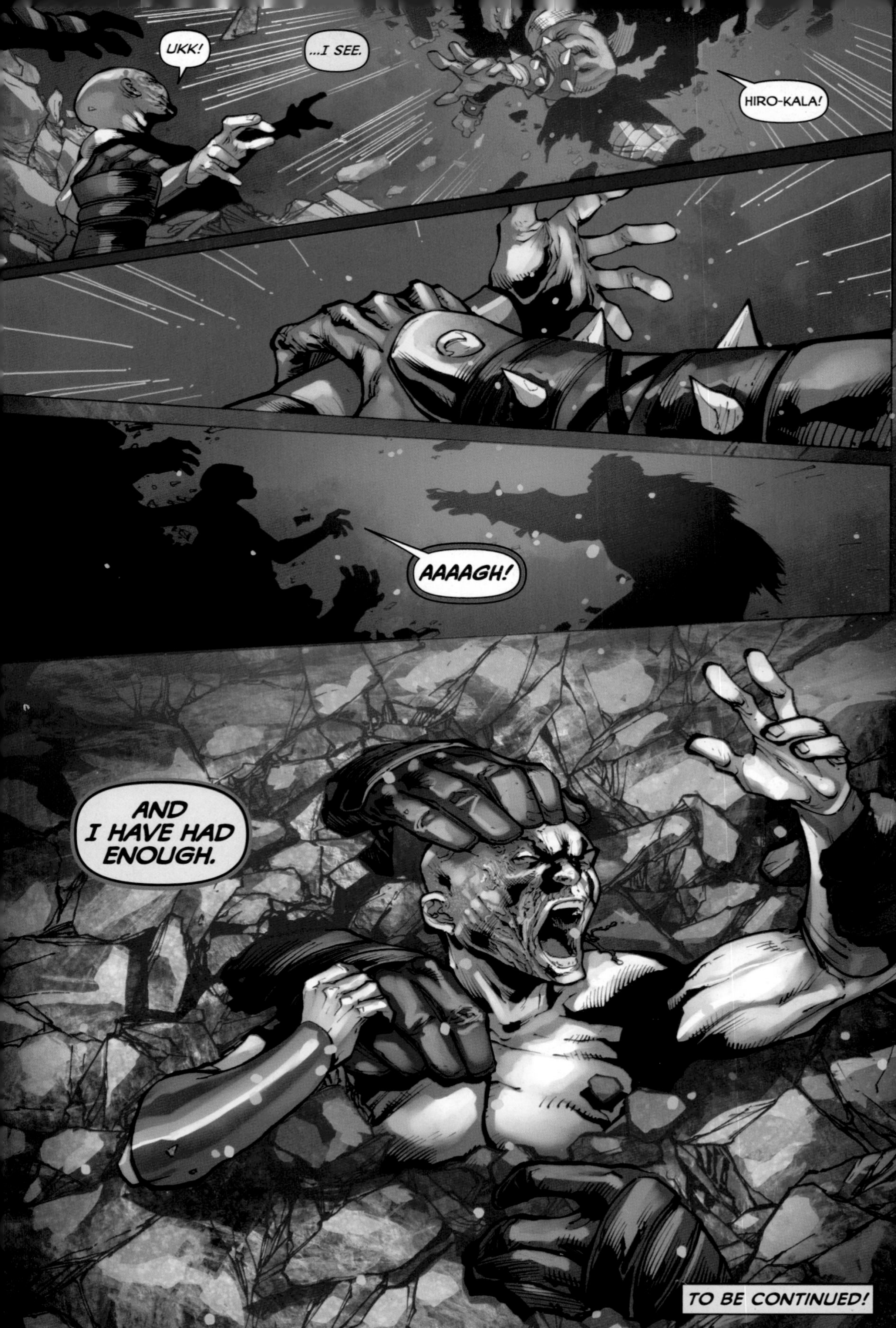
UKK!
...I SEE.
HIRO-KALA!
AAAAGH!
AND I HAVE HAD ENOUGH.
TO BE CONTINUED!

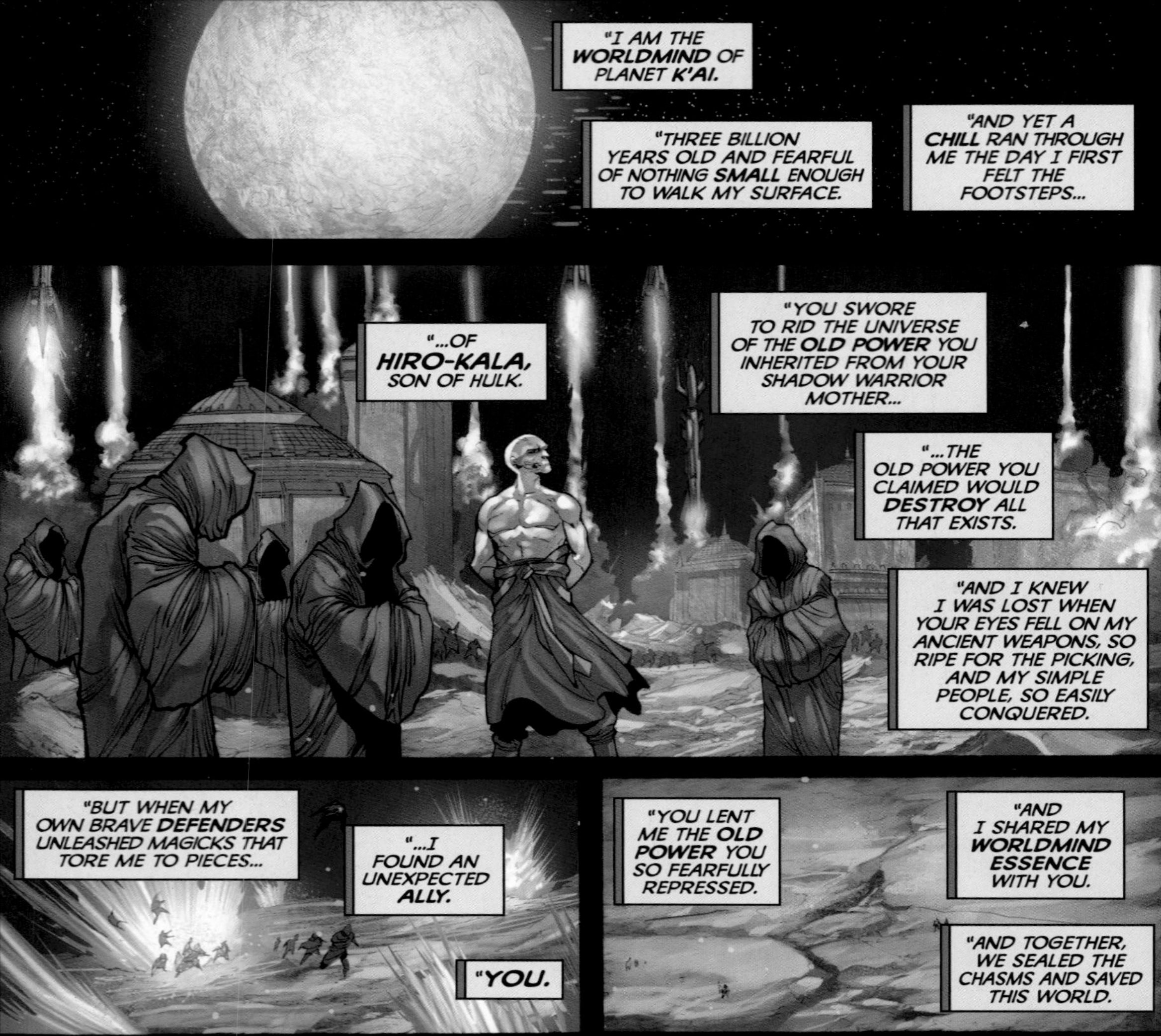
"I AM THE WORLDMIND OF PLANET K'AI.
"THREE BILLION YEARS OLD AND FEARFUL OF NOTHING SMALL ENOUGH TO WALK MY SURFACE.
"AND YET A CHILL RAN THROUGH ME THE DAY I FIRST FELT THE FOOTSTEPS...
"...OF HIRO-KALA, SON OF HULK.
"YOU SWORE TO RID THE UNIVERSE OF THE OLD POWER YOU INHERITED FROM YOUR SHADOW WARRIOR MOTHER...
"...THE OLD POWER YOU CLAIMED WOULD DESTROY ALL THAT EXISTS.
"AND I KNEW I WAS LOST WHEN YOUR EYES FELL ON MY ANCIENT WEAPONS, SO RIPE FOR THE PICKING, AND MY SIMPLE PEOPLE, SO EASILY CONQUERED.
"BUT WHEN MY OWN BRAVE DEFENDERS UNLEASHED MAGICKS THAT TORE ME TO PIECES...
"...I FOUND AN UNEXPECTED ALLY.
"YOU.
"YOU LENT ME THE OLD POWER YOU SO FEARFULLY REPRESSED.
"AND I SHARED MY WORLDMIND ESSENCE WITH YOU.
"AND TOGETHER, WE SEALED THE CHASMS AND SAVED THIS WORLD.

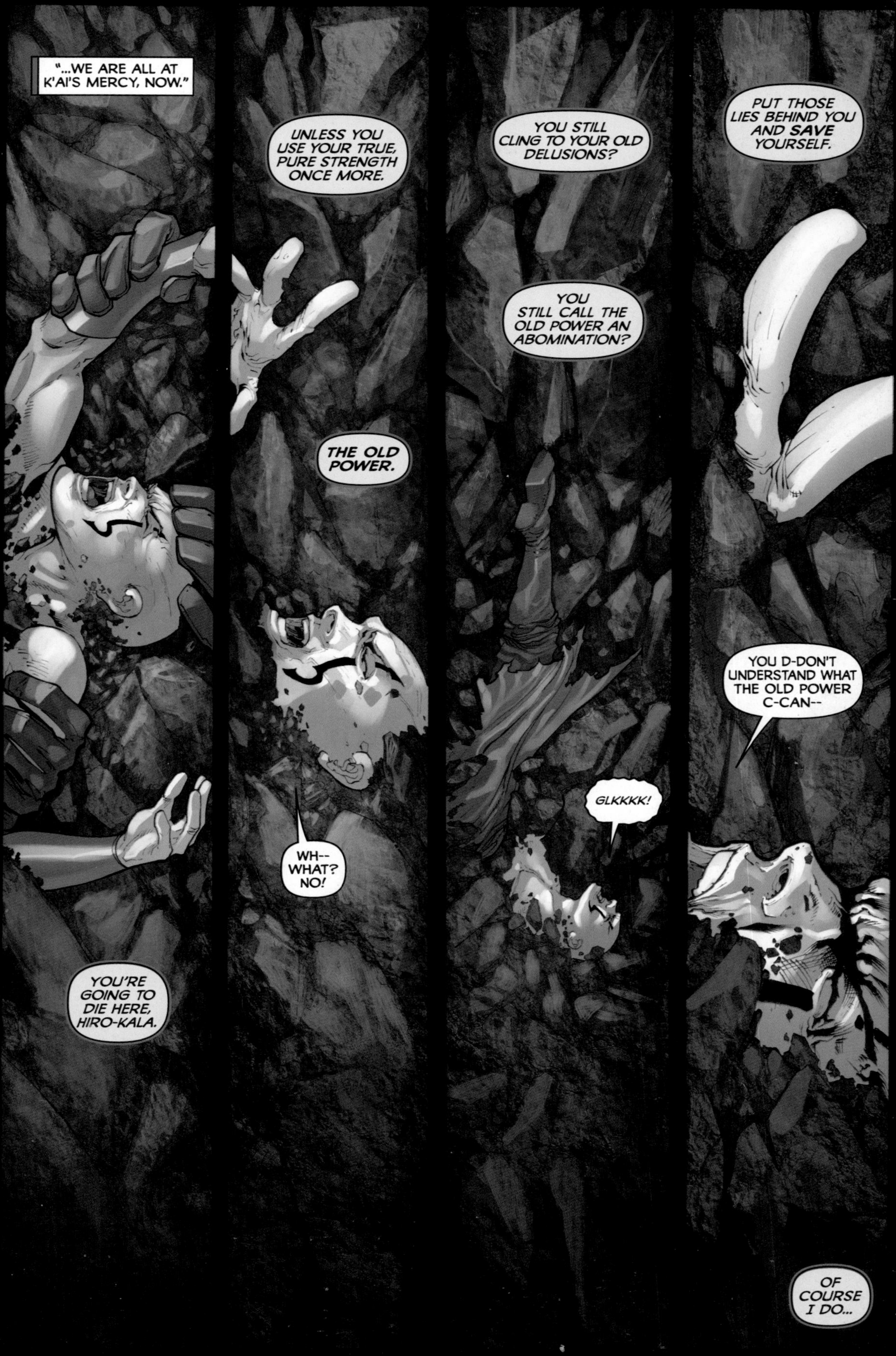
"...WE ARE ALL AT K'AI'S MERCY, NOW."
YOU'RE GOING TO DIE HERE, HIRO-KALA.
UNLESS YOU USE YOUR TRUE, PURE STRENGTH ONCE MORE.
THE OLD POWER.
WH-- WHAT? NO!
YOU STILL CLING TO YOUR OLD DELUSIONS?
YOU STILL CALL THE OLD POWER AN ABOMINATION?
GLKKKK!
PUT THOSE LIES BEHIND YOU AND SAVE YOURSELF.
YOU D-DON'T UNDERSTAND WHAT THE OLD POWER C-CAN--
OF COURSE I DO...

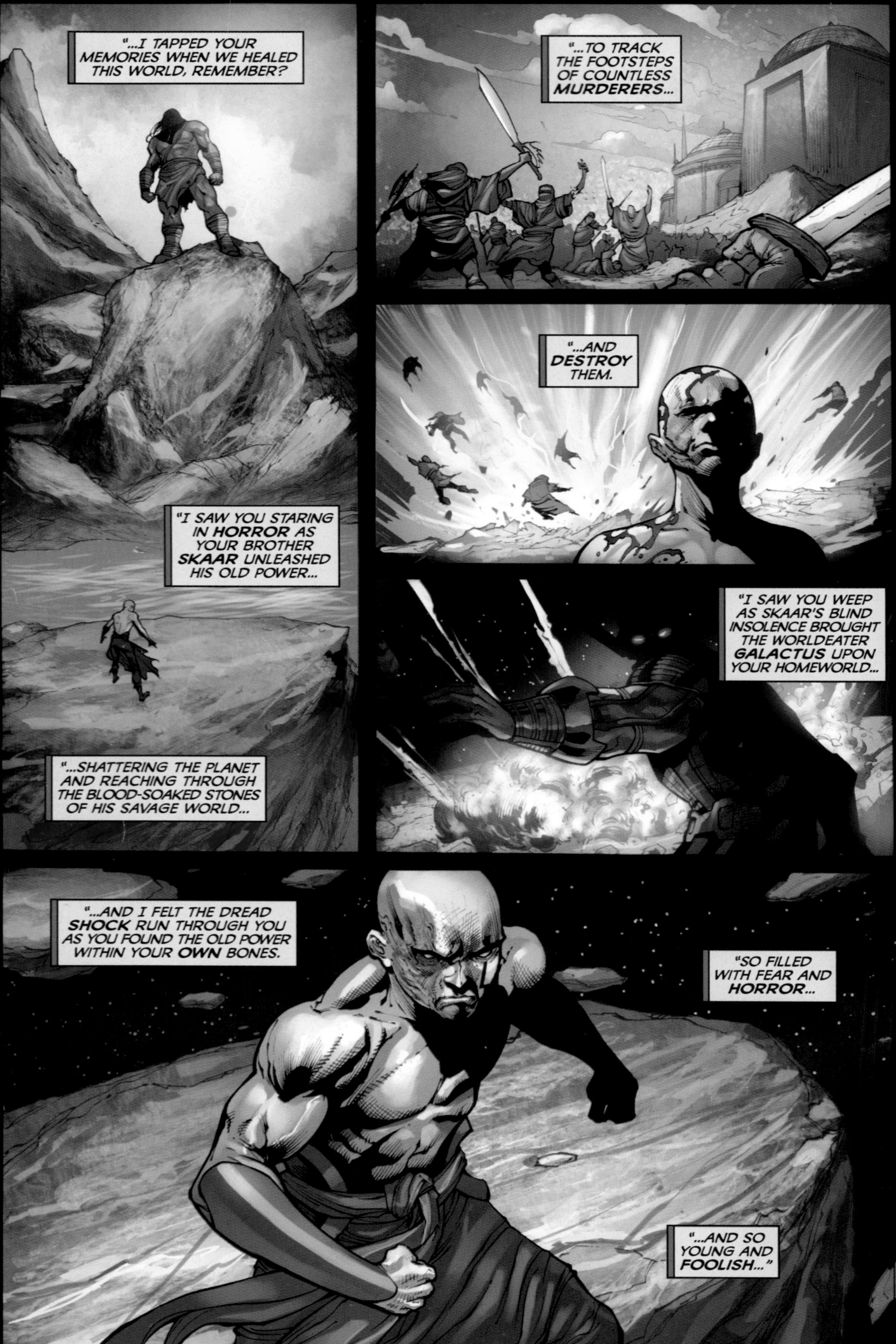
"...I TAPPED YOUR MEMORIES WHEN WE HEALED THIS WORLD, REMEMBER?
"...TO TRACK THE FOOTSTEPS OF COUNTLESS MURDERERS...
"...AND DESTROY THEM.
"I SAW YOU STARING IN HORROR AS YOUR BROTHER SKAAR UNLEASHED HIS OLD POWER...
"...SHATTERING THE PLANET AND REACHING THROUGH THE BLOOD-SOAKED STONES OF HIS SAVAGE WORLD...
"I SAW YOU WEEP AS SKAAR'S BLIND INSOLENCE BROUGHT THE WORLDEATER GALACTUS UPON YOUR HOMEWORLD...
"...AND I FELT THE DREAD SHOCK RUN THROUGH YOU AS YOU FOUND THE OLD POWER WITHIN YOUR OWN BONES.
"SO FILLED WITH FEAR AND HORROR...
"...AND SO YOUNG AND FOOLISH..."

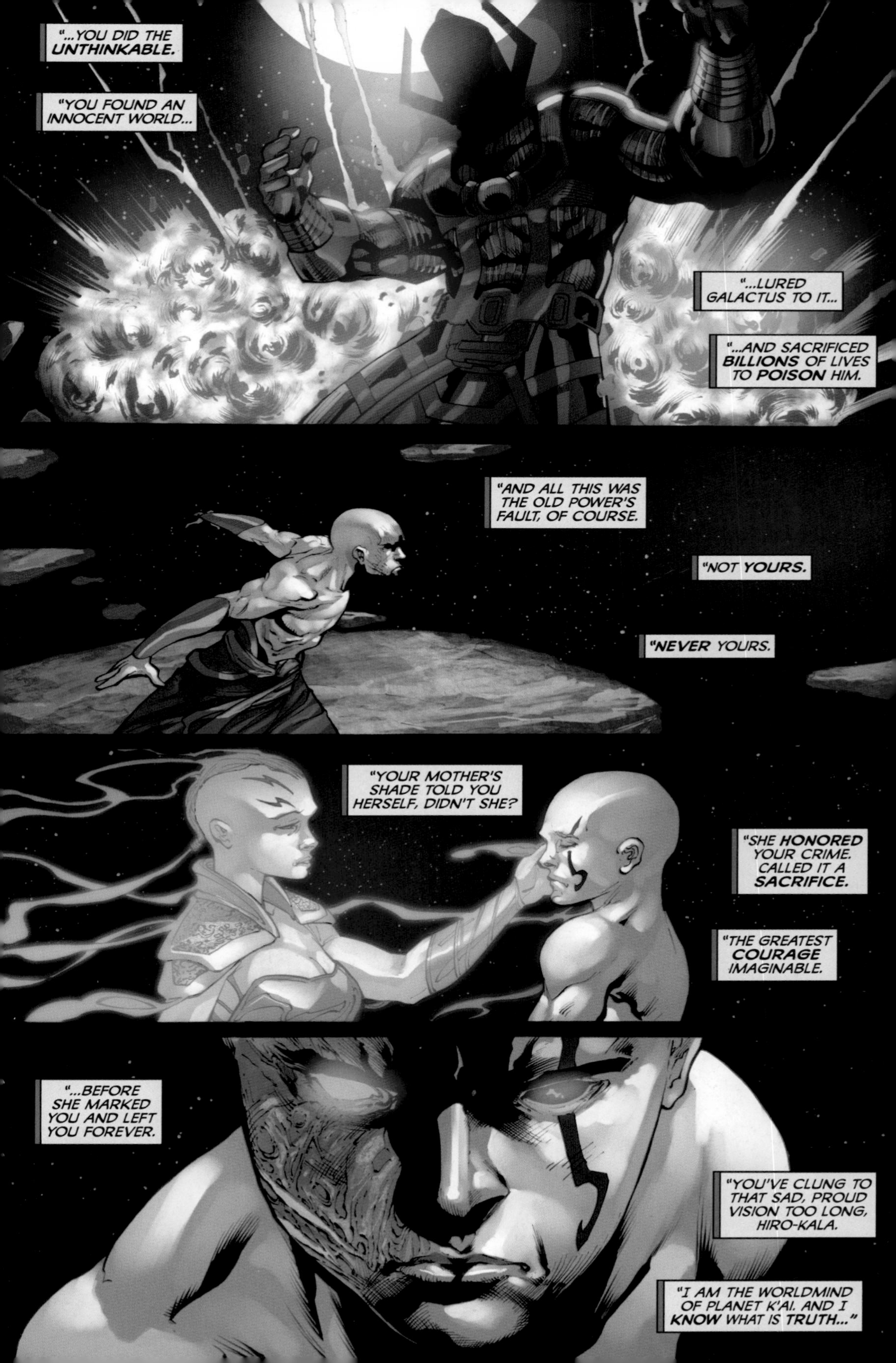
"...YOU DID THE UNTHINKABLE.
"YOU FOUND AN INNOCENT WORLD...
"...LURED GALACTUS TO IT...
"...AND SACRIFICED BILLIONS OF LIVES TO POISON HIM.
"AND ALL THIS WAS THE OLD POWER'S FAULT, OF COURSE.
"NOT YOURS.
"NEVER YOURS.
"YOUR MOTHER'S SHADE TOLD YOU HERSELF, DIDN'T SHE?
"SHE HONORED YOUR CRIME. CALLED IT A SACRIFICE.
"THE GREATEST COURAGE IMAGINABLE.
"...BEFORE SHE MARKED YOU AND LEFT YOU FOREVER.
"YOU'VE CLUNG TO THAT SAD, PROUD VISION TOO LONG, HIRO-KALA.
"I AM THE WORLDMIND OF PLANET K'AI. AND I KNOW WHAT IS TRUTH..."

...AND TODAY, SO WILL YOU...
...WHEN I REAWAKEN YOUR OLD POWER.
EMBRACE IT, CHILD...
...AND BECOME EVERYTHING...
AAAAAAGH!
...YOU WERE MEANT TO BE.
SSSKRRAAAAKKKK
AAH...!
HA. YOU SEE NOW, DON'T YOU?

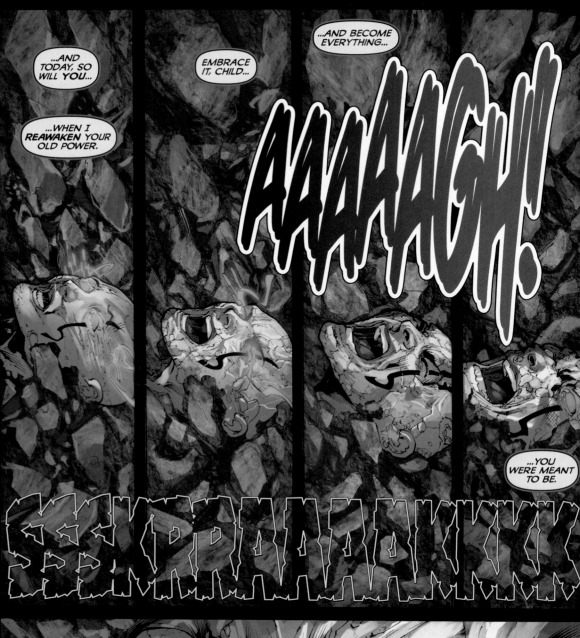

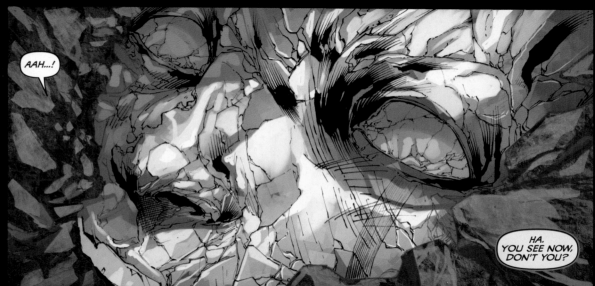

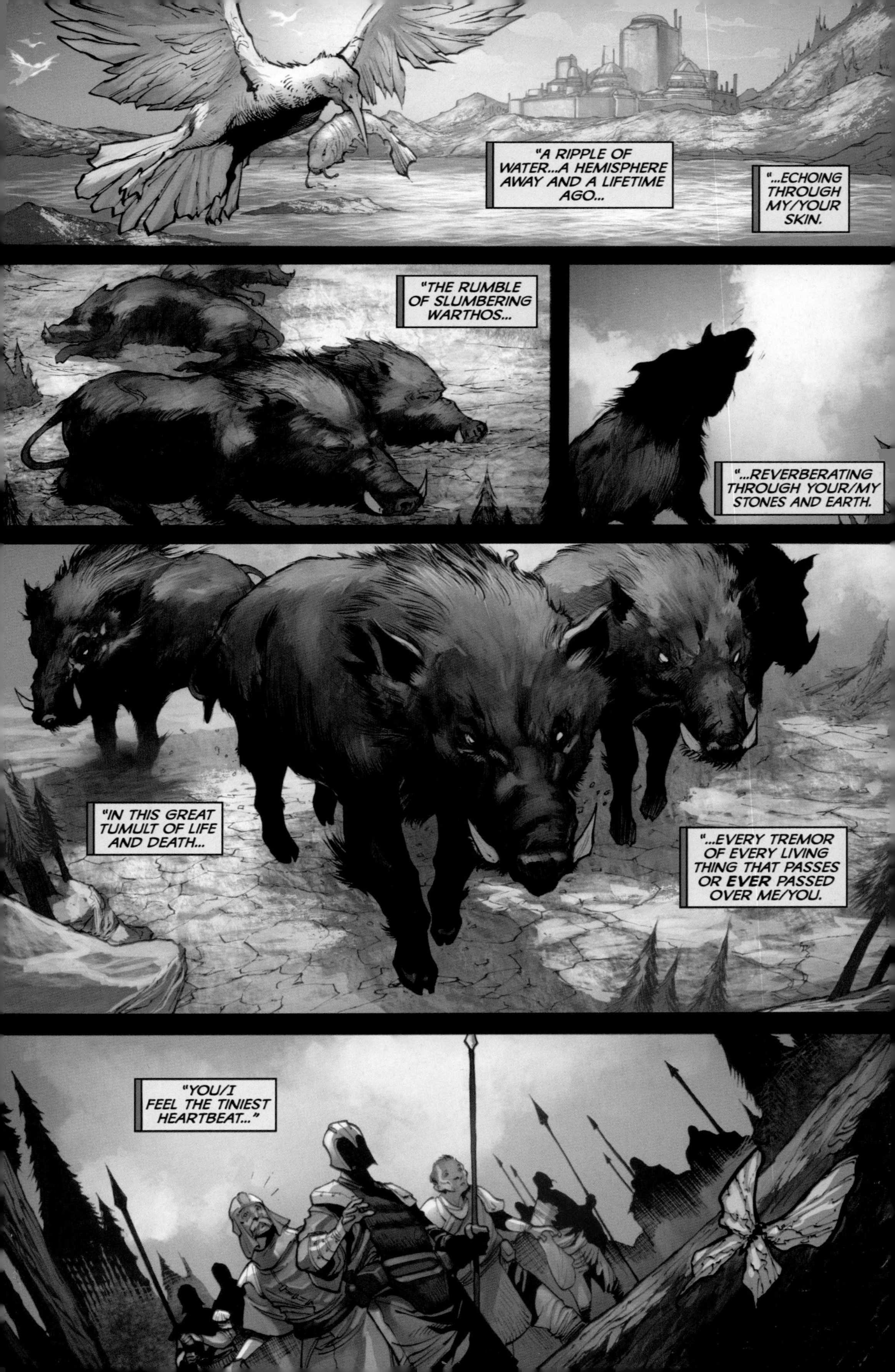
"A RIPPLE OF WATER...A HEMISPHERE AWAY AND A LIFETIME AGO...
"...ECHOING THROUGH MY/YOUR SKIN.
"THE RUMBLE OF SLUMBERING WARTHOS...
"...REVERBERATING THROUGH YOUR/MY STONES AND EARTH.
"IN THIS GREAT TUMULT OF LIFE AND DEATH...
"...EVERY TREMOR OF EVERY LIVING THING THAT PASSES OR **EVER** PASSED OVER ME/YOU.
"YOU/I FEEL THE TINIEST HEARTBEAT..."

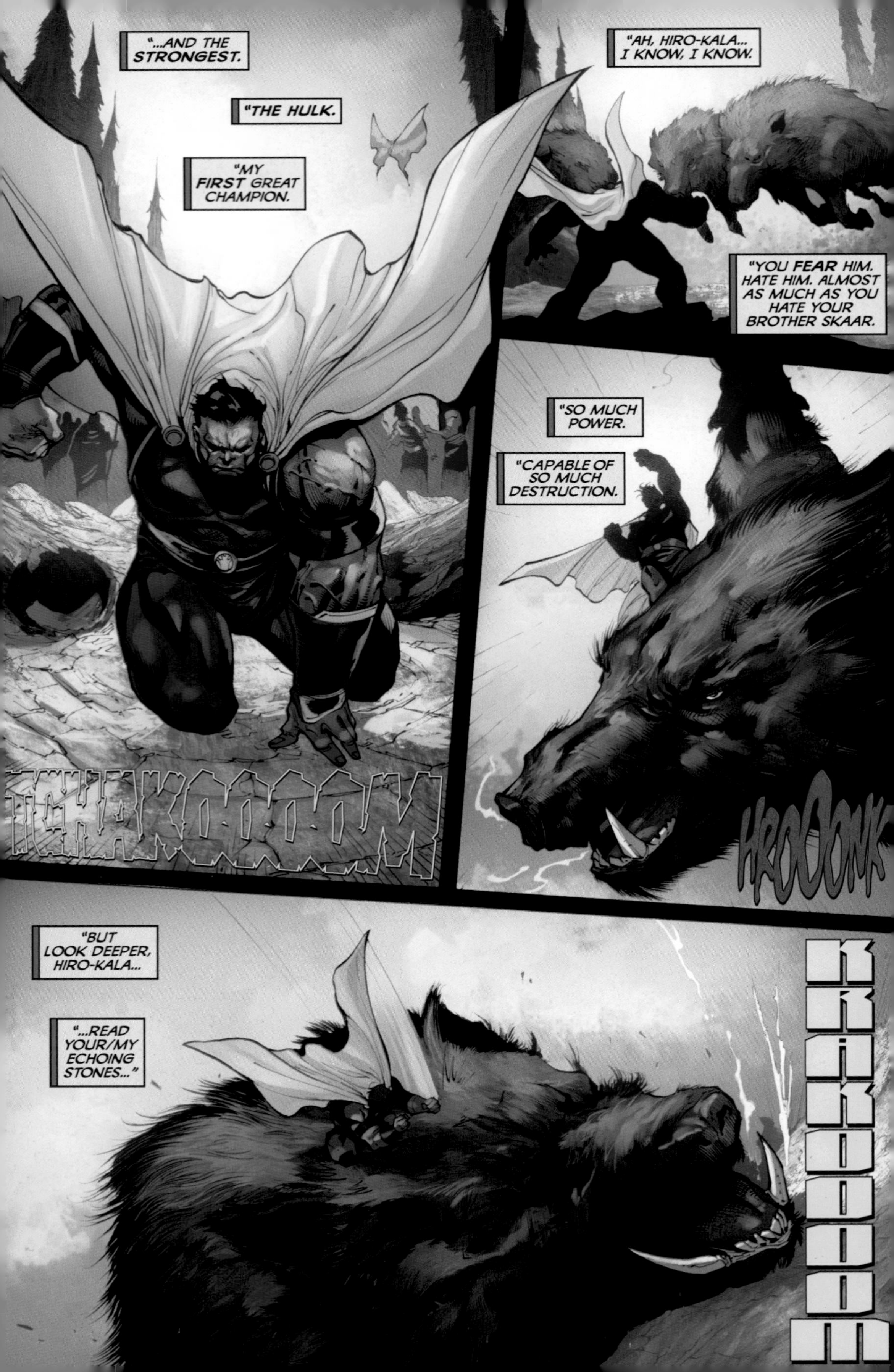
"...AND THE STRONGEST.
"THE HULK.
"MY FIRST GREAT CHAMPION.
CHAKOOOOM
"AH, HIRO-KALA... I KNOW, I KNOW.
"YOU FEAR HIM. HATE HIM. ALMOST AS MUCH AS YOU HATE YOUR BROTHER SKAAR.
"SO MUCH POWER.
"CAPABLE OF SO MUCH DESTRUCTION.
HROOONK
"BUT LOOK DEEPER, HIRO-KALA...
"...READ YOUR/MY ECHOING STONES..."
KRAKOOOOM

"...AND SEE WHAT IT CAN MEAN TO FIGHT FOR SOMETHING..."
JARELLA...
"...WHAT IT MEANS TO LIVE...
MY LOVE.
"...THE GLORY OF WHAT WAS...
...AND WHAT COULD BE AGAIN.

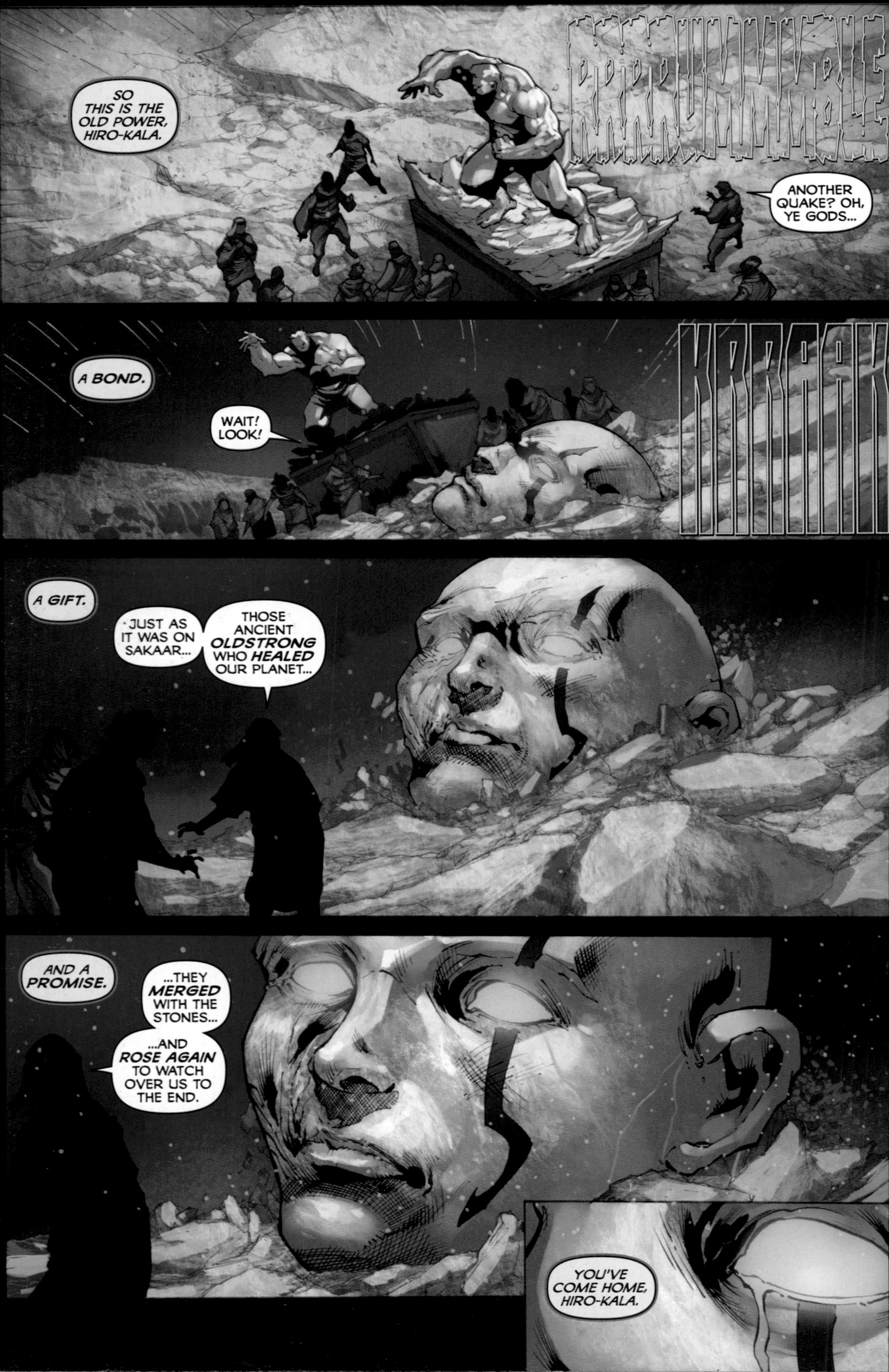
SO THIS IS THE OLD POWER, HIRO-KALA.
ANOTHER QUAKE? OH, YE GODS...
A BOND.
WAIT! LOOK!
KRRAAK
A GIFT.
JUST AS IT WAS ON SAKAAR...
THOSE ANCIENT OLDSTRONG WHO HEALED OUR PLANET...
AND A PROMISE.
...THEY MERGED WITH THE STONES...
...AND ROSE AGAIN TO WATCH OVER US TO THE END.
YOU'VE COME HOME, HIRO-KALA.

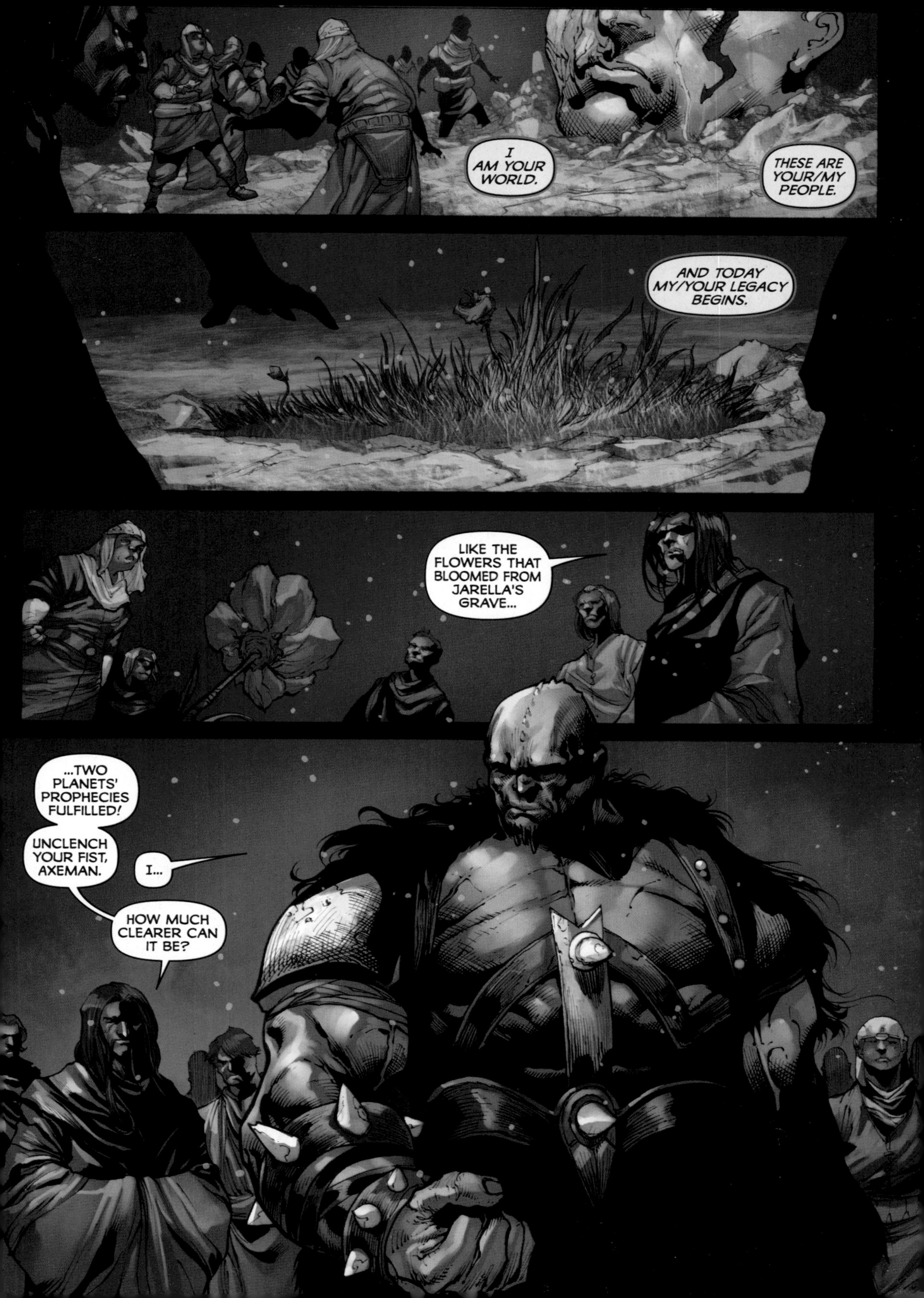
I AM YOUR WORLD.
THESE ARE YOUR/MY PEOPLE.
AND TODAY MY/YOUR LEGACY BEGINS.
LIKE THE FLOWERS THAT BLOOMED FROM JARELLA'S GRAVE...
...TWO PLANETS' PROPHECIES FULFILLED!
UNCLENCH YOUR FIST, AXEMAN.
I...
HOW MUCH CLEARER CAN IT BE?

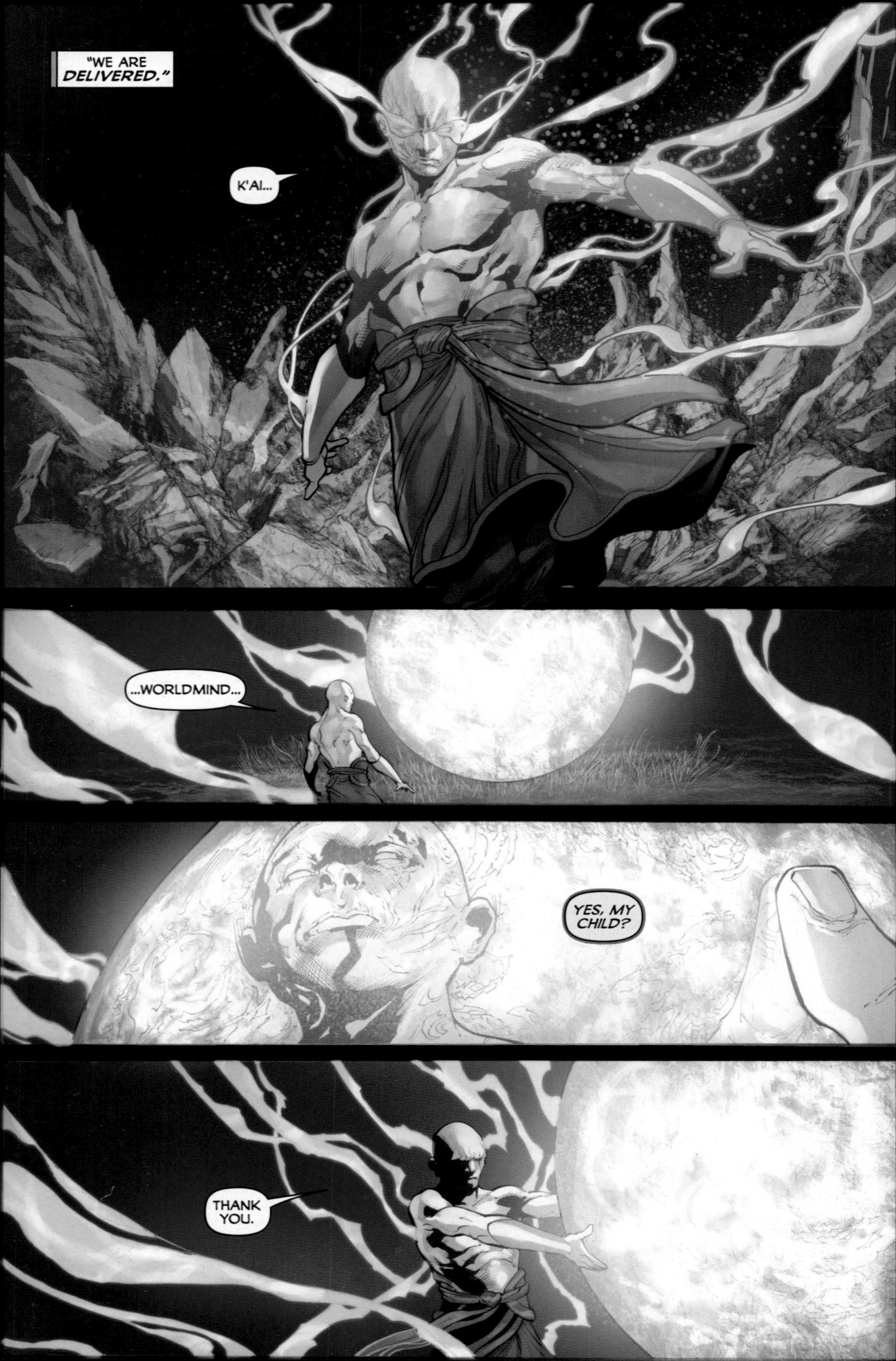
"WE ARE DELIVERED."
K'AI...
...WORLDMIND...
YES, MY CHILD?
THANK YOU.

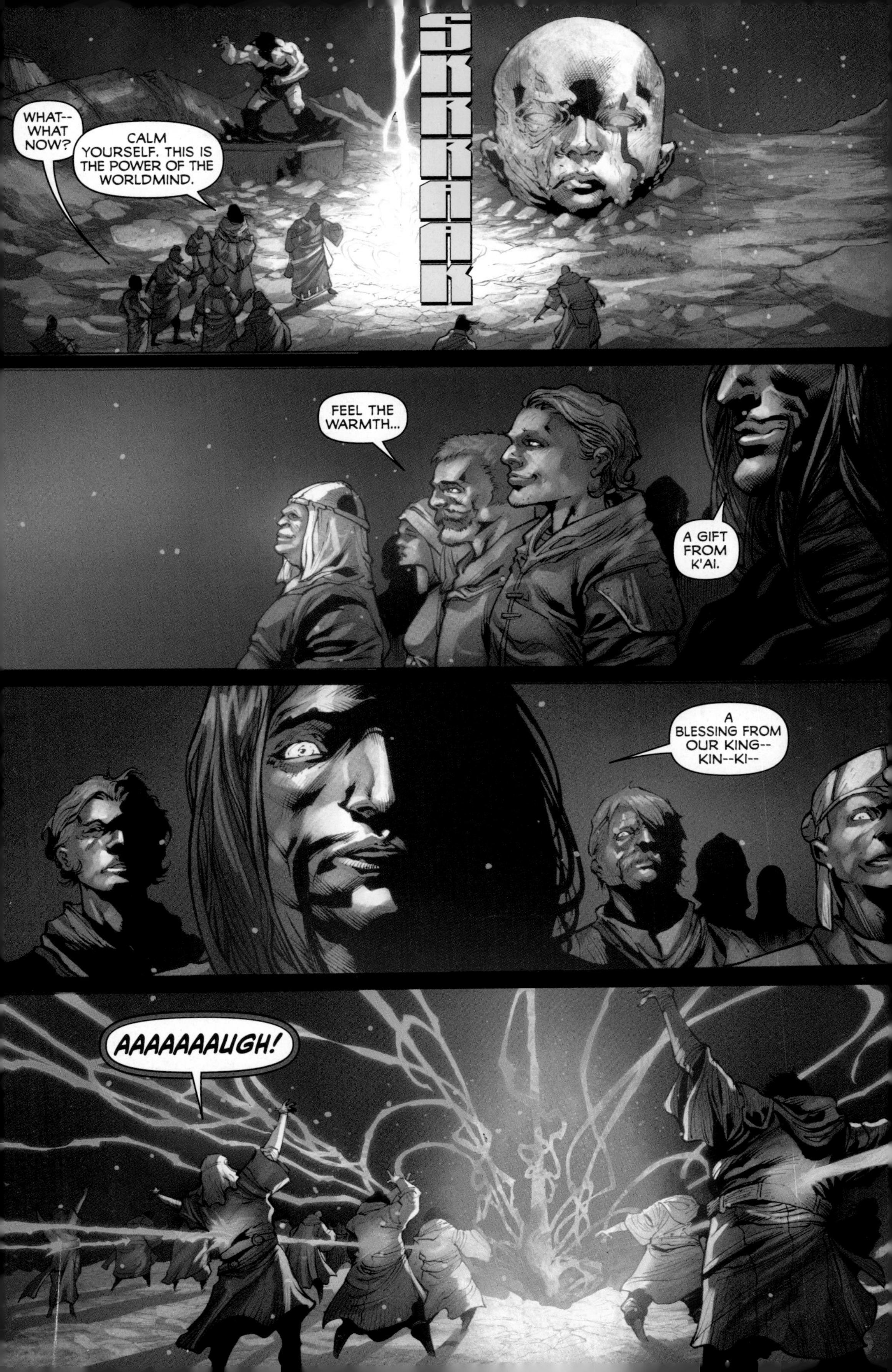
SKRAAK
WHAT-- WHAT NOW?
CALM YOURSELF. THIS IS THE POWER OF THE WORLDMIND.
FEEL THE WARMTH...
A GIFT FROM K'AI.
A BLESSING FROM OUR KING-- KIN--KI--
AAAAAAAUGH!

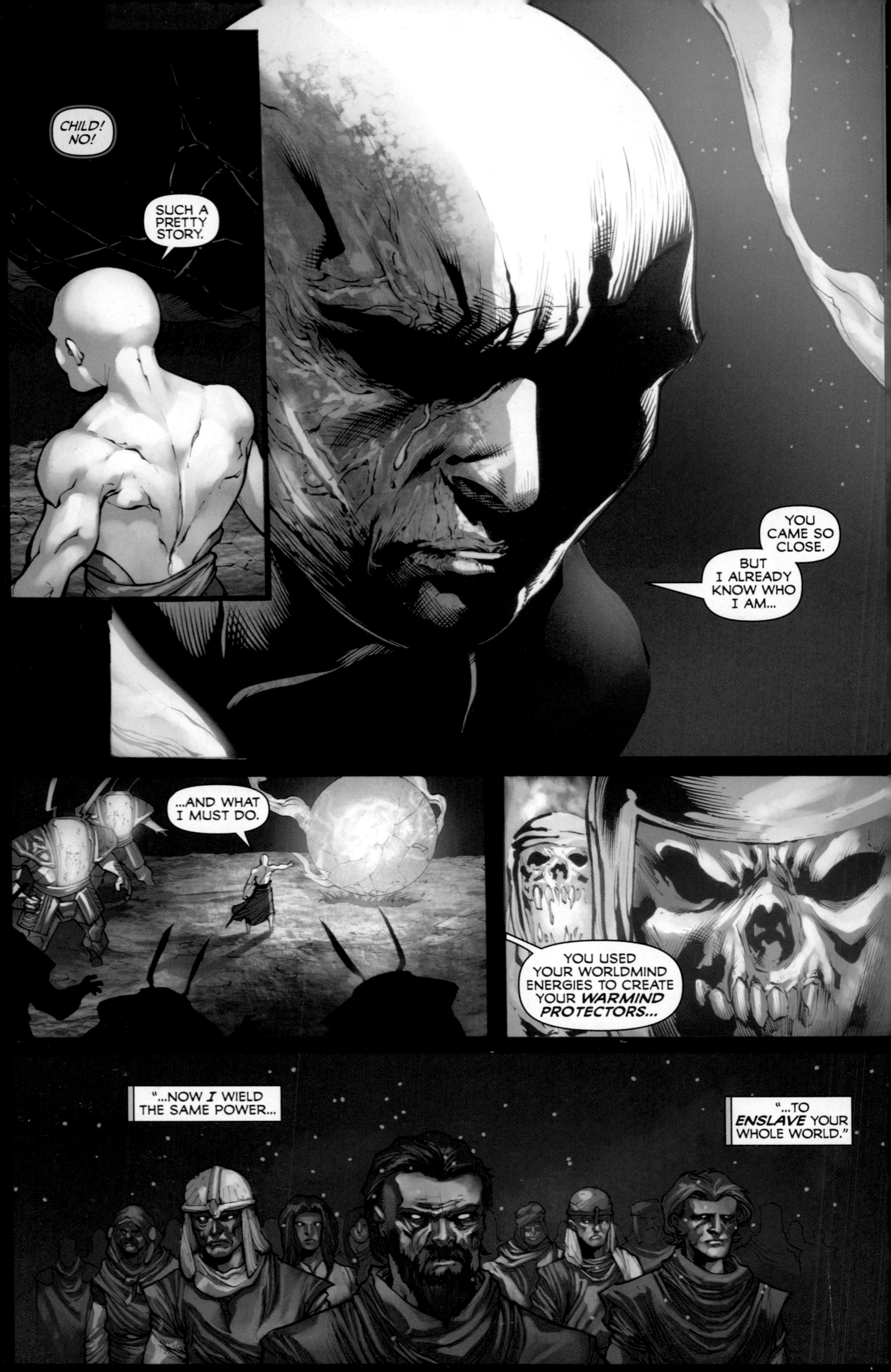

CHILD! NO!
SUCH A PRETTY STORY.
YOU CAME SO CLOSE.
BUT I ALREADY KNOW WHO I AM...
...AND WHAT I MUST DO.
YOU USED YOUR WORLDMIND ENERGIES TO CREATE YOUR *WARMIND PROTECTORS...*
"...NOW *I* WIELD THE SAME POWER...
"...TO *ENSLAVE* YOUR WHOLE WORLD."

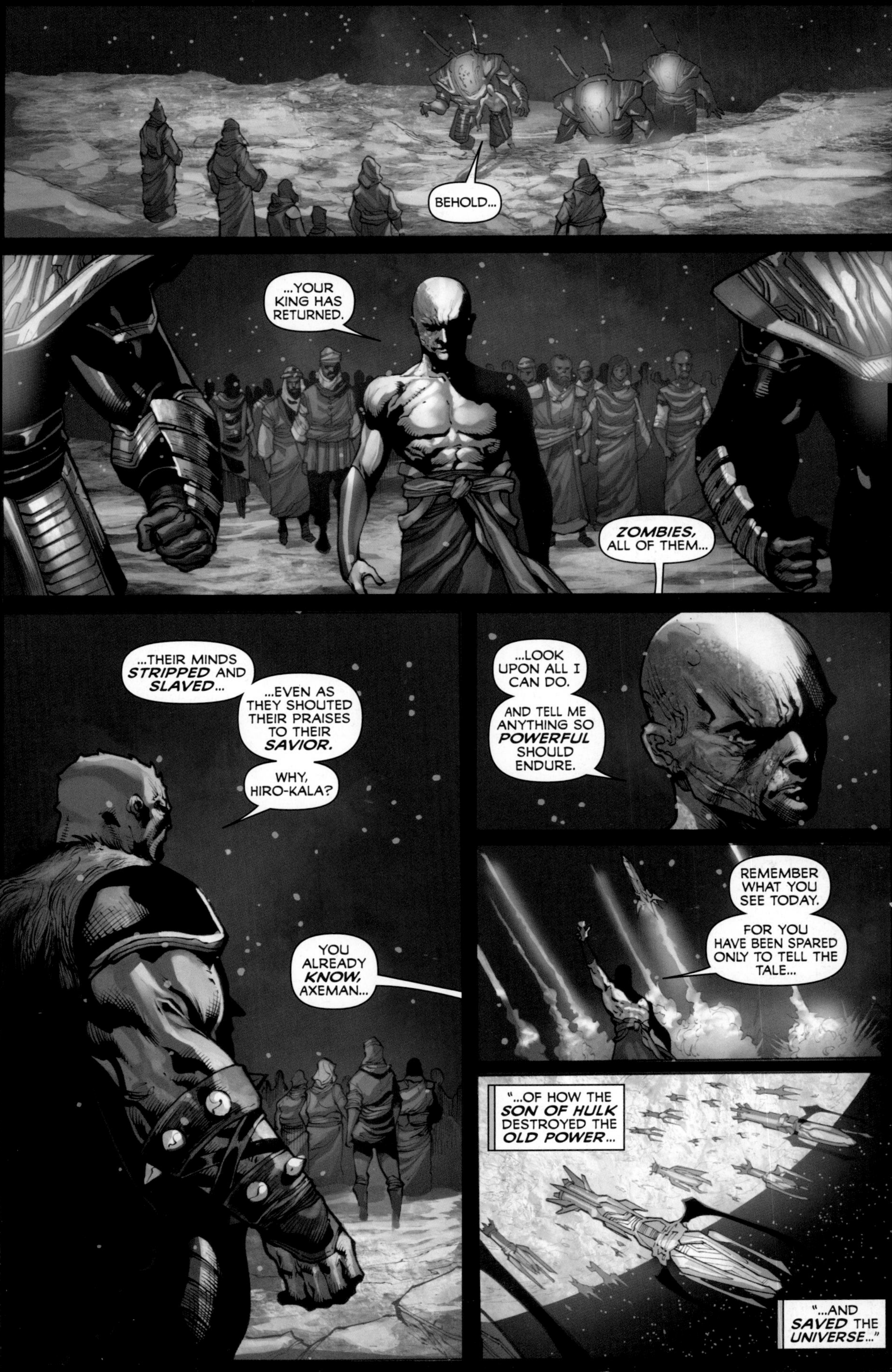
BEHOLD...
...YOUR KING HAS RETURNED.
ZOMBIES, ALL OF THEM...
...THEIR MINDS STRIPPED AND SLAVED...
...EVEN AS THEY SHOUTED THEIR PRAISES TO THEIR SAVIOR.
WHY, HIRO-KALA?
YOU ALREADY KNOW, AXEMAN...
...LOOK UPON ALL I CAN DO.
AND TELL ME ANYTHING SO POWERFUL SHOULD ENDURE.
REMEMBER WHAT YOU SEE TODAY.
FOR YOU HAVE BEEN SPARED ONLY TO TELL THE TALE...
"...OF HOW THE SON OF HULK DESTROYED THE OLD POWER...
"...AND SAVED THE UNIVERSE..."

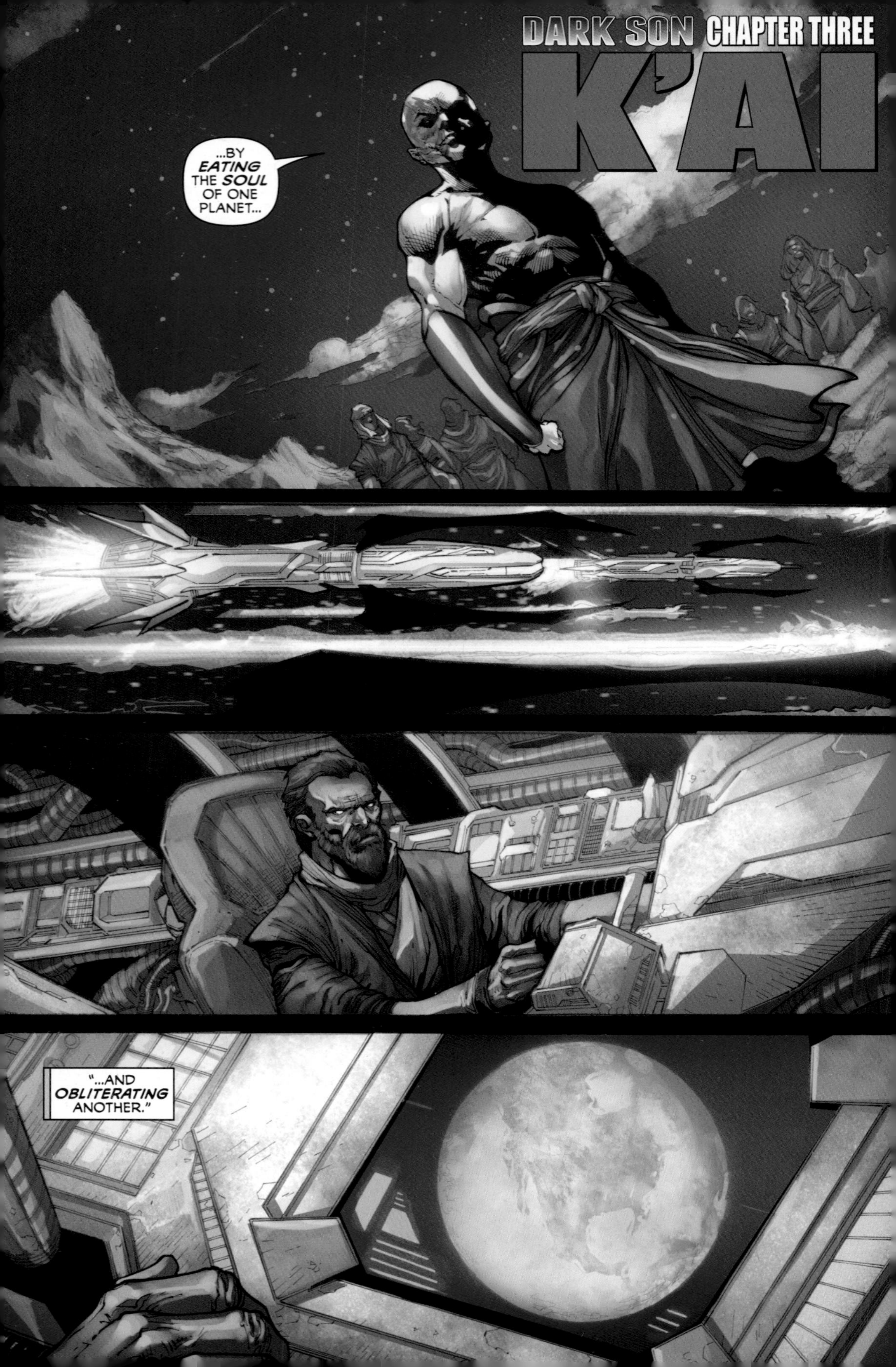
DARK SON CHAPTER THREE
K'AI
...BY EATING THE SOUL OF ONE PLANET...
"...AND OBLITERATING ANOTHER."

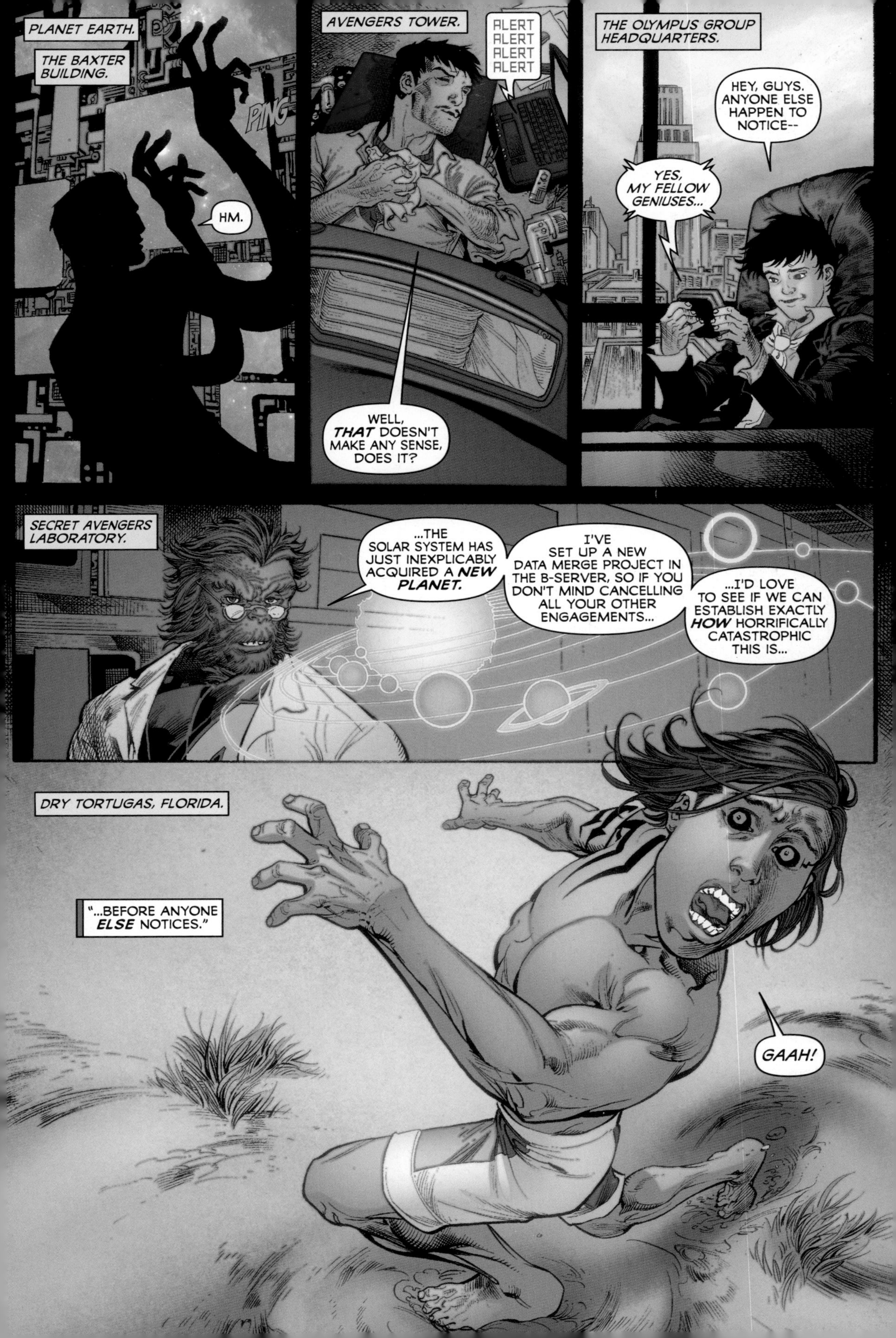
PLANET EARTH.
THE BAXTER BUILDING.
PING
HM.
AVENGERS TOWER.
ALERT ALERT ALERT ALERT
WELL, THAT DOESN'T MAKE ANY SENSE, DOES IT?
THE OLYMPUS GROUP HEADQUARTERS.
HEY, GUYS. ANYONE ELSE HAPPEN TO NOTICE--
YES, MY FELLOW GENIUSES...
SECRET AVENGERS LABORATORY.
...THE SOLAR SYSTEM HAS JUST INEXPLICABLY ACQUIRED A NEW PLANET.
I'VE SET UP A NEW DATA MERGE PROJECT IN THE B-SERVER, SO IF YOU DON'T MIND CANCELLING ALL YOUR OTHER ENGAGEMENTS...
...I'D LOVE TO SEE IF WE CAN ESTABLISH EXACTLY HOW HORRIFICALLY CATASTROPHIC THIS IS...
DRY TORTUGAS, FLORIDA.
"...BEFORE ANYONE ELSE NOTICES."
GAAH!

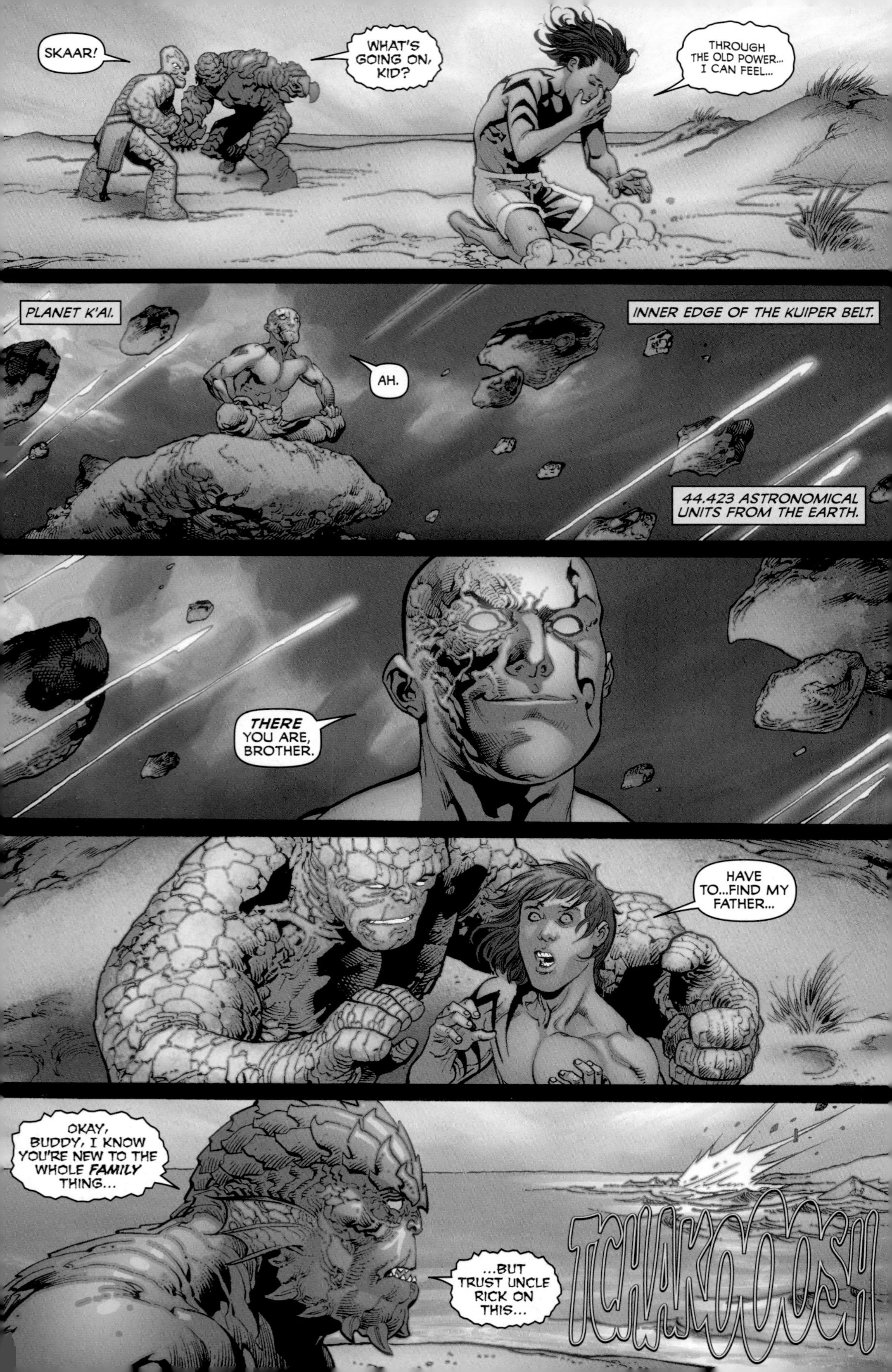
SKAAR!
WHAT'S GOING ON, KID?
THROUGH THE OLD POWER... I CAN FEEL...
PLANET K'AI.
INNER EDGE OF THE KUIPER BELT.
AH.
44.423 ASTRONOMICAL UNITS FROM THE EARTH.
THERE YOU ARE, BROTHER.
HAVE TO...FIND MY FATHER...
OKAY, BUDDY, I KNOW YOU'RE NEW TO THE WHOLE FAMILY THING...
...BUT TRUST UNCLE RICK ON THIS...
TCHAKOOOSH

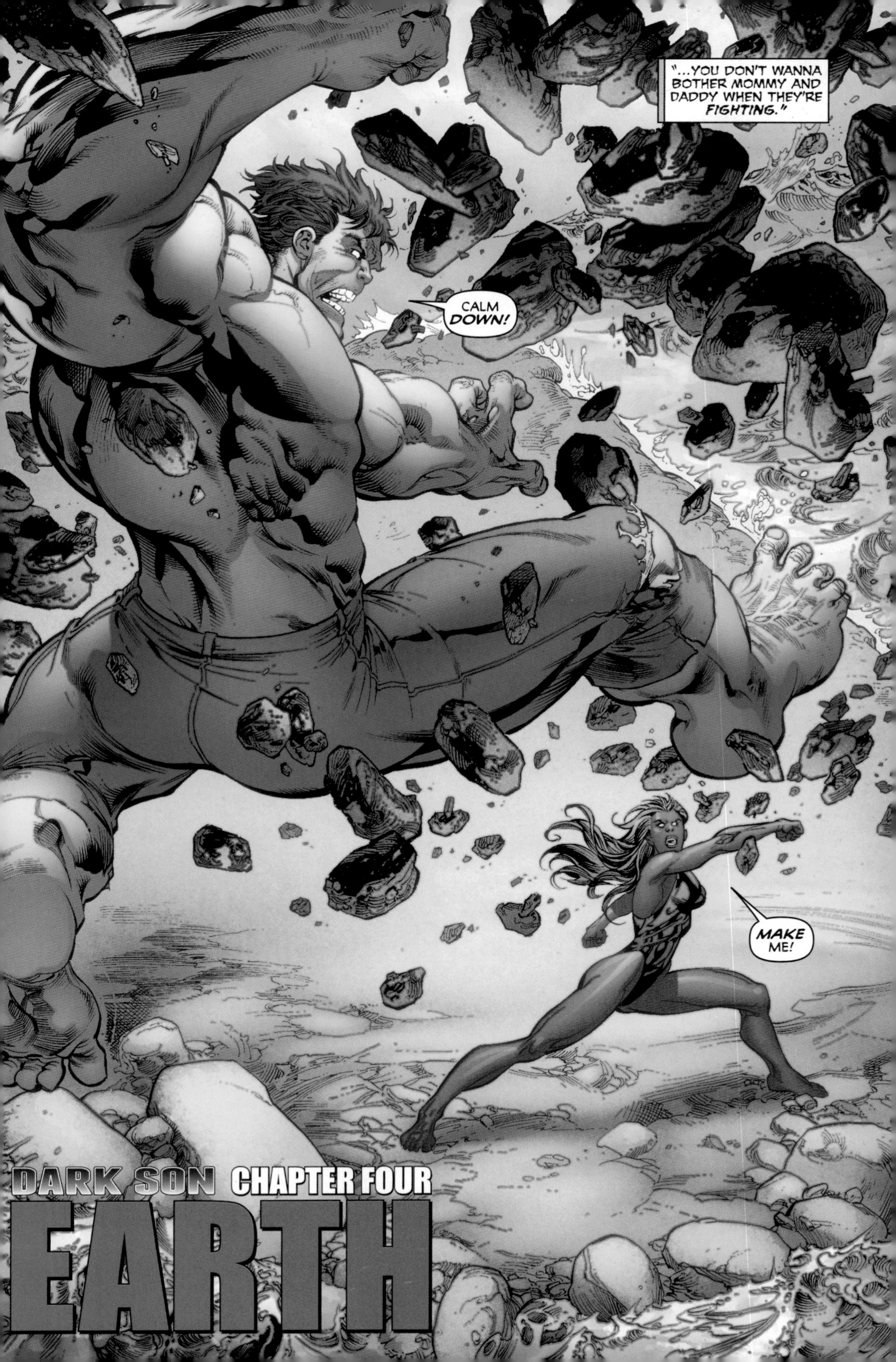
"...YOU DON'T WANNA BOTHER MOMMY AND DADDY WHEN THEY'RE *FIGHTING*."
CALM *DOWN!*
MAKE ME!
DARK SON CHAPTER FOUR
EARTH

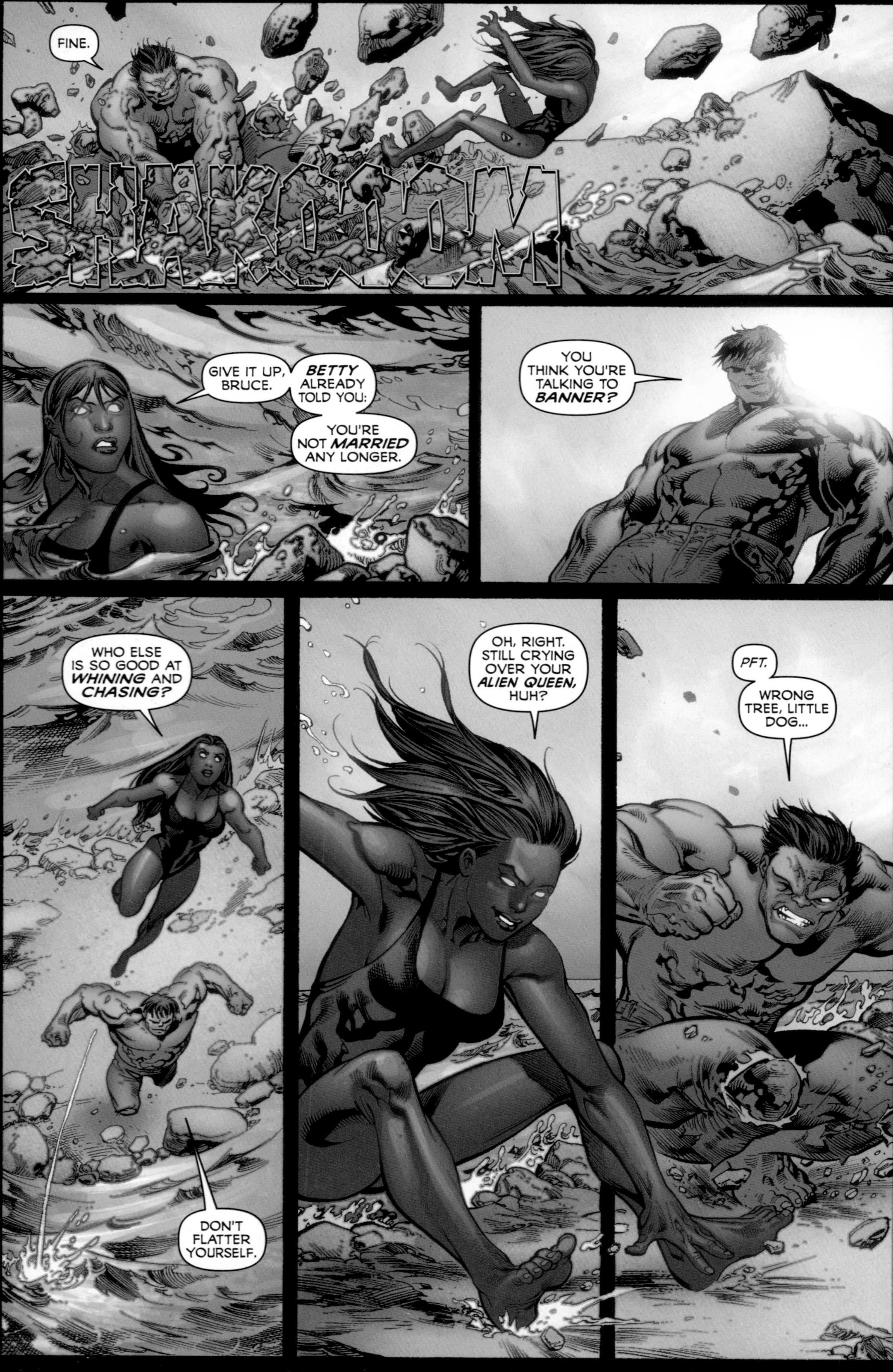
FINE.
SHRAKOOOM
GIVE IT UP, BRUCE.
BETTY ALREADY TOLD YOU:
YOU'RE NOT MARRIED ANY LONGER.
YOU THINK YOU'RE TALKING TO BANNER?
WHO ELSE IS SO GOOD AT WHINING AND CHASING?
DON'T FLATTER YOURSELF.
OH, RIGHT. STILL CRYING OVER YOUR ALIEN QUEEN, HUH?
PFT.
WRONG TREE, LITTLE DOG...

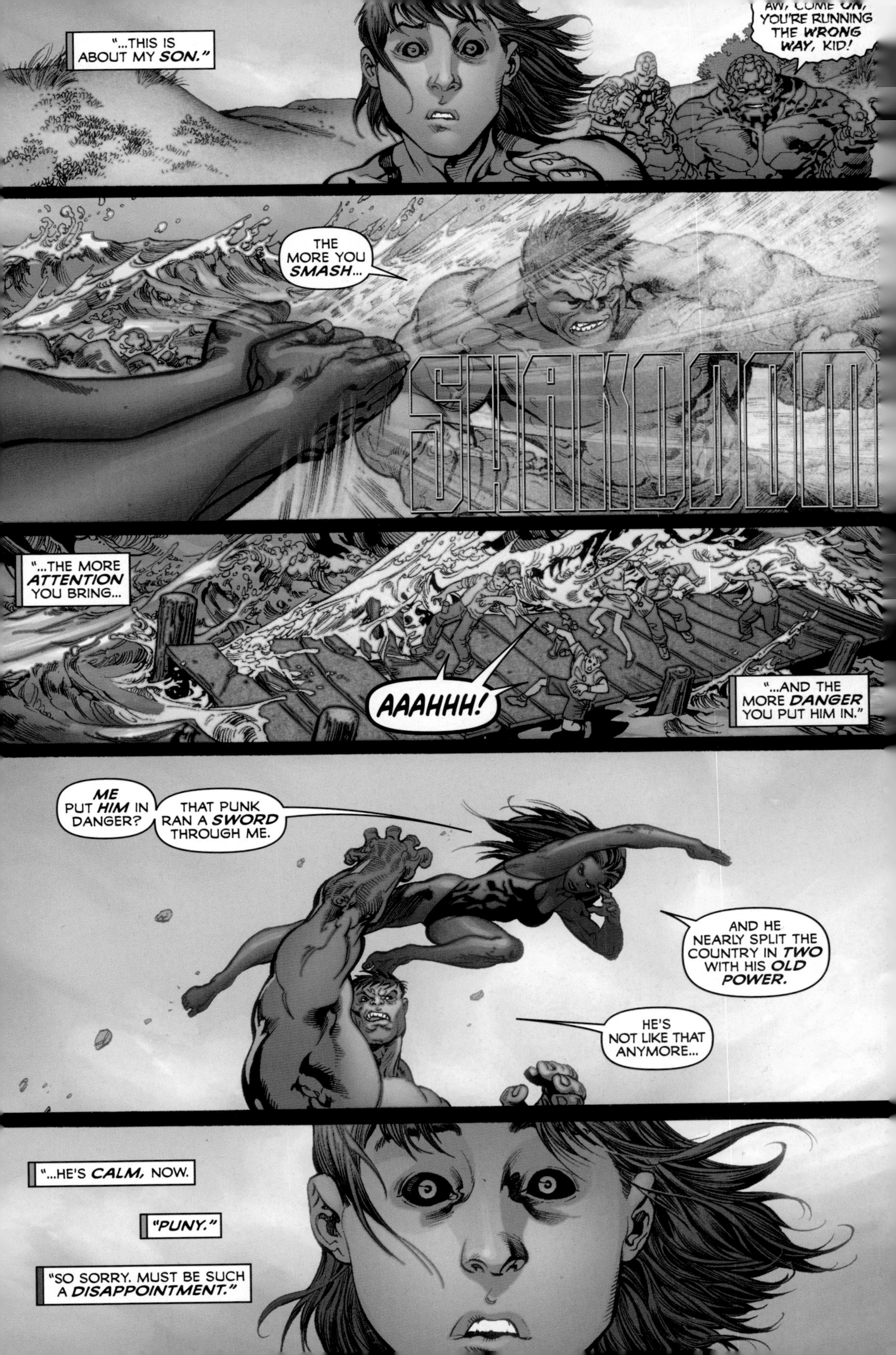
"...THIS IS ABOUT MY *SON.*"
AW, COME ON, YOU'RE RUNNING THE *WRONG WAY,* KID!
THE MORE YOU *SMASH*...
SHAKOOOM
"...THE MORE *ATTENTION* YOU BRING...
AAAHHH!
"...AND THE MORE *DANGER* YOU PUT HIM IN."
ME PUT *HIM* IN DANGER?
THAT PUNK RAN A *SWORD* THROUGH ME.
AND HE NEARLY SPLIT THE COUNTRY IN *TWO* WITH HIS *OLD POWER.*
HE'S NOT LIKE THAT ANYMORE...
"...HE'S *CALM,* NOW.
"PUNY."
"SO SORRY. MUST BE SUCH A *DISAPPOINTMENT.*"

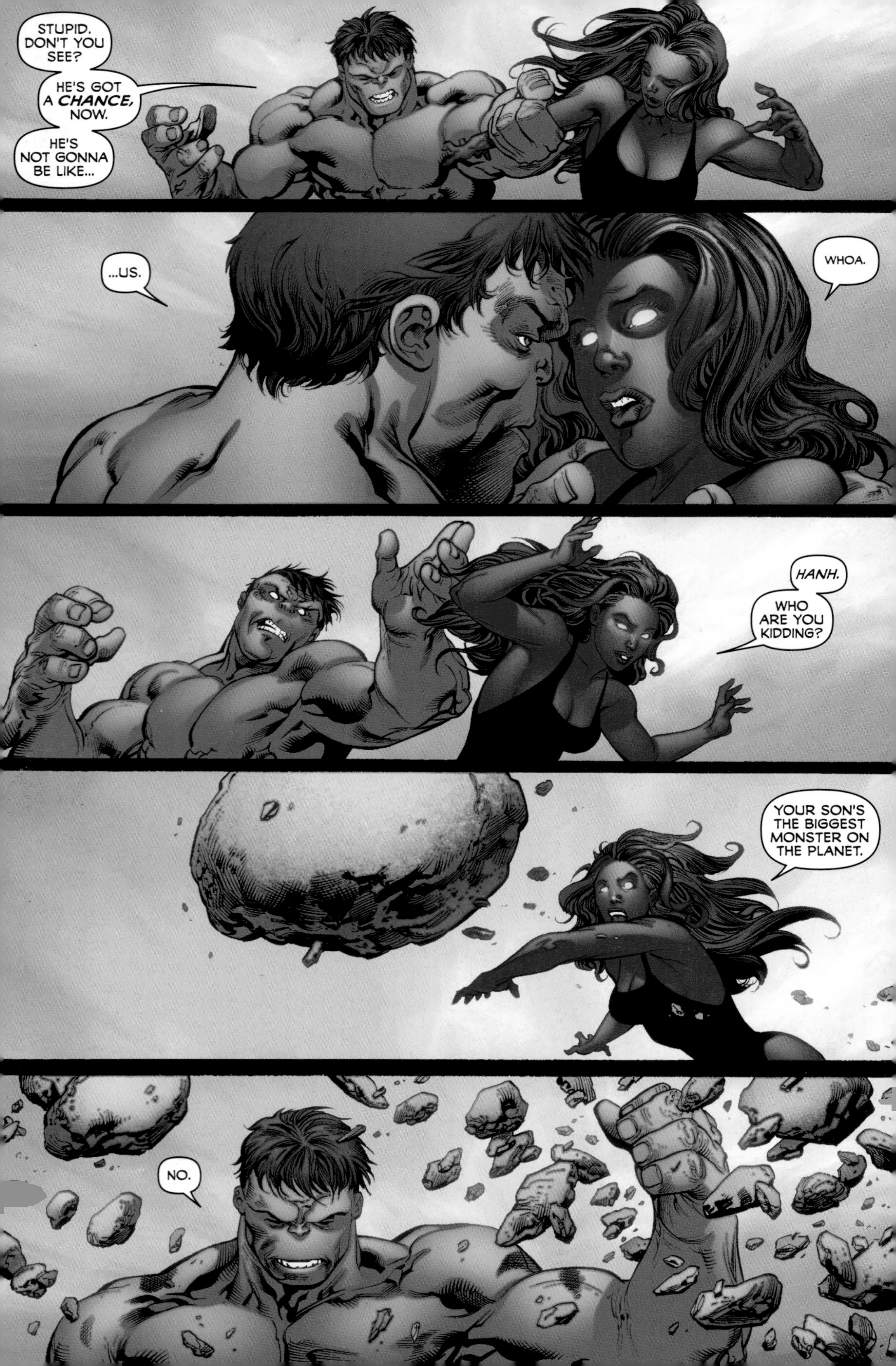
STUPID. DON'T YOU SEE?
HE'S GOT A *CHANCE,* NOW.
HE'S NOT GONNA BE LIKE...
...US.
WHOA.
HANH.
WHO ARE YOU KIDDING?
YOUR SON'S THE BIGGEST MONSTER ON THE PLANET.
NO.

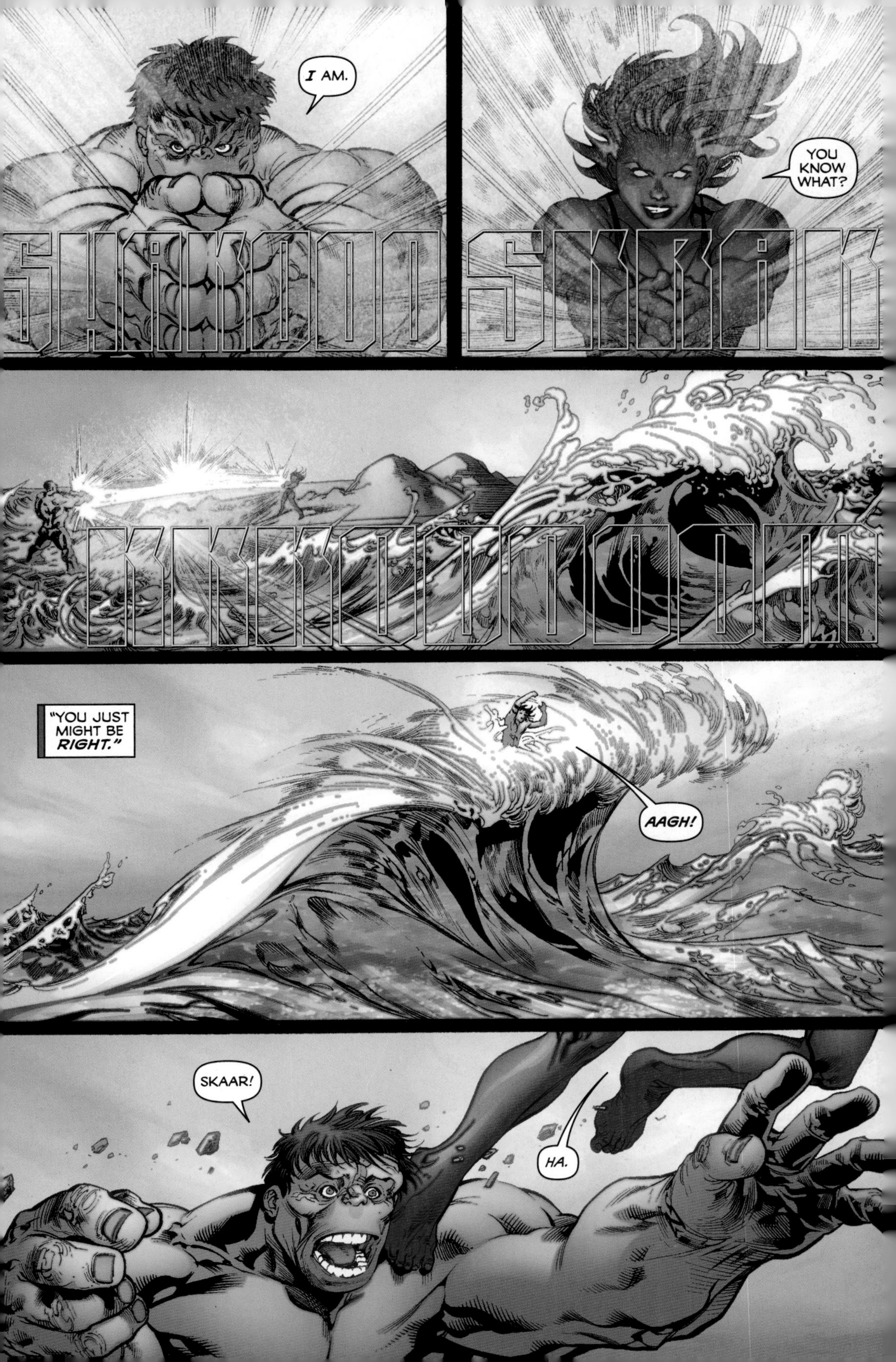
I AM.
YOU KNOW WHAT?
"YOU JUST MIGHT BE RIGHT."
AAGH!
SKAAR!
HA.

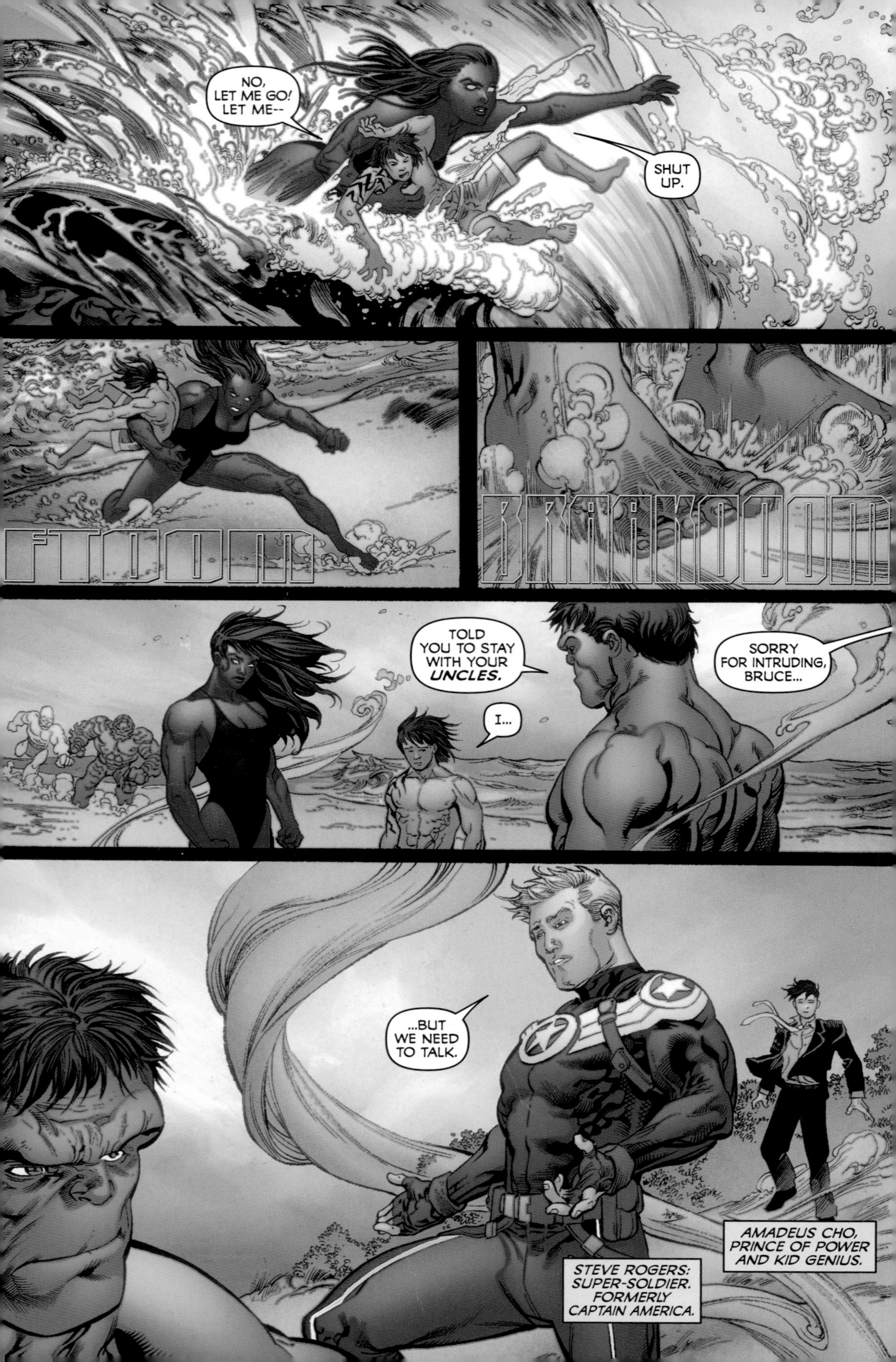
NO, LET ME GO! LET ME--
SHUT UP.
FTOOM
BRAAKOOOM
TOLD YOU TO STAY WITH YOUR UNCLES.
I...
SORRY FOR INTRUDING, BRUCE...
...BUT WE NEED TO TALK.
AMADEUS CHO, PRINCE OF POWER AND KID GENIUS.
STEVE ROGERS: SUPER-SOLDIER. FORMERLY CAPTAIN AMERICA.

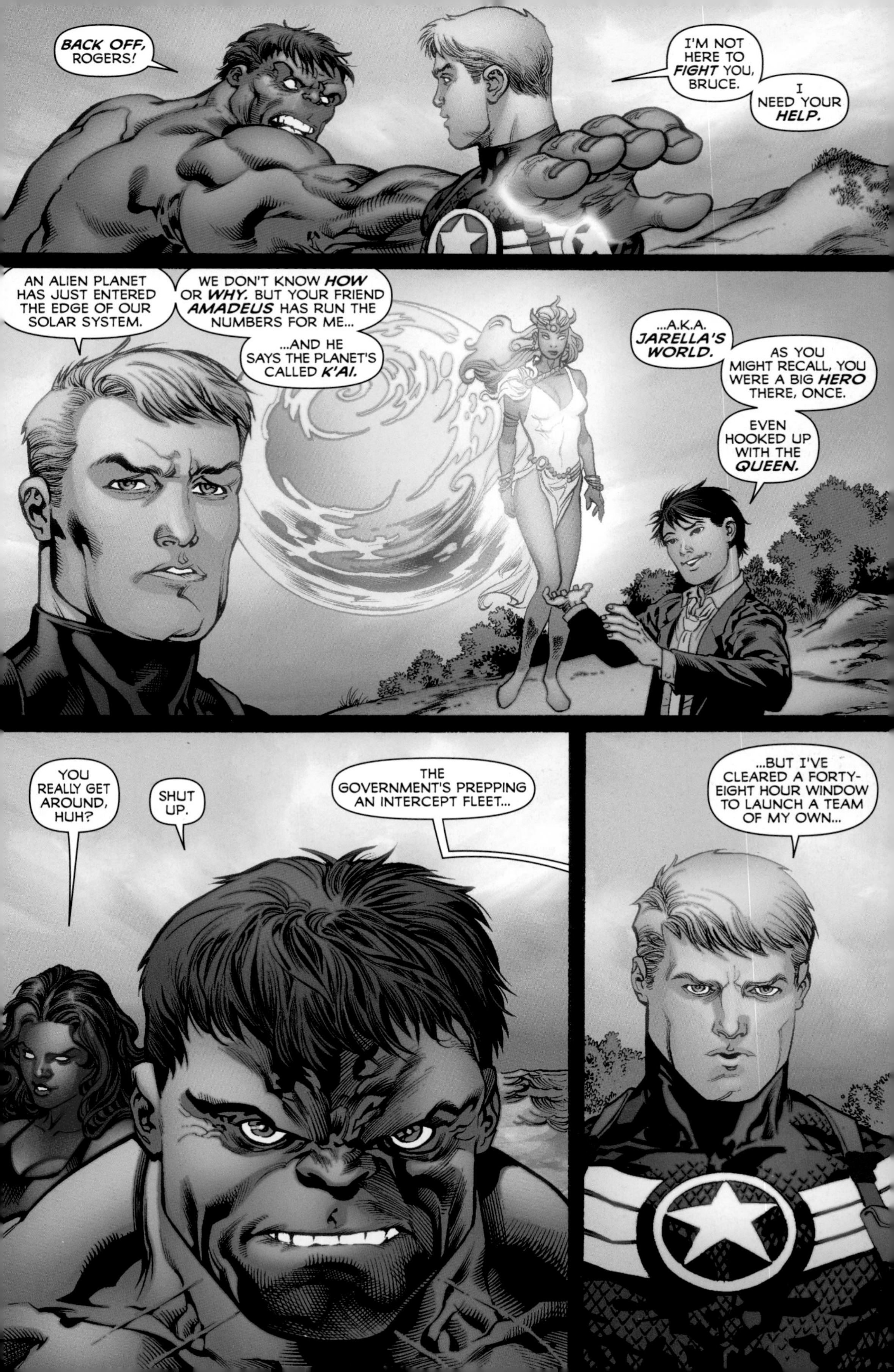
BACK OFF, ROGERS!
I'M NOT HERE TO FIGHT YOU, BRUCE.
I NEED YOUR HELP.
AN ALIEN PLANET HAS JUST ENTERED THE EDGE OF OUR SOLAR SYSTEM.
WE DON'T KNOW HOW OR WHY. BUT YOUR FRIEND AMADEUS HAS RUN THE NUMBERS FOR ME...
...AND HE SAYS THE PLANET'S CALLED K'AI.
...A.K.A. JARELLA'S WORLD.
AS YOU MIGHT RECALL, YOU WERE A BIG HERO THERE, ONCE.
EVEN HOOKED UP WITH THE QUEEN.
YOU REALLY GET AROUND, HUH?
SHUT UP.
THE GOVERNMENT'S PREPPING AN INTERCEPT FLEET...
...BUT I'VE CLEARED A FORTY-EIGHT HOUR WINDOW TO LAUNCH A TEAM OF MY OWN...

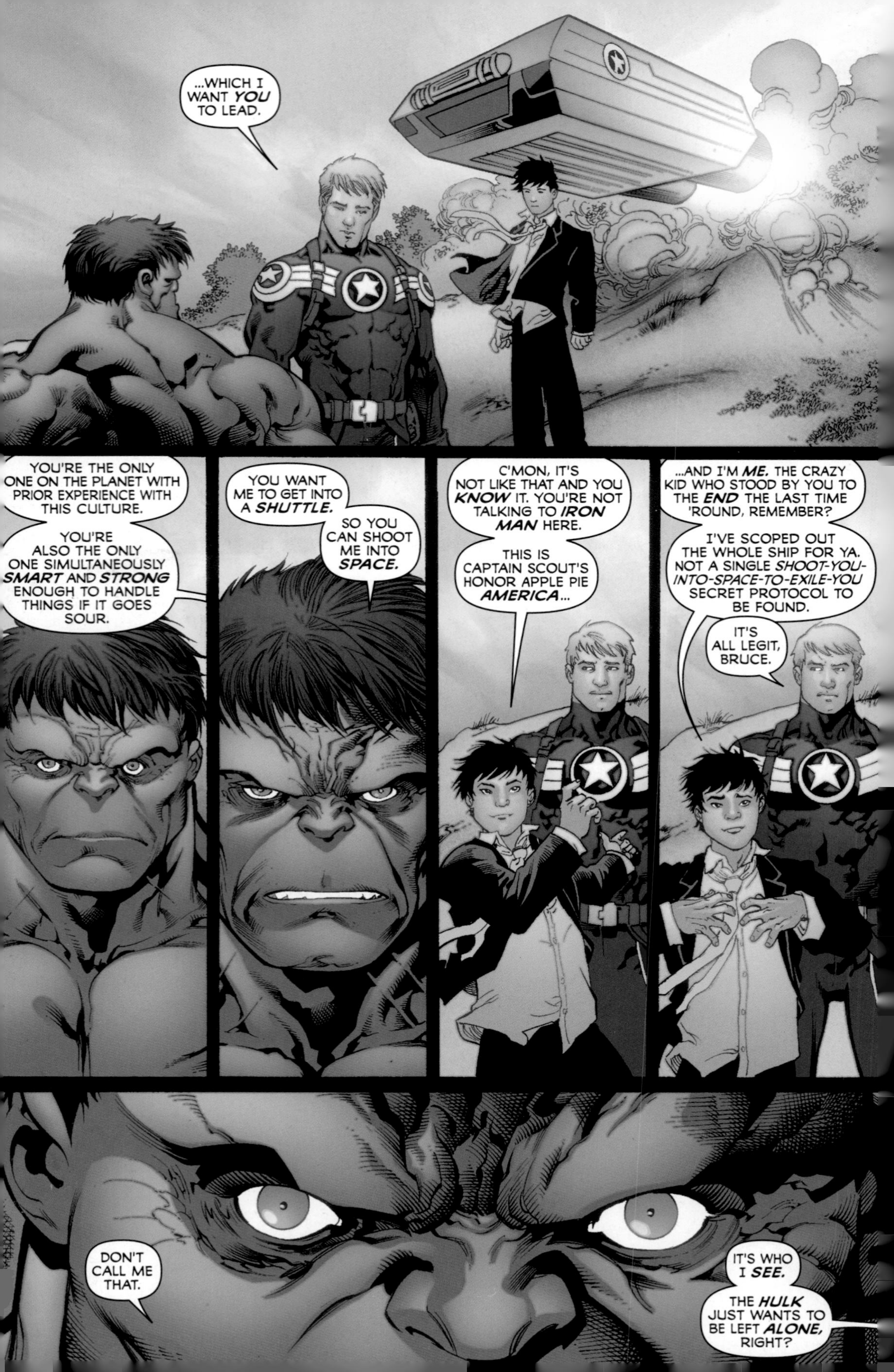
...WHICH I WANT YOU TO LEAD.
YOU'RE THE ONLY ONE ON THE PLANET WITH PRIOR EXPERIENCE WITH THIS CULTURE.
YOU'RE ALSO THE ONLY ONE SIMULTANEOUSLY SMART AND STRONG ENOUGH TO HANDLE THINGS IF IT GOES SOUR.
YOU WANT ME TO GET INTO A SHUTTLE.
SO YOU CAN SHOOT ME INTO SPACE.
C'MON, IT'S NOT LIKE THAT AND YOU KNOW IT. YOU'RE NOT TALKING TO IRON MAN HERE.
THIS IS CAPTAIN SCOUT'S HONOR APPLE PIE AMERICA...
...AND I'M ME. THE CRAZY KID WHO STOOD BY YOU TO THE END THE LAST TIME 'ROUND, REMEMBER?
I'VE SCOPED OUT THE WHOLE SHIP FOR YA. NOT A SINGLE SHOOT-YOU-INTO-SPACE-TO-EXILE-YOU SECRET PROTOCOL TO BE FOUND.
IT'S ALL LEGIT, BRUCE.
DON'T CALL ME THAT.
IT'S WHO I SEE.
THE HULK JUST WANTS TO BE LEFT ALONE, RIGHT?

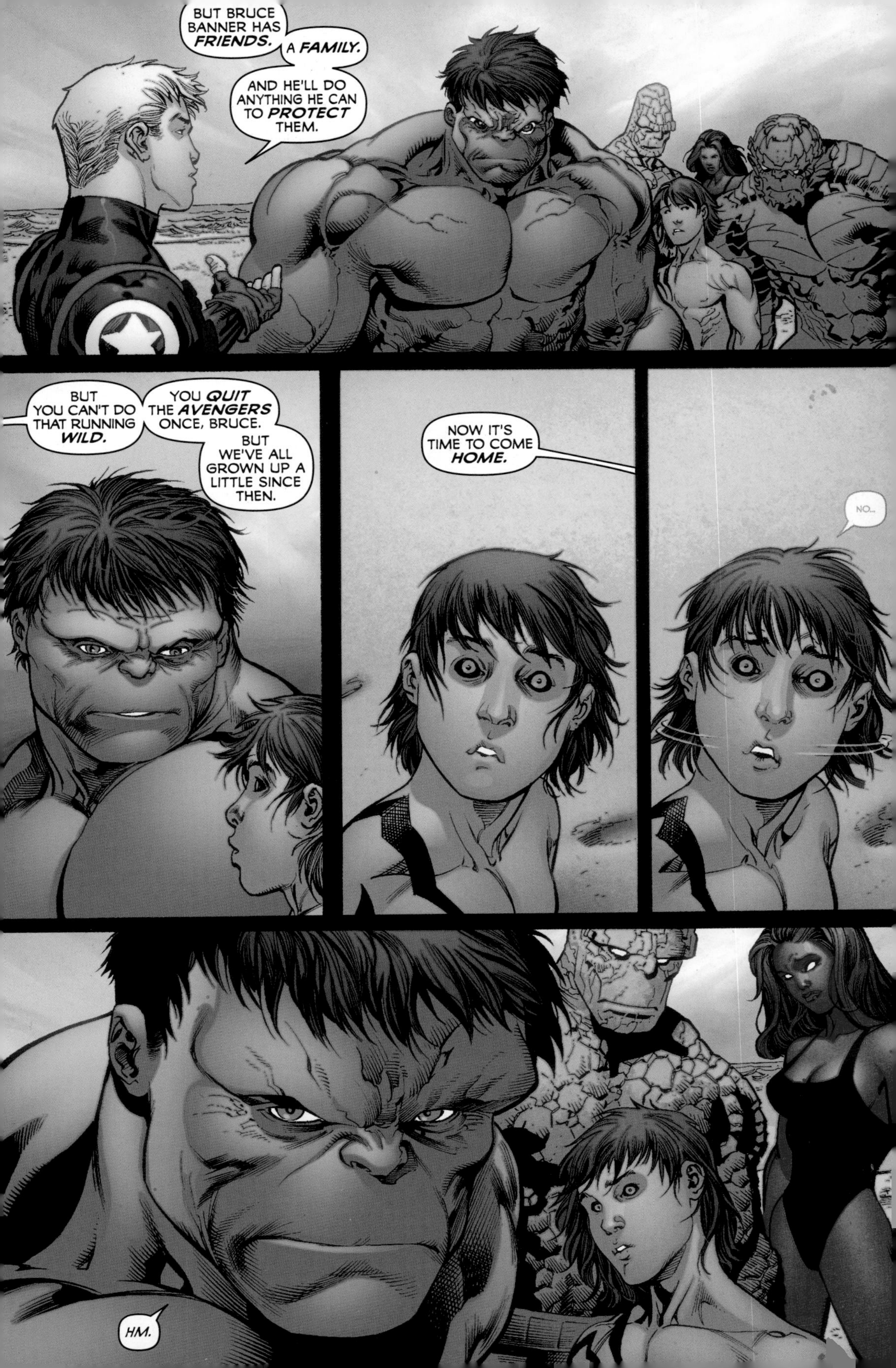
BUT BRUCE BANNER HAS FRIENDS.
A FAMILY.
AND HE'LL DO ANYTHING HE CAN TO PROTECT THEM.
BUT YOU CAN'T DO THAT RUNNING WILD.
YOU QUIT THE AVENGERS ONCE, BRUCE.
BUT WE'VE ALL GROWN UP A LITTLE SINCE THEN.
NOW IT'S TIME TO COME HOME.
NO...
HM.

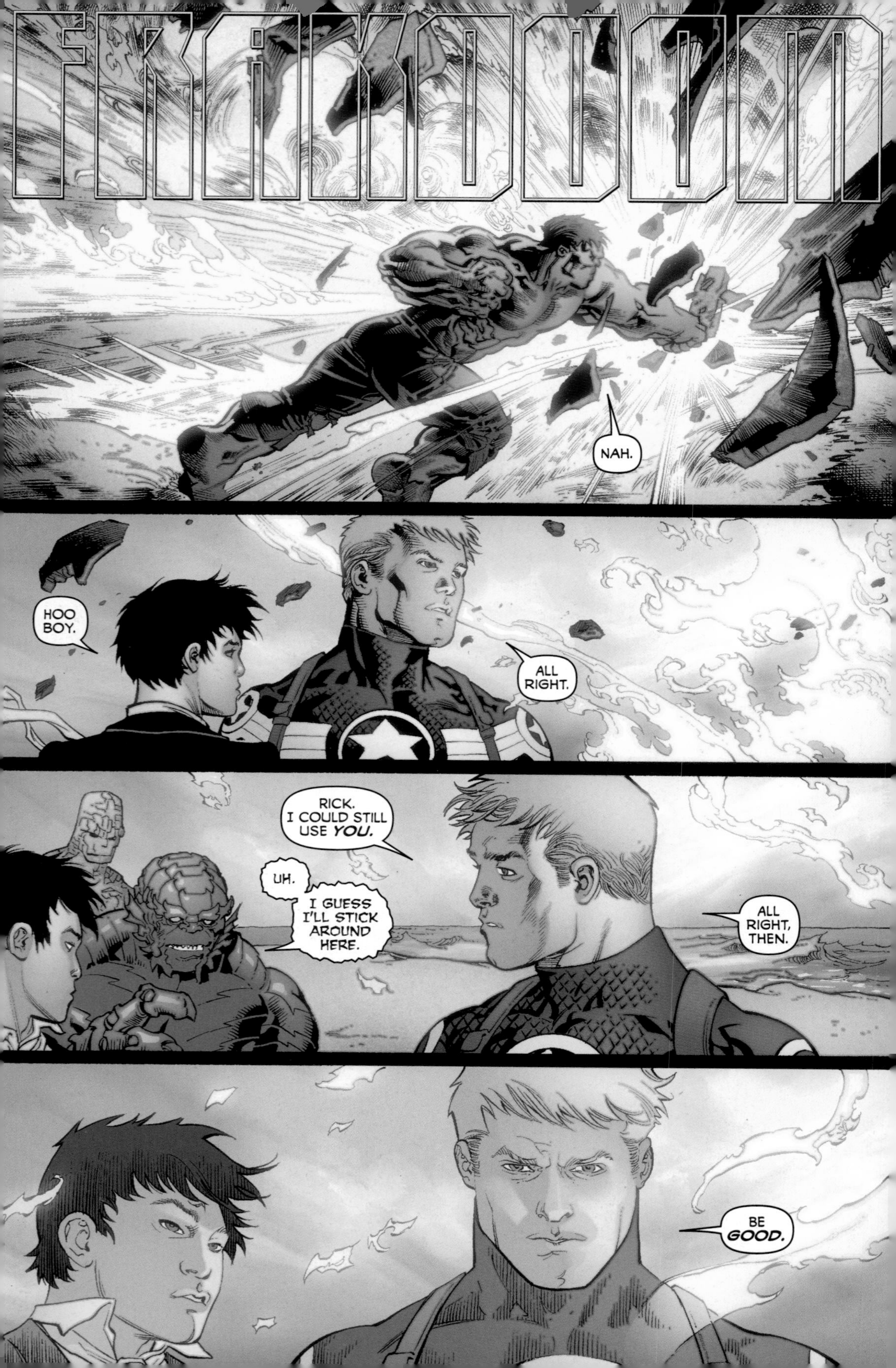
FRAKDOOM
NAH.
HOO BOY.
ALL RIGHT.
RICK. I COULD STILL USE *YOU.*
UH.
I GUESS I'LL STICK AROUND HERE.
ALL RIGHT, THEN.
BE *GOOD.*

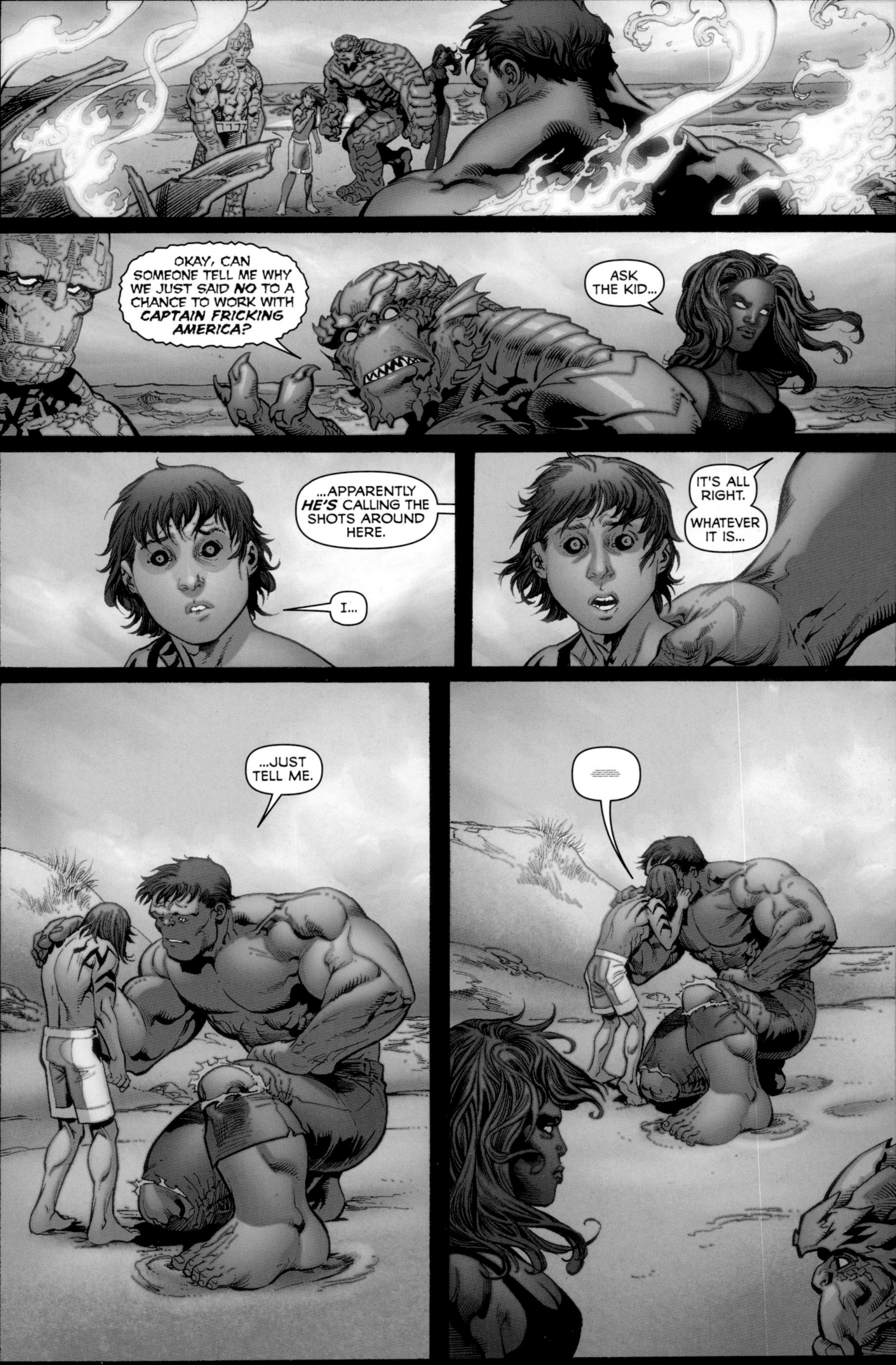
OKAY, CAN SOMEONE TELL ME WHY WE JUST SAID NO TO A CHANCE TO WORK WITH CAPTAIN FRICKING AMERICA?
ASK THE KID...
...APPARENTLY HE'S CALLING THE SHOTS AROUND HERE.
I...
IT'S ALL RIGHT.
WHATEVER IT IS...
...JUST TELL ME.

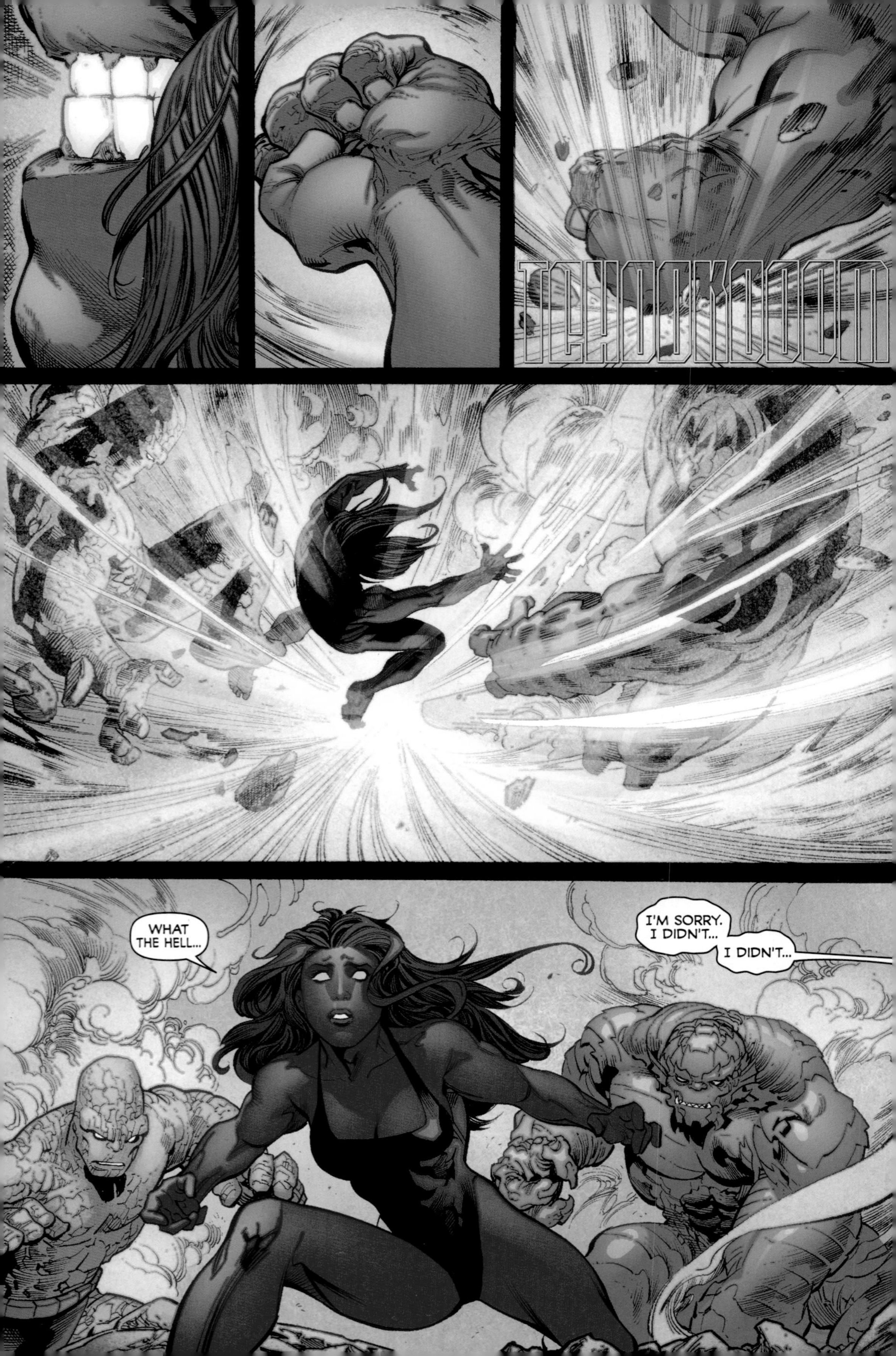
TCHOOKOOOM
WHAT THE HELL...
I'M SORRY. I DIDN'T...
I DIDN'T...

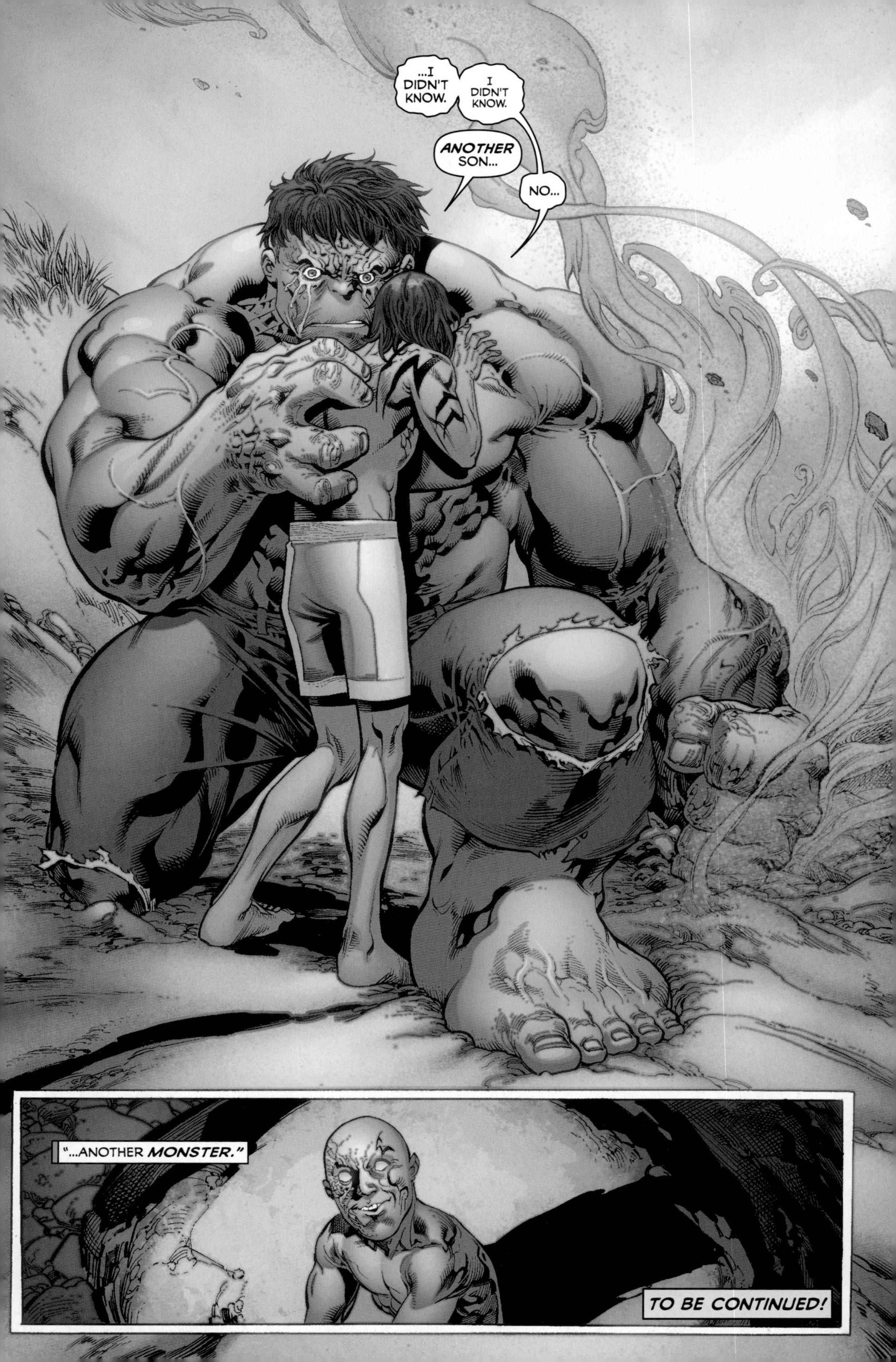
...I DIDN'T KNOW.
I DIDN'T KNOW.
ANOTHER SON...
NO...
"...ANOTHER MONSTER."
TO BE CONTINUED!

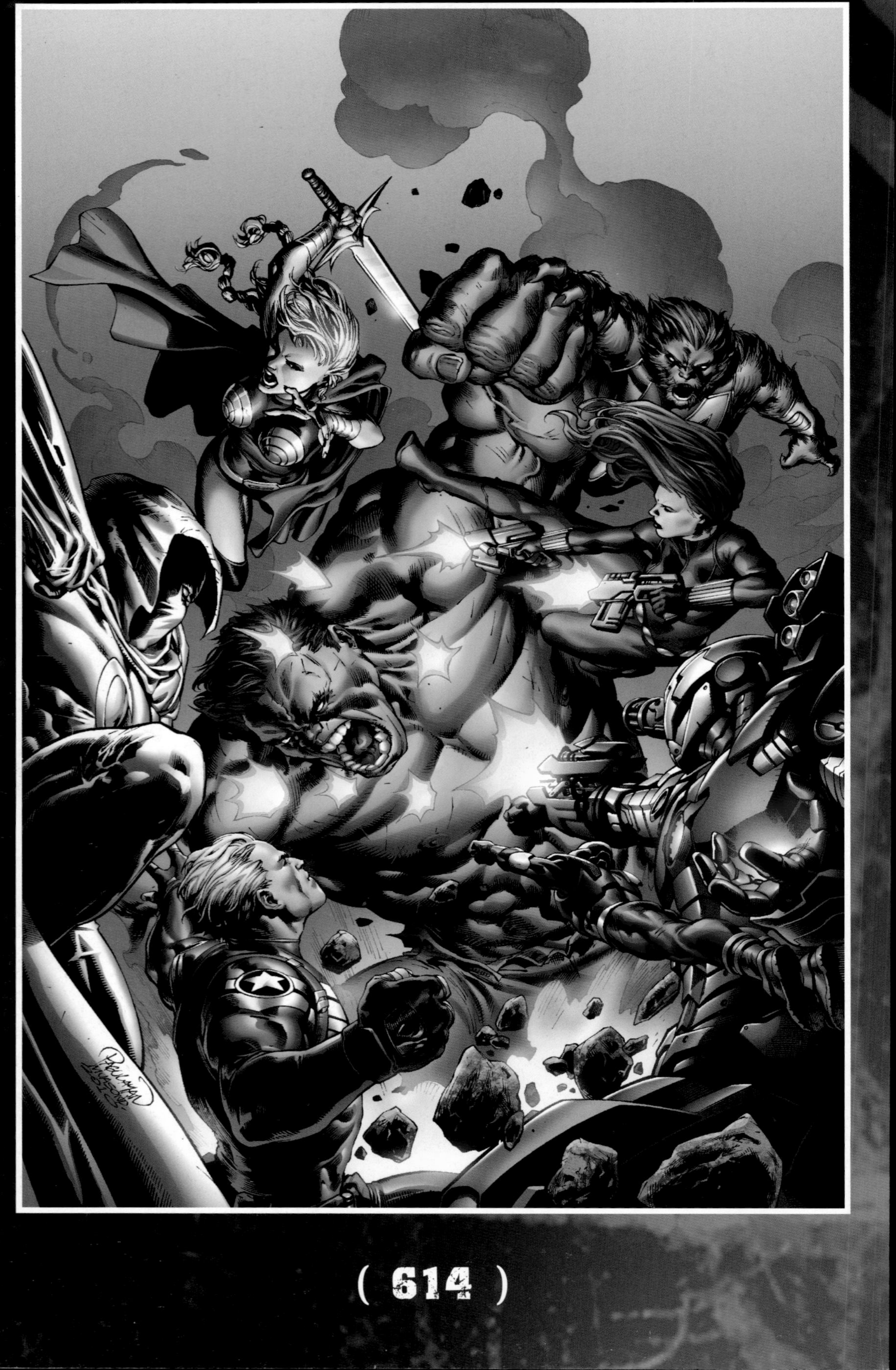

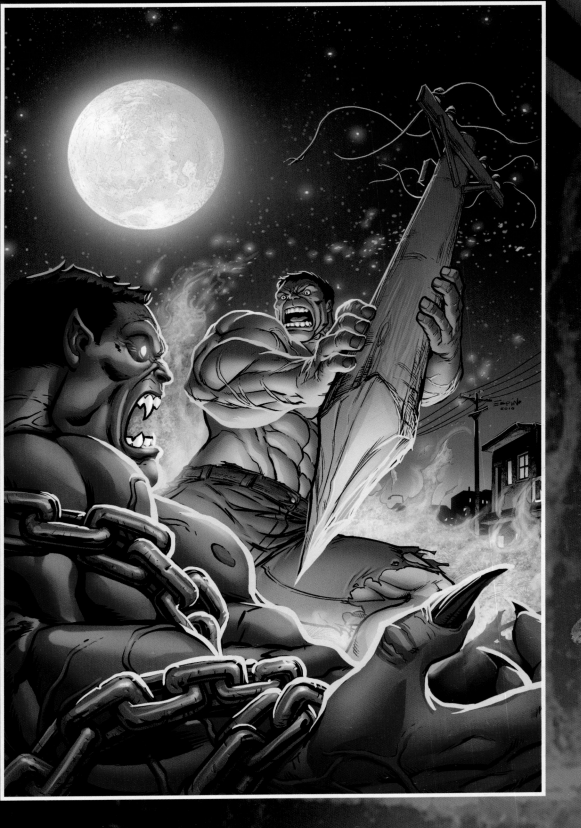

(614 VAMPIRE VARIANT)

BY SALVADOR ESPIN

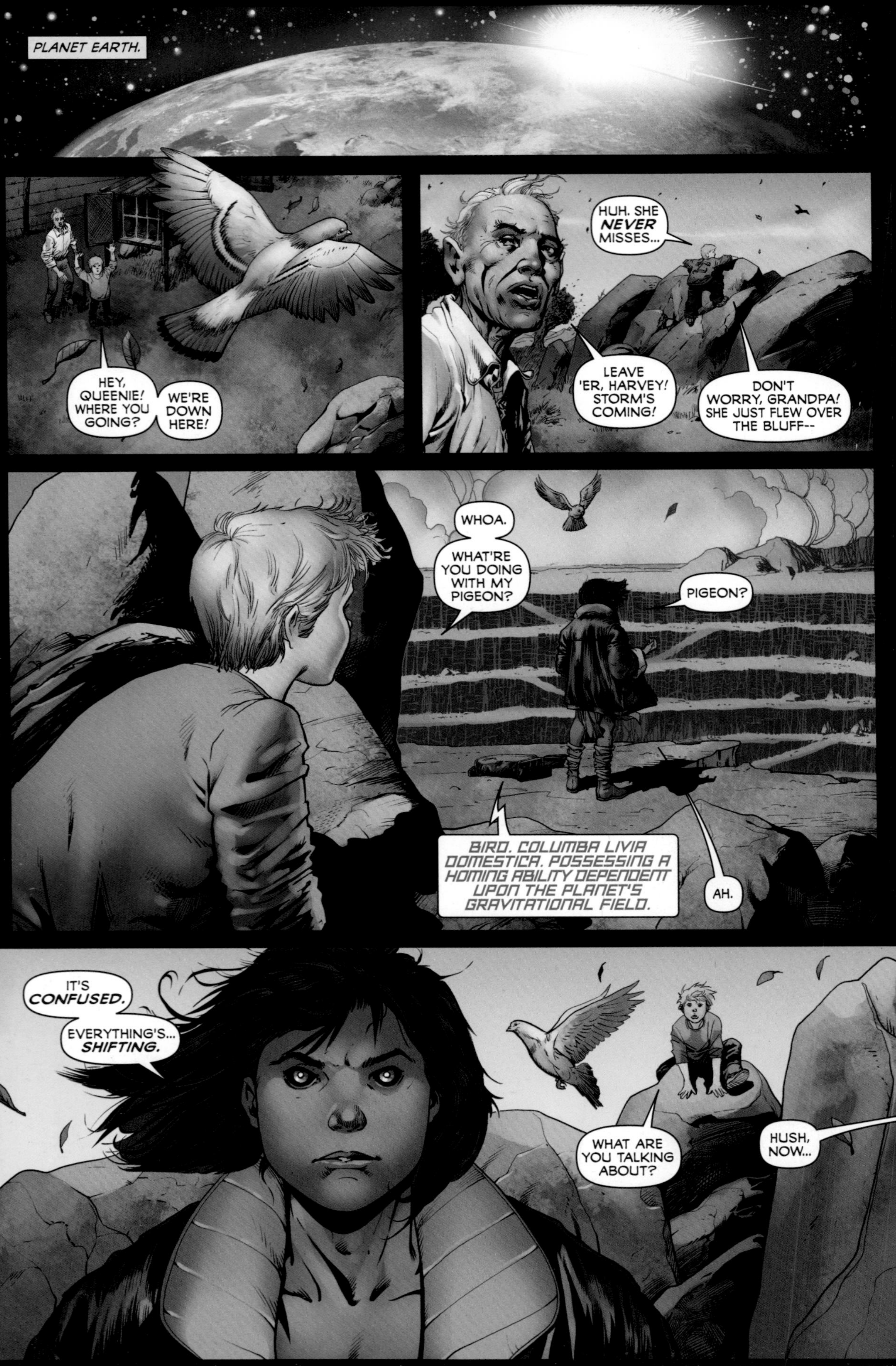
PLANET EARTH.
HEY, QUEENIE! WHERE YOU GOING?
WE'RE DOWN HERE!
HUH. SHE NEVER MISSES...
LEAVE 'ER, HARVEY! STORM'S COMING!
DON'T WORRY, GRANDPA! SHE JUST FLEW OVER THE BLUFF--
WHOA.
WHAT'RE YOU DOING WITH MY PIGEON?
PIGEON?
BIRD. COLUMBA LIVIA DOMESTICA. POSSESSING A HOMING ABILITY DEPENDENT UPON THE PLANET'S GRAVITATIONAL FIELD.
AH.
IT'S CONFUSED.
EVERYTHING'S... SHIFTING.
WHAT ARE YOU TALKING ABOUT?
HUSH, NOW...

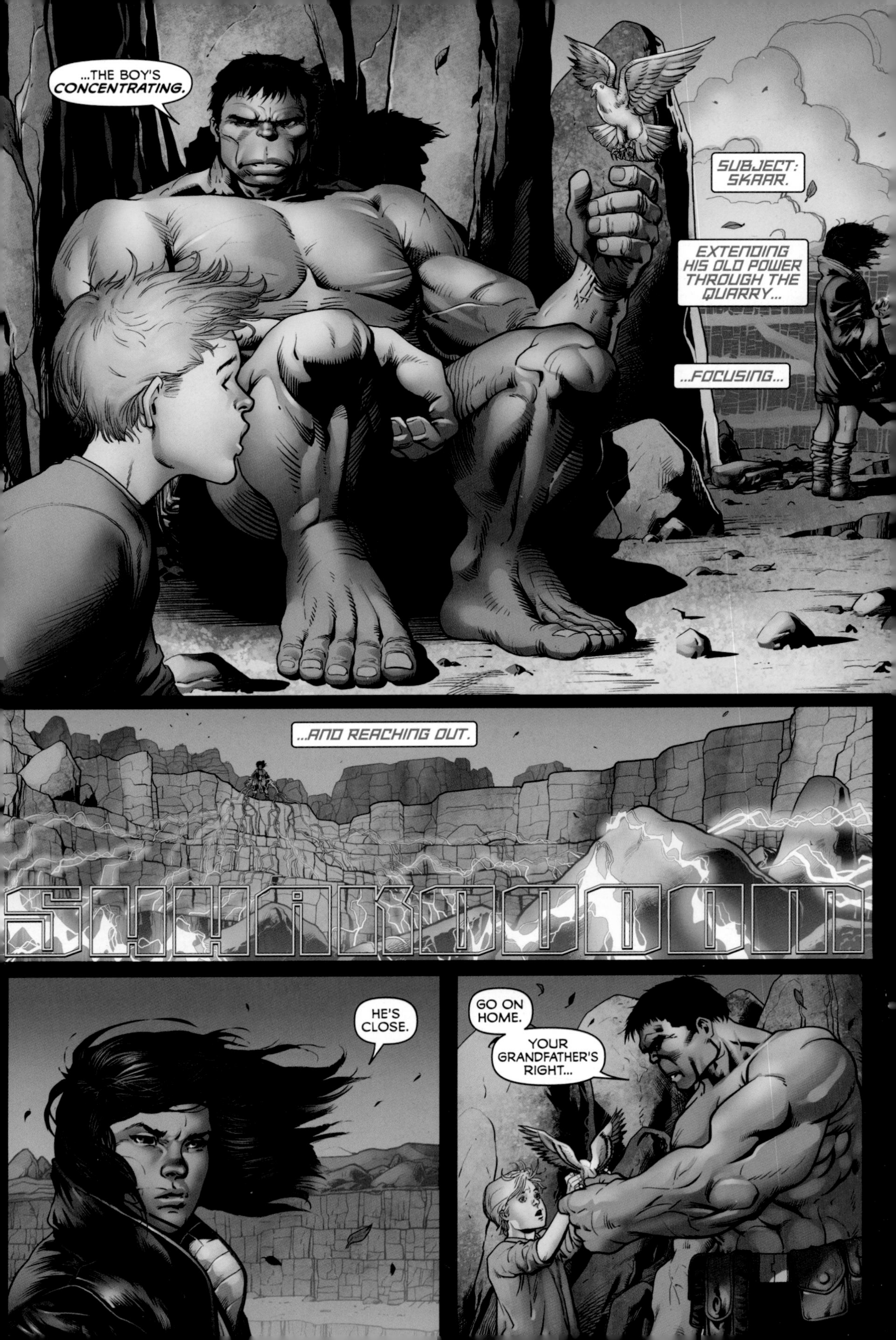
...THE BOY'S CONCENTRATING.
SUBJECT: SKAAR.
EXTENDING HIS OLD POWER THROUGH THE QUARRY...
...FOCUSING...
...AND REACHING OUT.
SHKRAKOOOOOM
HE'S CLOSE.
GO ON HOME.
YOUR GRANDFATHER'S RIGHT...

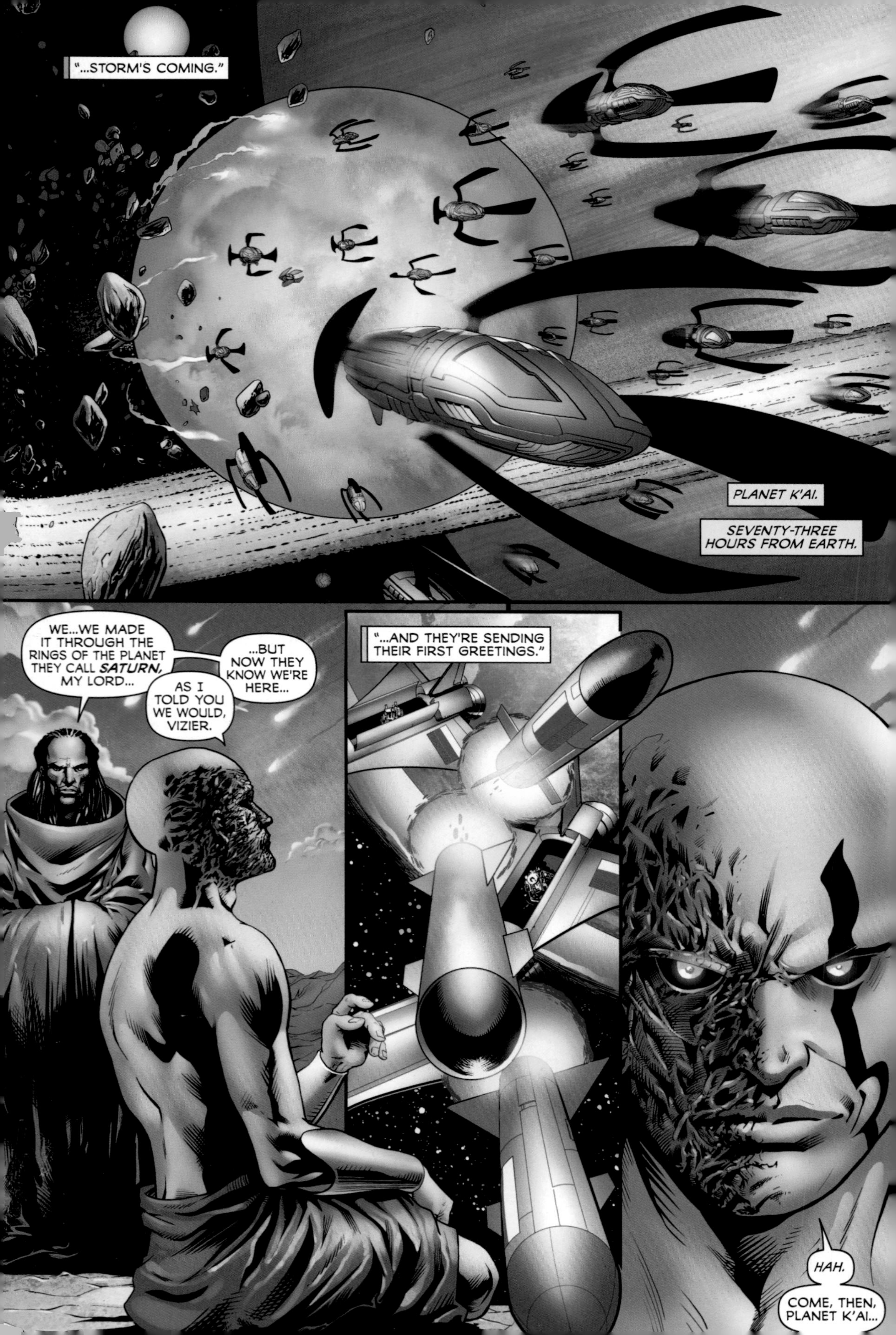
"...STORM'S COMING."
PLANET K'AI.
SEVENTY-THREE HOURS FROM EARTH.
WE...WE MADE IT THROUGH THE RINGS OF THE PLANET THEY CALL *SATURN,* MY LORD...
...BUT NOW THEY KNOW WE'RE HERE...
AS I TOLD YOU WE WOULD, VIZIER.
"...AND THEY'RE SENDING THEIR FIRST GREETINGS."
HAH.
COME, THEN, PLANET K'AI...

...LET'S SEND OUR *OWN* WELCOME.

"MY FELLOW AMERICANS...

"...THREE HOURS AGO, AN ALIEN PLANET THE SIZE OF *MARS* WAS DISCOVERED WITHIN OUR SOLAR SYSTEM...

"...AND IT APPEARS TO BE ON A *COLLISION COURSE* WITH *EARTH.*

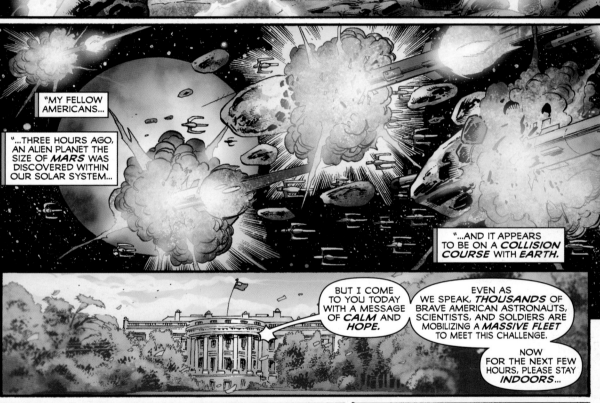

BUT I COME TO YOU TODAY WITH A MESSAGE OF *CALM* AND *HOPE.*

EVEN AS WE SPEAK, *THOUSANDS* OF BRAVE AMERICAN ASTRONAUTS, SCIENTISTS, AND SOLDIERS ARE MOBILIZING A *MASSIVE FLEET* TO MEET THIS CHALLENGE.

NOW FOR THE NEXT FEW HOURS, PLEASE STAY *INDOORS*...

...THE *WIND STORMS* CAUSED BY THE INCOMING PLANET'S GRAVITATIONAL FIELD MAY *INCREASE* BEFORE THEY *LESSEN.*

BUT LET ME BE *CLEAR*...

...THE UNITED STATES HAS THE TECHNOLOGY, THE EXPERTISE, AND THE WILL TO HANDLE THIS CRISIS.

SO GO AHEAD. CALL YOUR GRANDMOTHER.

EMBRACE YOUR CHILDREN.

PRAY.

BUT I ASSURE YOU...

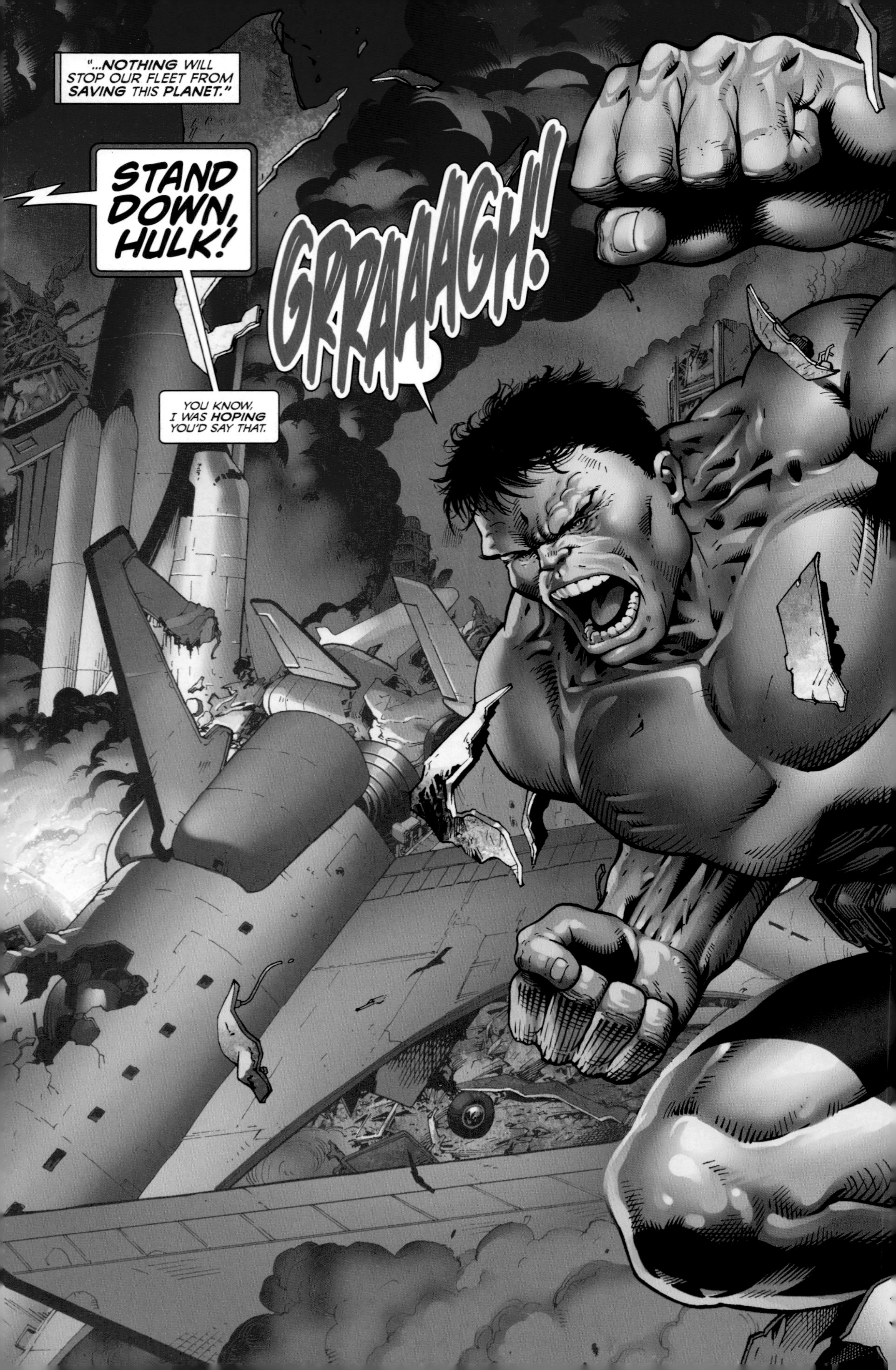
"...NOTHING WILL STOP OUR FLEET FROM SAVING THIS PLANET."
STAND DOWN, HULK!
YOU KNOW, I WAS HOPING YOU'D SAY THAT.
GRRAAAGH!!

KRAKKOOOM

CAPE CANAVERAL.

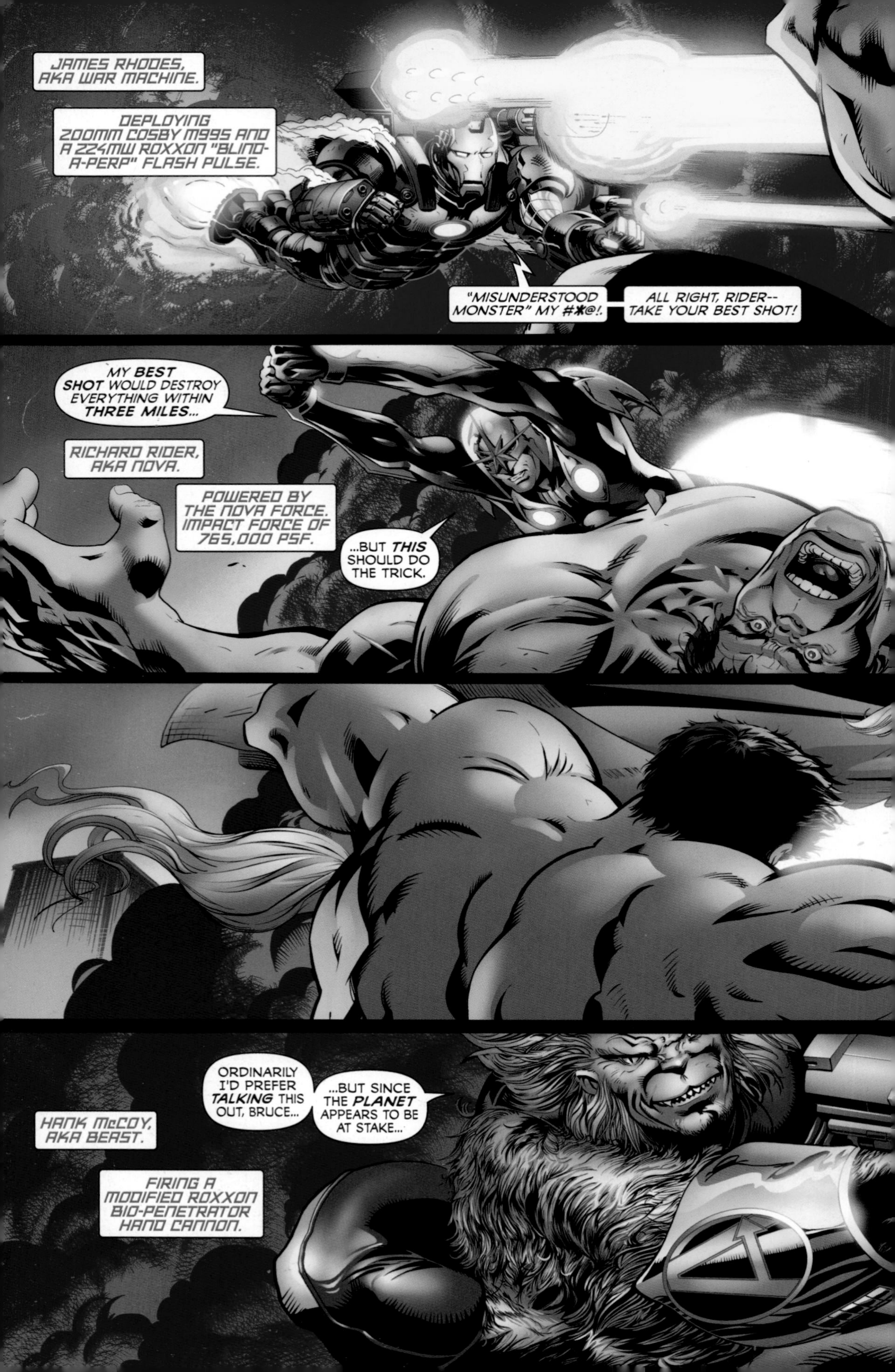
JAMES RHODES, AKA WAR MACHINE.
DEPLOYING 200MM COSBY M995 AND A 224MW ROXXON "BLIND-A-PERP" FLASH PULSE.
"MISUNDERSTOOD MONSTER" MY #*@!.
ALL RIGHT, RIDER-- TAKE YOUR BEST SHOT!
MY BEST SHOT WOULD DESTROY EVERYTHING WITHIN THREE MILES...
RICHARD RIDER, AKA NOVA.
POWERED BY THE NOVA FORCE. IMPACT FORCE OF 765,000 PSF.
...BUT THIS SHOULD DO THE TRICK.
ORDINARILY I'D PREFER TALKING THIS OUT, BRUCE...
...BUT SINCE THE PLANET APPEARS TO BE AT STAKE...
HANK McCOY, AKA BEAST.
FIRING A MODIFIED ROXXON BIO-PENETRATOR HAND CANNON.

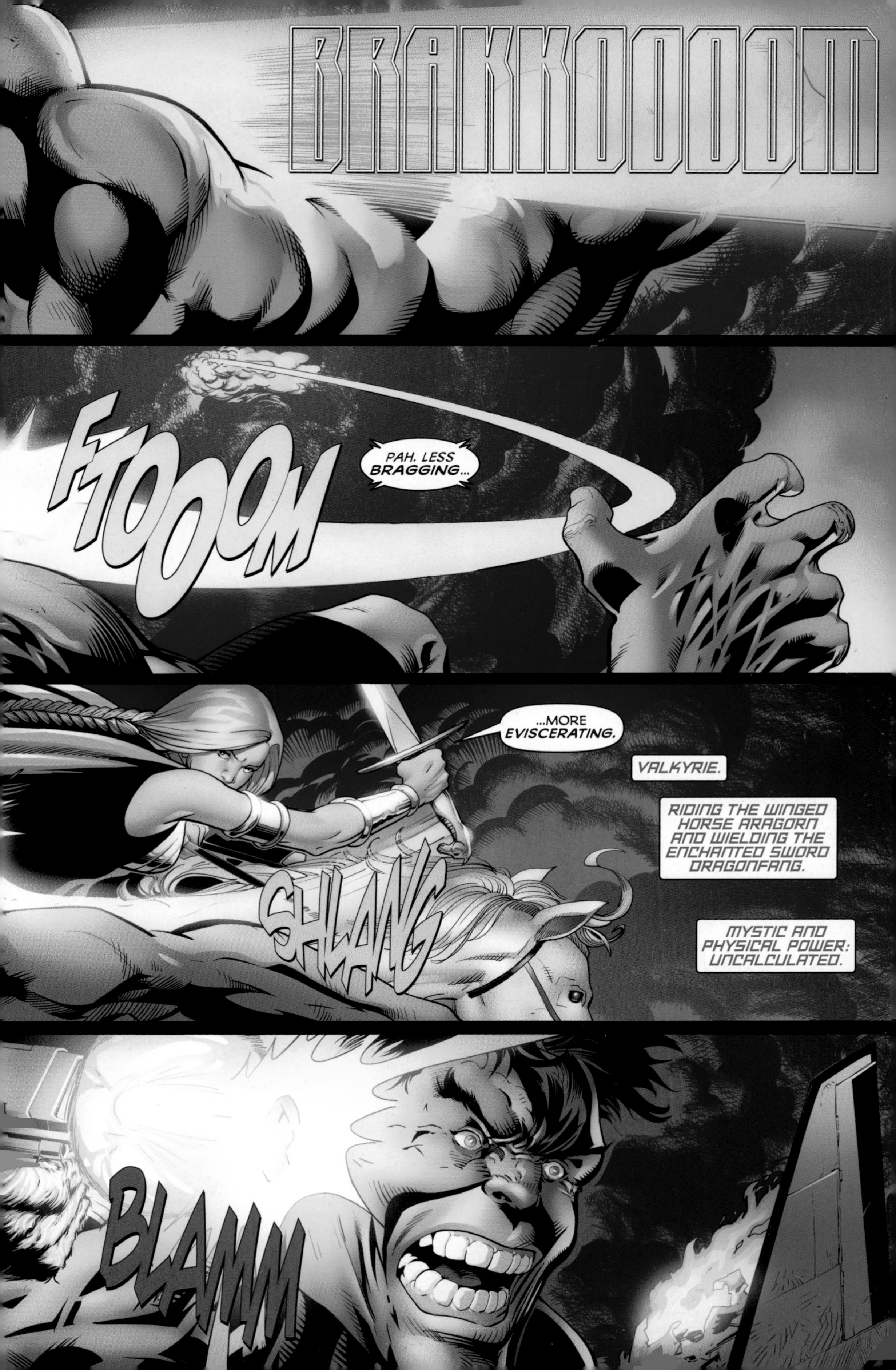
BRAKKOOOOM
FTOOOM
PAH. LESS BRAGGING...
...MORE EVISCERATING.
VALKYRIE.
RIDING THE WINGED HORSE ARAGORN AND WIELDING THE ENCHANTED SWORD DRAGONFANG.
SHLANG
MYSTIC AND PHYSICAL POWER: UNCALCULATED.
BLAMM

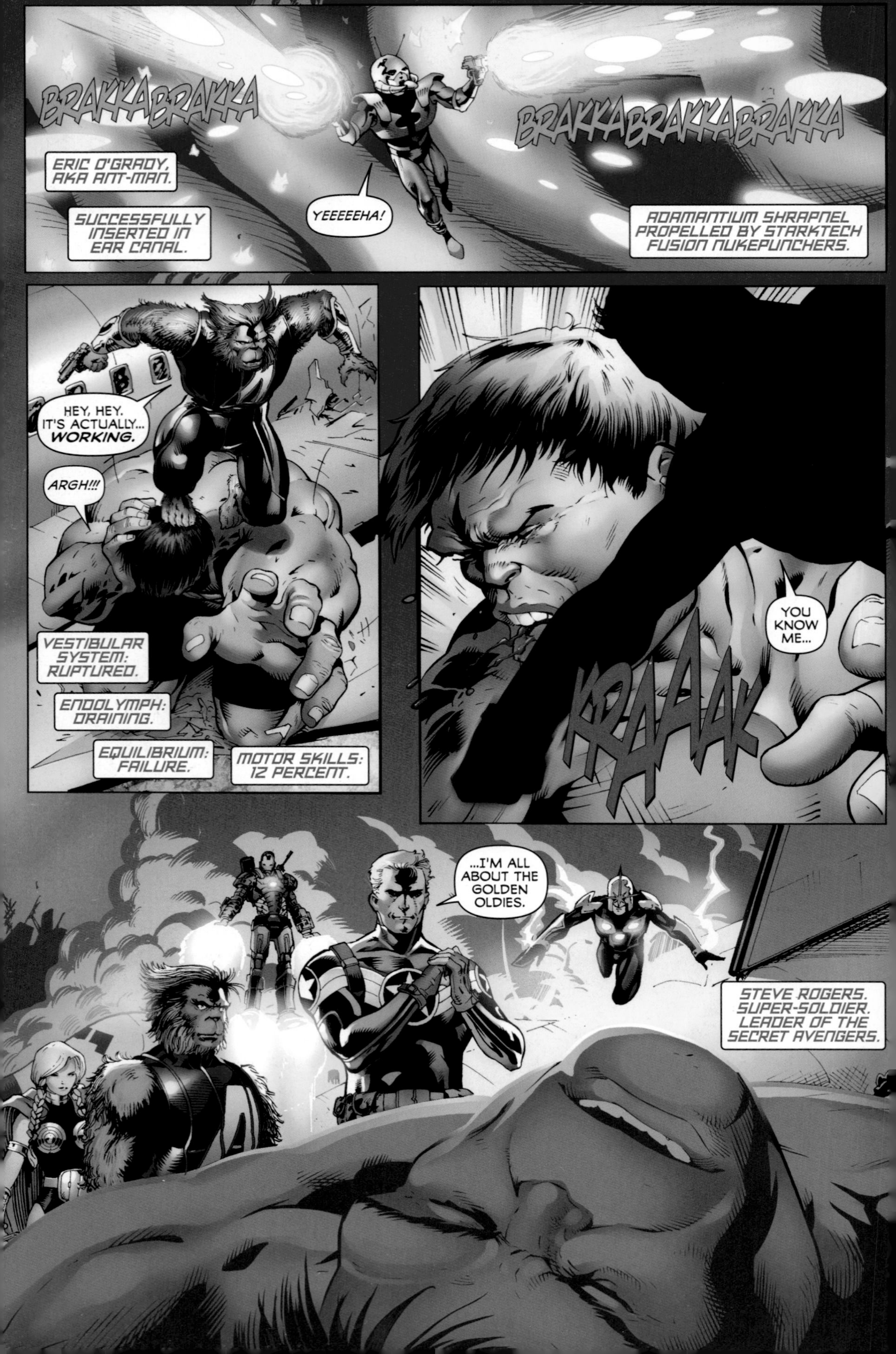
BRAKKABRAKKA
ERIC O'GRADY, AKA ANT-MAN.
SUCCESSFULLY INSERTED IN EAR CANAL.
YEEEEEHA!
BRAKKABRAKKABRAKKA
ADAMANTIUM SHRAPNEL PROPELLED BY STARKTECH FUSION NUKEPUNCHERS.
HEY, HEY. IT'S ACTUALLY... WORKING.
ARGH!!!
VESTIBULAR SYSTEM: RUPTURED.
ENDOLYMPH: DRAINING.
EQUILIBRIUM: FAILURE.
MOTOR SKILLS: 12 PERCENT.
YOU KNOW ME...
KRAAAK
...I'M ALL ABOUT THE GOLDEN OLDIES.
STEVE ROGERS. SUPER-SOLDIER. LEADER OF THE SECRET AVENGERS.

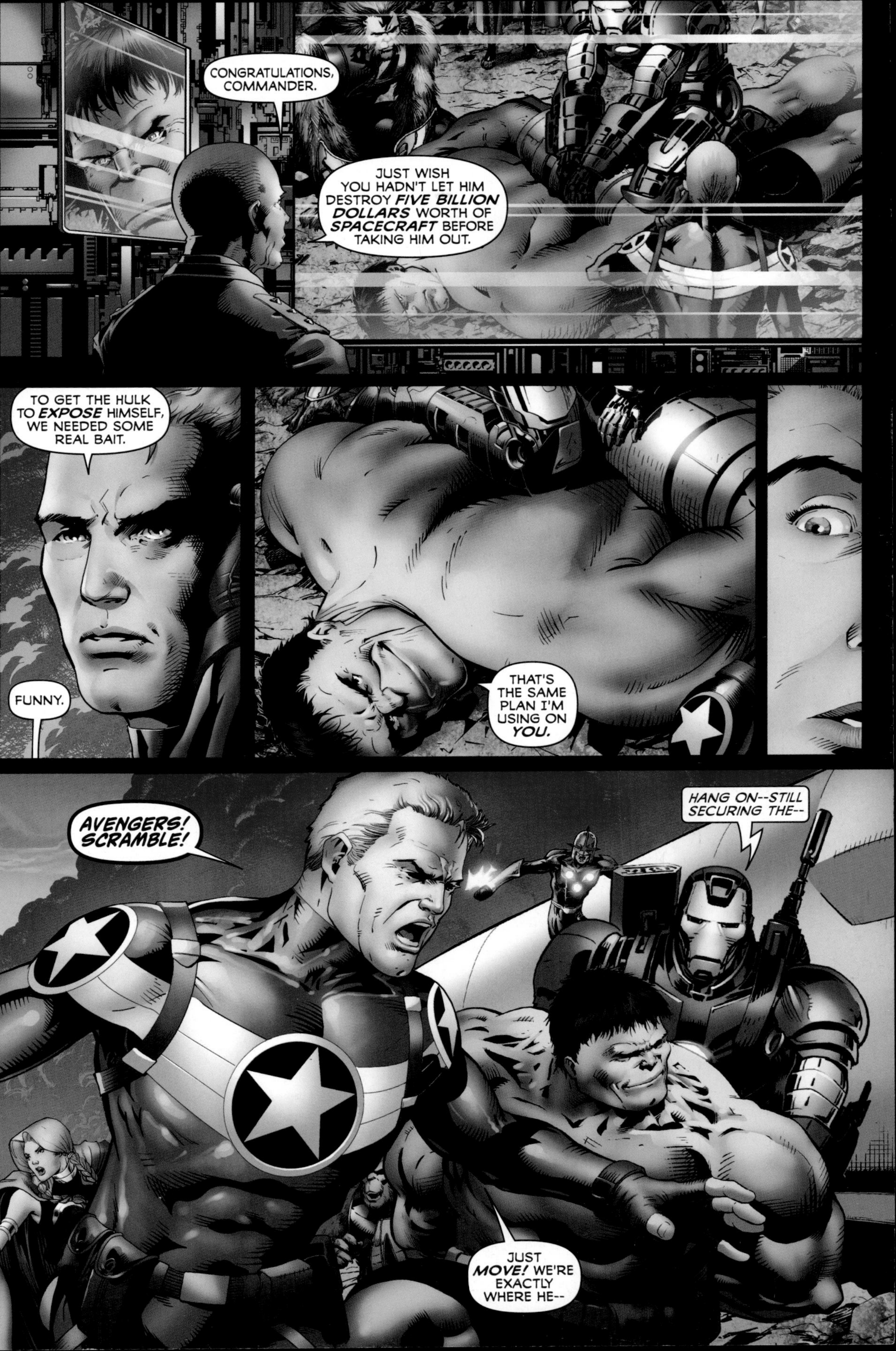
CONGRATULATIONS, COMMANDER.
JUST WISH YOU HADN'T LET HIM DESTROY FIVE BILLION DOLLARS WORTH OF SPACECRAFT BEFORE TAKING HIM OUT.
TO GET THE HULK TO EXPOSE HIMSELF, WE NEEDED SOME REAL BAIT.
FUNNY.
THAT'S THE SAME PLAN I'M USING ON YOU.
AVENGERS! SCRAMBLE!
HANG ON--STILL SECURING THE--
JUST MOVE! WE'RE EXACTLY WHERE HE--

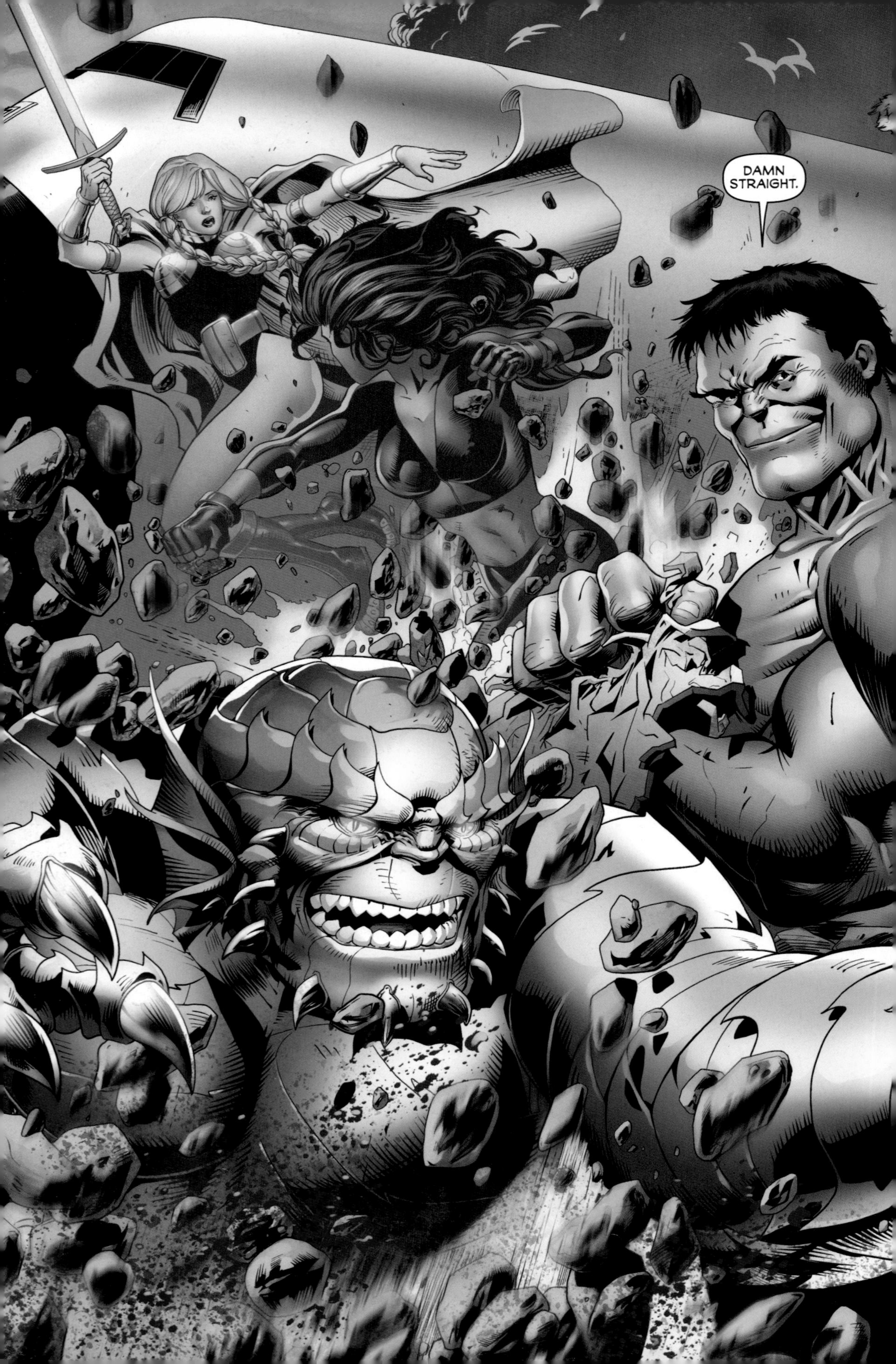
DAMN STRAIGHT.

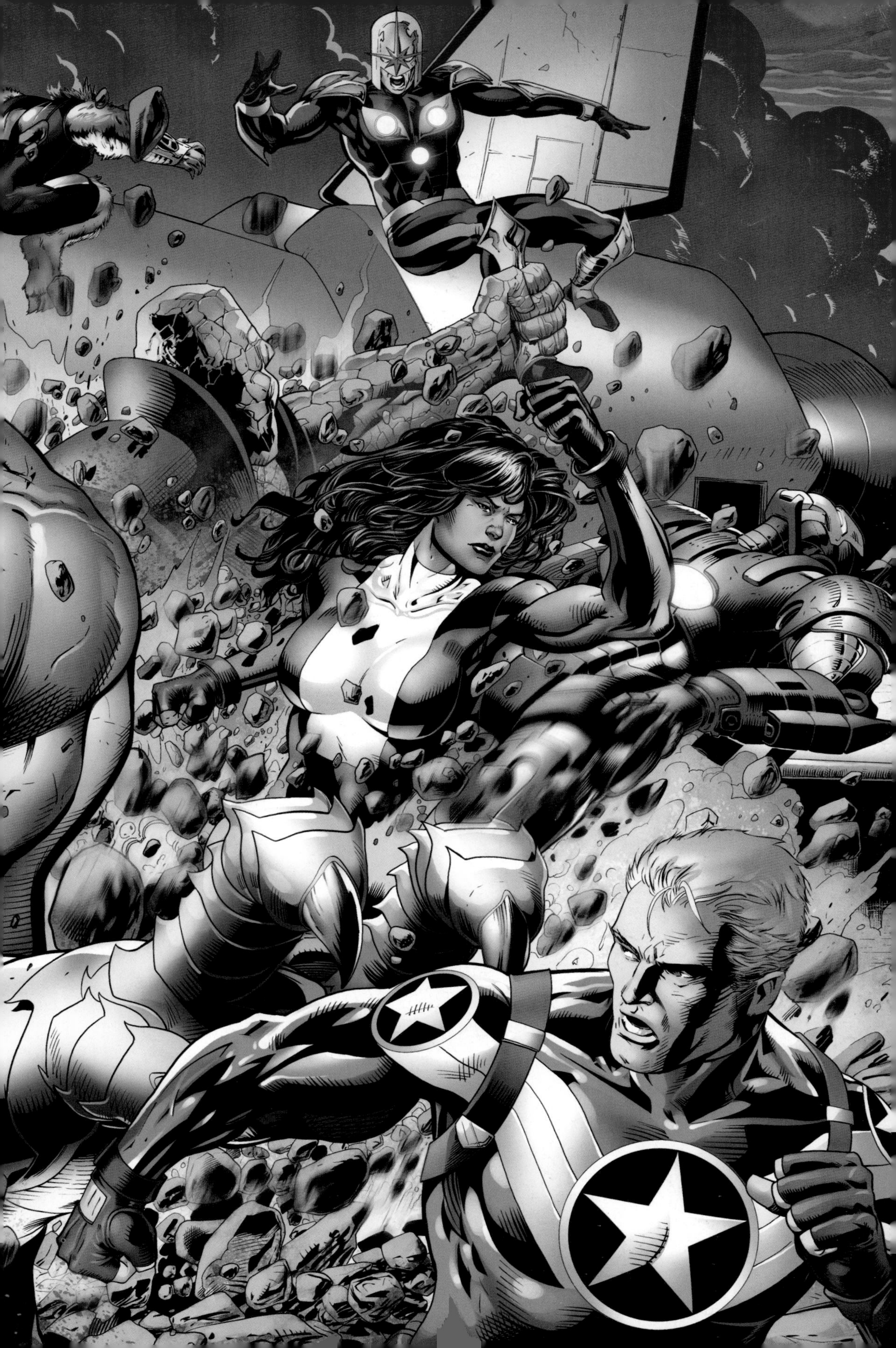

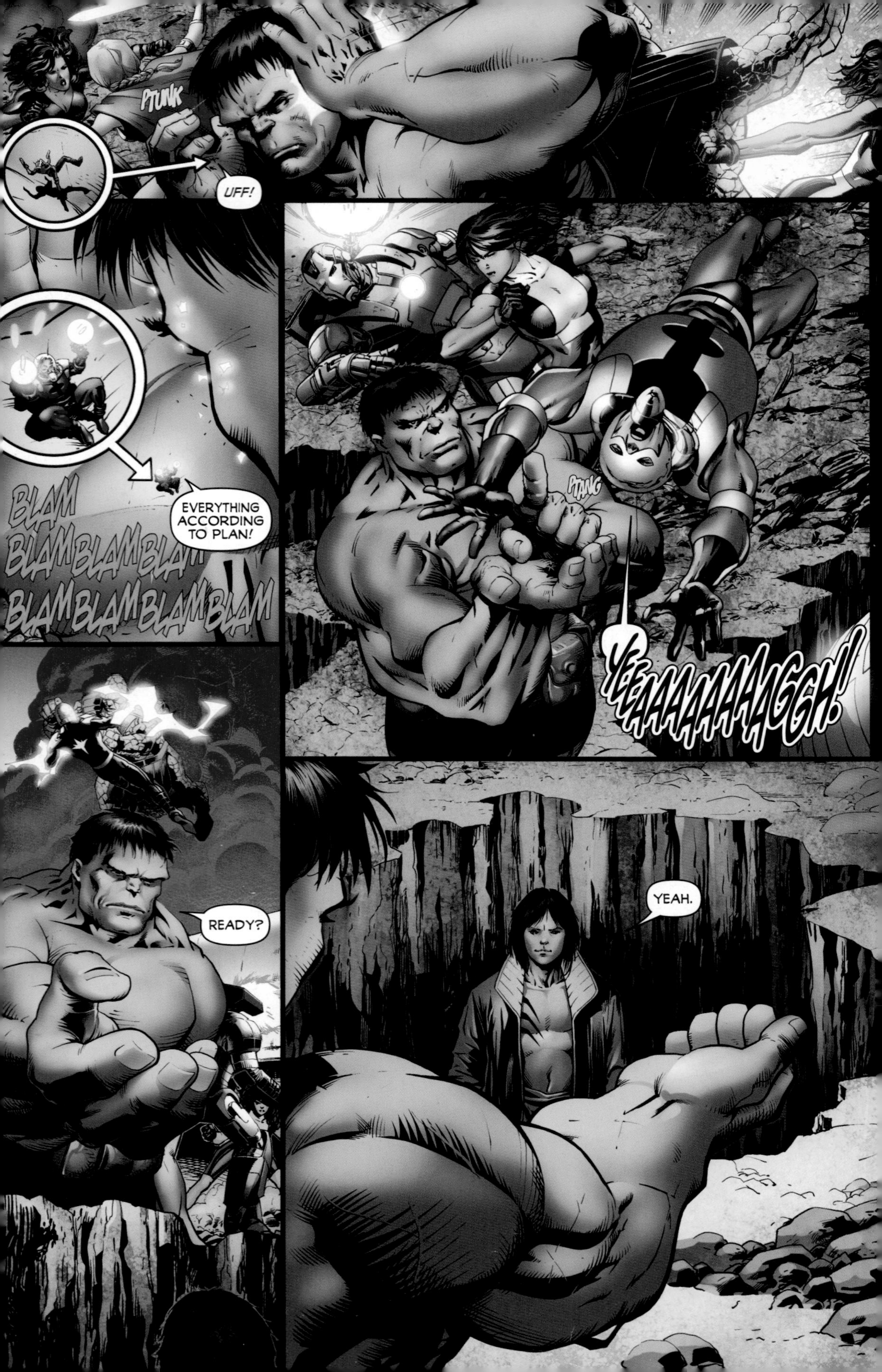
PTUNK
UFF!
BLAM
BLAM BLAM BLAM
BLAM BLAM BLAM BLAM
EVERYTHING ACCORDING TO PLAN!
PTANG
YEAAAAAAAGGH!
READY?
YEAH.

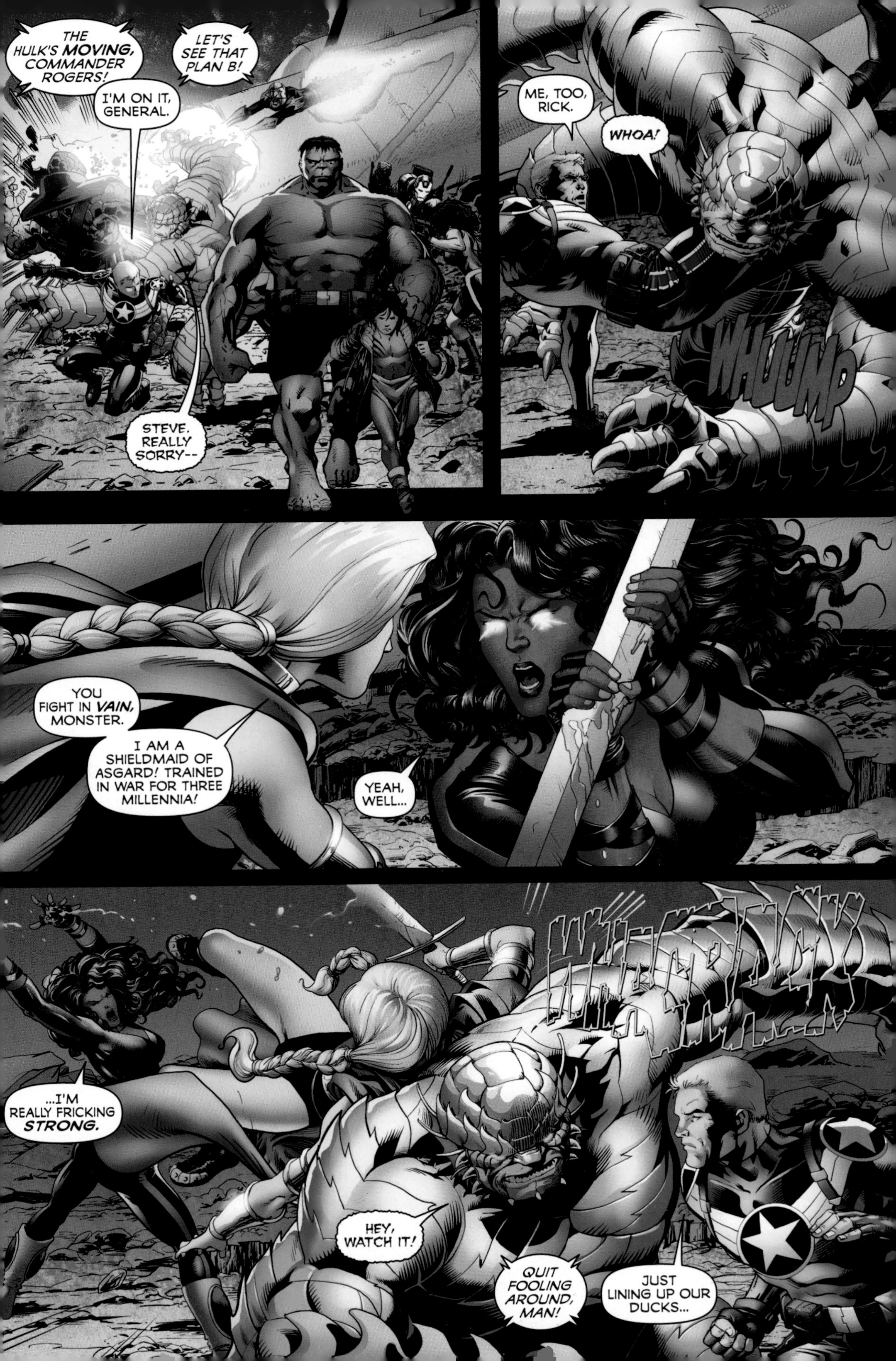
THE HULK'S **MOVING,** COMMANDER ROGERS!
LET'S SEE THAT PLAN B!
I'M ON IT, GENERAL.
STEVE. REALLY SORRY--
ME, TOO, RICK.
WHOA!
WHUUMP
YOU FIGHT IN ***VAIN,*** MONSTER.
I AM A SHIELDMAID OF ASGARD! TRAINED IN WAR FOR THREE MILLENNIA!
YEAH, WELL...
...I'M REALLY FRICKING ***STRONG.***
HEY, WATCH IT!
QUIT FOOLING AROUND, MAN!
JUST LINING UP OUR DUCKS...

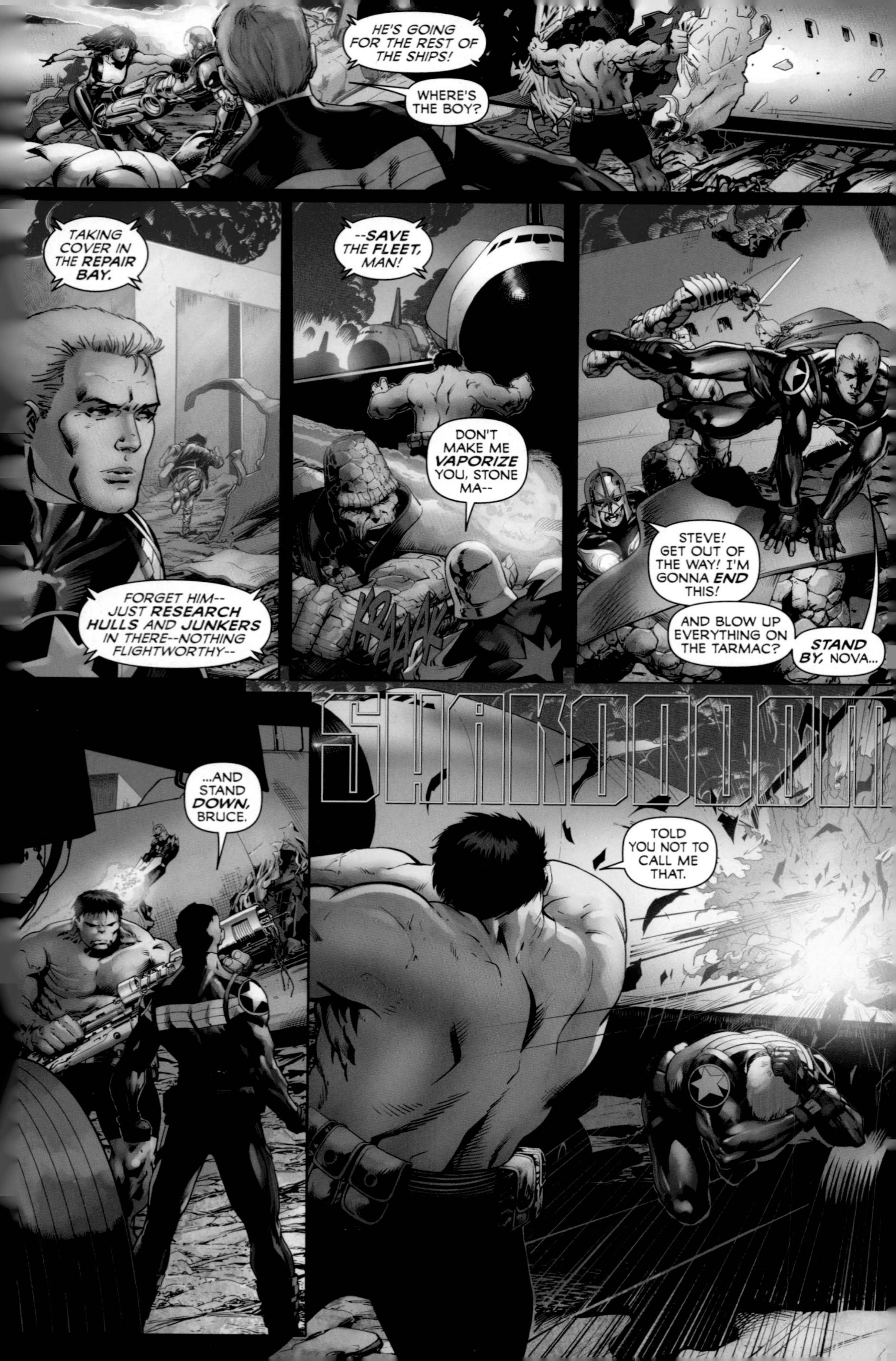
HE'S GOING FOR THE REST OF THE SHIPS!
WHERE'S THE BOY?
TAKING COVER IN THE REPAIR BAY.
FORGET HIM-- JUST RESEARCH HULLS AND JUNKERS IN THERE--NOTHING FLIGHTWORTHY--
--SAVE THE FLEET, MAN!
DON'T MAKE ME VAPORIZE YOU, STONE MA--
KRAAAK
STEVE! GET OUT OF THE WAY! I'M GONNA END THIS!
AND BLOW UP EVERYTHING ON THE TARMAC?
STAND BY, NOVA...
...AND STAND DOWN, BRUCE.
TOLD YOU NOT TO CALL ME THAT.

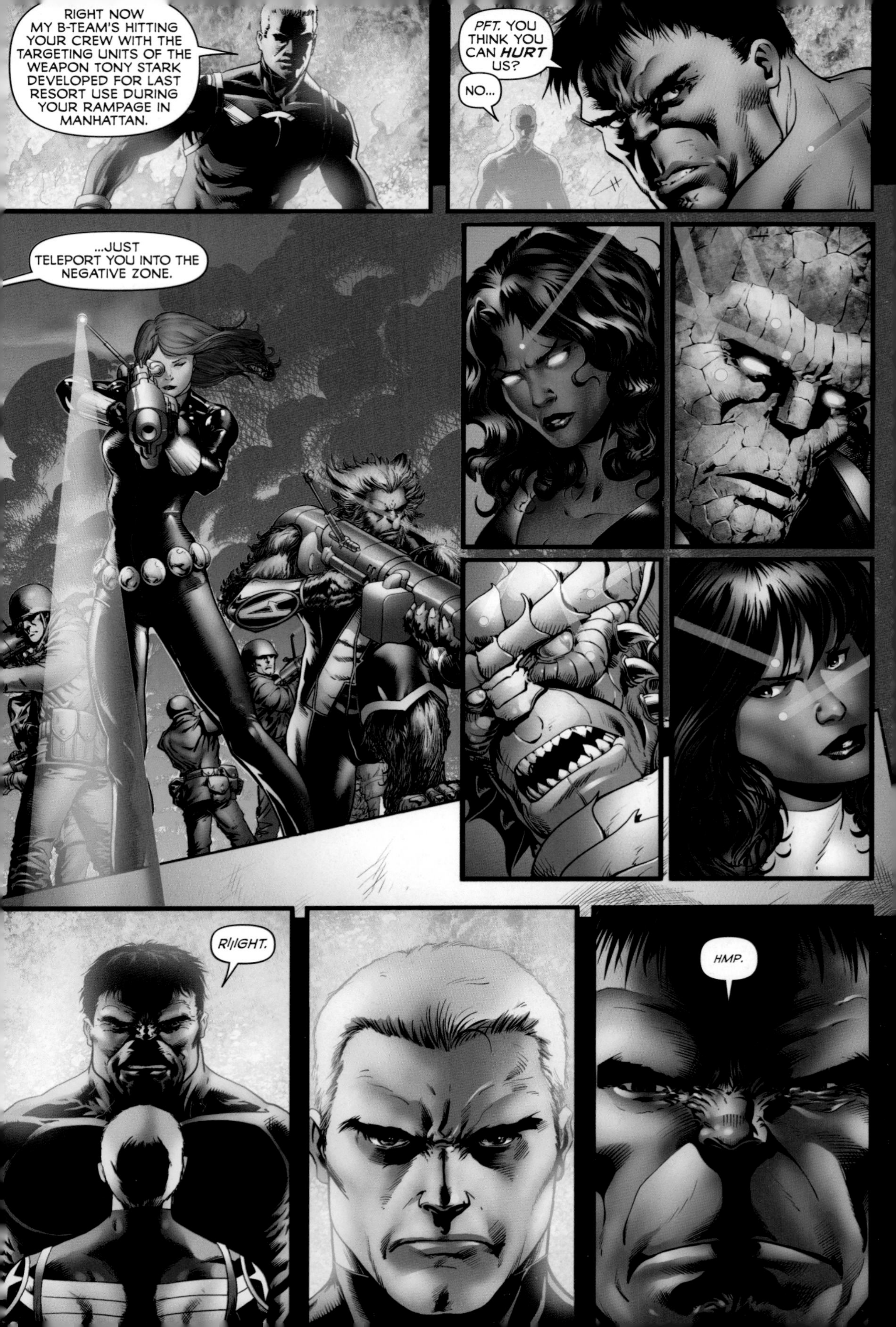
RIGHT NOW MY B-TEAM'S HITTING YOUR CREW WITH THE TARGETING UNITS OF THE WEAPON TONY STARK DEVELOPED FOR LAST RESORT USE DURING YOUR RAMPAGE IN MANHATTAN.
PFT. YOU THINK YOU CAN HURT US?
NO...
...JUST TELEPORT YOU INTO THE NEGATIVE ZONE.
RIIIGHT.
HMP.

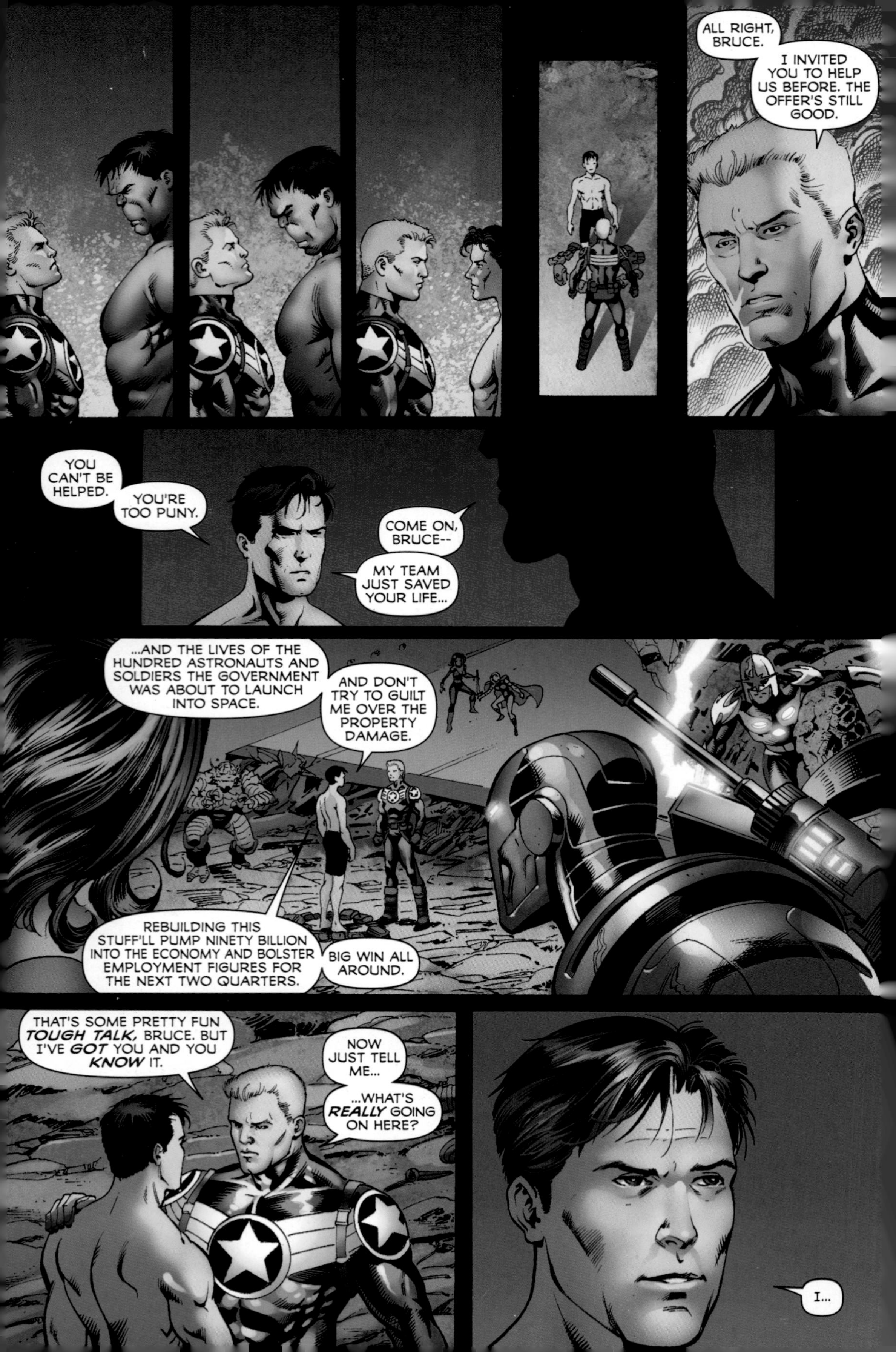
ALL RIGHT, BRUCE.
I INVITED YOU TO HELP US BEFORE. THE OFFER'S STILL GOOD.
YOU CAN'T BE HELPED.
YOU'RE TOO PUNY.
COME ON, BRUCE--
MY TEAM JUST SAVED YOUR LIFE...
...AND THE LIVES OF THE HUNDRED ASTRONAUTS AND SOLDIERS THE GOVERNMENT WAS ABOUT TO LAUNCH INTO SPACE.
AND DON'T TRY TO GUILT ME OVER THE PROPERTY DAMAGE.
REBUILDING THIS STUFF'LL PUMP NINETY BILLION INTO THE ECONOMY AND BOLSTER EMPLOYMENT FIGURES FOR THE NEXT TWO QUARTERS.
BIG WIN ALL AROUND.
THAT'S SOME PRETTY FUN TOUGH TALK, BRUCE. BUT I'VE GOT YOU AND YOU KNOW IT.
NOW JUST TELL ME...
...WHAT'S REALLY GOING ON HERE?
I...

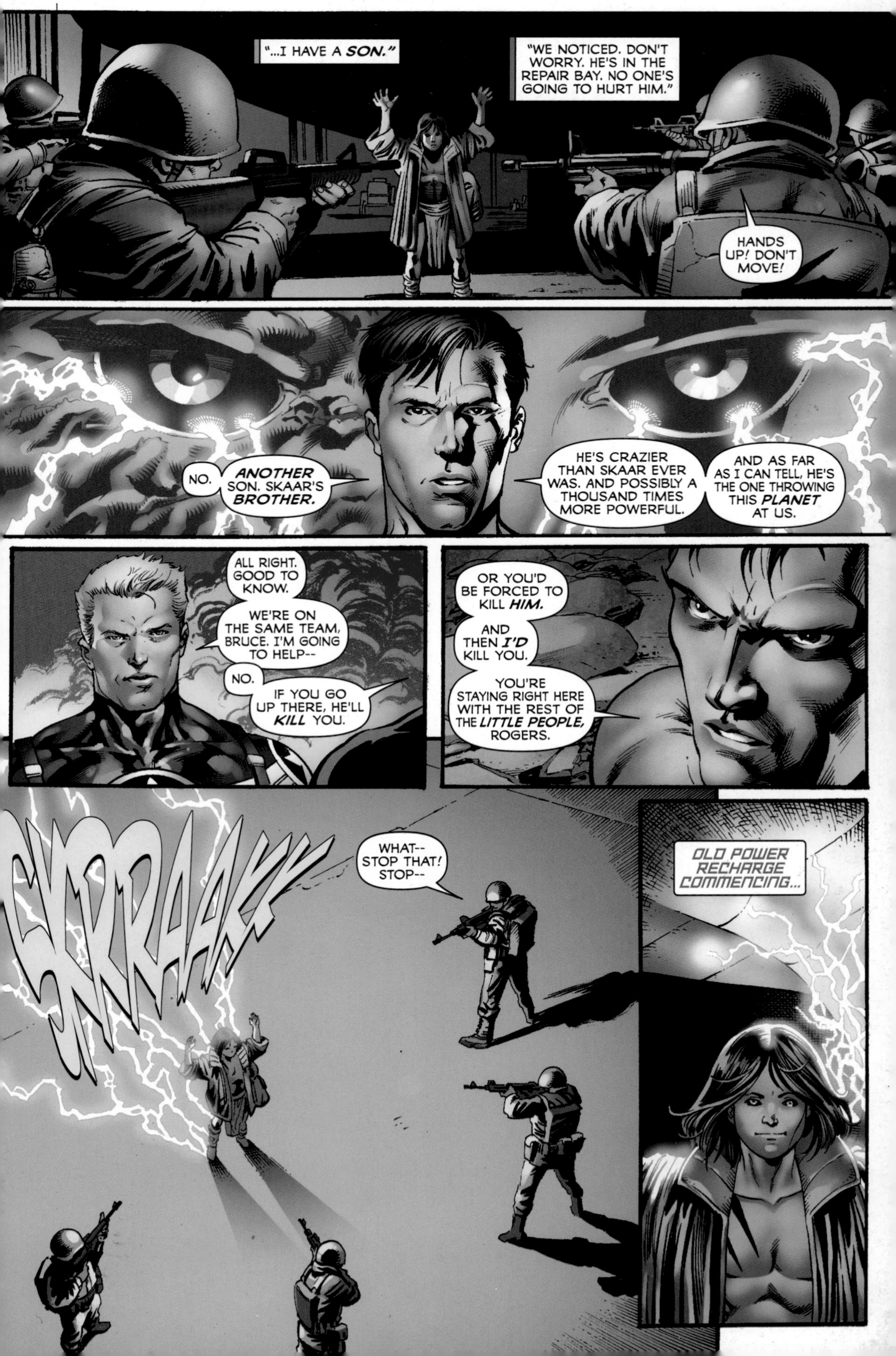
"...I HAVE A SON."
"WE NOTICED. DON'T WORRY. HE'S IN THE REPAIR BAY. NO ONE'S GOING TO HURT HIM."
HANDS UP! DON'T MOVE!
NO.
ANOTHER SON. SKAAR'S BROTHER.
HE'S CRAZIER THAN SKAAR EVER WAS. AND POSSIBLY A THOUSAND TIMES MORE POWERFUL.
AND AS FAR AS I CAN TELL, HE'S THE ONE THROWING THIS PLANET AT US.
ALL RIGHT. GOOD TO KNOW.
WE'RE ON THE SAME TEAM, BRUCE. I'M GOING TO HELP--
NO.
IF YOU GO UP THERE, HE'LL KILL YOU.
OR YOU'D BE FORCED TO KILL HIM.
AND THEN I'D KILL YOU.
YOU'RE STAYING RIGHT HERE WITH THE REST OF THE LITTLE PEOPLE, ROGERS.
SKRRAAKK!
WHAT-- STOP THAT! STOP--
OLD POWER RECHARGE COMMENCING...

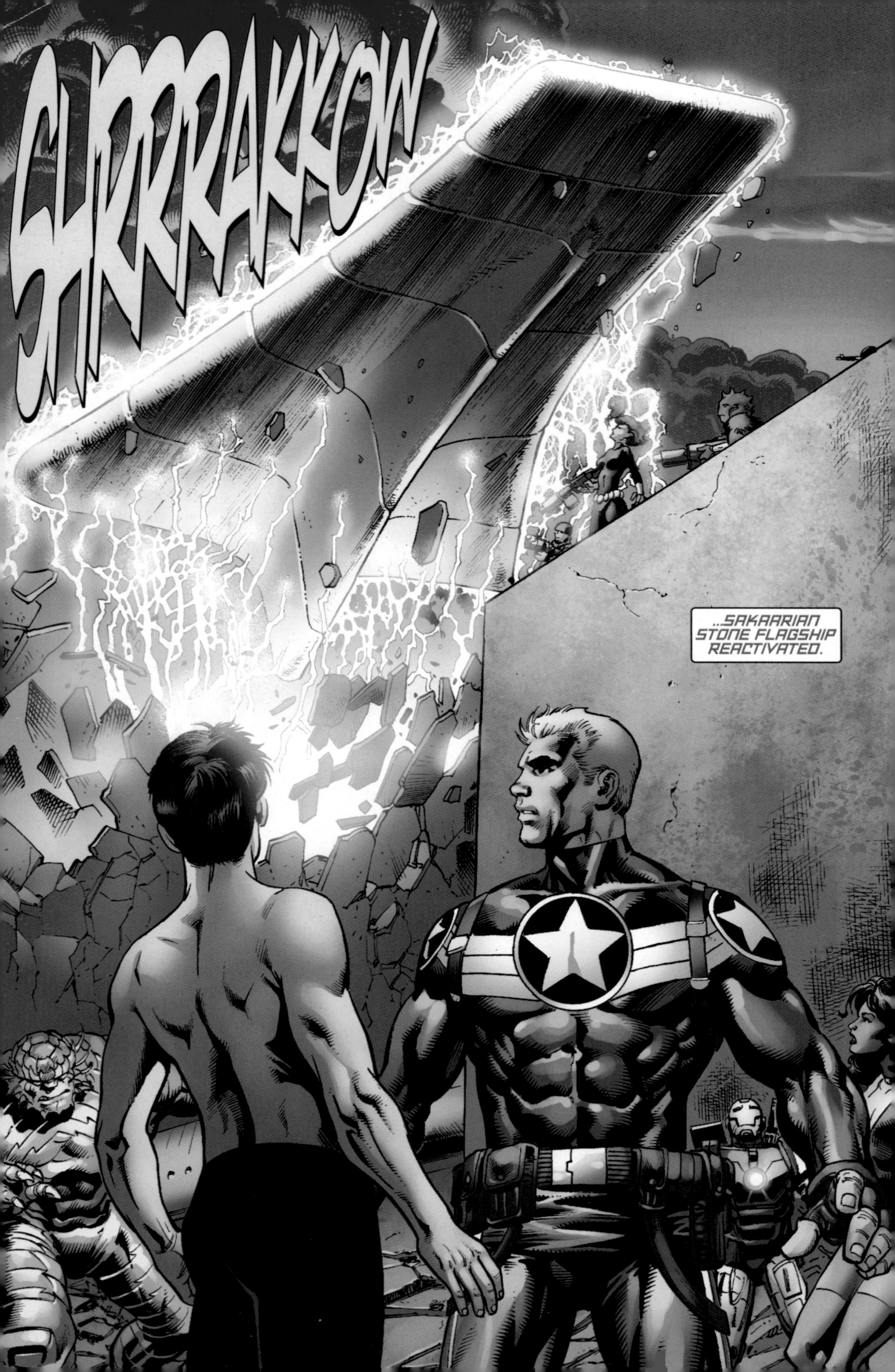
SHRRAKKOW
...SAKAARIAN STONE FLAGSHIP REACTIVATED.

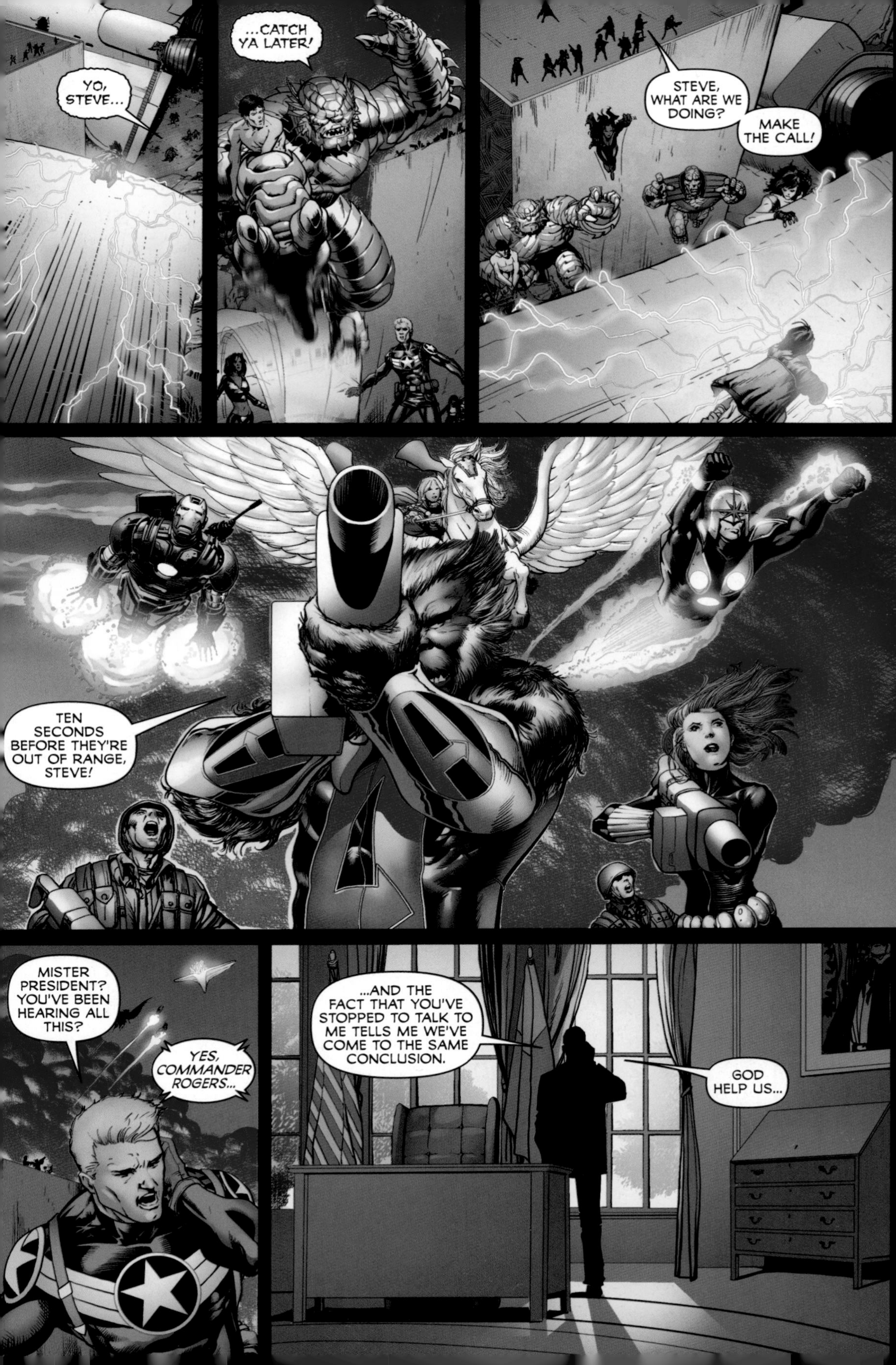
YO, STEVE...
...CATCH YA LATER!
STEVE, WHAT ARE WE DOING?
MAKE THE CALL!
TEN SECONDS BEFORE THEY'RE OUT OF RANGE, STEVE!
MISTER PRESIDENT? YOU'VE BEEN HEARING ALL THIS?
YES, COMMANDER ROGERS...
...AND THE FACT THAT YOU'VE STOPPED TO TALK TO ME TELLS ME WE'VE COME TO THE SAME CONCLUSION.
GOD HELP US...

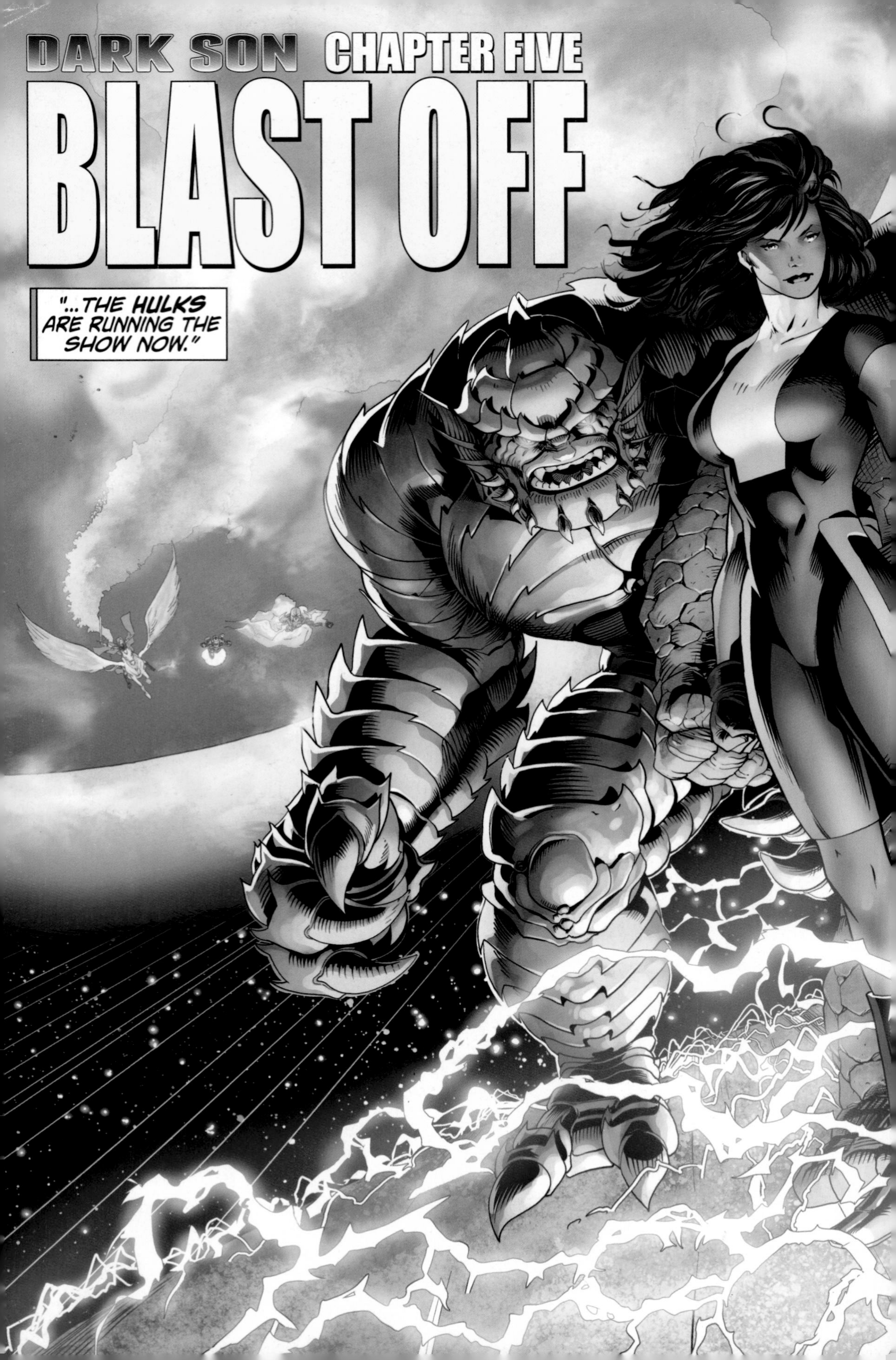
DARK SON CHAPTER FIVE
BLAST OFF
"...THE HULKS ARE RUNNING THE SHOW NOW."

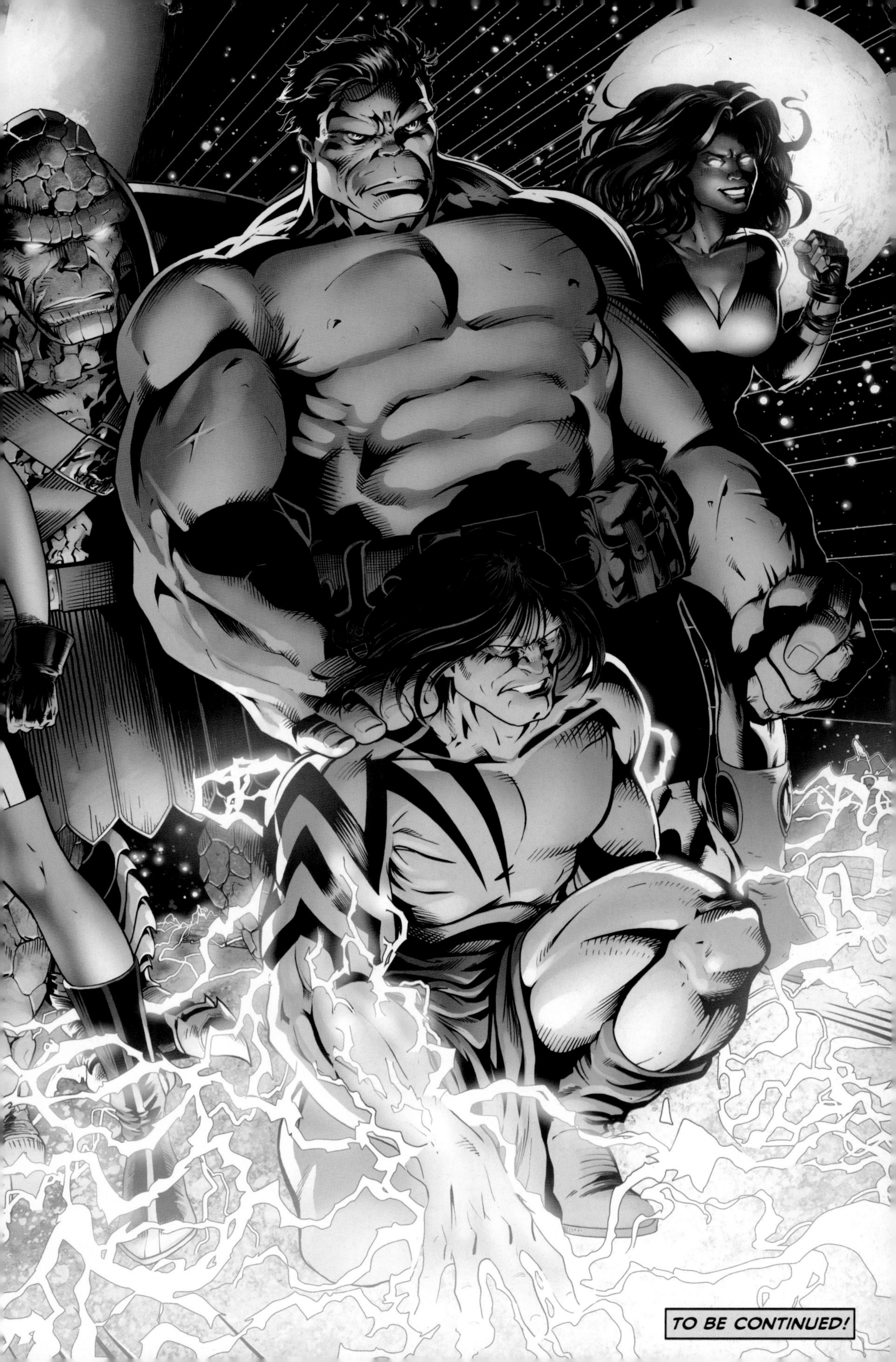
TO BE CONTINUED!

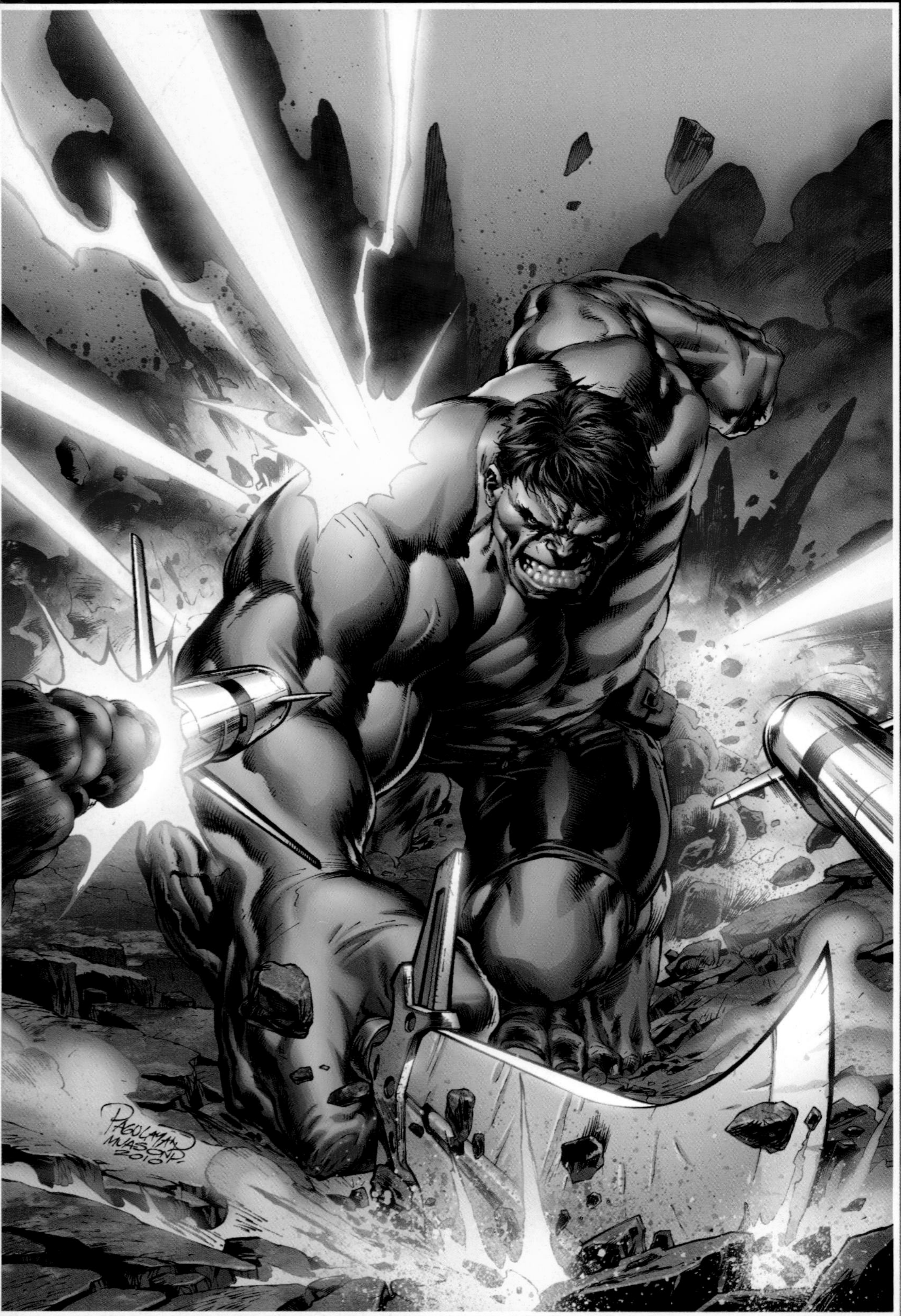

(615)

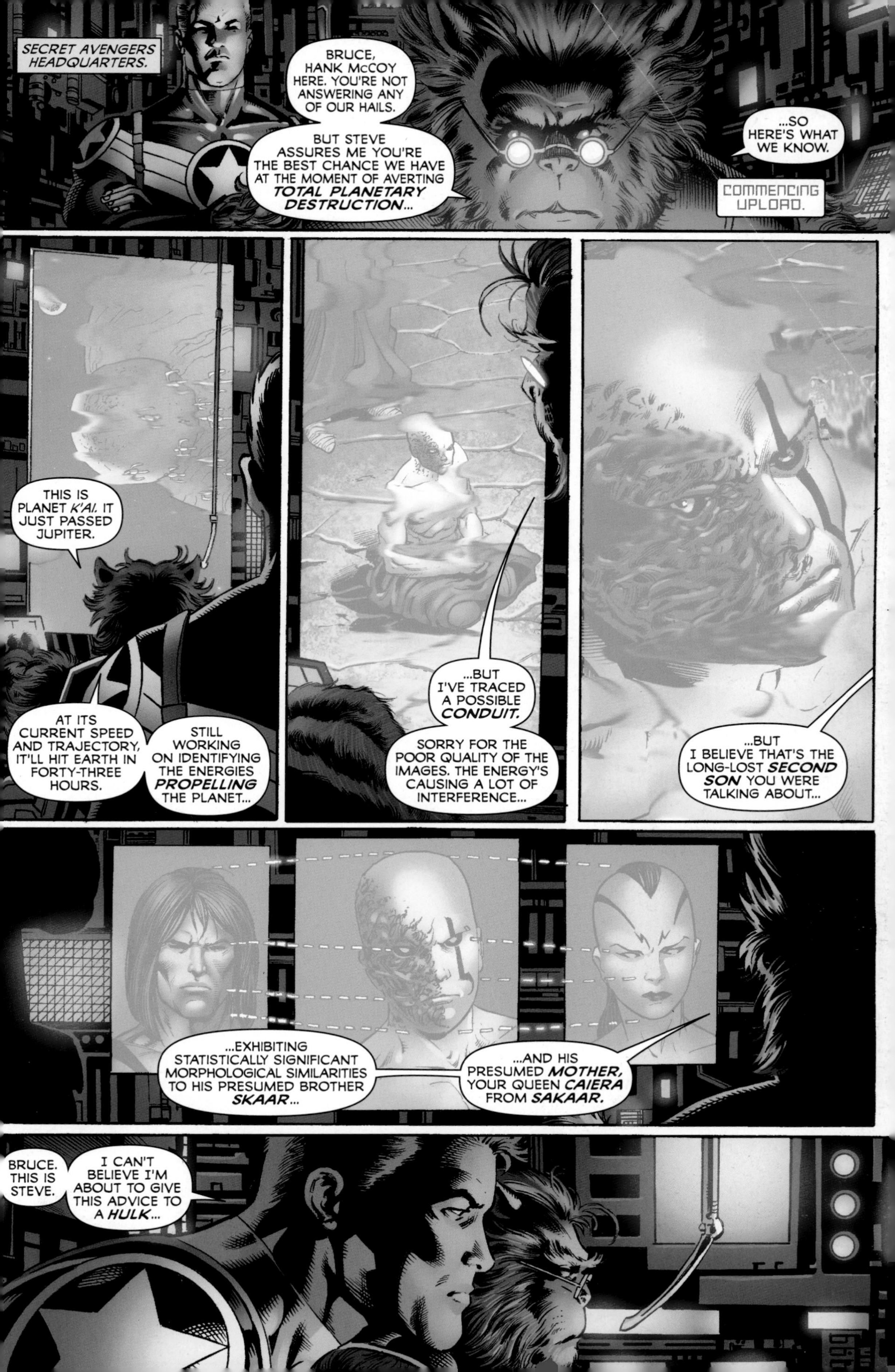
SECRET AVENGERS HEADQUARTERS.
BRUCE, HANK McCOY HERE. YOU'RE NOT ANSWERING ANY OF OUR HAILS.
BUT STEVE ASSURES ME YOU'RE THE BEST CHANCE WE HAVE AT THE MOMENT OF AVERTING TOTAL PLANETARY DESTRUCTION...
...SO HERE'S WHAT WE KNOW.
COMMENCING UPLOAD.
THIS IS PLANET K'AI. IT JUST PASSED JUPITER.
AT ITS CURRENT SPEED AND TRAJECTORY, IT'LL HIT EARTH IN FORTY-THREE HOURS.
STILL WORKING ON IDENTIFYING THE ENERGIES PROPELLING THE PLANET...
...BUT I'VE TRACED A POSSIBLE CONDUIT.
SORRY FOR THE POOR QUALITY OF THE IMAGES. THE ENERGY'S CAUSING A LOT OF INTERFERENCE...
...BUT I BELIEVE THAT'S THE LONG-LOST SECOND SON YOU WERE TALKING ABOUT...
...EXHIBITING STATISTICALLY SIGNIFICANT MORPHOLOGICAL SIMILARITIES TO HIS PRESUMED BROTHER SKAAR...
...AND HIS PRESUMED MOTHER, YOUR QUEEN CAIERA FROM SAKAAR.
BRUCE. THIS IS STEVE.
I CAN'T BELIEVE I'M ABOUT TO GIVE THIS ADVICE TO A HULK...

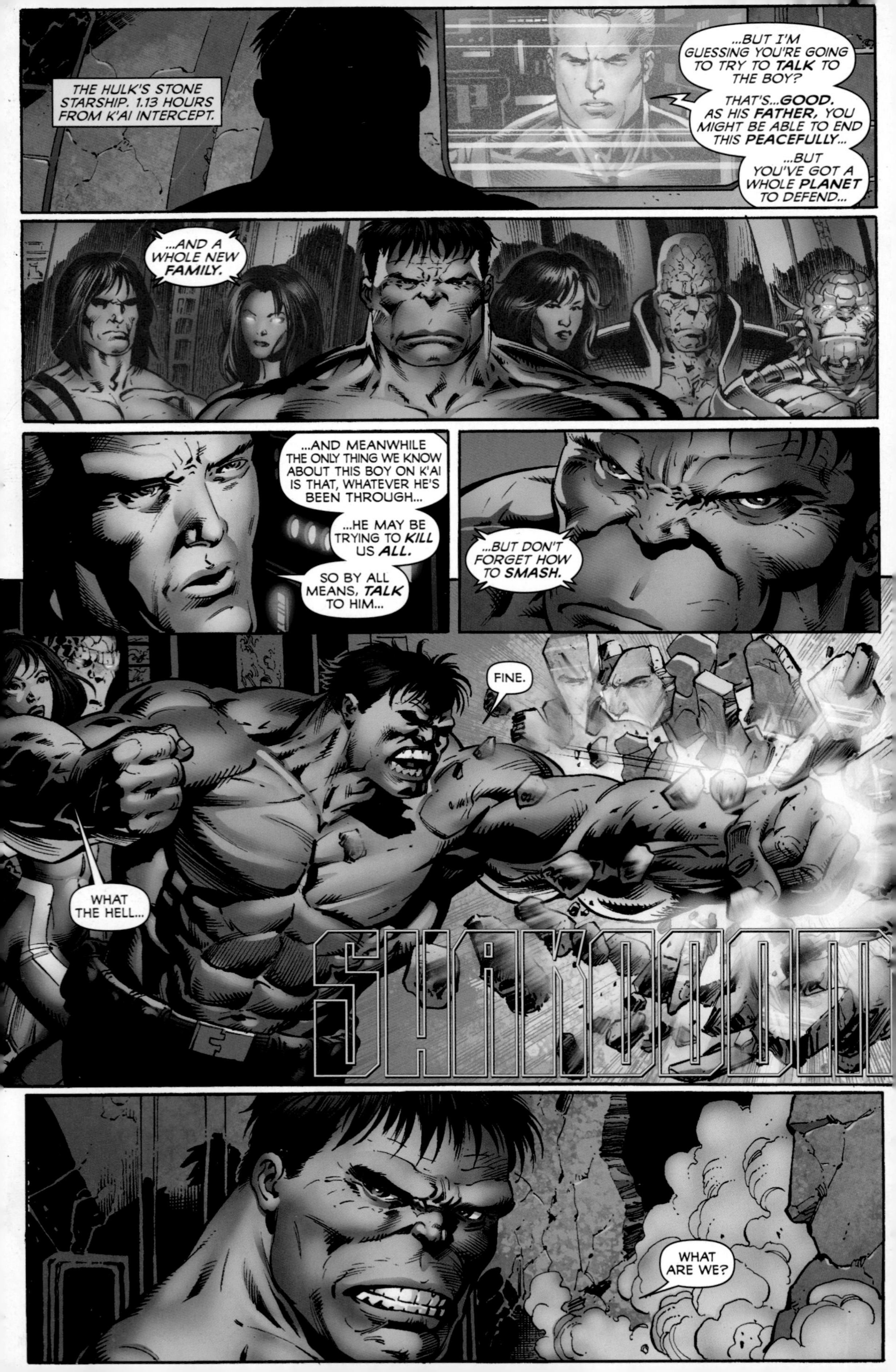
THE HULK'S STONE STARSHIP. 1.13 HOURS FROM K'AI INTERCEPT.
...BUT I'M GUESSING YOU'RE GOING TO TRY TO TALK TO THE BOY?
THAT'S...GOOD. AS HIS FATHER, YOU MIGHT BE ABLE TO END THIS PEACEFULLY...
...BUT YOU'VE GOT A WHOLE PLANET TO DEFEND...
...AND A WHOLE NEW FAMILY.
...AND MEANWHILE THE ONLY THING WE KNOW ABOUT THIS BOY ON K'AI IS THAT, WHATEVER HE'S BEEN THROUGH...
...HE MAY BE TRYING TO KILL US ALL.
SO BY ALL MEANS, TALK TO HIM...
...BUT DON'T FORGET HOW TO SMASH.
FINE.
WHAT THE HELL...
SHAKOOOM
WHAT ARE WE?

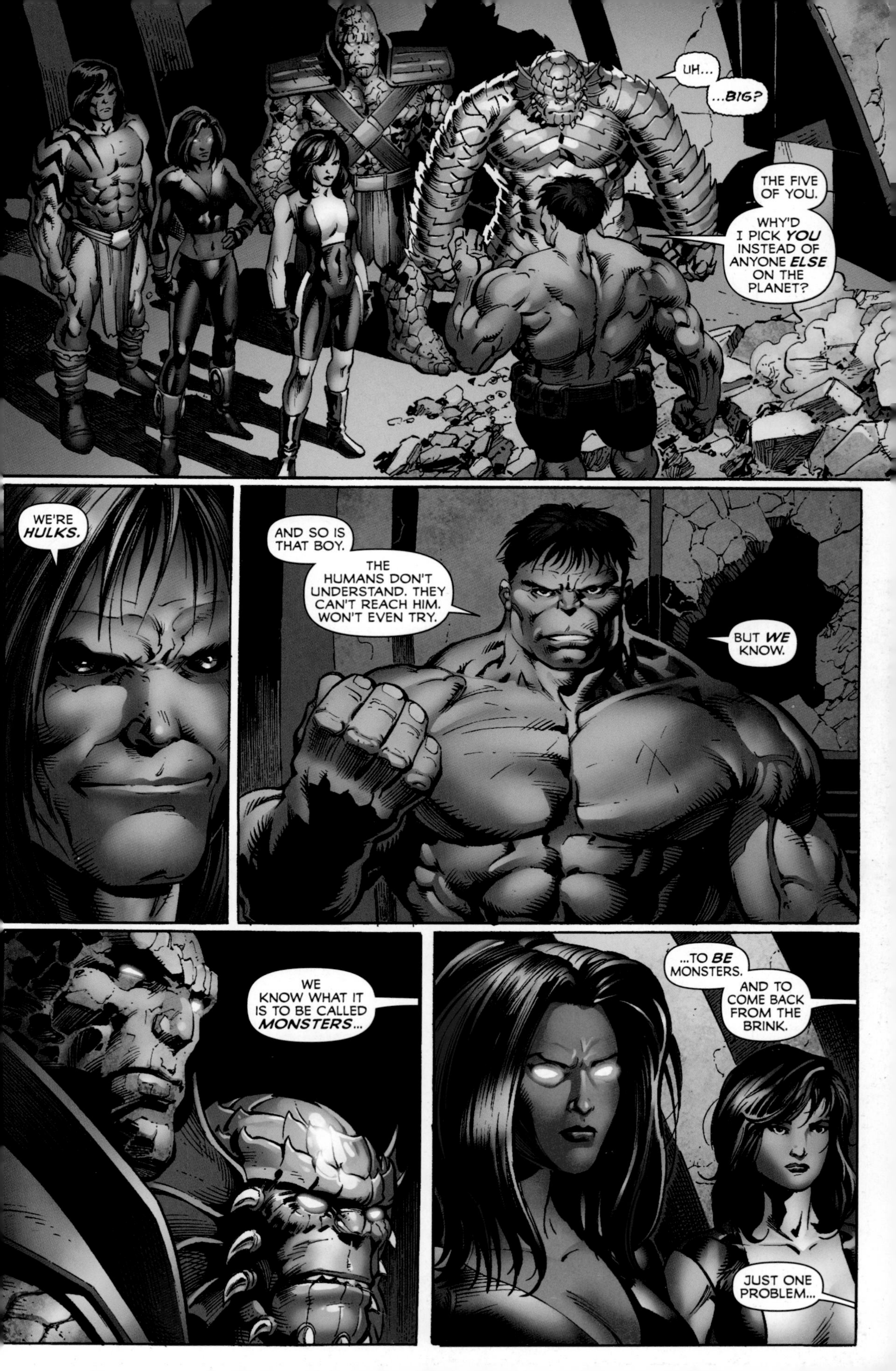
UH...
...BIG?
THE FIVE OF YOU.
WHY'D I PICK YOU INSTEAD OF ANYONE ELSE ON THE PLANET?
WE'RE HULKS.
AND SO IS THAT BOY.
THE HUMANS DON'T UNDERSTAND. THEY CAN'T REACH HIM. WON'T EVEN TRY.
BUT WE KNOW.
WE KNOW WHAT IT IS TO BE CALLED MONSTERS...
...TO BE MONSTERS.
AND TO COME BACK FROM THE BRINK.
JUST ONE PROBLEM...

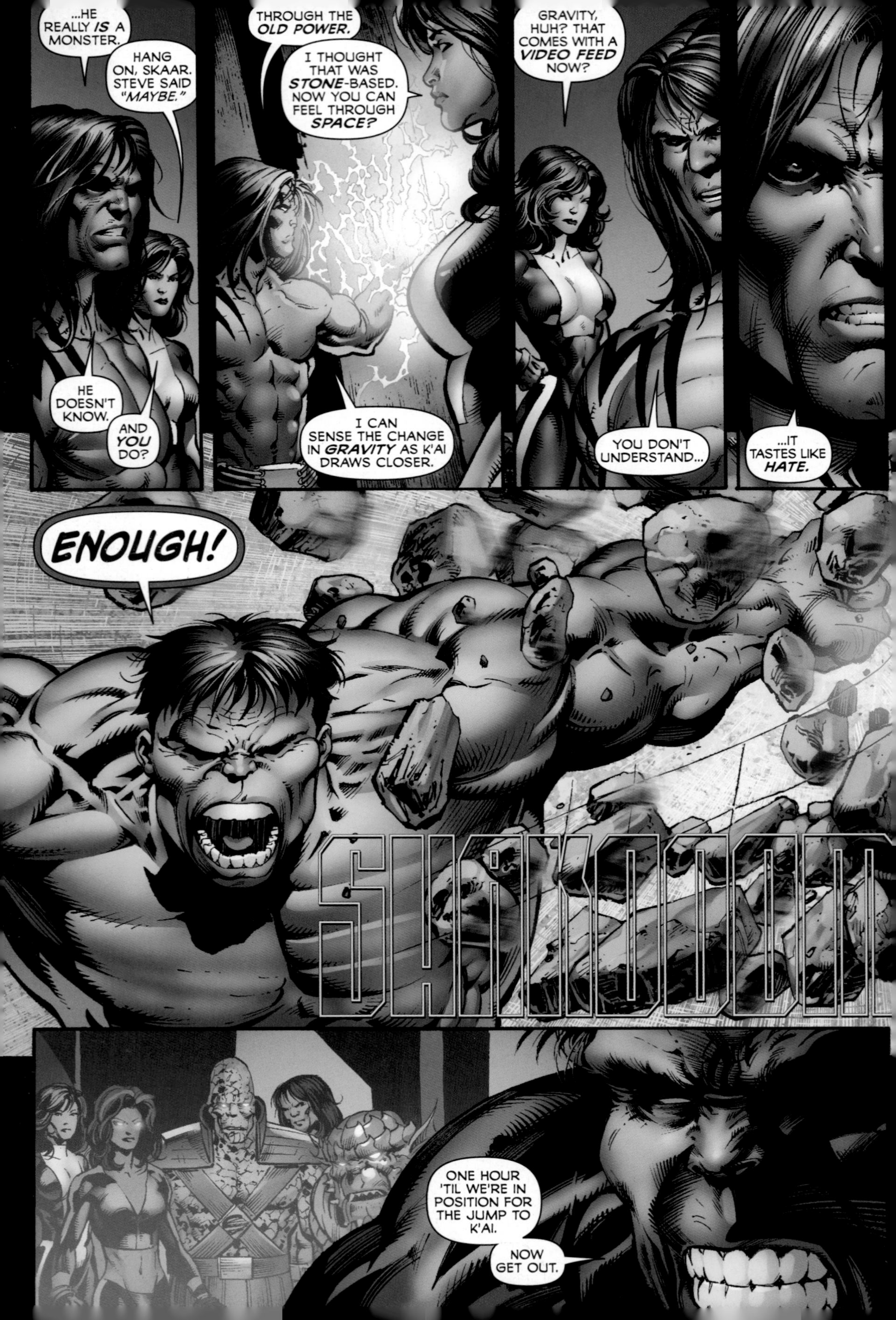

...HE REALLY *IS* A MONSTER.
HANG ON, SKAAR. STEVE SAID *"MAYBE."*
HE DOESN'T KNOW.
AND *YOU* DO?
THROUGH THE *OLD POWER.*
I THOUGHT THAT WAS *STONE*-BASED. NOW YOU CAN FEEL THROUGH *SPACE?*
I CAN SENSE THE CHANGE IN *GRAVITY* AS K'AI DRAWS CLOSER.
GRAVITY, HUH? THAT COMES WITH A *VIDEO FEED* NOW?
YOU DON'T UNDERSTAND...
...IT TASTES LIKE *HATE.*
ENOUGH!
ONE HOUR 'TIL WE'RE IN POSITION FOR THE JUMP TO K'AI.
NOW GET OUT.

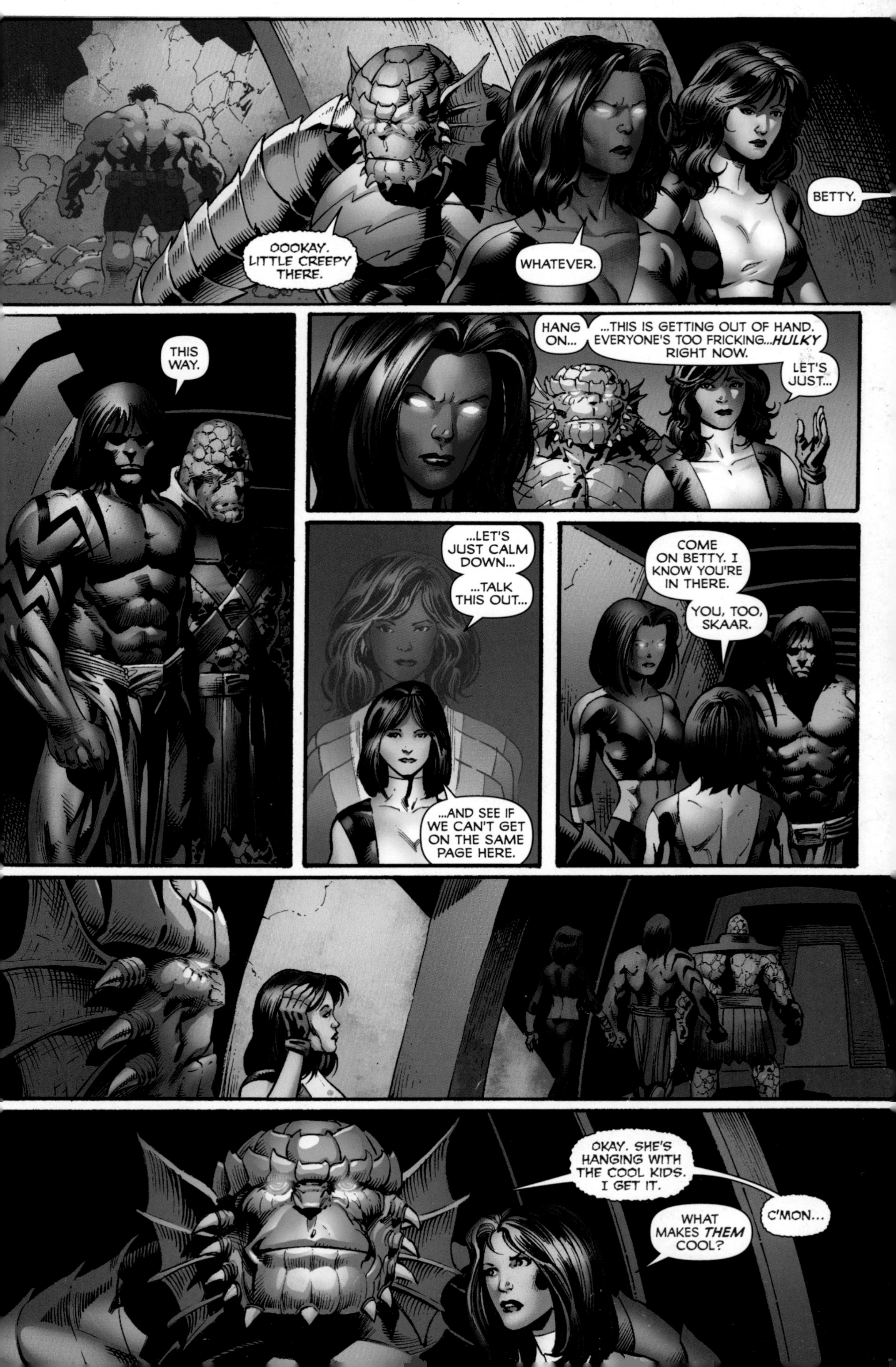
OOOKAY. LITTLE CREEPY THERE.
WHATEVER.
BETTY.
THIS WAY.
HANG ON...
...THIS IS GETTING OUT OF HAND. EVERYONE'S TOO FRICKING...HULKY RIGHT NOW.
LET'S JUST...
...LET'S JUST CALM DOWN...
...TALK THIS OUT...
...AND SEE IF WE CAN'T GET ON THE SAME PAGE HERE.
COME ON BETTY. I KNOW YOU'RE IN THERE.
YOU, TOO, SKAAR.
OKAY. SHE'S HANGING WITH THE COOL KIDS. I GET IT.
C'MON...
WHAT MAKES THEM COOL?

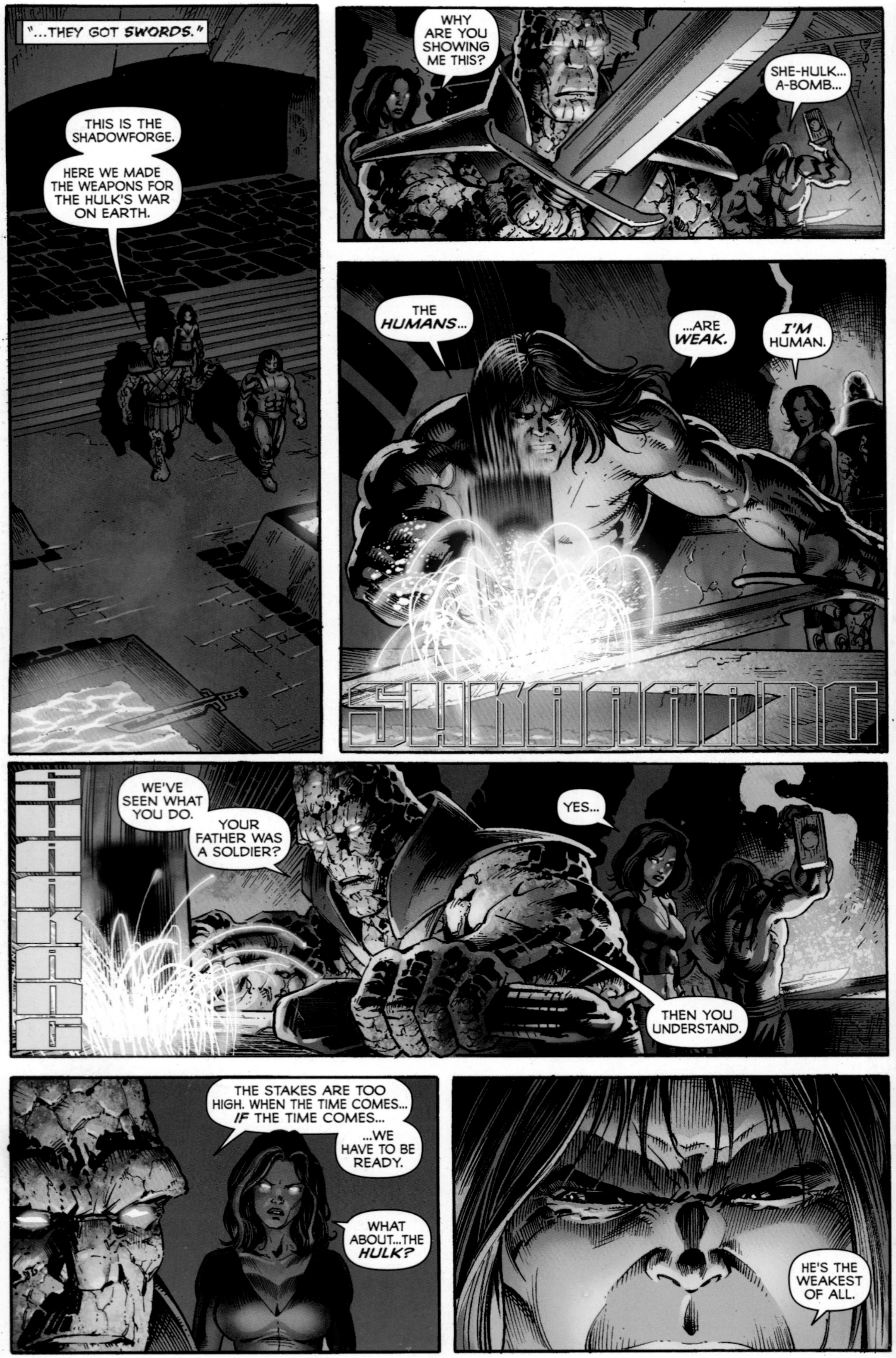
"...THEY GOT SWORDS."
THIS IS THE SHADOWFORGE.
HERE WE MADE THE WEAPONS FOR THE HULK'S WAR ON EARTH.
WHY ARE YOU SHOWING ME THIS?
SHE-HULK... A-BOMB...
THE HUMANS...
...ARE WEAK.
I'M HUMAN.
SHKAAAANNG
SHIIIKANG
WE'VE SEEN WHAT YOU DO.
YOUR FATHER WAS A SOLDIER?
YES...
THEN YOU UNDERSTAND.
THE STAKES ARE TOO HIGH. WHEN THE TIME COMES... IF THE TIME COMES...
...WE HAVE TO BE READY.
WHAT ABOUT...THE HULK?
HE'S THE WEAKEST OF ALL.

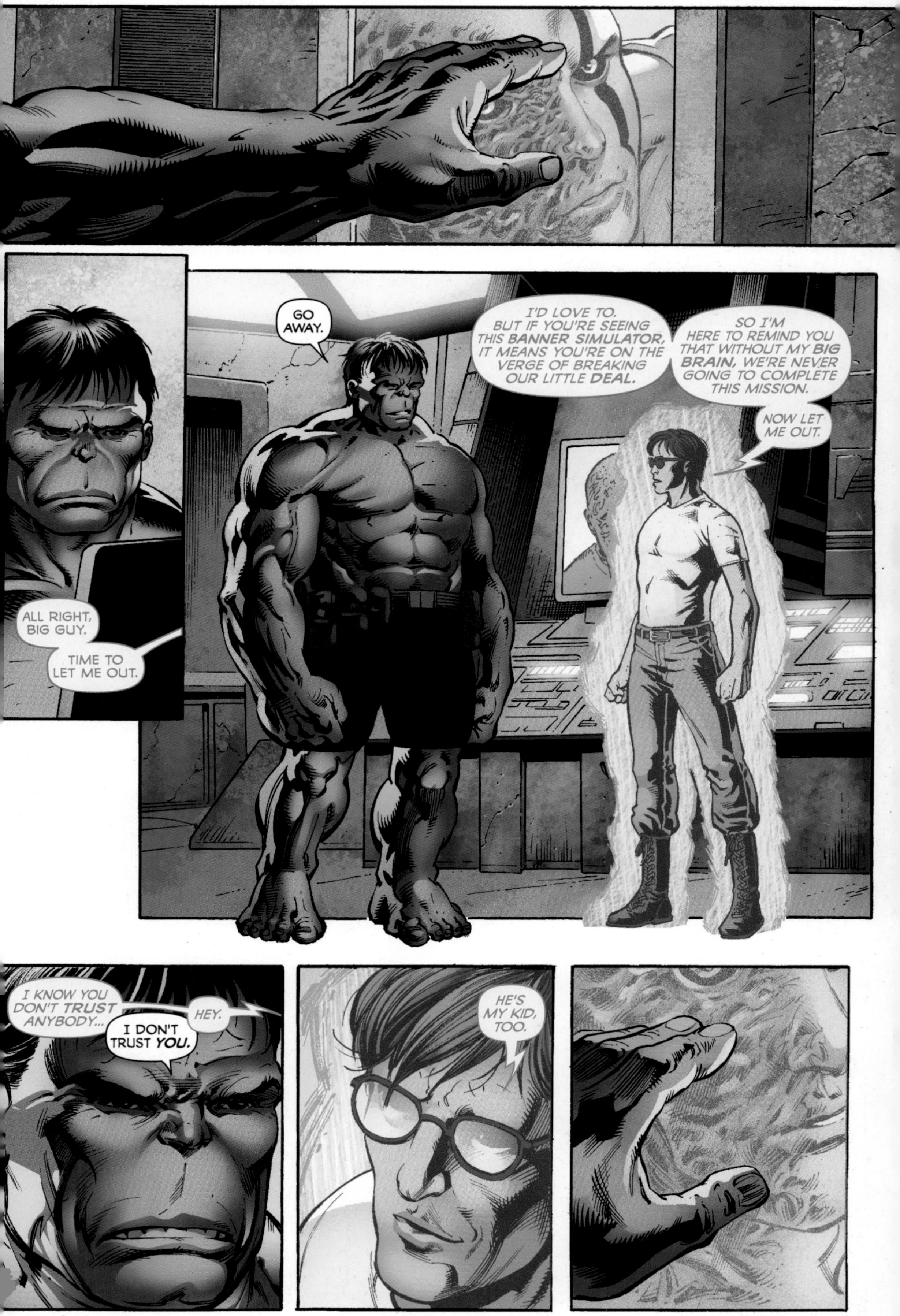
ALL RIGHT, BIG GUY.
TIME TO LET ME OUT.
GO AWAY.
I'D LOVE TO. BUT IF YOU'RE SEEING THIS BANNER SIMULATOR, IT MEANS YOU'RE ON THE VERGE OF BREAKING OUR LITTLE DEAL.
SO I'M HERE TO REMIND YOU THAT WITHOUT MY BIG BRAIN, WE'RE NEVER GOING TO COMPLETE THIS MISSION.
NOW LET ME OUT.
I KNOW YOU DON'T TRUST ANYBODY...
HEY.
I DON'T TRUST YOU.
HE'S MY KID, TOO.

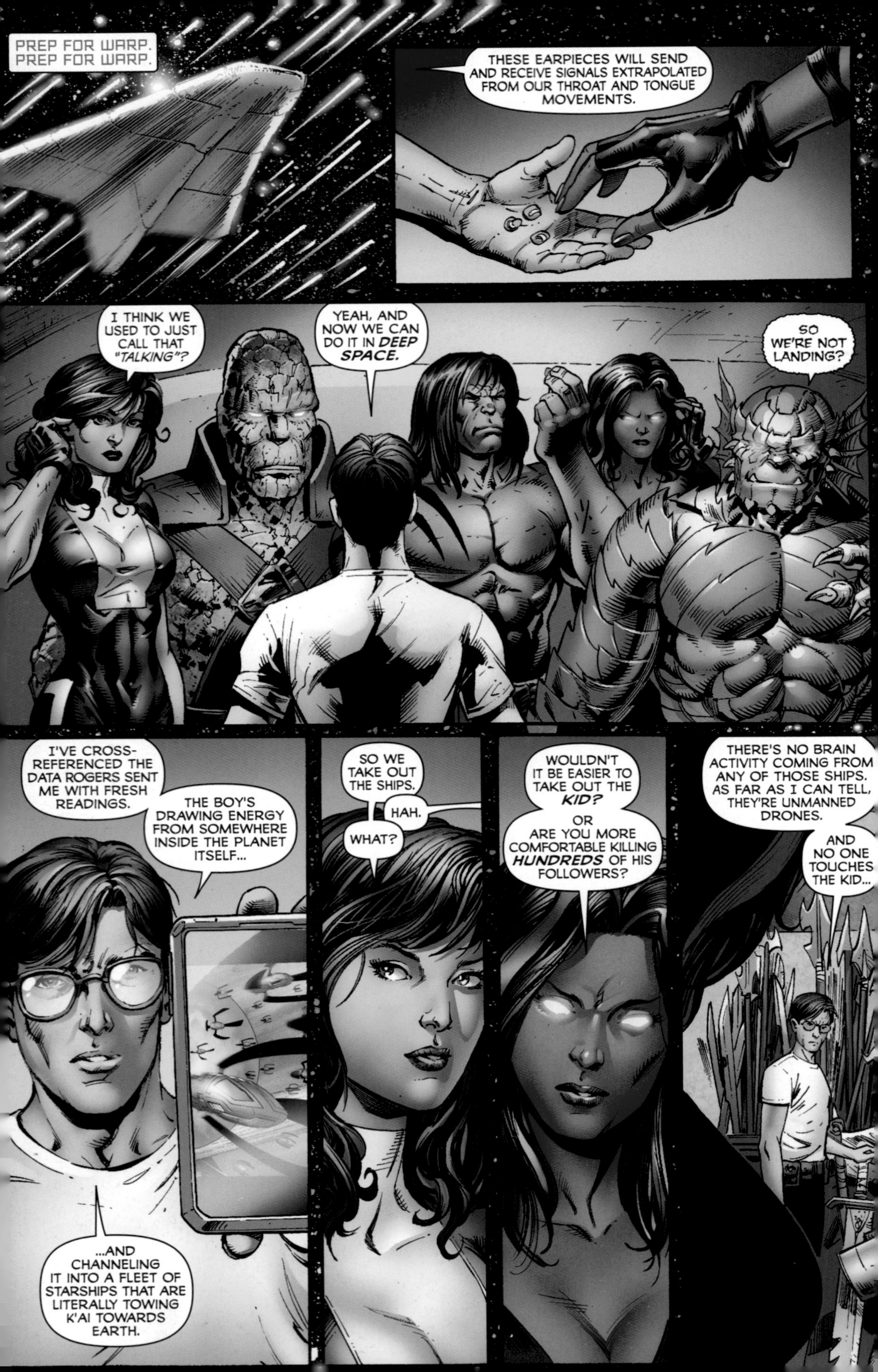

PREP FOR WARP. PREP FOR WARP.
THESE EARPIECES WILL SEND AND RECEIVE SIGNALS EXTRAPOLATED FROM OUR THROAT AND TONGUE MOVEMENTS.
I THINK WE USED TO JUST CALL THAT "TALKING"?
YEAH, AND NOW WE CAN DO IT IN DEEP SPACE.
SO WE'RE NOT LANDING?
I'VE CROSS-REFERENCED THE DATA ROGERS SENT ME WITH FRESH READINGS.
THE BOY'S DRAWING ENERGY FROM SOMEWHERE INSIDE THE PLANET ITSELF...
...AND CHANNELING IT INTO A FLEET OF STARSHIPS THAT ARE LITERALLY TOWING K'AI TOWARDS EARTH.
SO WE TAKE OUT THE SHIPS.
HAH.
WHAT?
WOULDN'T IT BE EASIER TO TAKE OUT THE KID?
OR ARE YOU MORE COMFORTABLE KILLING HUNDREDS OF HIS FOLLOWERS?
THERE'S NO BRAIN ACTIVITY COMING FROM ANY OF THOSE SHIPS. AS FAR AS I CAN TELL, THEY'RE UNMANNED DRONES.
AND NO ONE TOUCHES THE KID...

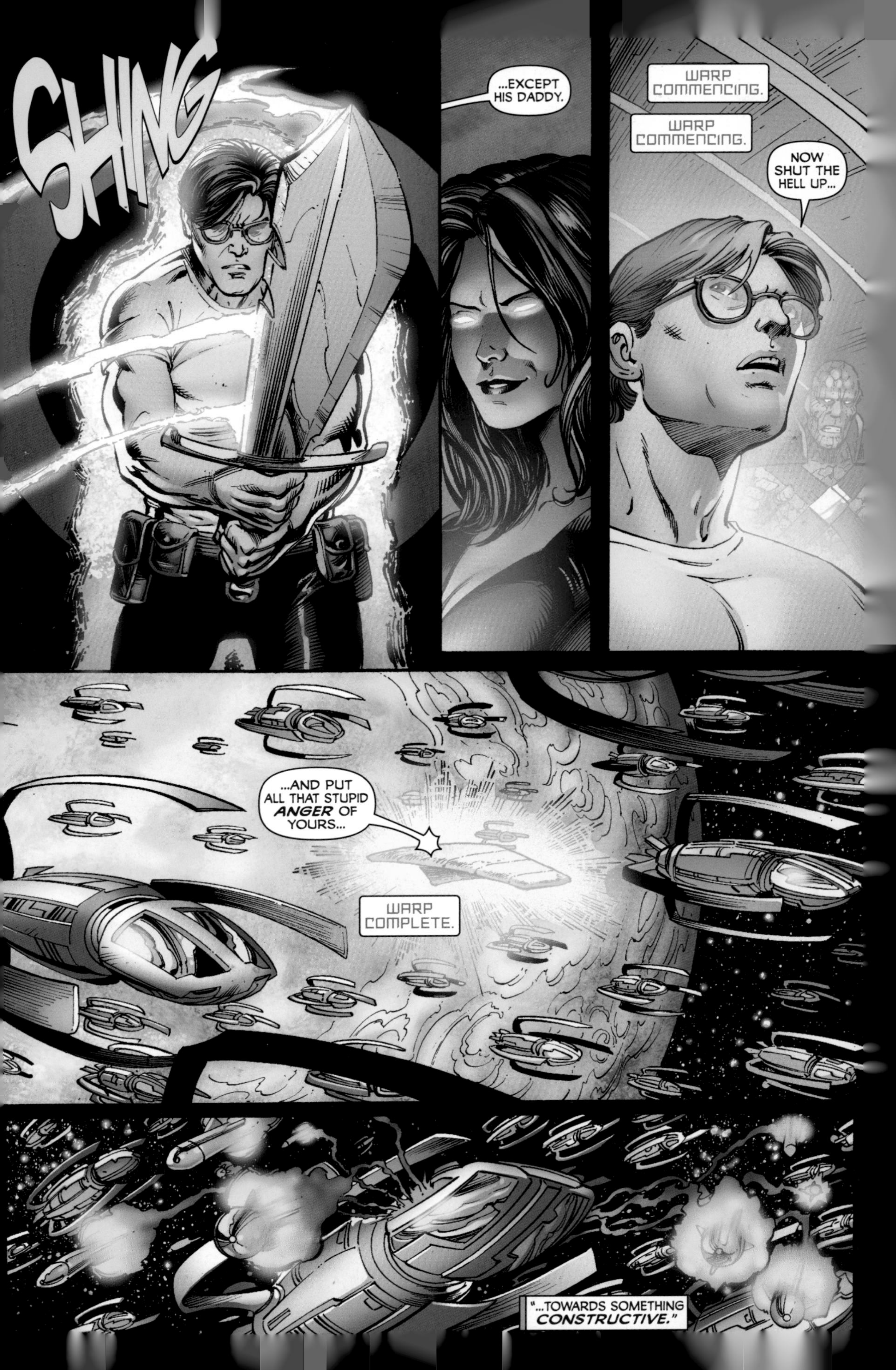
SHING
...EXCEPT HIS DADDY.
WARP COMMENCING.
WARP COMMENCING.
NOW SHUT THE HELL UP...
...AND PUT ALL THAT STUPID ANGER OF YOURS...
WARP COMPLETE.
"...TOWARDS SOMETHING CONSTRUCTIVE."

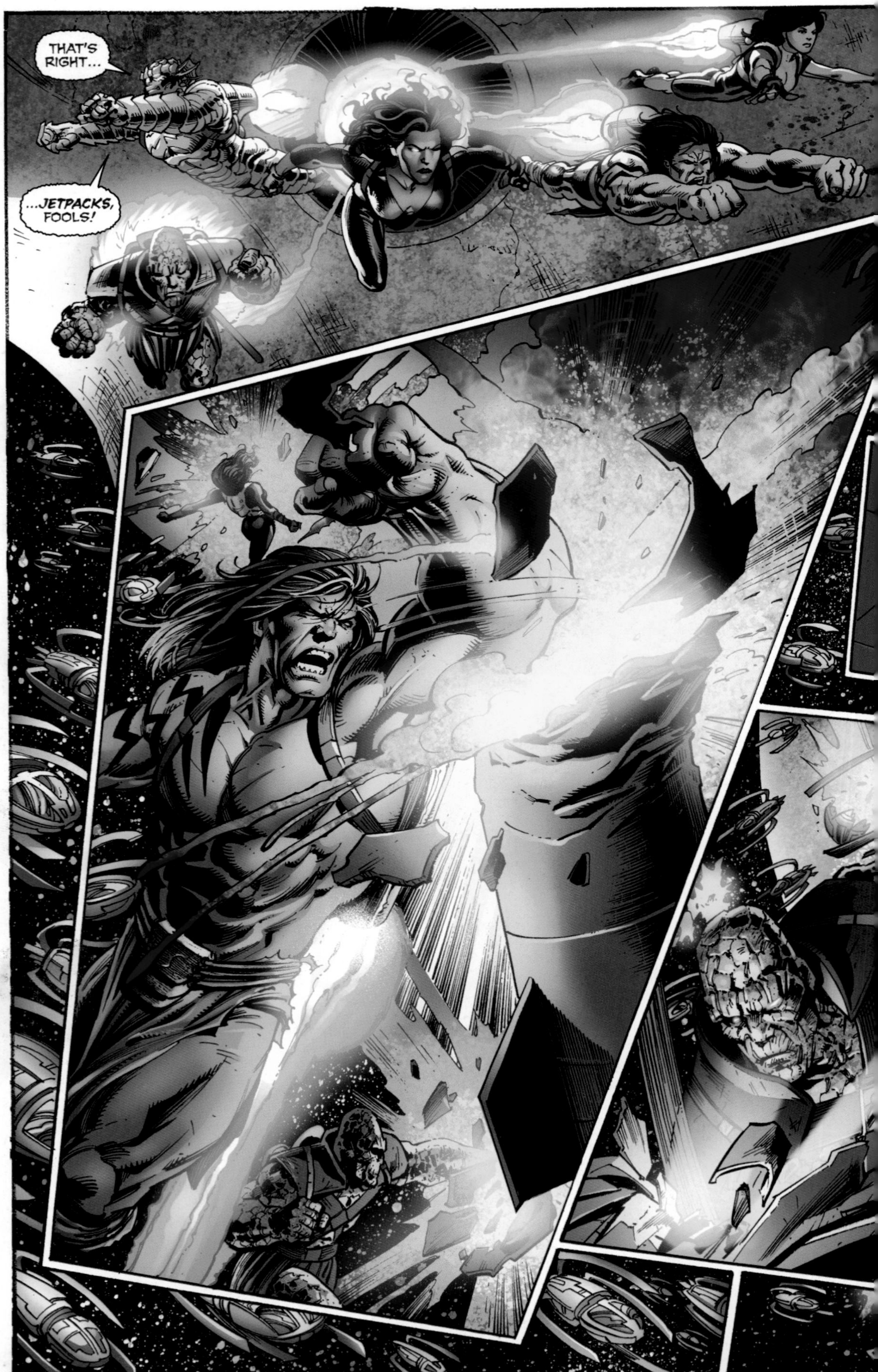
THAT'S RIGHT...
...JETPACKS, FOOLS!

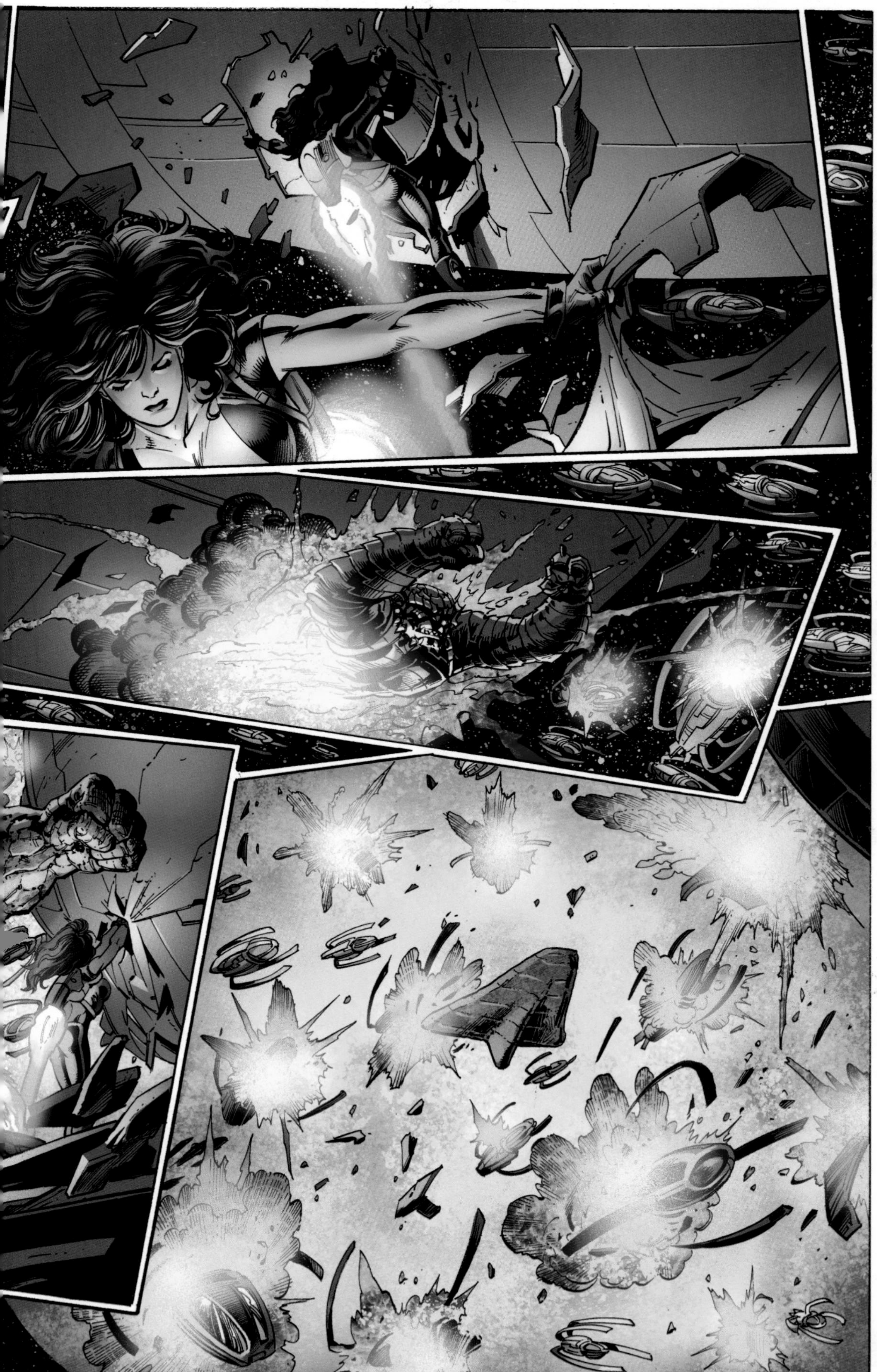

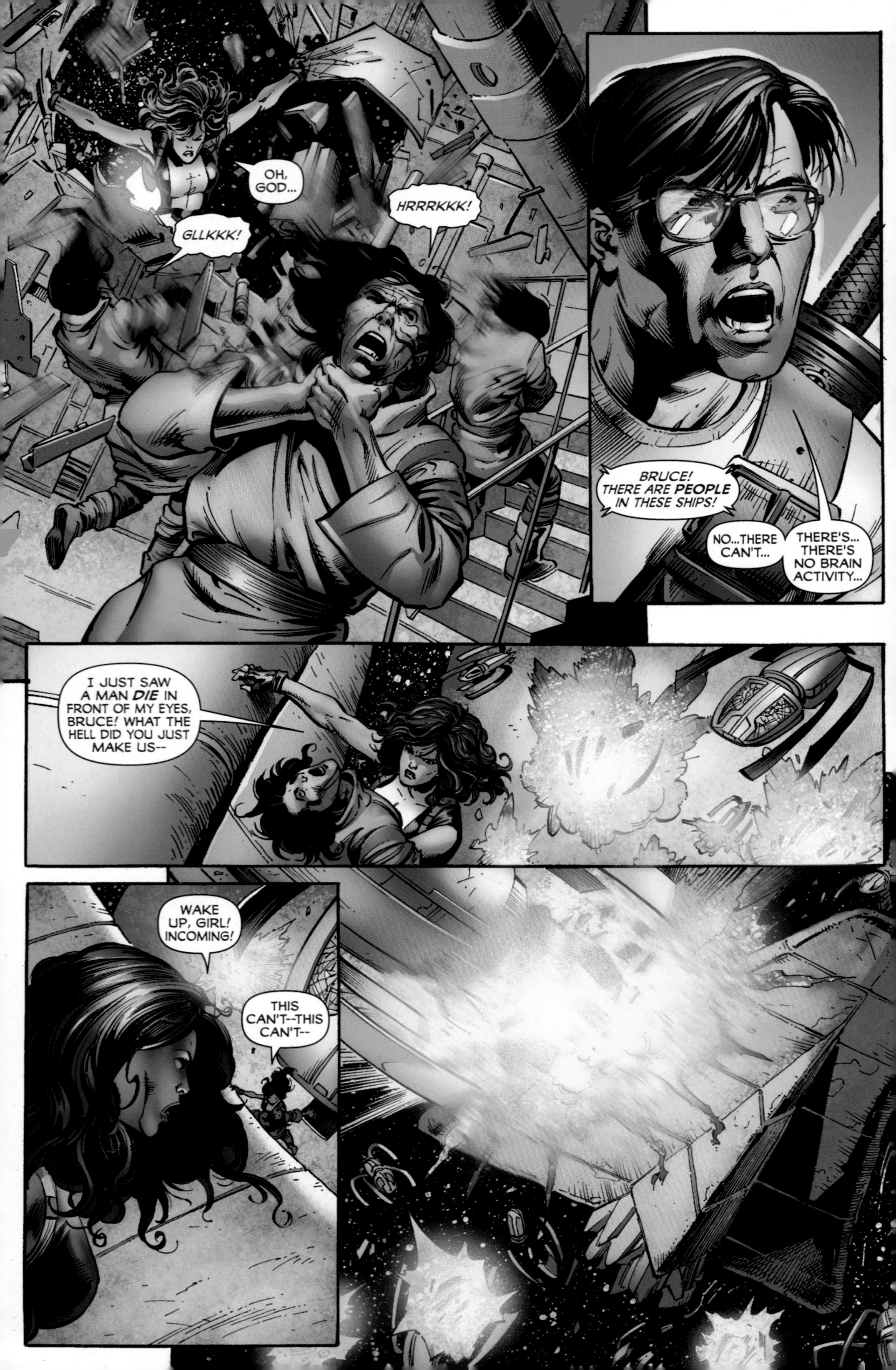
OH, GOD...
HRRRKKK!
GLLKKK!
BRUCE! THERE ARE PEOPLE IN THESE SHIPS!
NO...THERE CAN'T...
THERE'S... THERE'S NO BRAIN ACTIVITY...
I JUST SAW A MAN DIE IN FRONT OF MY EYES, BRUCE! WHAT THE HELL DID YOU JUST MAKE US--
WAKE UP, GIRL! INCOMING!
THIS CAN'T--THIS CAN'T--

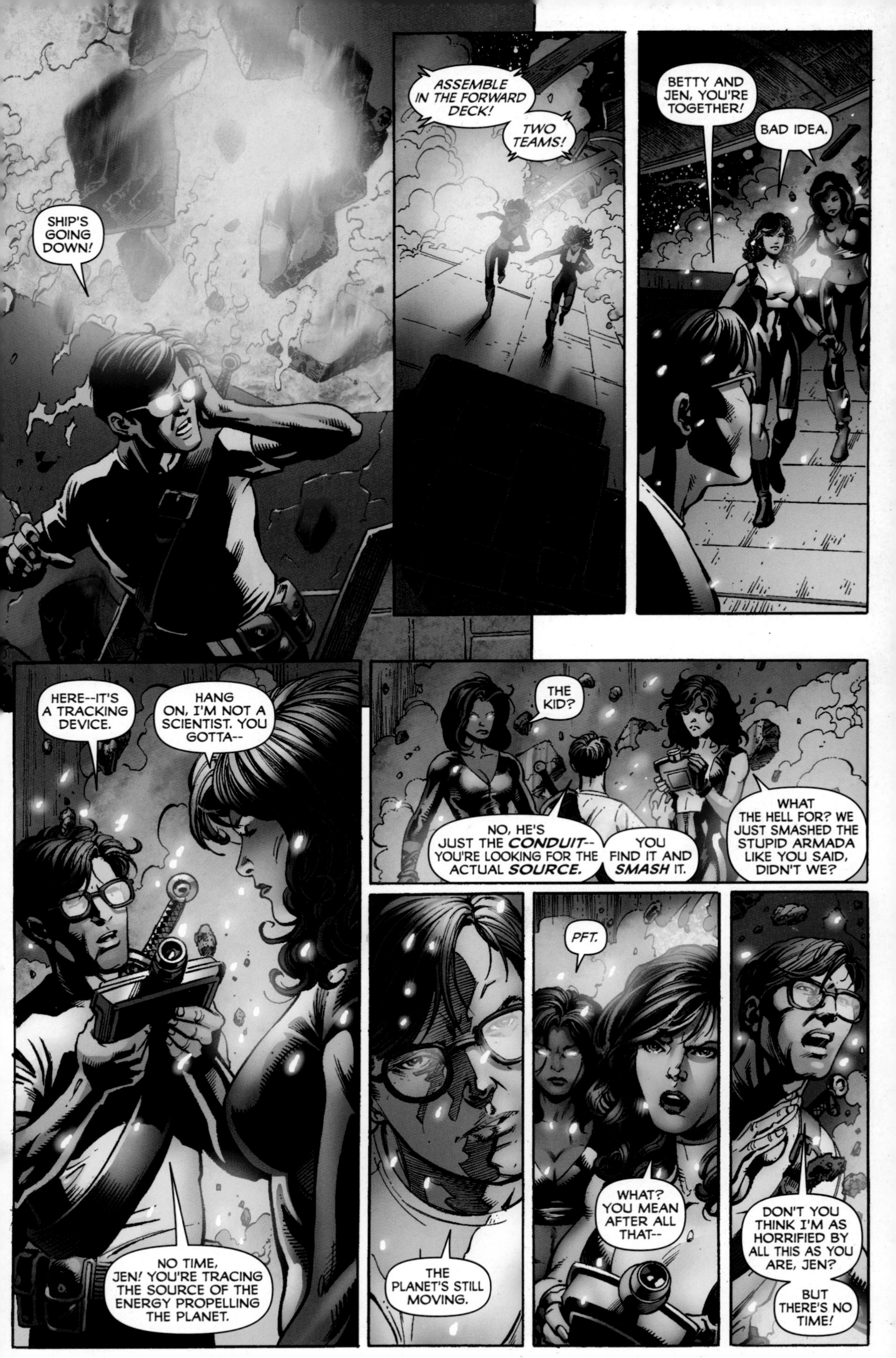
SHIP'S GOING DOWN!
ASSEMBLE IN THE FORWARD DECK!
TWO TEAMS!
BETTY AND JEN, YOU'RE TOGETHER!
BAD IDEA.
HERE--IT'S A TRACKING DEVICE.
HANG ON, I'M NOT A SCIENTIST. YOU GOTTA--
NO TIME, JEN! YOU'RE TRACING THE SOURCE OF THE ENERGY PROPELLING THE PLANET.
THE KID?
NO, HE'S JUST THE *CONDUIT*-- YOU'RE LOOKING FOR THE ACTUAL *SOURCE.*
YOU FIND IT AND *SMASH* IT.
WHAT THE HELL FOR? WE JUST SMASHED THE STUPID ARMADA LIKE YOU SAID, DIDN'T WE?
THE PLANET'S STILL MOVING.
PFT.
WHAT? YOU MEAN AFTER ALL THAT--
DON'T YOU THINK I'M AS HORRIFIED BY ALL THIS AS YOU ARE, JEN?
BUT THERE'S NO TIME!

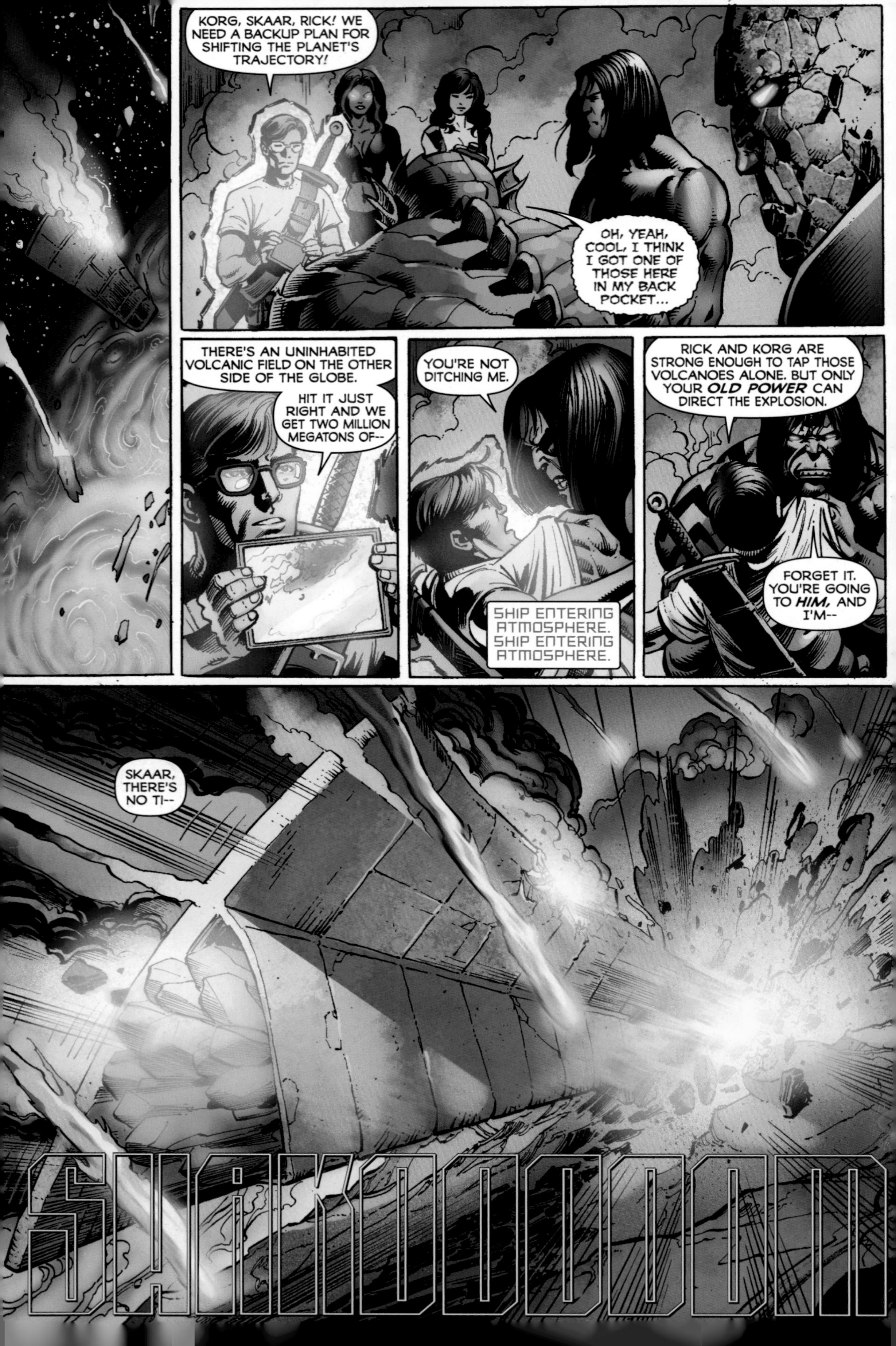
KORG, SKAAR, RICK! WE NEED A BACKUP PLAN FOR SHIFTING THE PLANET'S TRAJECTORY!
OH, YEAH, COOL, I THINK I GOT ONE OF THOSE HERE IN MY BACK POCKET...
THERE'S AN UNINHABITED VOLCANIC FIELD ON THE OTHER SIDE OF THE GLOBE.
HIT IT JUST RIGHT AND WE GET TWO MILLION MEGATONS OF--
YOU'RE NOT DITCHING ME.
SHIP ENTERING ATMOSPHERE. SHIP ENTERING ATMOSPHERE.
RICK AND KORG ARE STRONG ENOUGH TO TAP THOSE VOLCANOES ALONE. BUT ONLY YOUR *OLD POWER* CAN DIRECT THE EXPLOSION.
FORGET IT. YOU'RE GOING TO *HIM,* AND I'M--
SKAAR, THERE'S NO TI--
SKAKOOOOOM

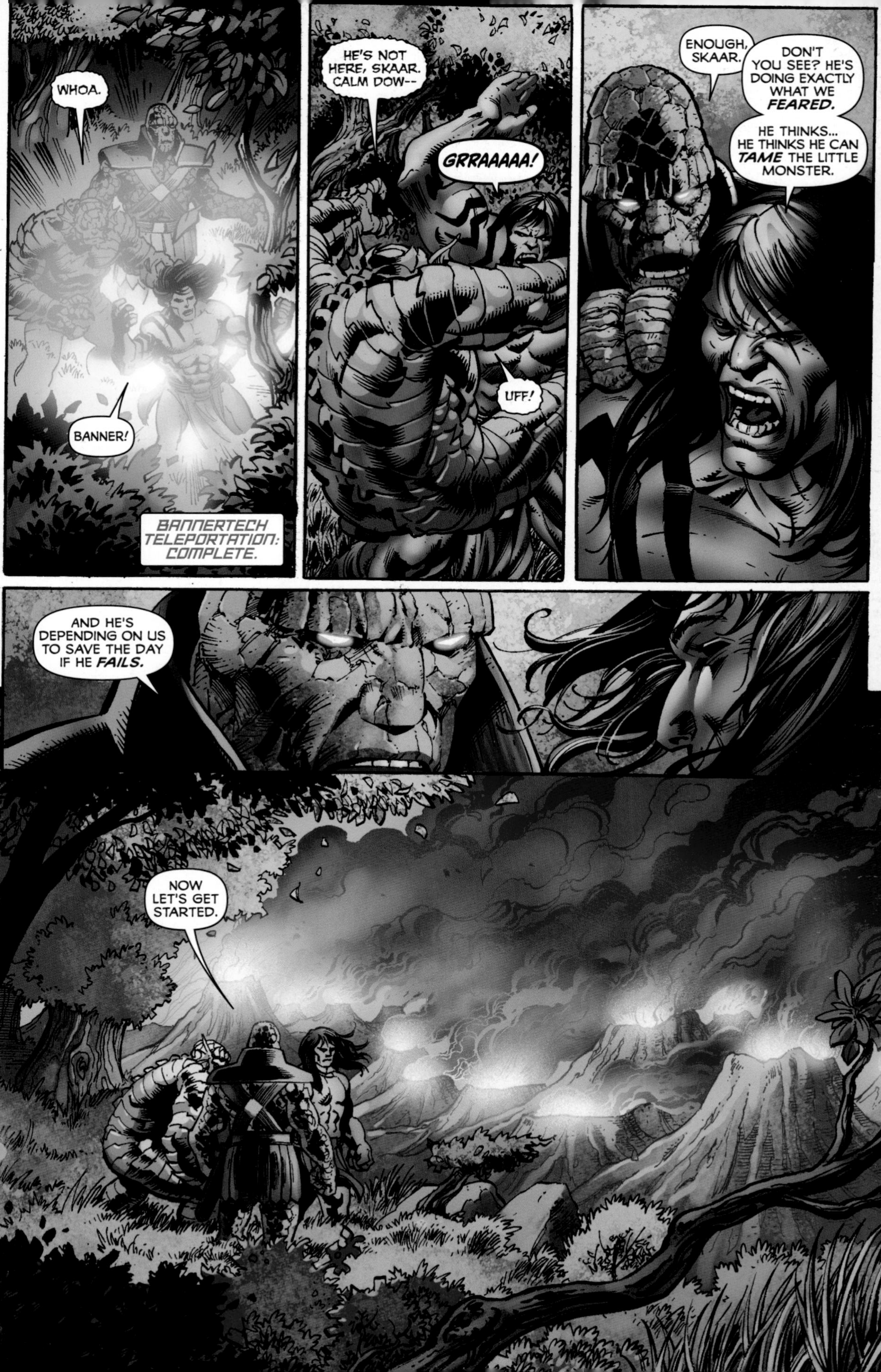
WHOA.
BANNER!
BANNERTECH TELEPORTATION: COMPLETE.
HE'S NOT HERE, SKAAR. CALM DOW--
GRRAAAAA!
UFF!
ENOUGH, SKAAR.
DON'T YOU SEE? HE'S DOING EXACTLY WHAT WE FEARED.
HE THINKS... HE THINKS HE CAN TAME THE LITTLE MONSTER.
AND HE'S DEPENDING ON US TO SAVE THE DAY IF HE FAILS.
NOW LET'S GET STARTED.

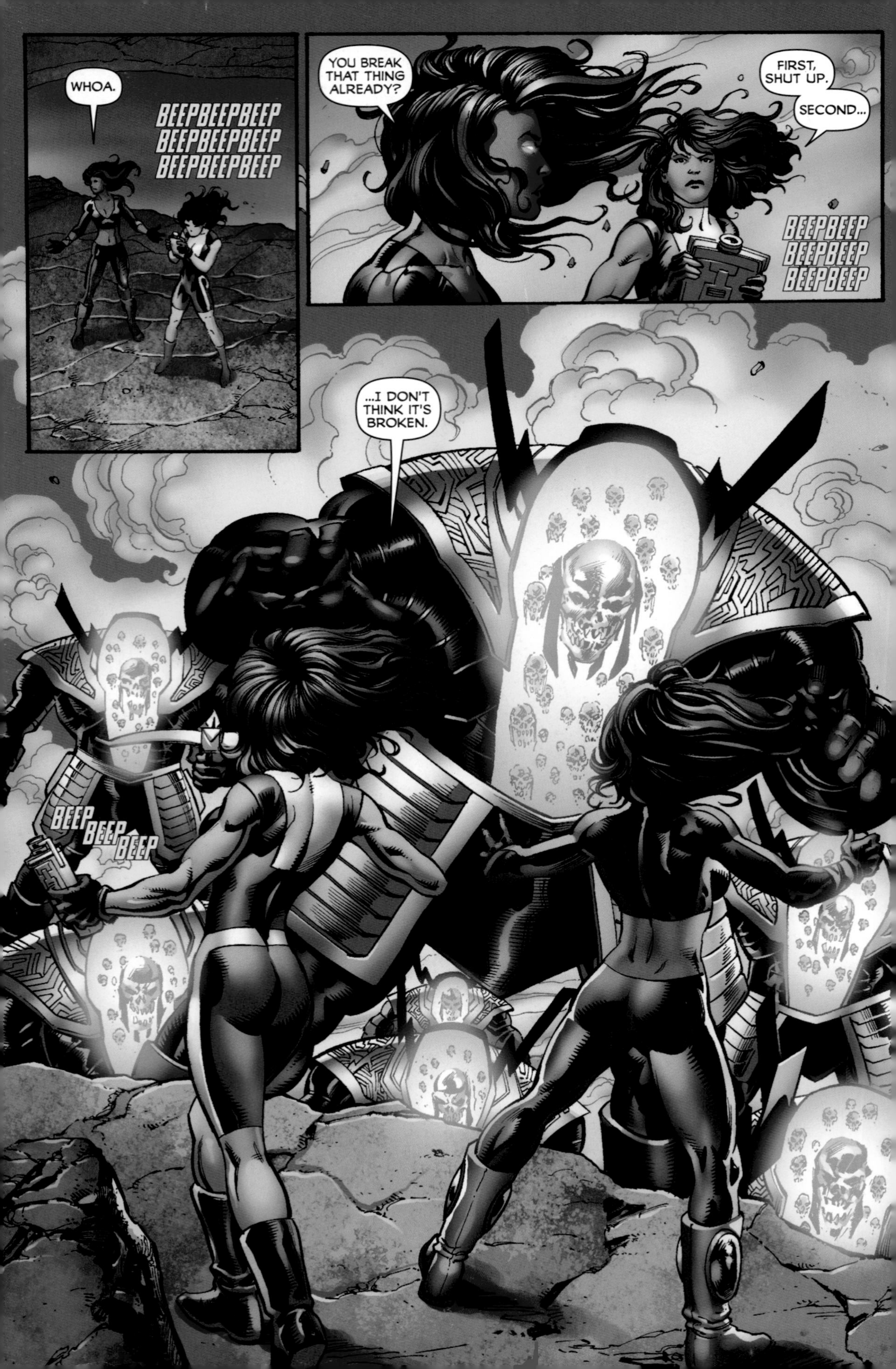
WHOA.
BEEPBEEPBEEP BEEPBEEPBEEP BEEPBEEPBEEP
YOU BREAK THAT THING ALREADY?
FIRST, SHUT UP.
SECOND...
BEEPBEEP BEEPBEEP BEEPBEEP
...I DON'T THINK IT'S BROKEN.
BEEP BEEP BEEP

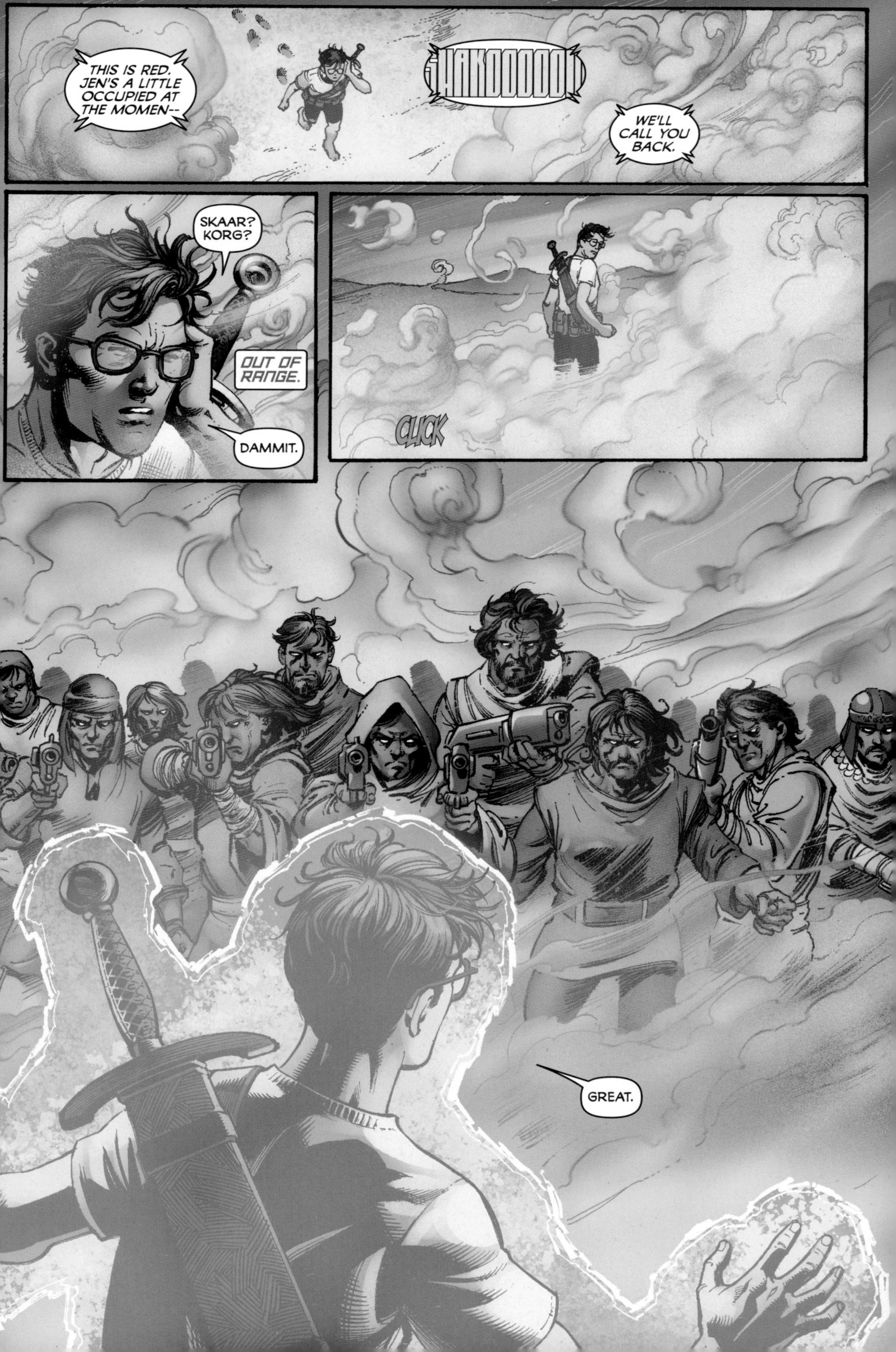
THIS IS RED. JEN'S A LITTLE OCCUPIED AT THE MOMEN--
¡HAKOOOOO!
WE'LL CALL YOU BACK.
SKAAR? KORG?
OUT OF RANGE.
DAMMIT.
CLICK
GREAT.

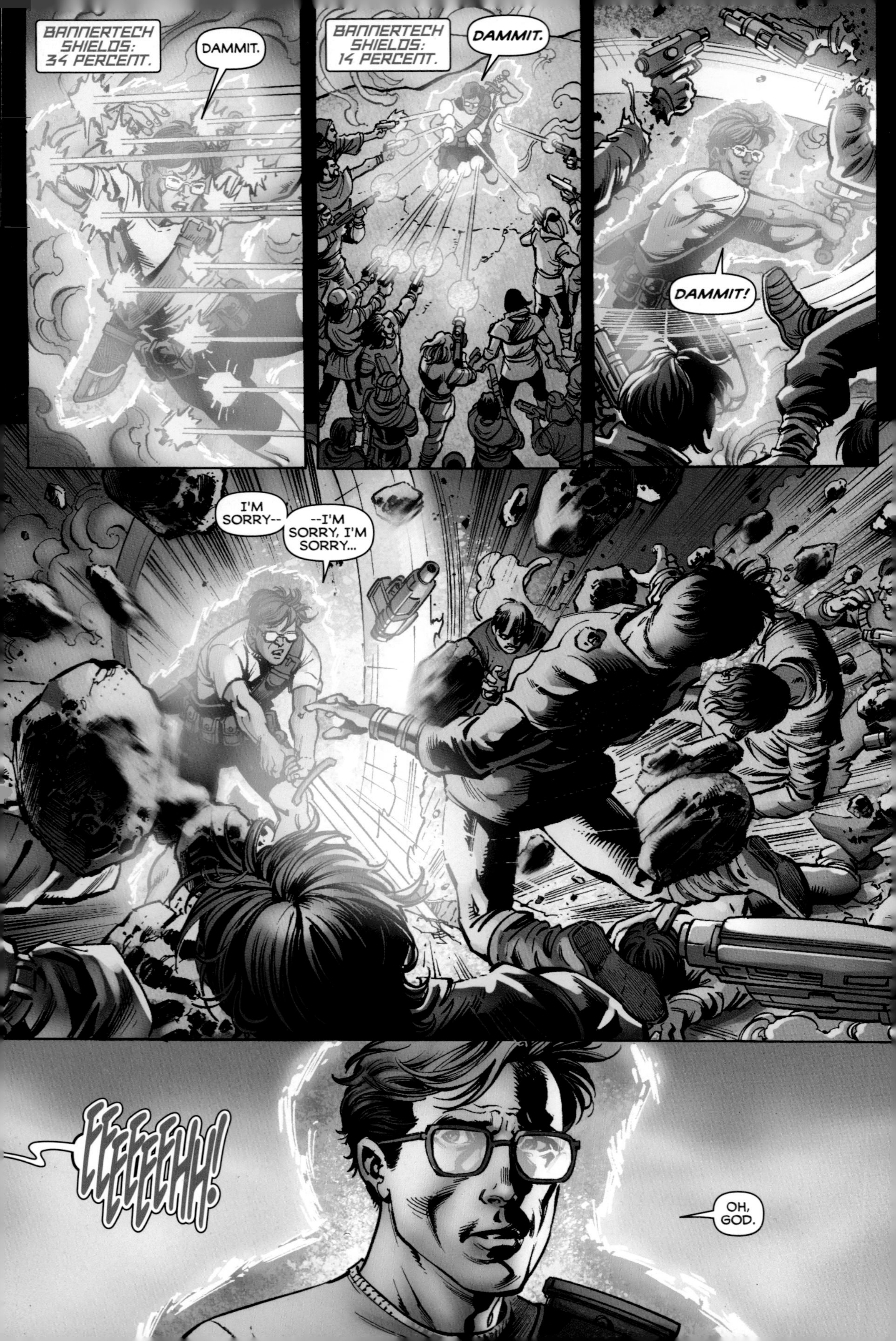
BANNERTECH SHIELDS: 34 PERCENT.
DAMMIT.
BANNERTECH SHIELDS: 14 PERCENT.
DAMMIT.
DAMMIT!
I'M SORRY--
--I'M SORRY, I'M SORRY...
EEEEEEHH!
OH, GOD.

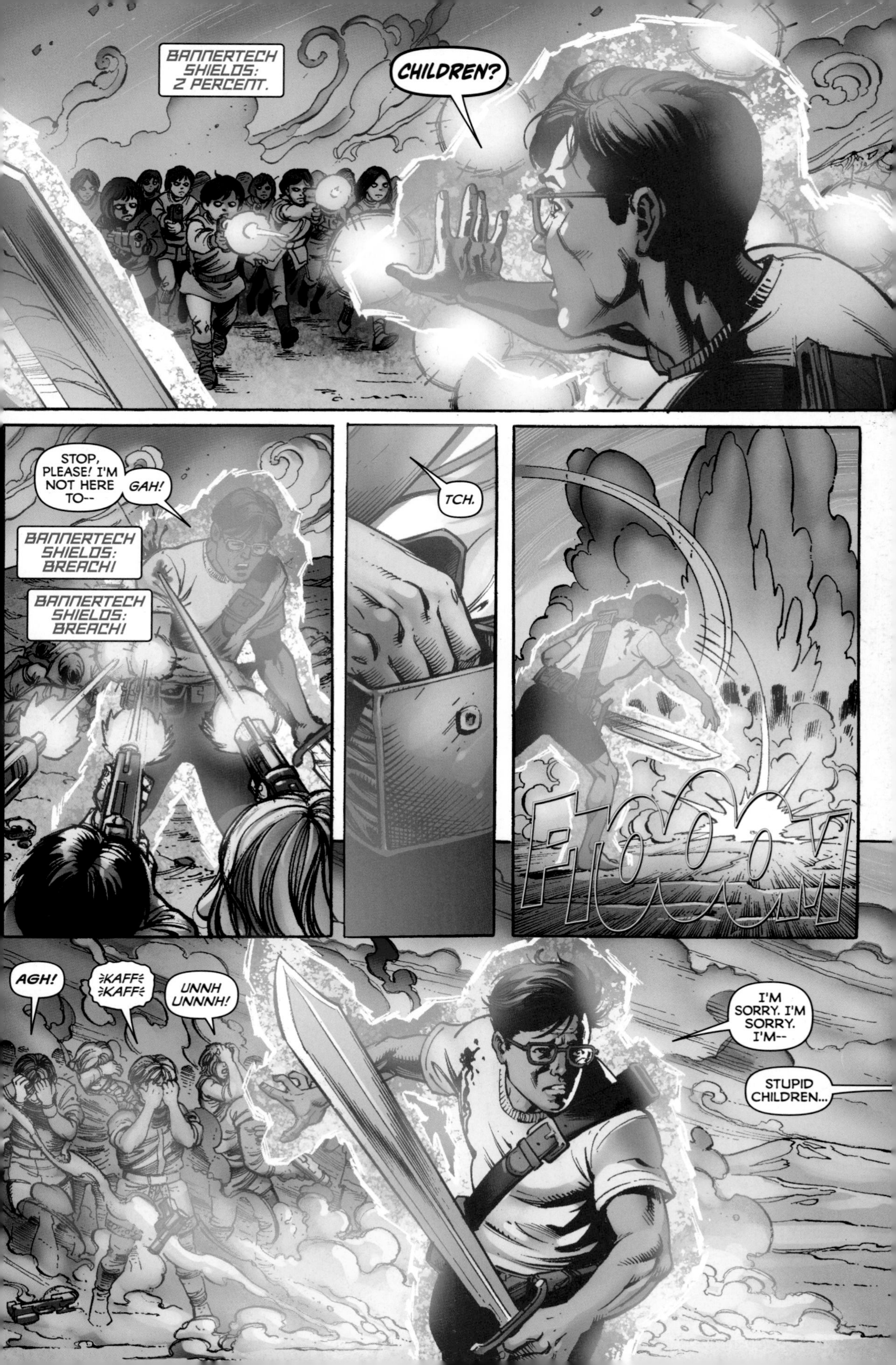
BANNERTECH SHIELDS: 2 PERCENT.
CHILDREN?
STOP, PLEASE! I'M NOT HERE TO--
GAH!
BANNERTECH SHIELDS: BREACH!
BANNERTECH SHIELDS: BREACH!
TCH.
FHOOOOM
AGH!
KAFF KAFF
UNNH UNNNH!
I'M SORRY. I'M SORRY. I'M--
STUPID CHILDREN...

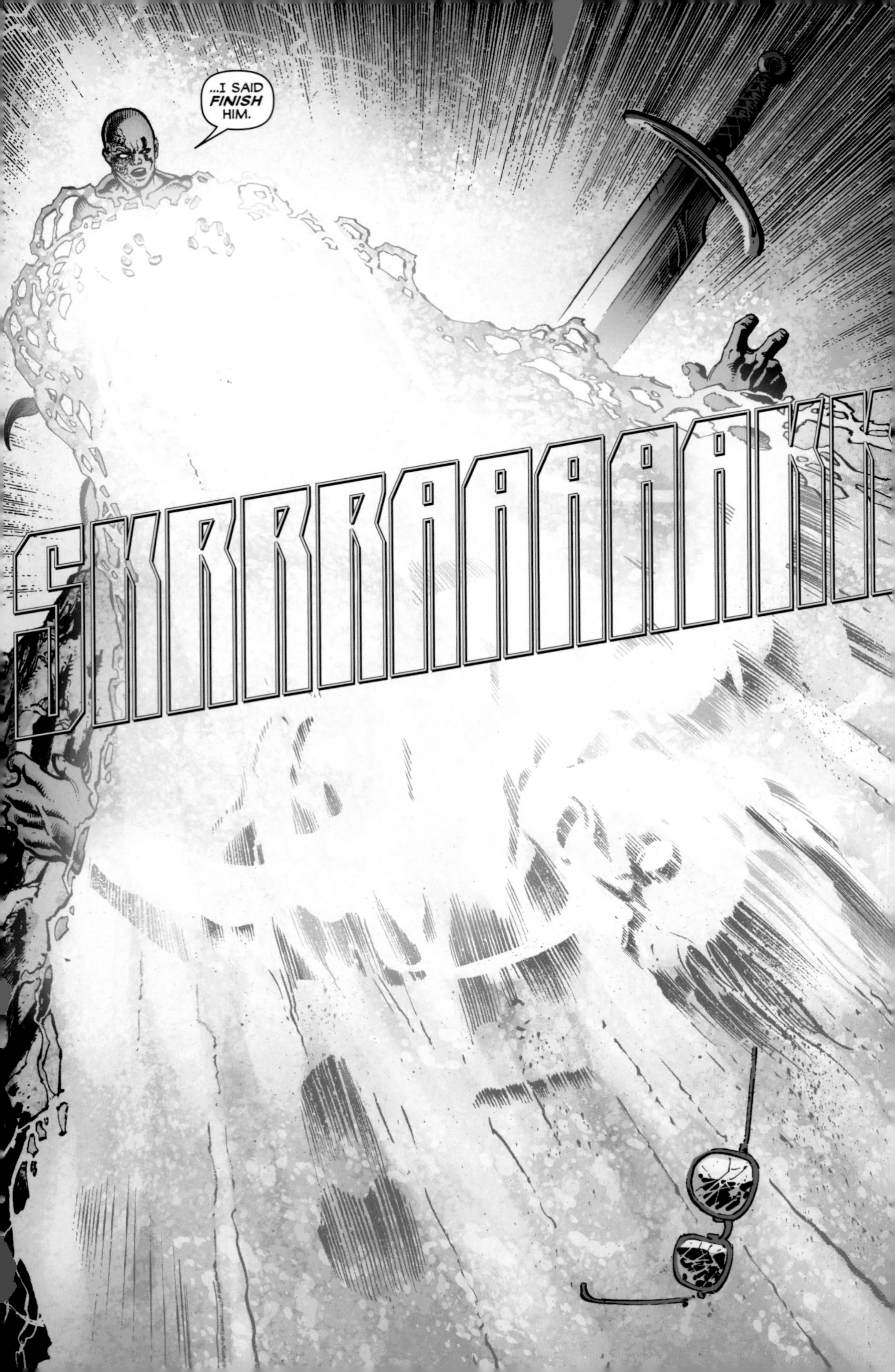
...I SAID *FINISH* HIM.
SKRRRAAAAAKK

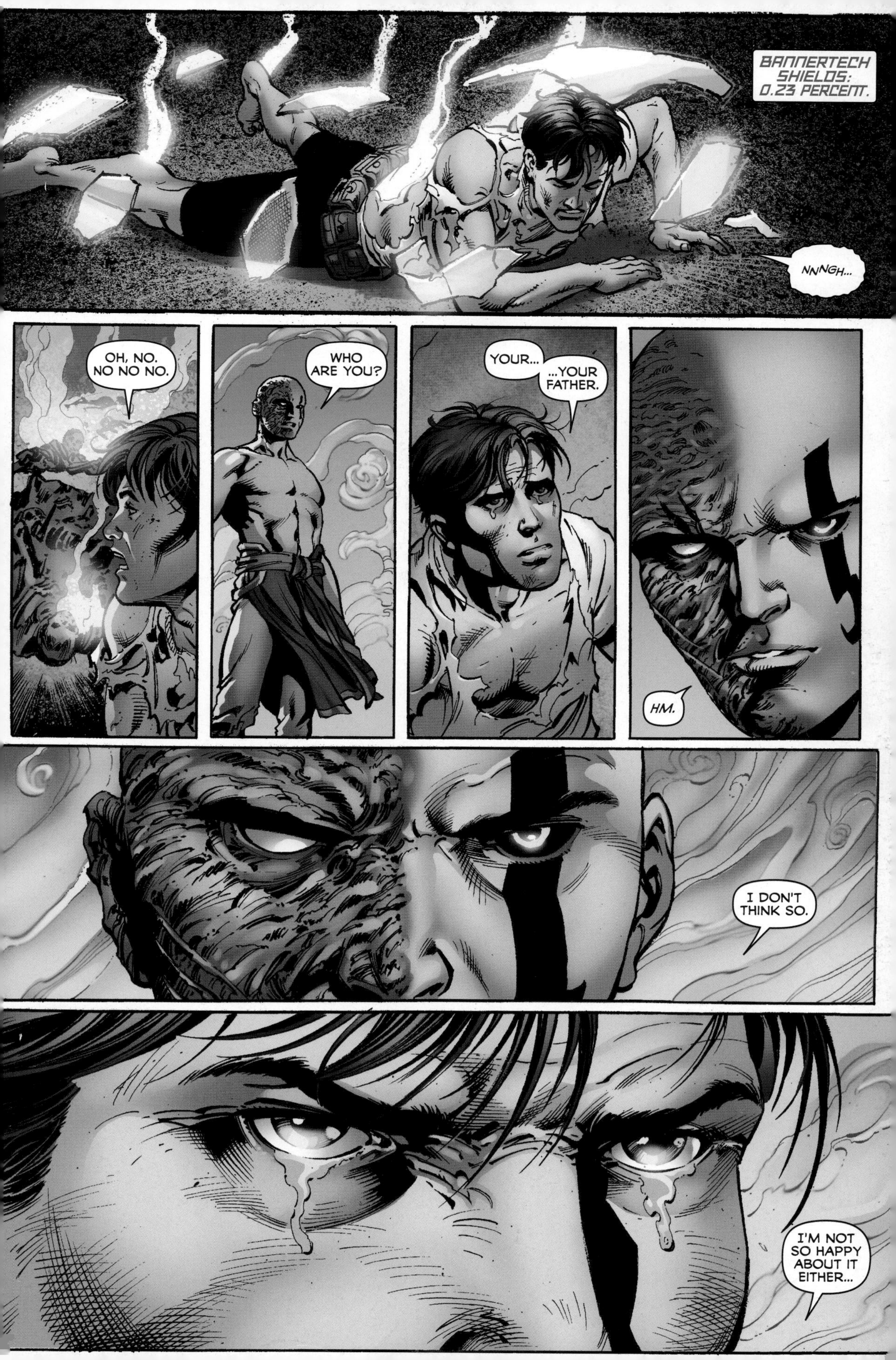

BANNERTECH SHIELDS: 0.23 PERCENT.
NNNGH...
OH, NO. NO NO NO.
WHO ARE YOU?
YOUR...
...YOUR FATHER.
HM.
I DON'T THINK SO.
I'M NOT SO HAPPY ABOUT IT EITHER...

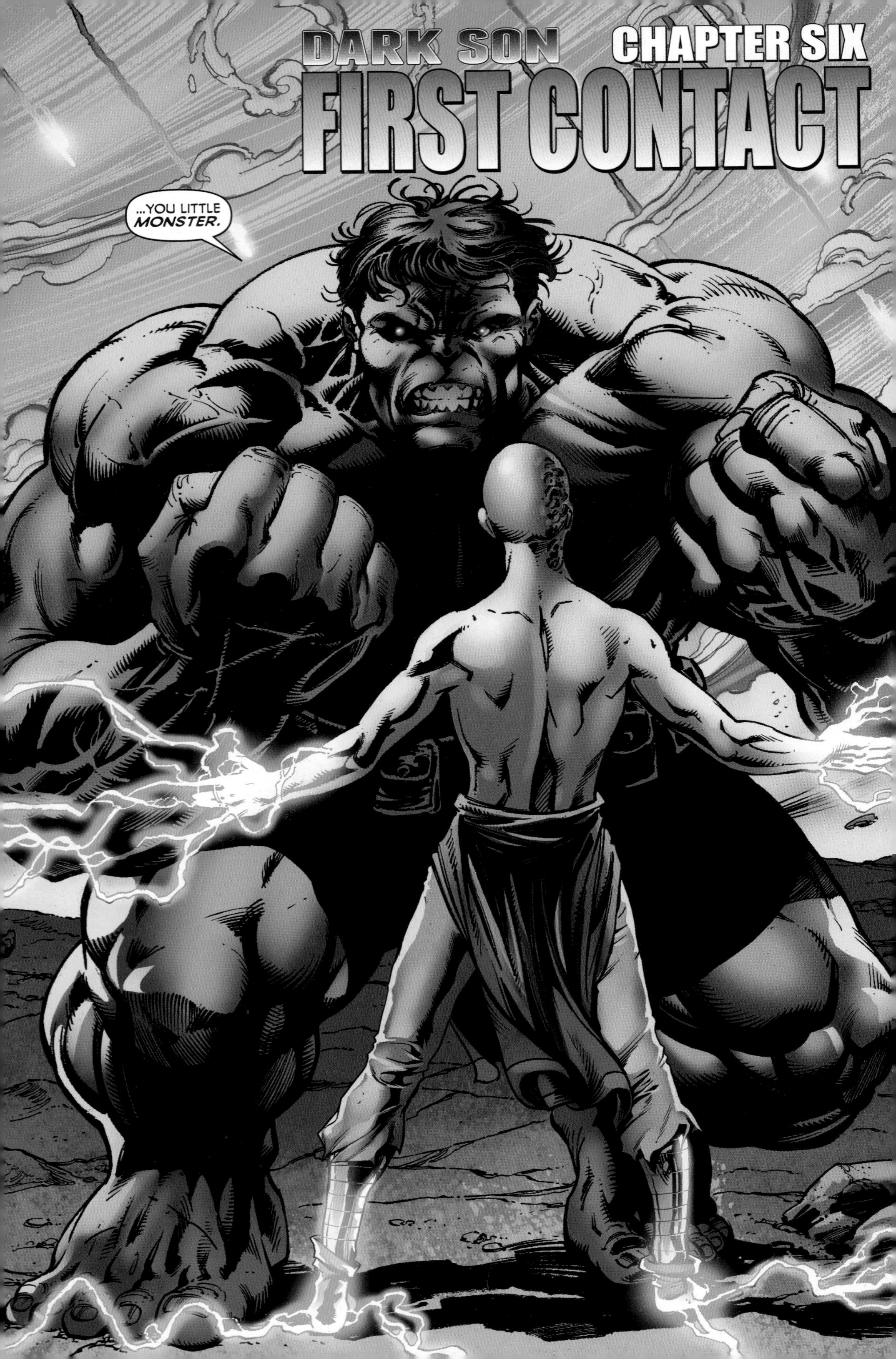
DARK SON
CHAPTER SIX
FIRST CONTACT
...YOU LITTLE MONSTER.

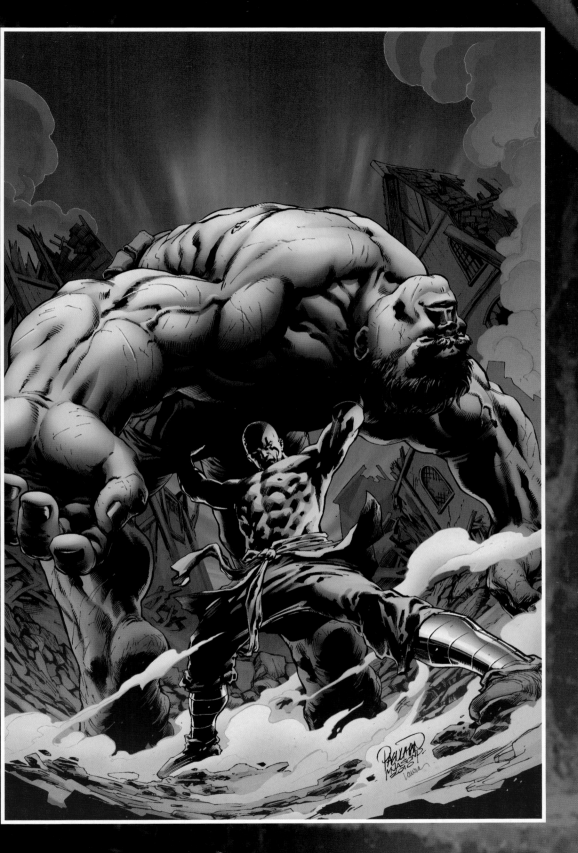

(616)

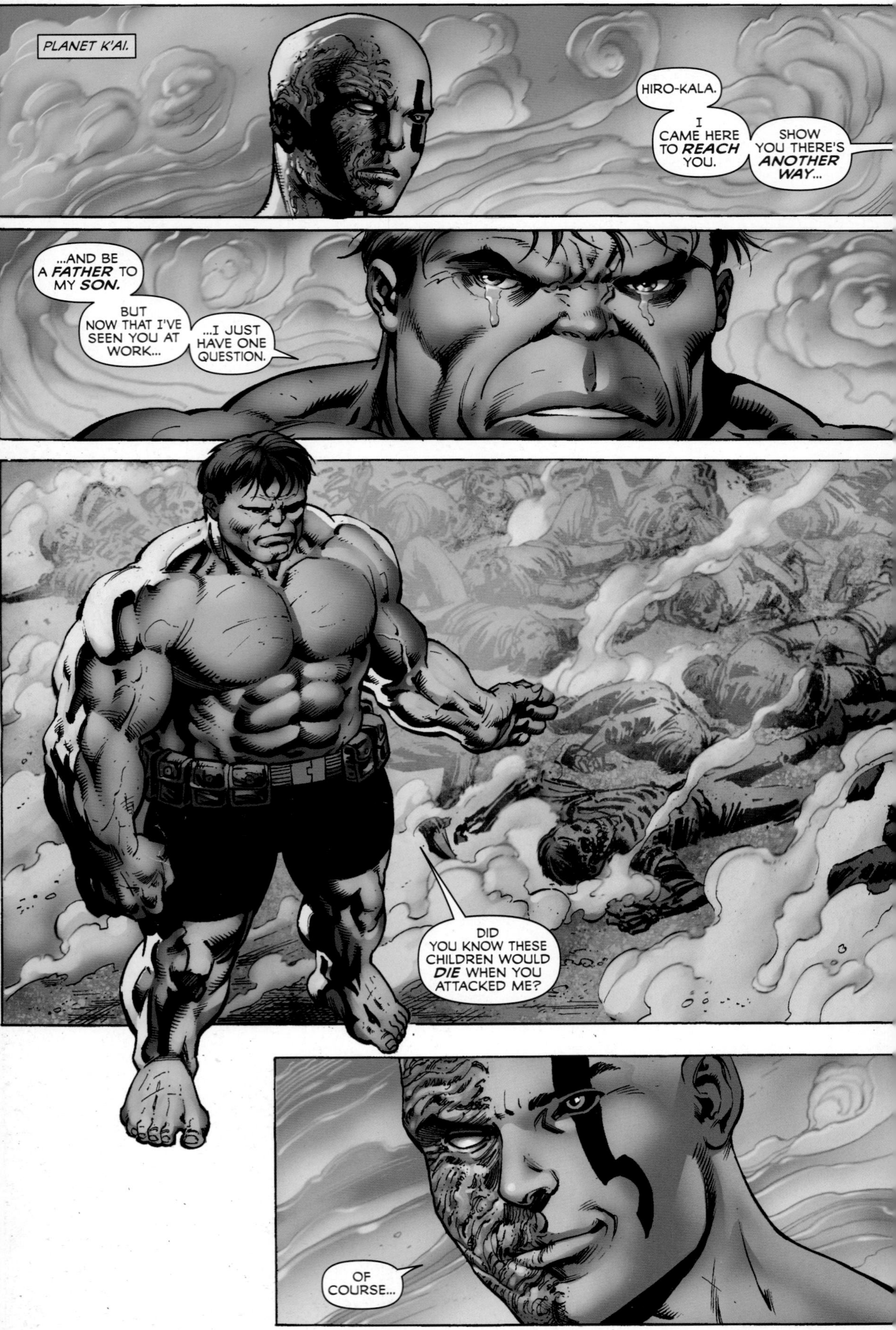
PLANET K'AI.
HIRO-KALA.
I CAME HERE TO REACH YOU.
SHOW YOU THERE'S ANOTHER WAY...
...AND BE A FATHER TO MY SON.
BUT NOW THAT I'VE SEEN YOU AT WORK...
...I JUST HAVE ONE QUESTION.
DID YOU KNOW THESE CHILDREN WOULD DIE WHEN YOU ATTACKED ME?
OF COURSE...

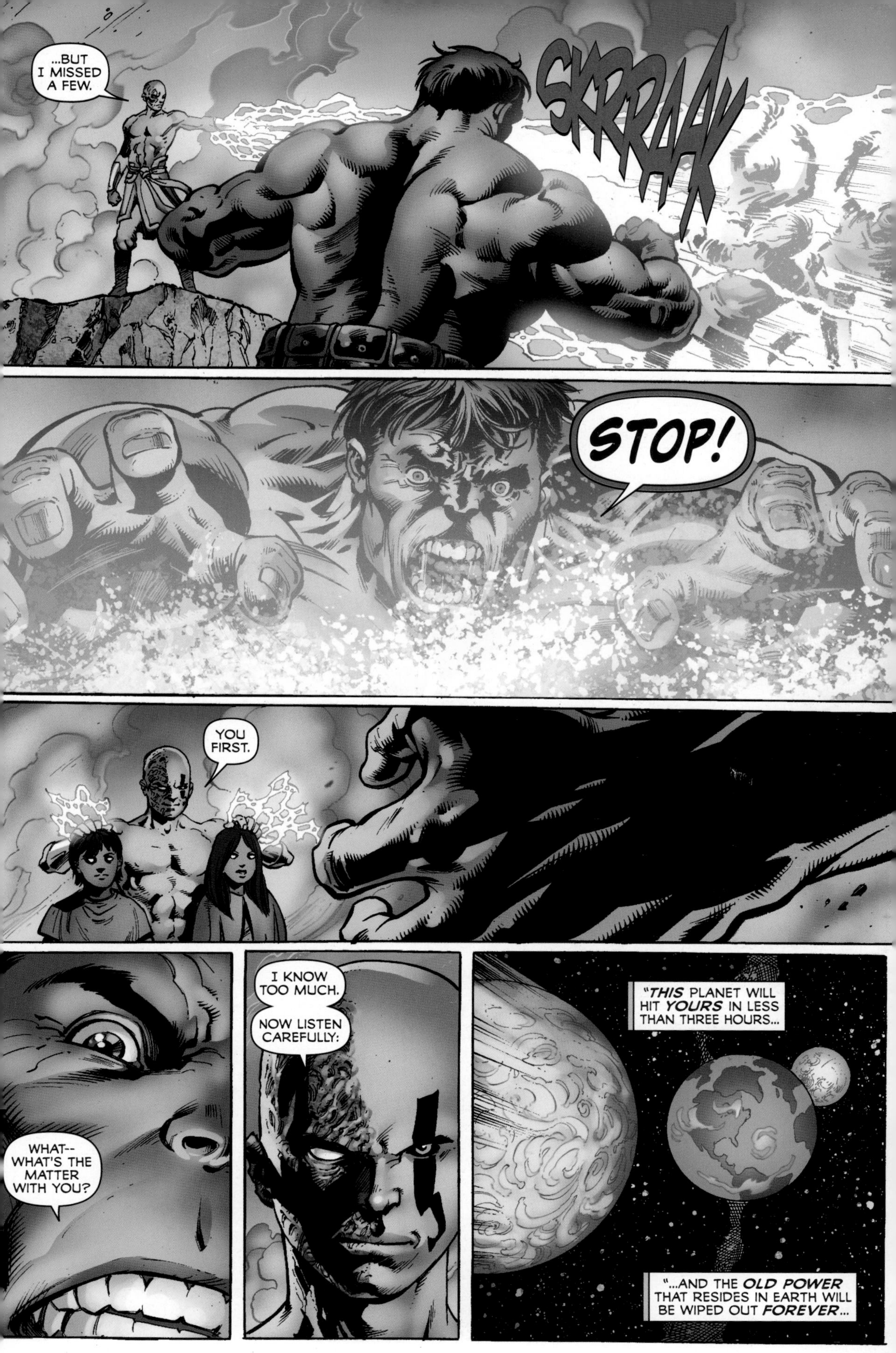
...BUT I MISSED A FEW.
SKRRAAK
STOP!
YOU FIRST.
WHAT-- WHAT'S THE MATTER WITH YOU?
I KNOW TOO MUCH.
NOW LISTEN CAREFULLY:
"*THIS* PLANET WILL HIT *YOURS* IN LESS THAN THREE HOURS...
"...AND THE *OLD POWER* THAT RESIDES IN EARTH WILL BE WIPED OUT *FOREVER*...

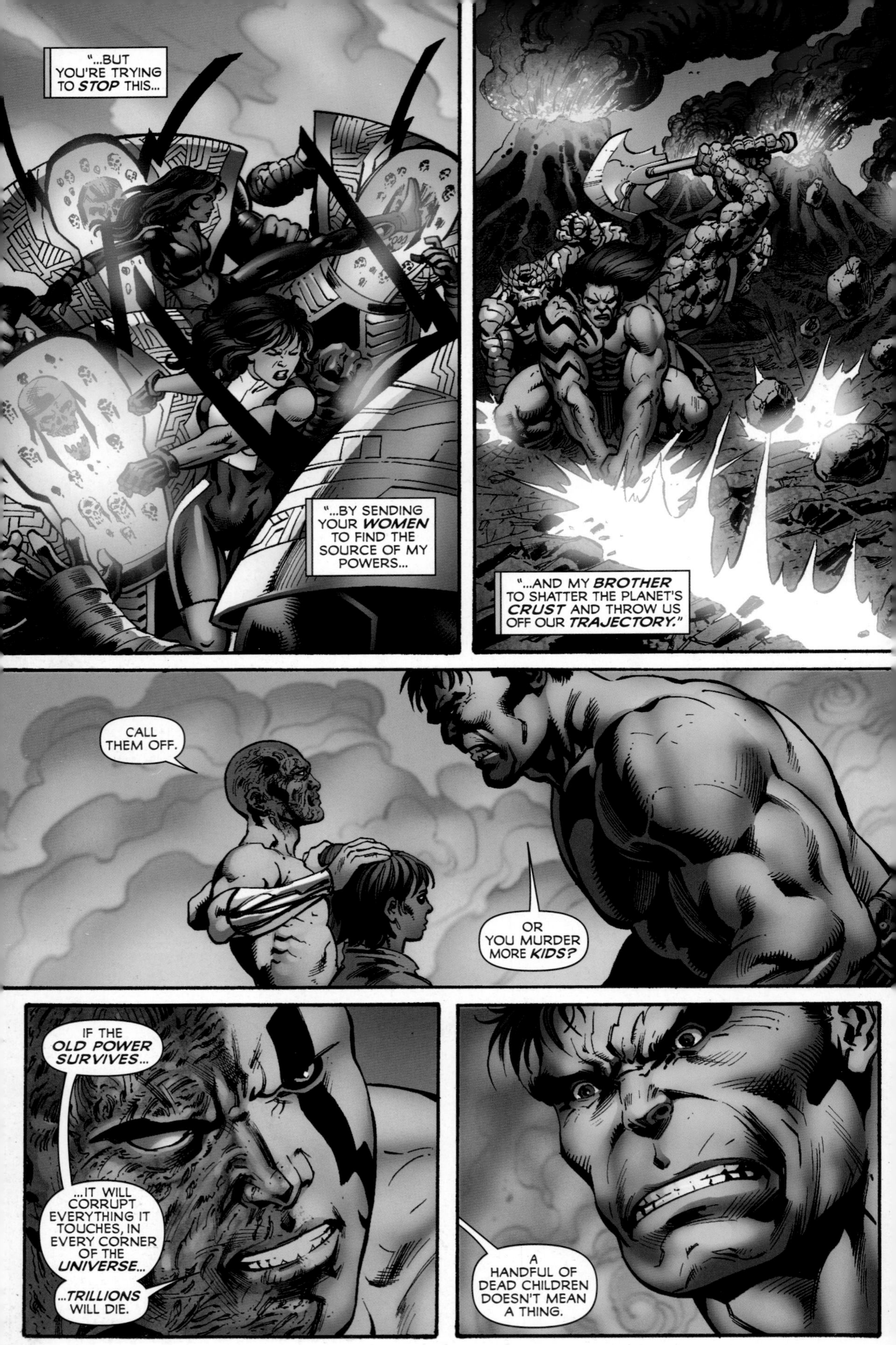
"...BUT YOU'RE TRYING TO *STOP* THIS...
"...BY SENDING YOUR *WOMEN* TO FIND THE SOURCE OF MY POWERS...
"...AND MY *BROTHER* TO SHATTER THE PLANET'S *CRUST* AND THROW US OFF OUR *TRAJECTORY.*"
CALL THEM OFF.
OR YOU MURDER MORE *KIDS?*
IF THE *OLD POWER SURVIVES...*
...IT WILL CORRUPT EVERYTHING IT TOUCHES, IN EVERY CORNER OF THE *UNIVERSE...*
...*TRILLIONS* WILL DIE.
A HANDFUL OF DEAD CHILDREN DOESN'T MEAN A THING.

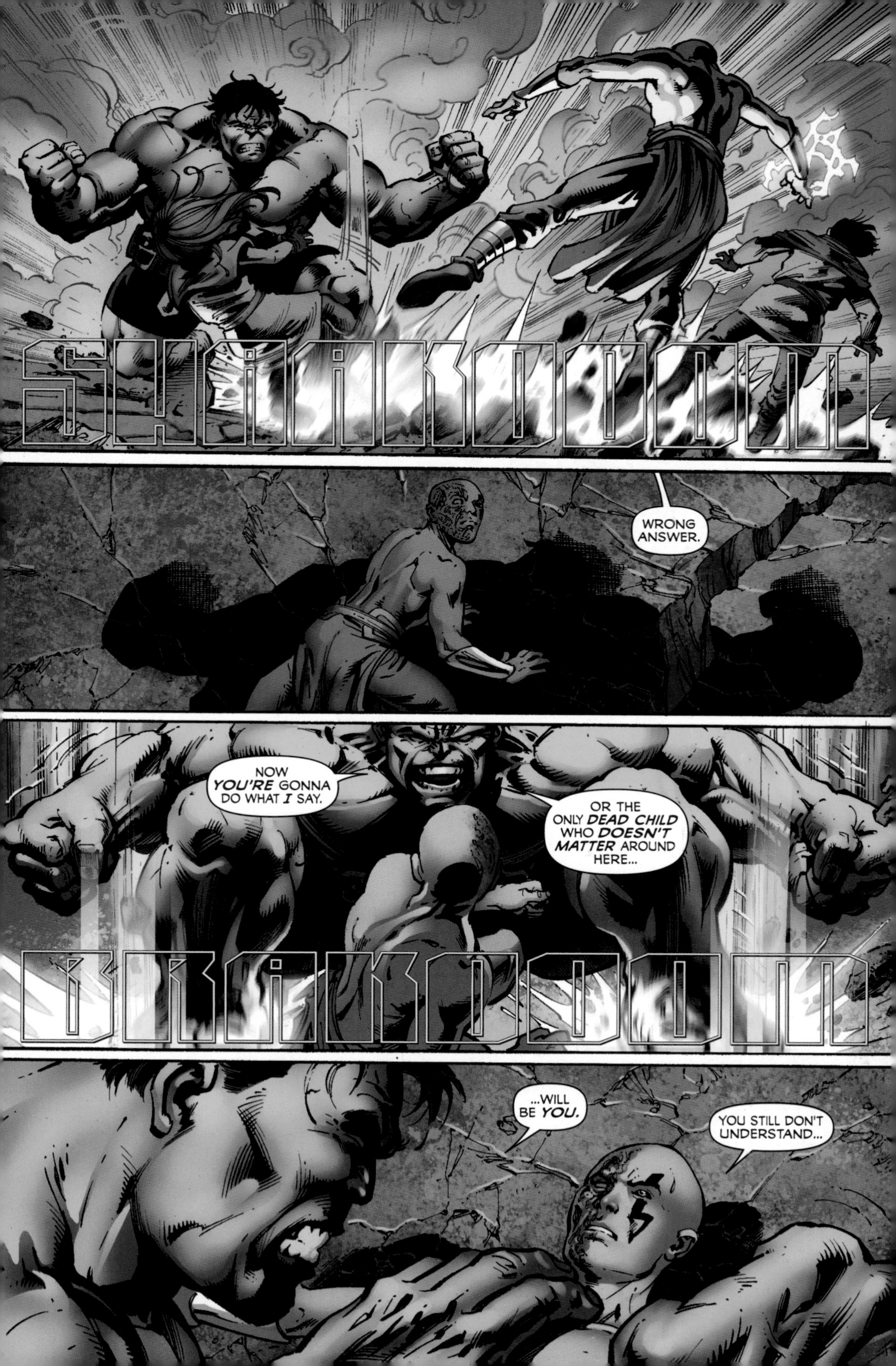
WRONG ANSWER.
NOW YOU'RE GONNA DO WHAT I SAY.
OR THE ONLY DEAD CHILD WHO DOESN'T MATTER AROUND HERE...
...WILL BE YOU.
YOU STILL DON'T UNDERSTAND...

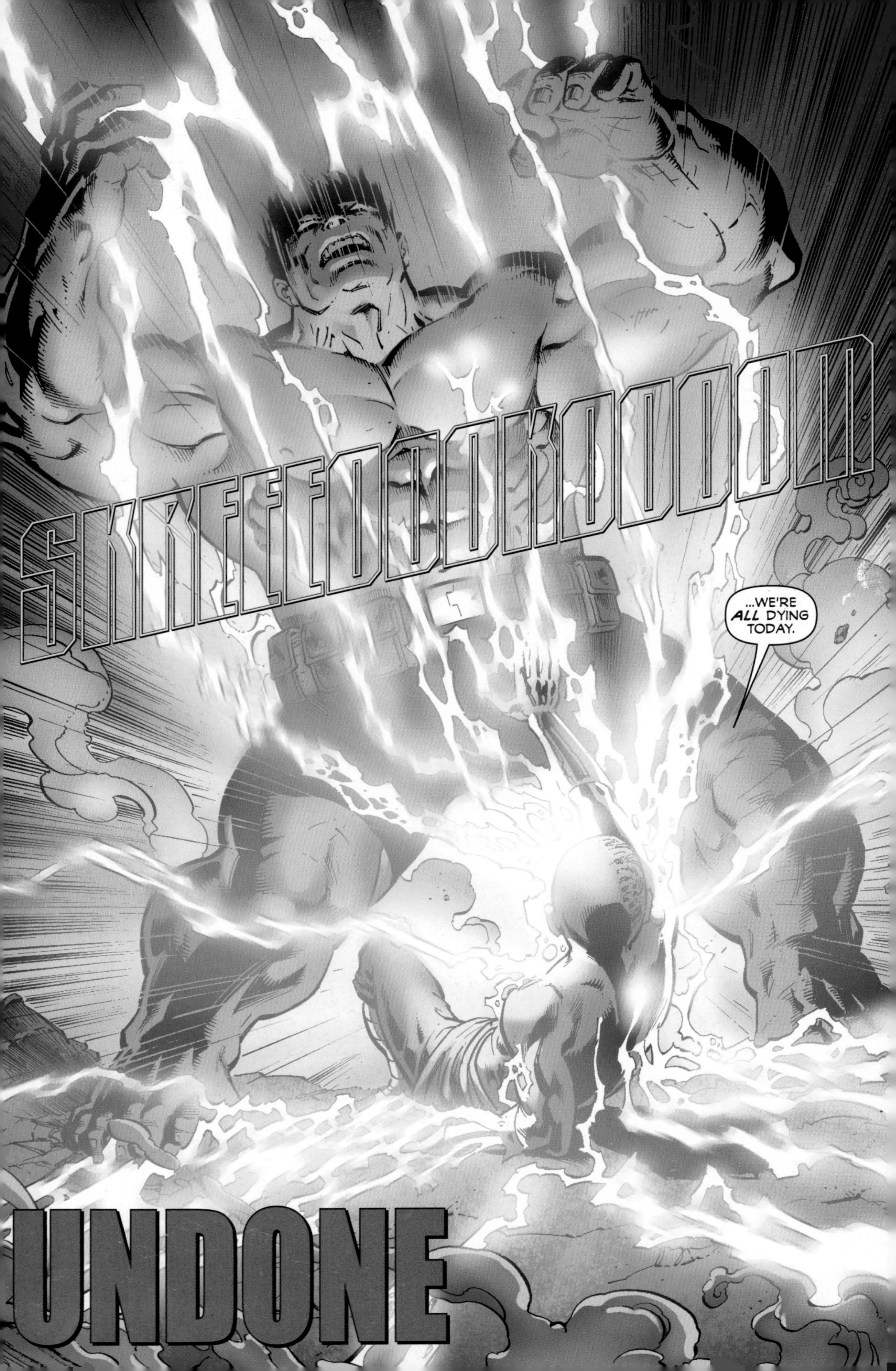
SKREEEDOOKOOOOOM
...WE'RE ALL DYING TODAY.
UNDONE

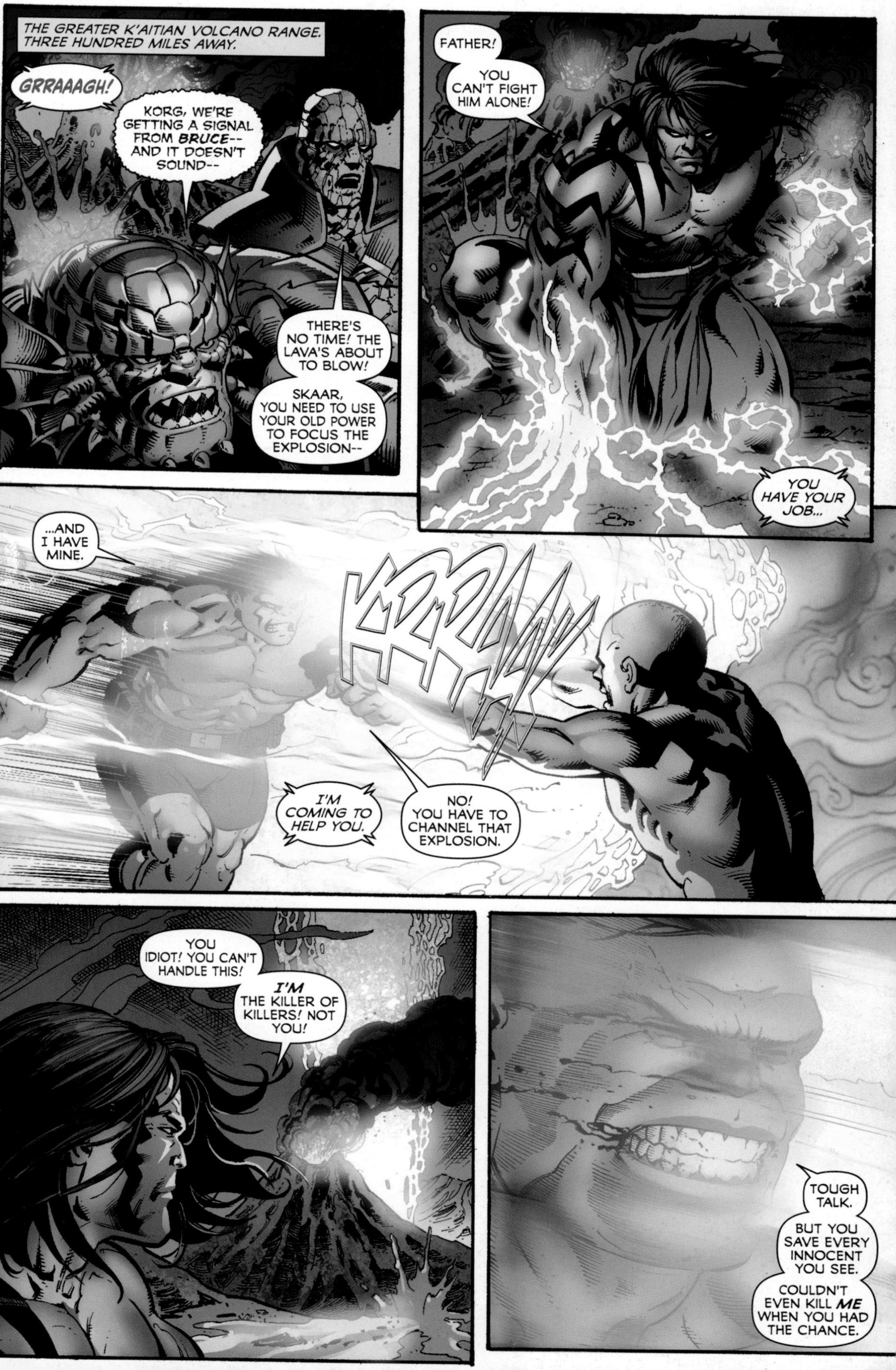
THE GREATER K'AITIAN VOLCANO RANGE. THREE HUNDRED MILES AWAY.
GRRAAAGH!
KORG, WE'RE GETTING A SIGNAL FROM BRUCE-- AND IT DOESN'T SOUND--
THERE'S NO TIME! THE LAVA'S ABOUT TO BLOW!
SKAAR, YOU NEED TO USE YOUR OLD POWER TO FOCUS THE EXPLOSION--
FATHER!
YOU CAN'T FIGHT HIM ALONE!
YOU HAVE YOUR JOB...
...AND I HAVE MINE.
KRRAAM
I'M COMING TO HELP YOU.
NO! YOU HAVE TO CHANNEL THAT EXPLOSION.
YOU IDIOT! YOU CAN'T HANDLE THIS!
I'M THE KILLER OF KILLERS! NOT YOU!
TOUGH TALK.
BUT YOU SAVE EVERY INNOCENT YOU SEE.
COULDN'T EVEN KILL ME WHEN YOU HAD THE CHANCE.

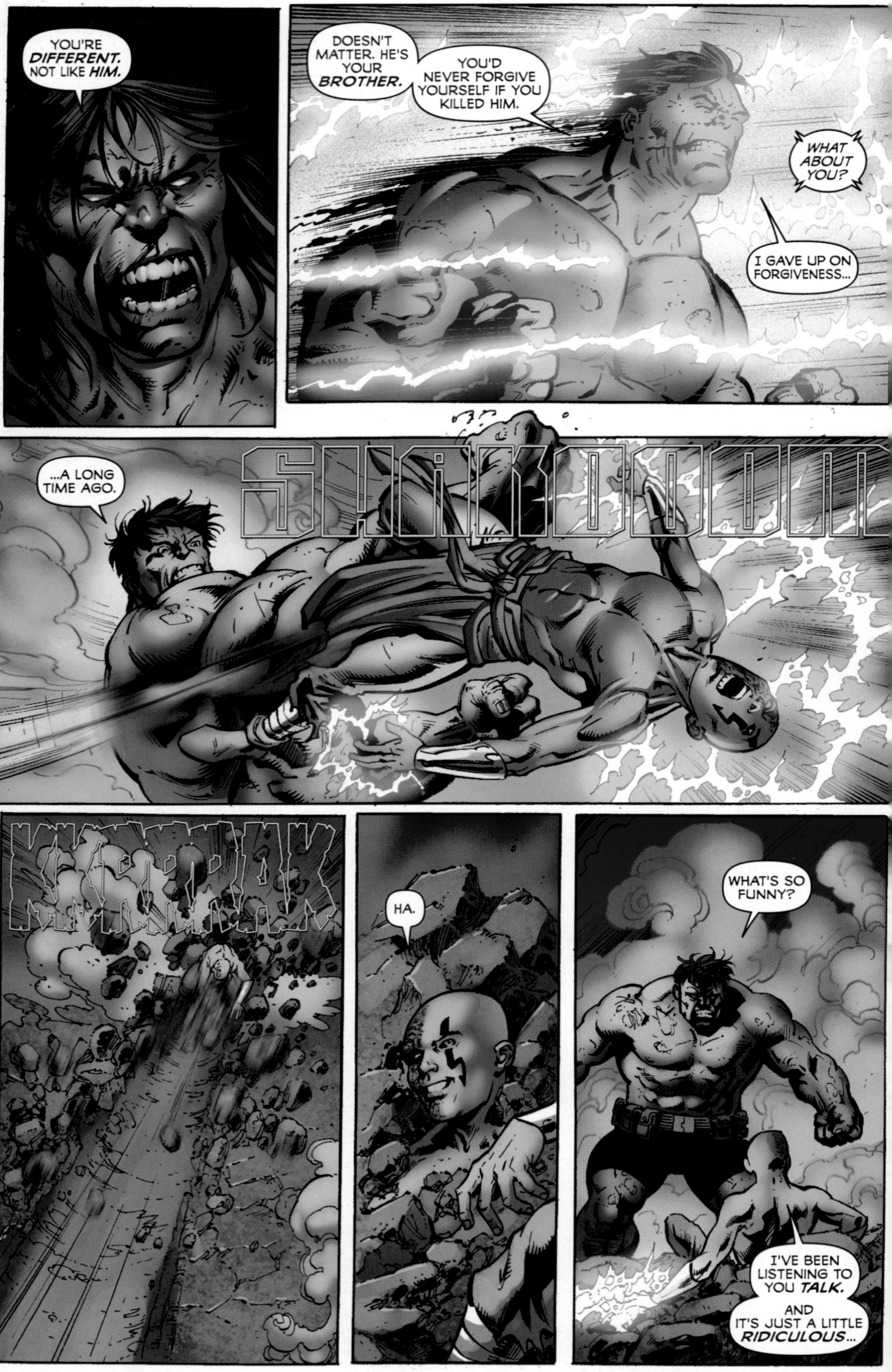
YOU'RE *DIFFERENT.* NOT LIKE *HIM.*
DOESN'T MATTER. HE'S YOUR *BROTHER.*
YOU'D NEVER FORGIVE YOURSELF IF YOU KILLED HIM.
WHAT ABOUT YOU?
I GAVE UP ON FORGIVENESS...
...A LONG TIME AGO.
HA.
WHAT'S SO FUNNY?
I'VE BEEN LISTENING TO YOU *TALK.*
AND IT'S JUST A LITTLE *RIDICULOUS*...

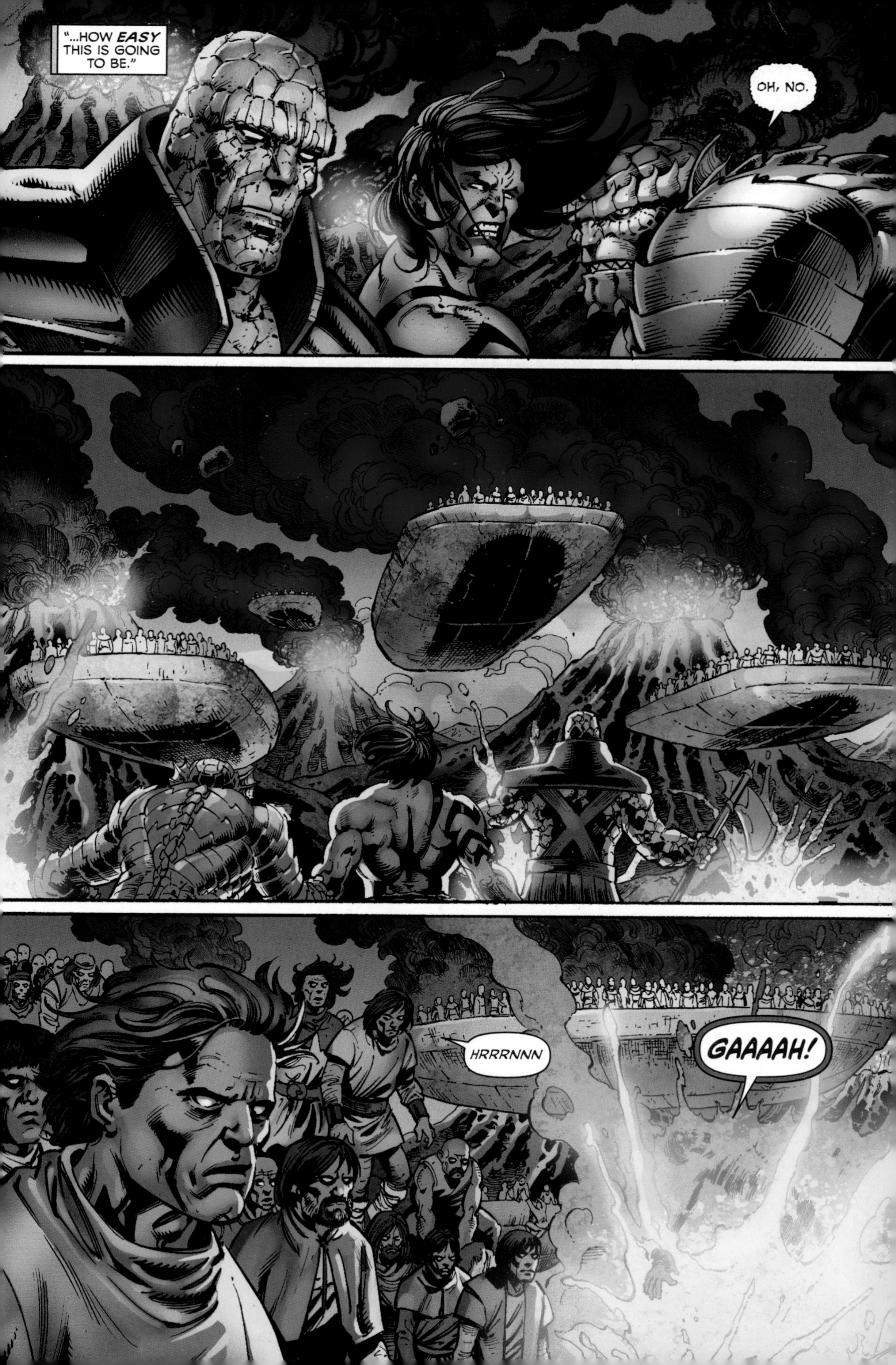
"...HOW EASY THIS IS GOING TO BE."
OH, NO.
HRRRNNN
GAAAAH!

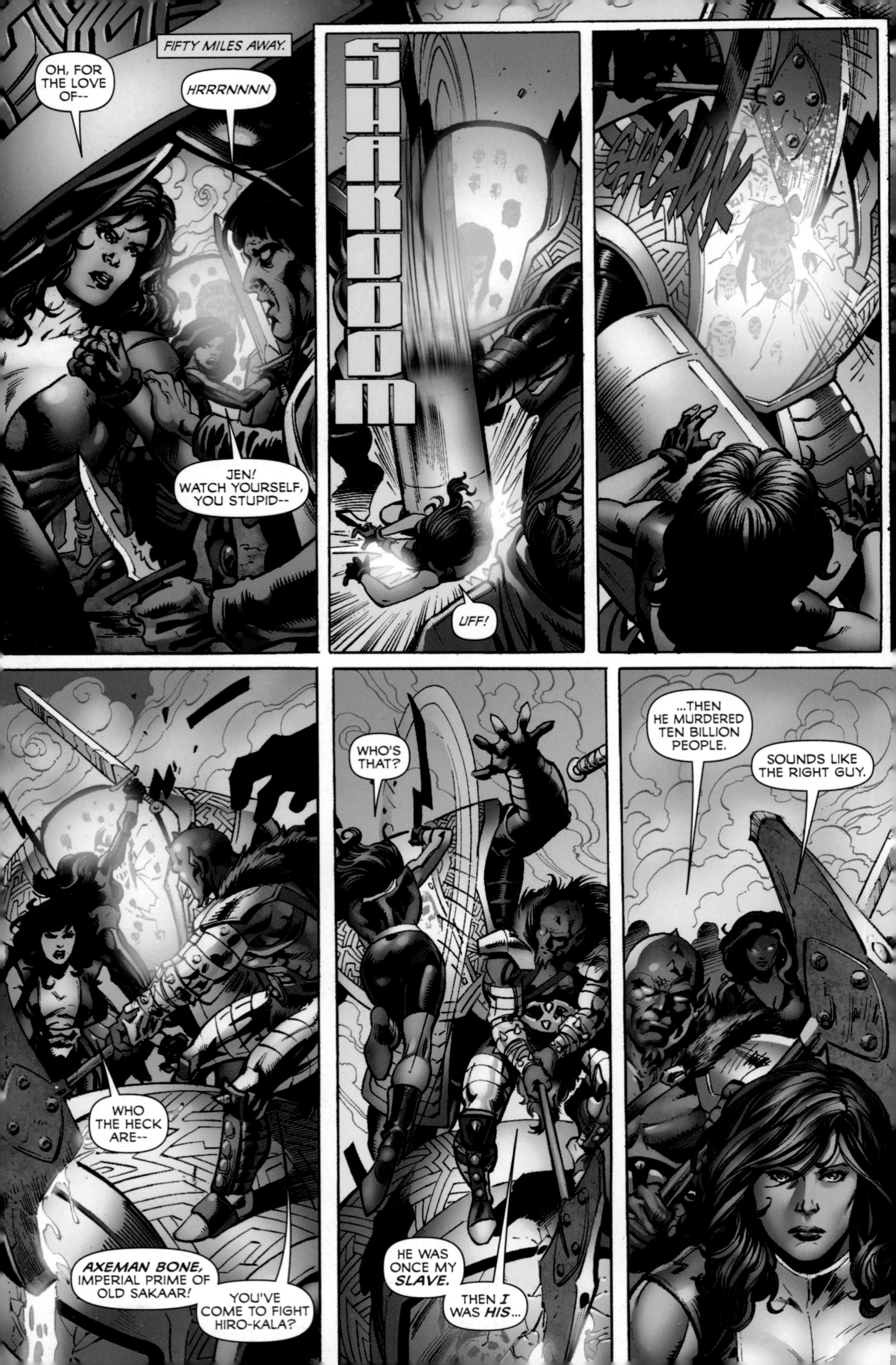
FIFTY MILES AWAY.
OH, FOR THE LOVE OF--
HRRRNNNN
JEN! WATCH YOURSELF, YOU STUPID--
SHAKOOM
UFF!
SHCHUNK
WHO THE HECK ARE--
AXEMAN BONE, IMPERIAL PRIME OF OLD SAKAAR!
YOU'VE COME TO FIGHT HIRO-KALA?
WHO'S THAT?
HE WAS ONCE MY SLAVE.
THEN I WAS HIS...
...THEN HE MURDERED TEN BILLION PEOPLE.
SOUNDS LIKE THE RIGHT GUY.

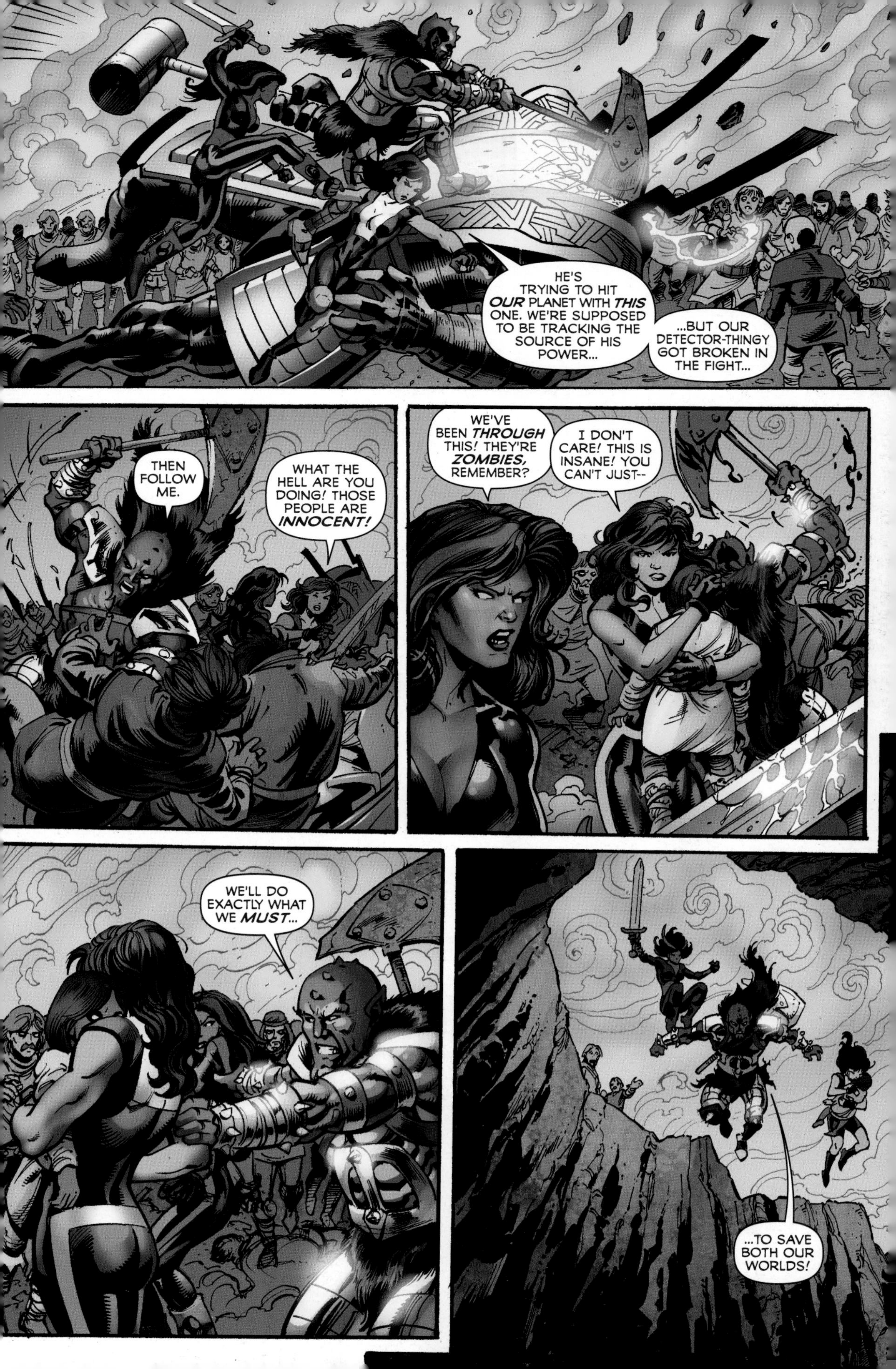
HE'S TRYING TO HIT *OUR* PLANET WITH *THIS* ONE. WE'RE SUPPOSED TO BE TRACKING THE SOURCE OF HIS POWER...
...BUT OUR DETECTOR-THINGY GOT BROKEN IN THE FIGHT...
WHAT THE HELL ARE YOU DOING! THOSE PEOPLE ARE *INNOCENT!*
THEN FOLLOW ME.
WE'VE BEEN *THROUGH* THIS! THEY'RE *ZOMBIES,* REMEMBER?
I DON'T CARE! THIS IS INSANE! YOU CAN'T JUST--
WE'LL DO EXACTLY WHAT WE *MUST*...
...TO SAVE BOTH OUR WORLDS!

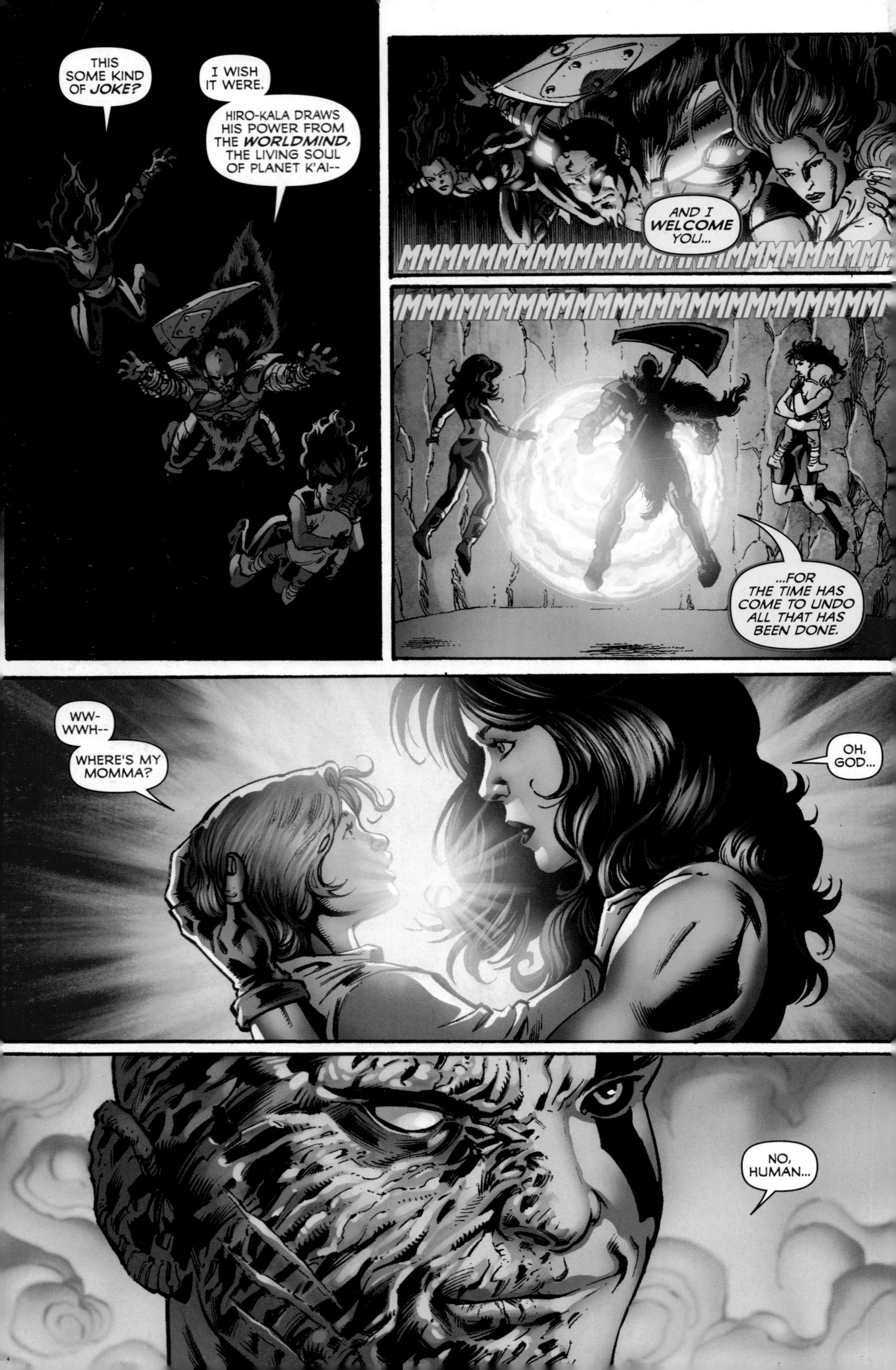
THIS SOME KIND OF JOKE?
I WISH IT WERE.
HIRO-KALA DRAWS HIS POWER FROM THE WORLDMIND, THE LIVING SOUL OF PLANET K'AI--
AND I WELCOME YOU...
MMMMMMMMMMMMMMMMMMMMMMMMMMMMM
MMMMMMMMMMMMMMMMMMMMMMMMMMM
...FOR THE TIME HAS COME TO UNDO ALL THAT HAS BEEN DONE.
WW-WWH--
WHERE'S MY MOMMA?
OH, GOD...
NO, HUMAN...

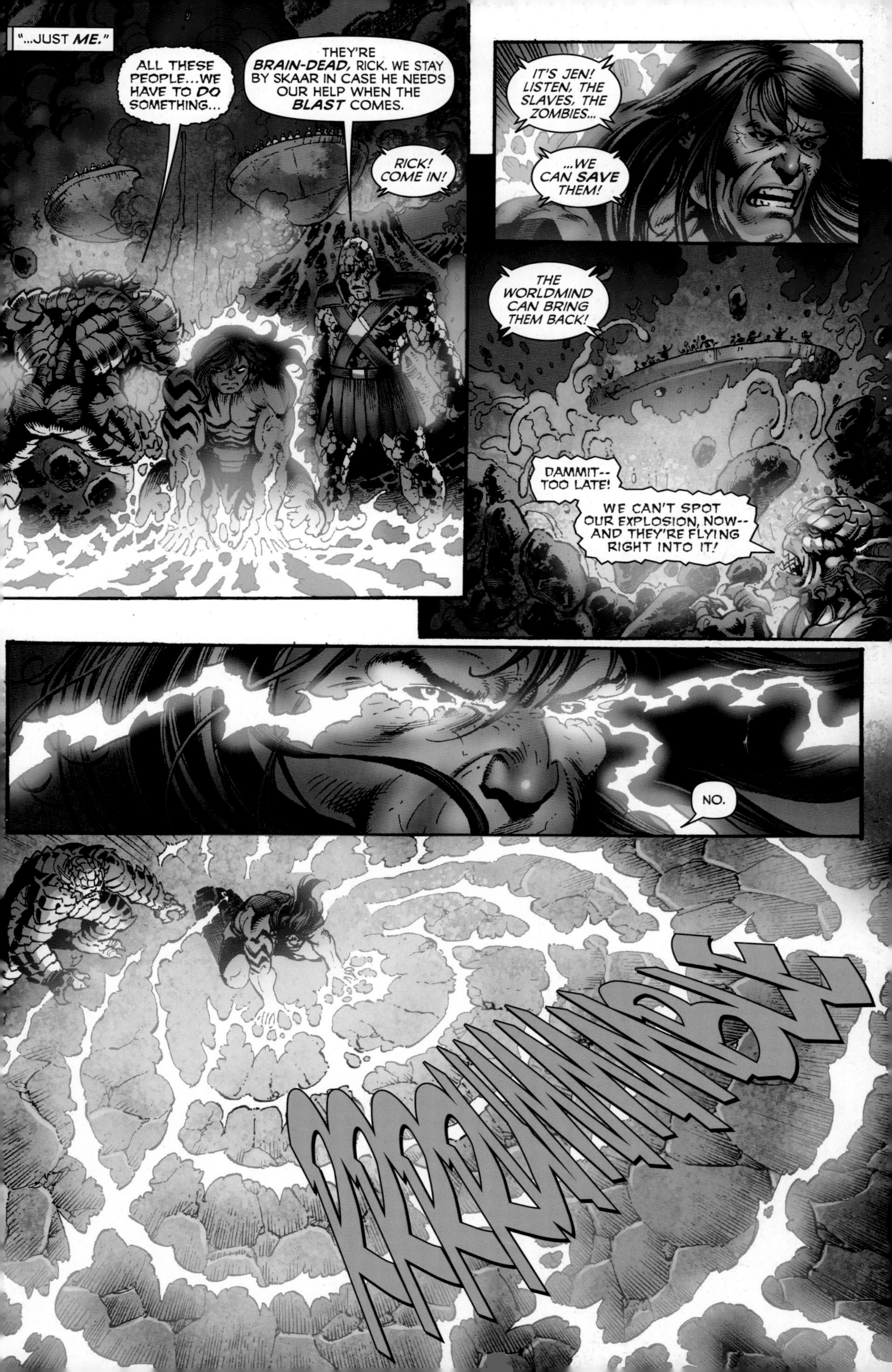
"...JUST ME."
ALL THESE PEOPLE...WE HAVE TO DO SOMETHING...
THEY'RE BRAIN-DEAD, RICK. WE STAY BY SKAAR IN CASE HE NEEDS OUR HELP WHEN THE BLAST COMES.
RICK! COME IN!
IT'S JEN! LISTEN, THE SLAVES, THE ZOMBIES...
...WE CAN SAVE THEM!
THE WORLDMIND CAN BRING THEM BACK!
DAMMIT-- TOO LATE!
WE CAN'T SPOT OUR EXPLOSION, NOW-- AND THEY'RE FLYING RIGHT INTO IT!
NO.

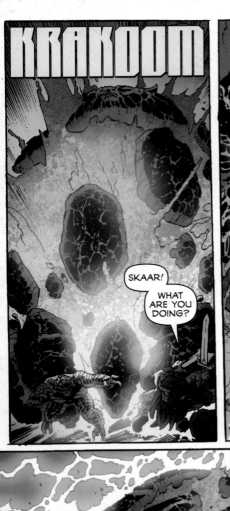

KRAKDOOM

SKAAR! WHAT ARE YOU DOING?

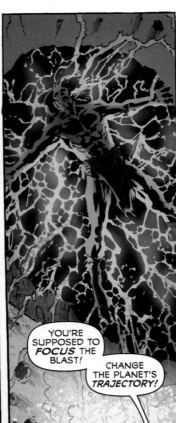

YOU'RE SUPPOSED TO *FOCUS* THE BLAST!

CHANGE THE PLANET'S *TRAJECTORY!*

NO.

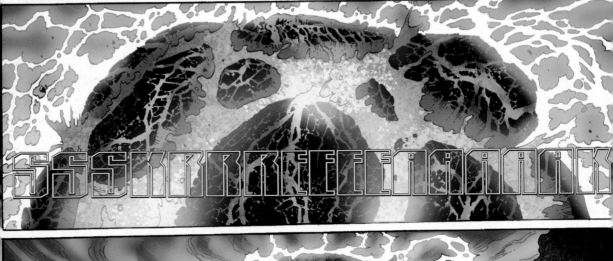

SSSKRRBBEEENNNK

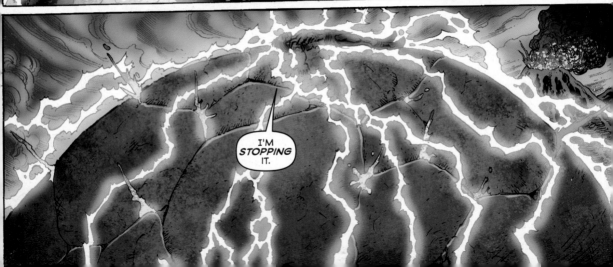

I'M *STOPPING* IT.

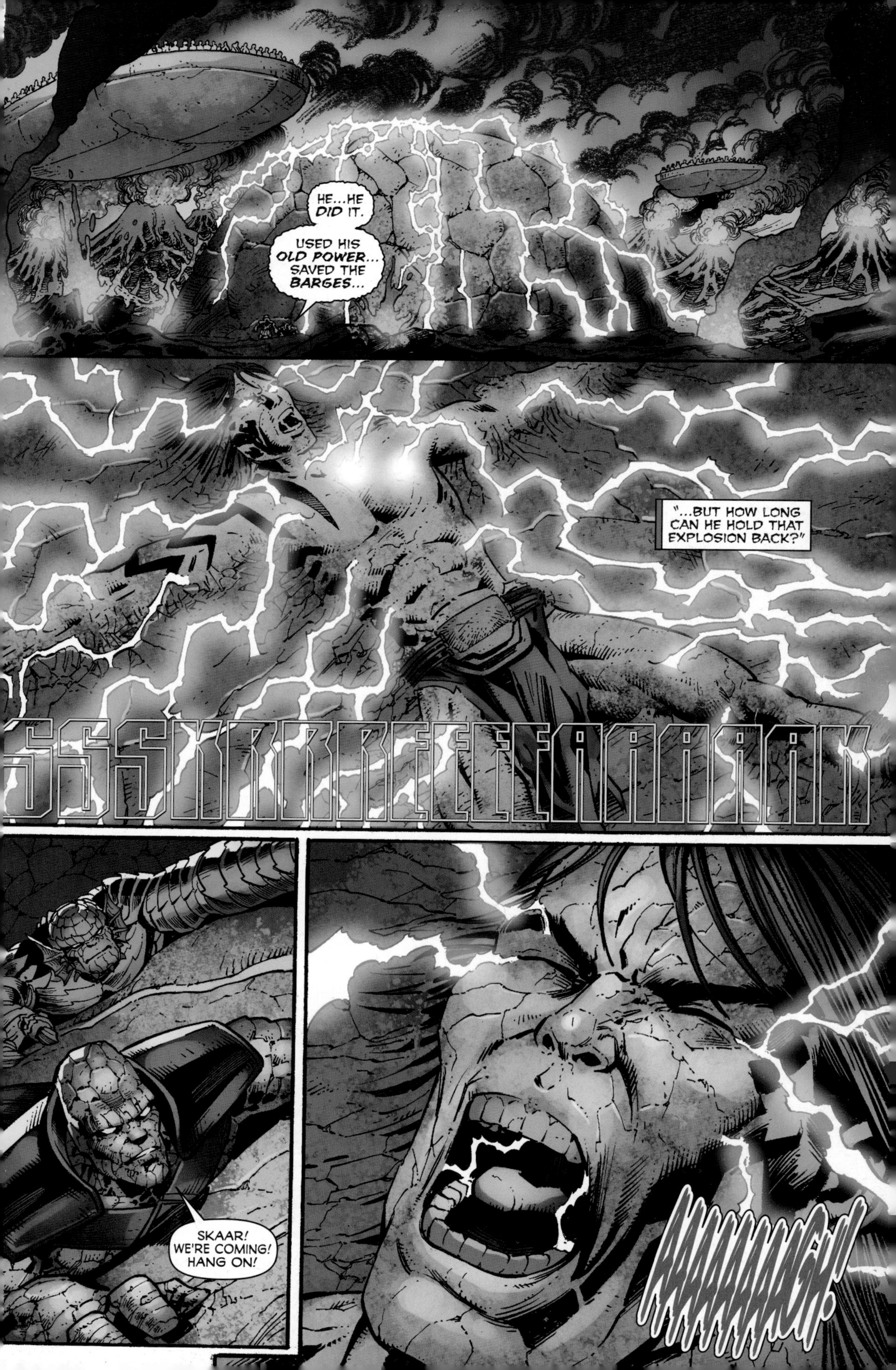
HE...HE DID IT.
USED HIS OLD POWER... SAVED THE BARGES...
"...BUT HOW LONG CAN HE HOLD THAT EXPLOSION BACK?"
SSSKRRRREEEEAAAAAK
SKAAR! WE'RE COMING! HANG ON!
AAAAAAAAGH!

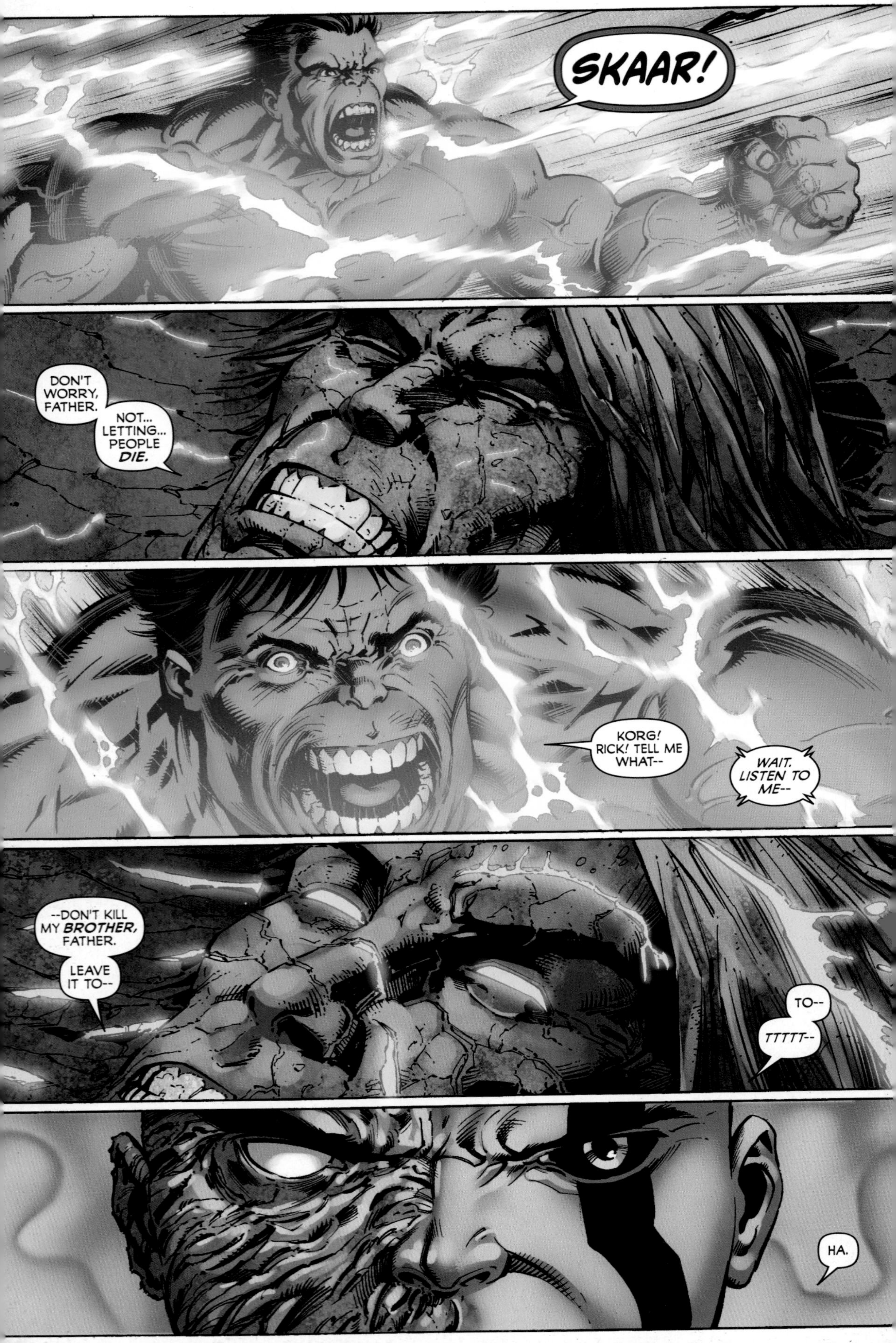
SKAAR!
DON'T WORRY, FATHER.
NOT... LETTING... PEOPLE *DIE.*
KORG! RICK! TELL ME WHAT--
WAIT. LISTEN TO ME--
--DON'T KILL MY *BROTHER,* FATHER.
LEAVE IT TO--
TO--
TTTTT--
HA.

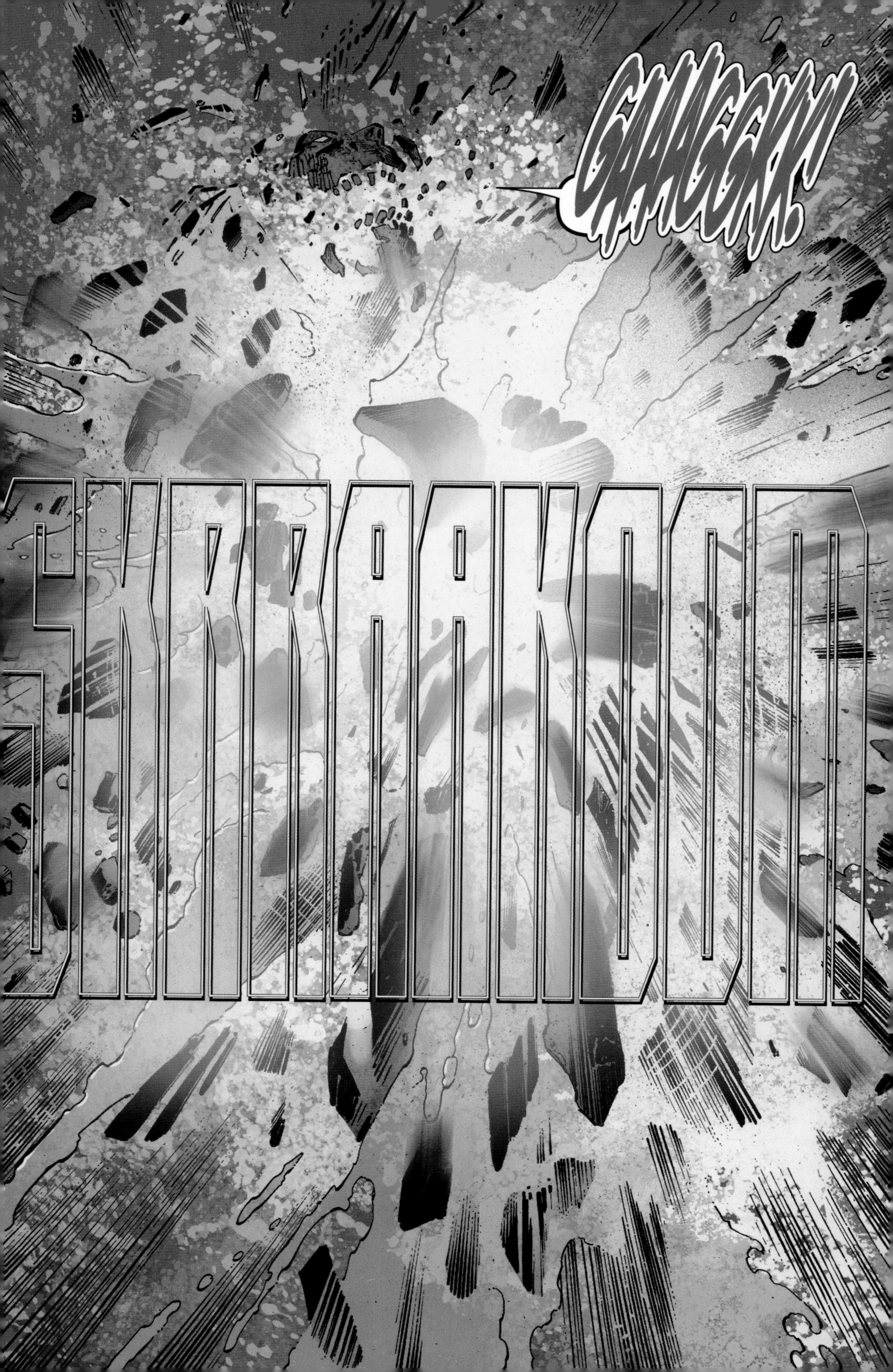
GAAGGKK!
SKRRAAKOOM

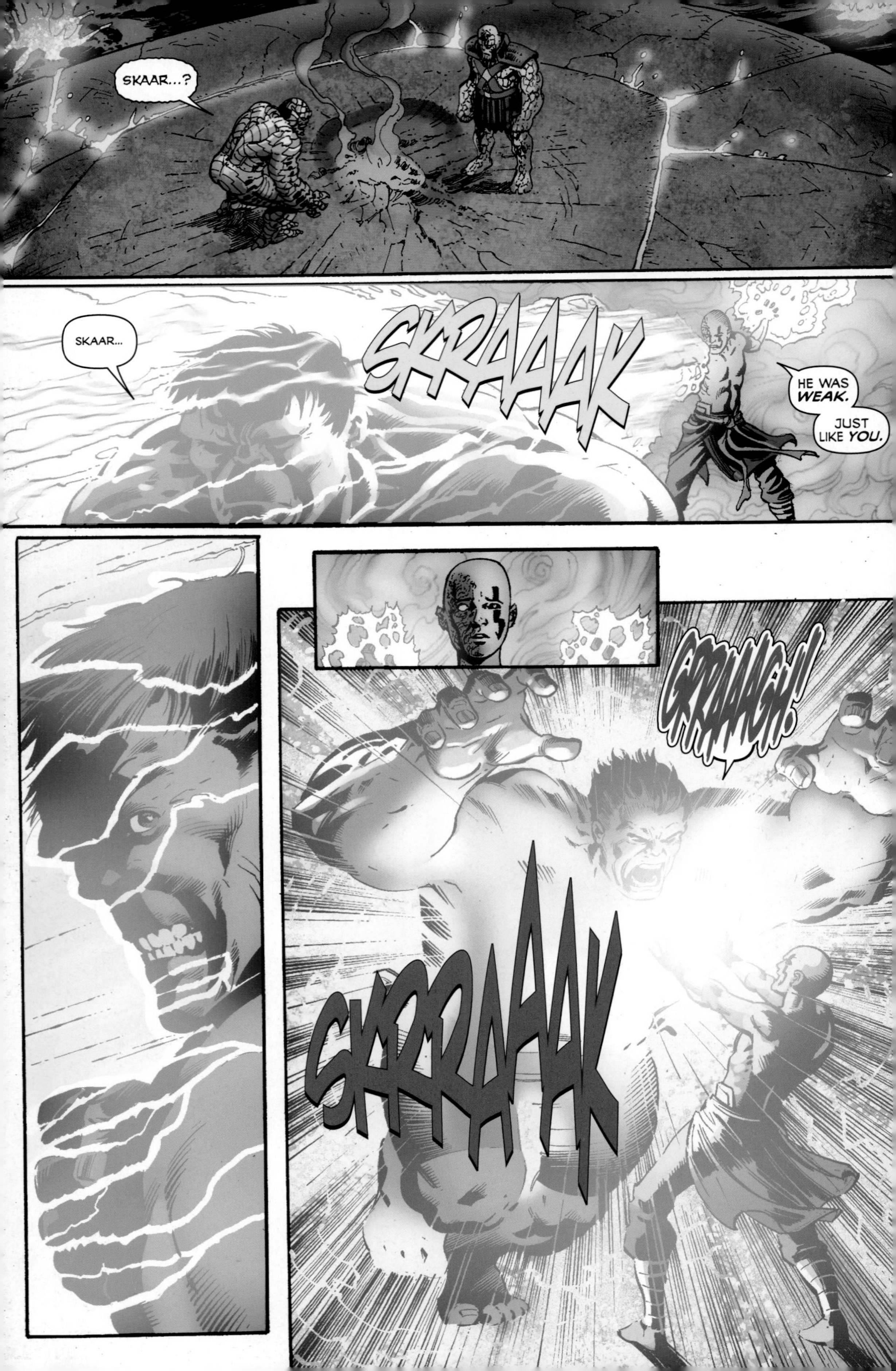

SKAAR...?
SKAAR...
SKRAAAK
HE WAS WEAK.
JUST LIKE YOU.
GRRAAAGH!
SKRRAAAK

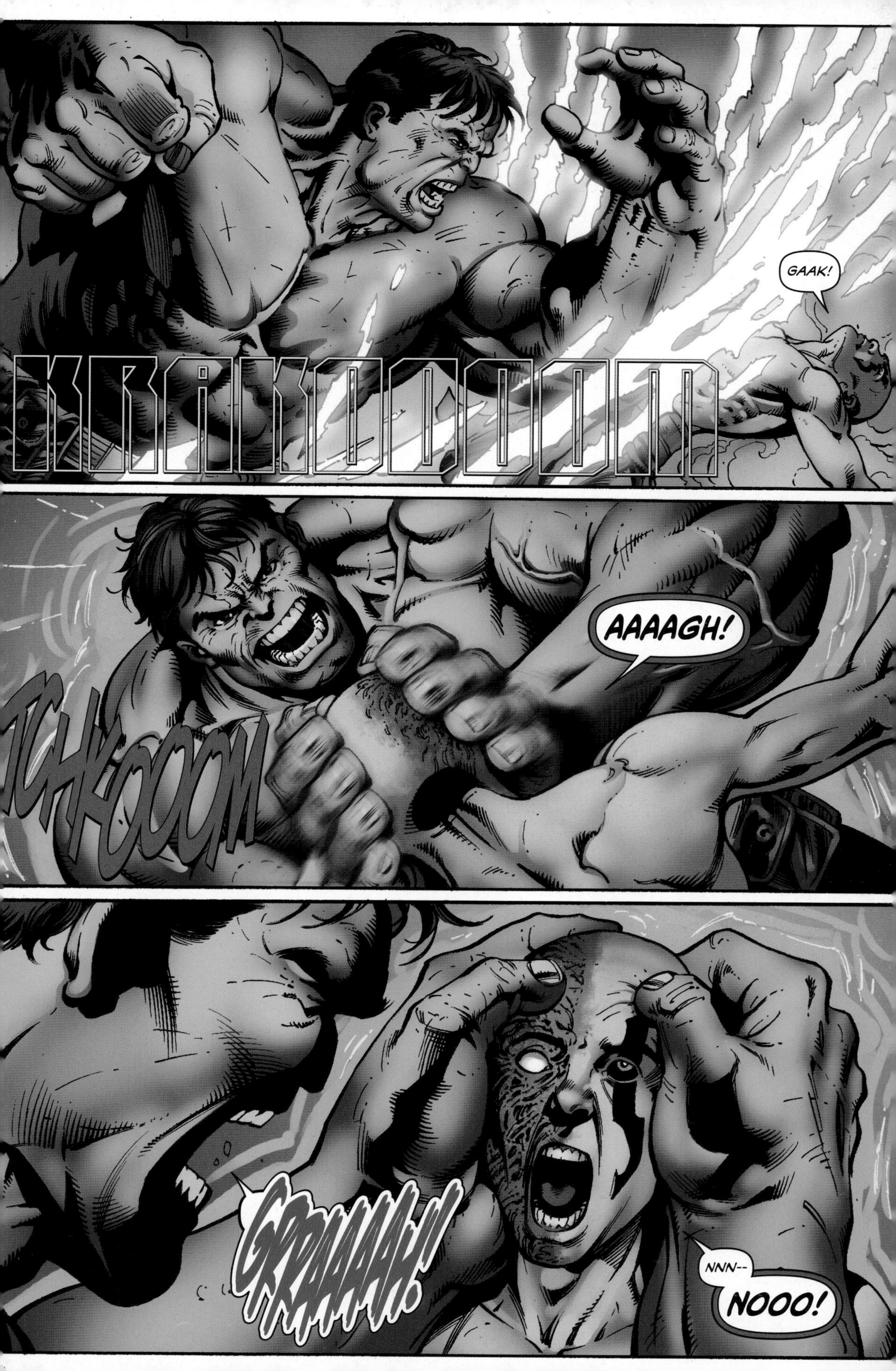
GAAK!
KRAKOOOOM
AAAAGH!
TCHKOOOM
GRAAAAH!
NNN--
NOOO!

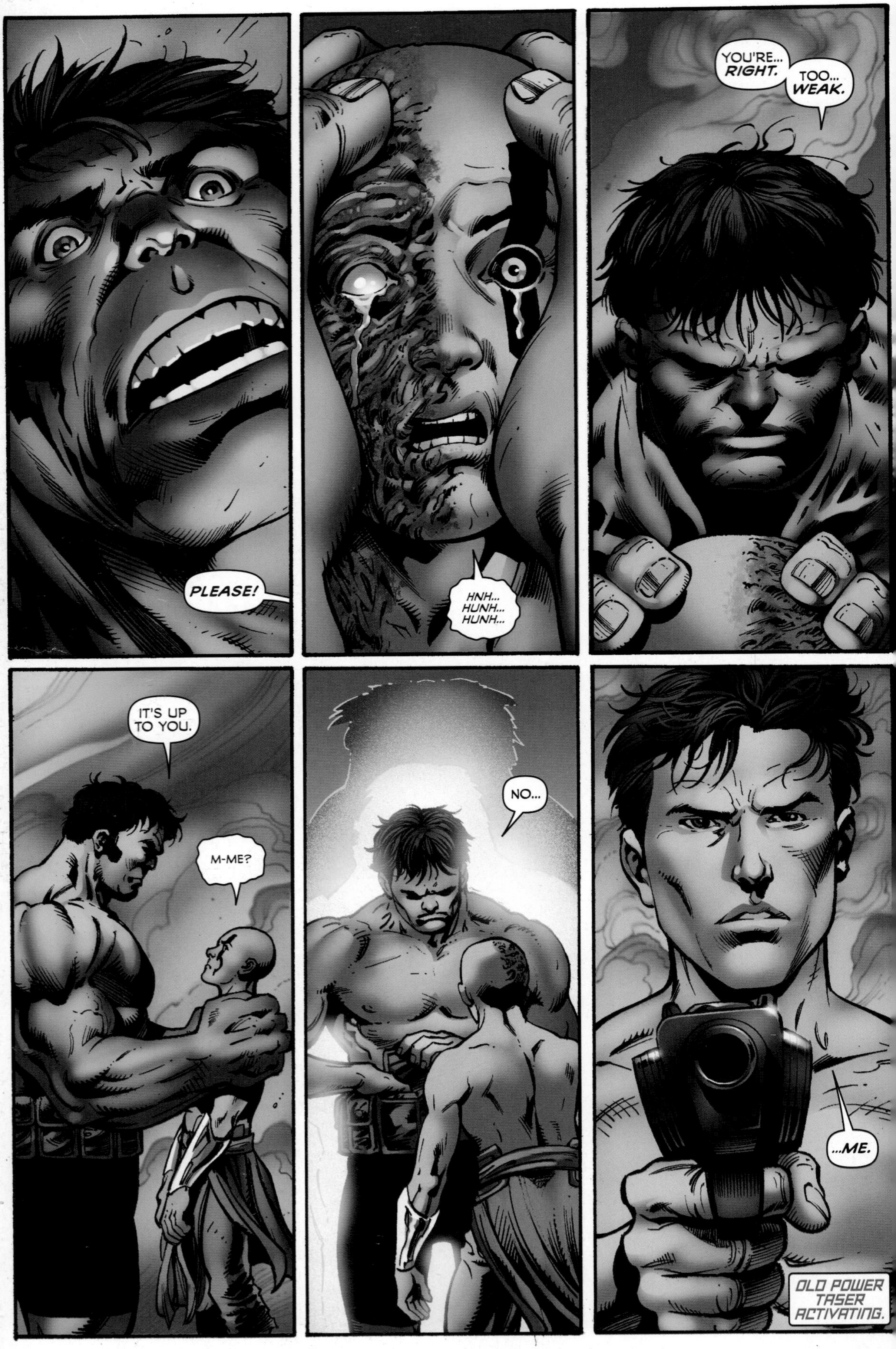
PLEASE!
HNH... HUNH... HUNH...
YOU'RE... RIGHT.
TOO... WEAK.
IT'S UP TO YOU.
M-ME?
NO...
...ME.
OLD POWER TASER ACTIVATING.

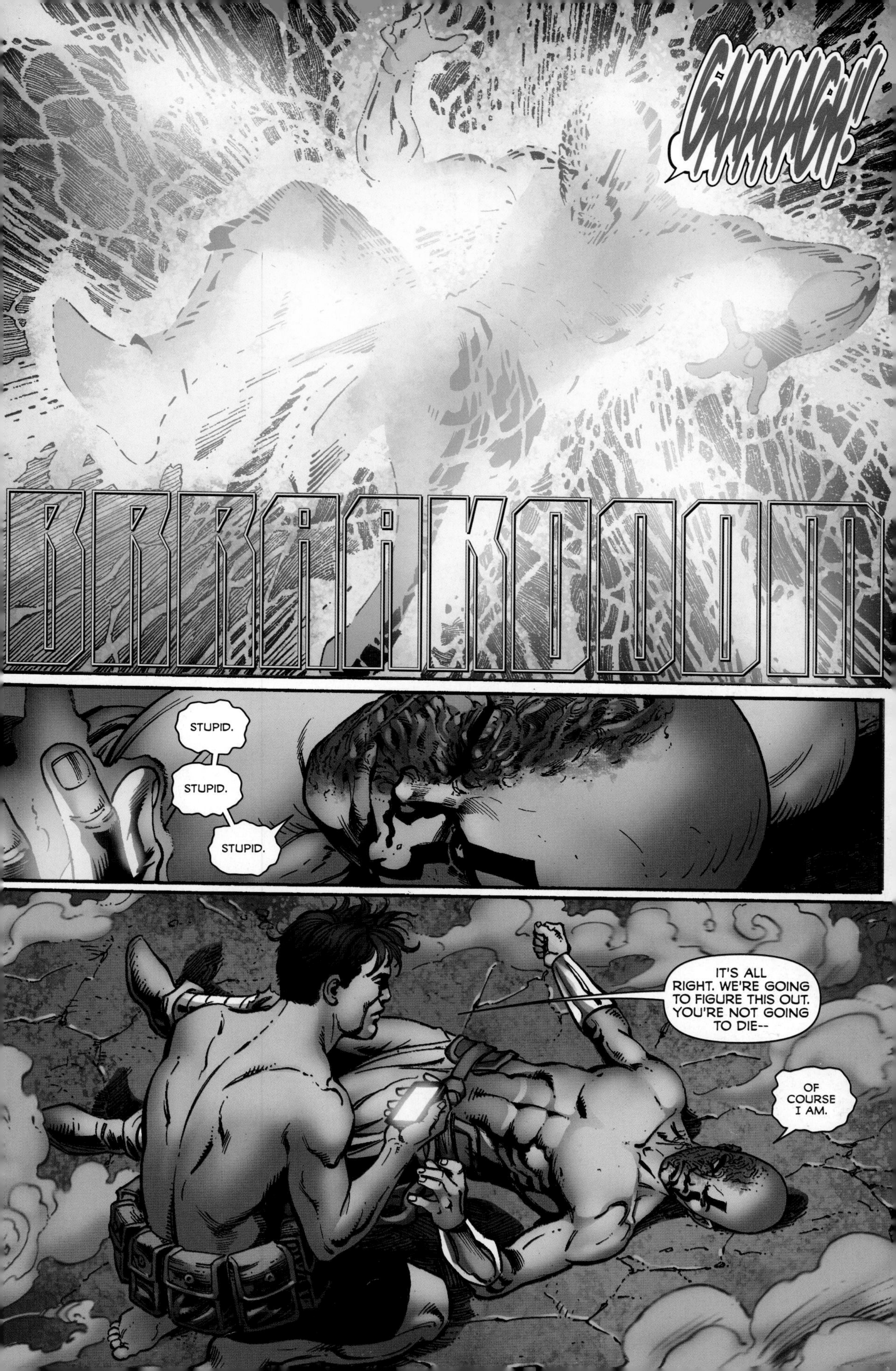
GAAAAAGH!!
BRRAAKOOOM
STUPID.
STUPID.
STUPID.
IT'S ALL RIGHT. WE'RE GOING TO FIGURE THIS OUT. YOU'RE NOT GOING TO DIE--
OF COURSE I AM.

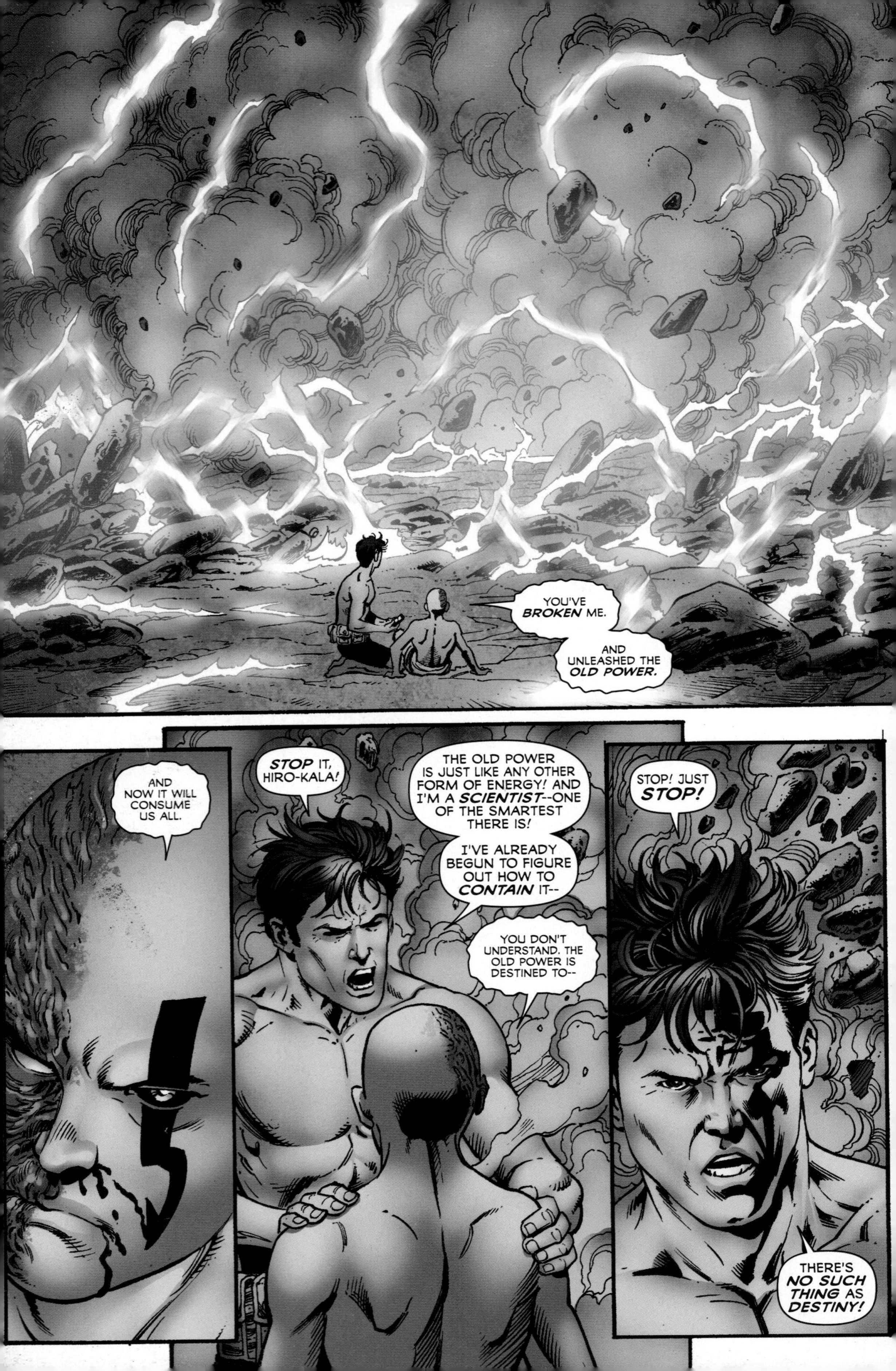
YOU'VE BROKEN ME.
AND UNLEASHED THE OLD POWER.
AND NOW IT WILL CONSUME US ALL.
STOP IT, HIRO-KALA!
THE OLD POWER IS JUST LIKE ANY OTHER FORM OF ENERGY! AND I'M A SCIENTIST--ONE OF THE SMARTEST THERE IS!
I'VE ALREADY BEGUN TO FIGURE OUT HOW TO CONTAIN IT--
YOU DON'T UNDERSTAND. THE OLD POWER IS DESTINED TO--
STOP! JUST STOP!
THERE'S NO SUCH THING AS DESTINY!

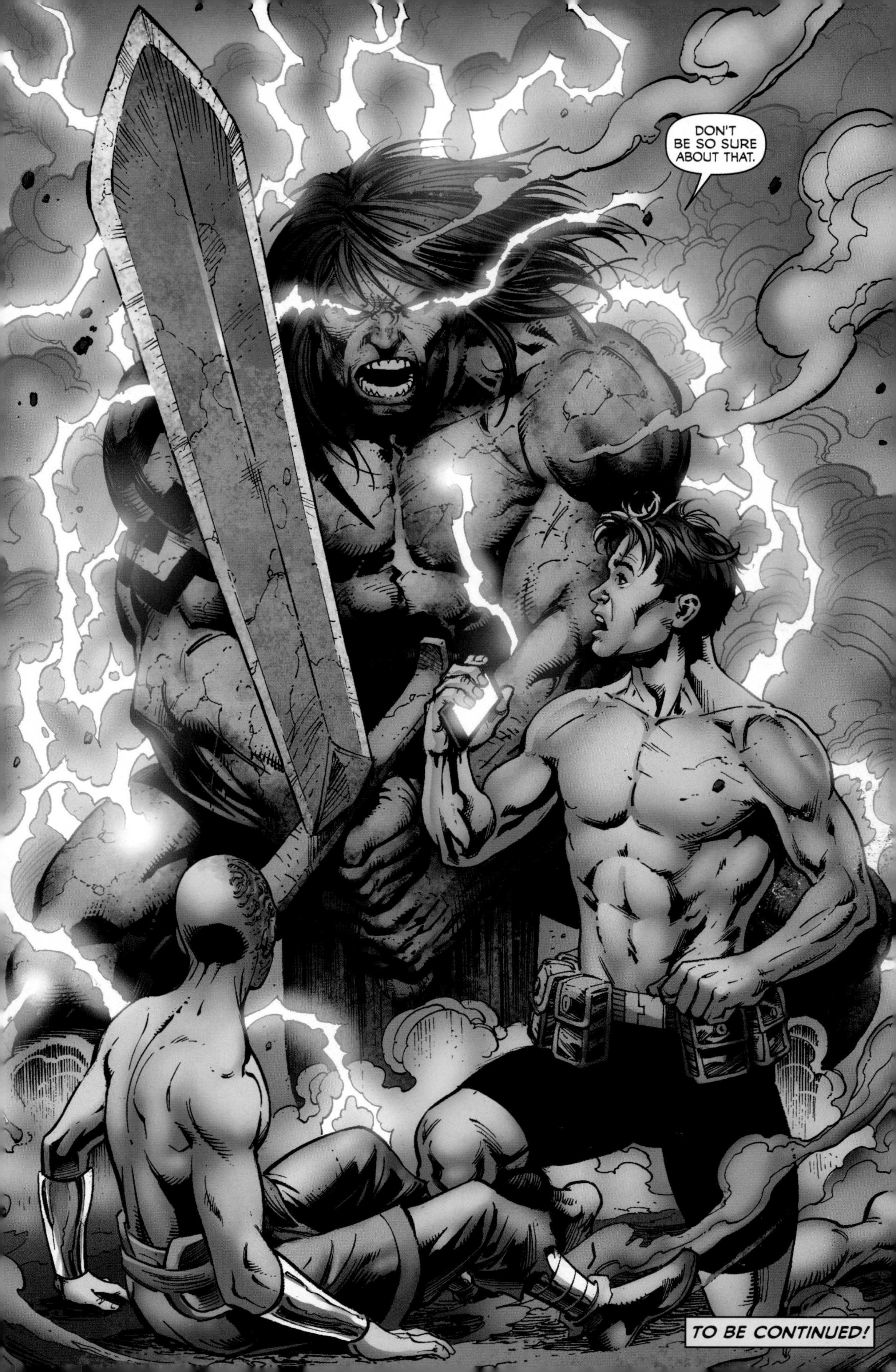
DON'T BE SO SURE ABOUT THAT.
TO BE CONTINUED!

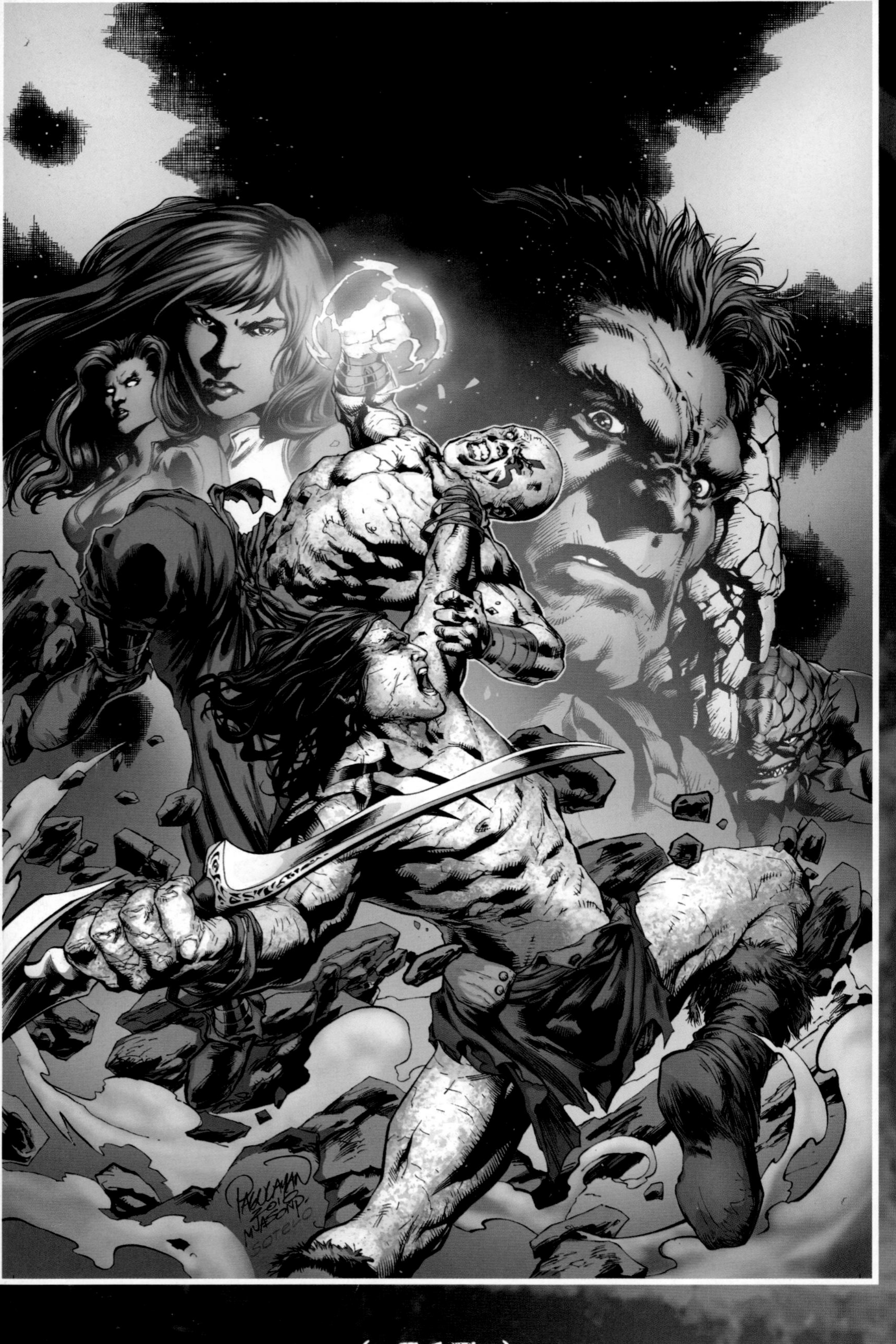

(617)

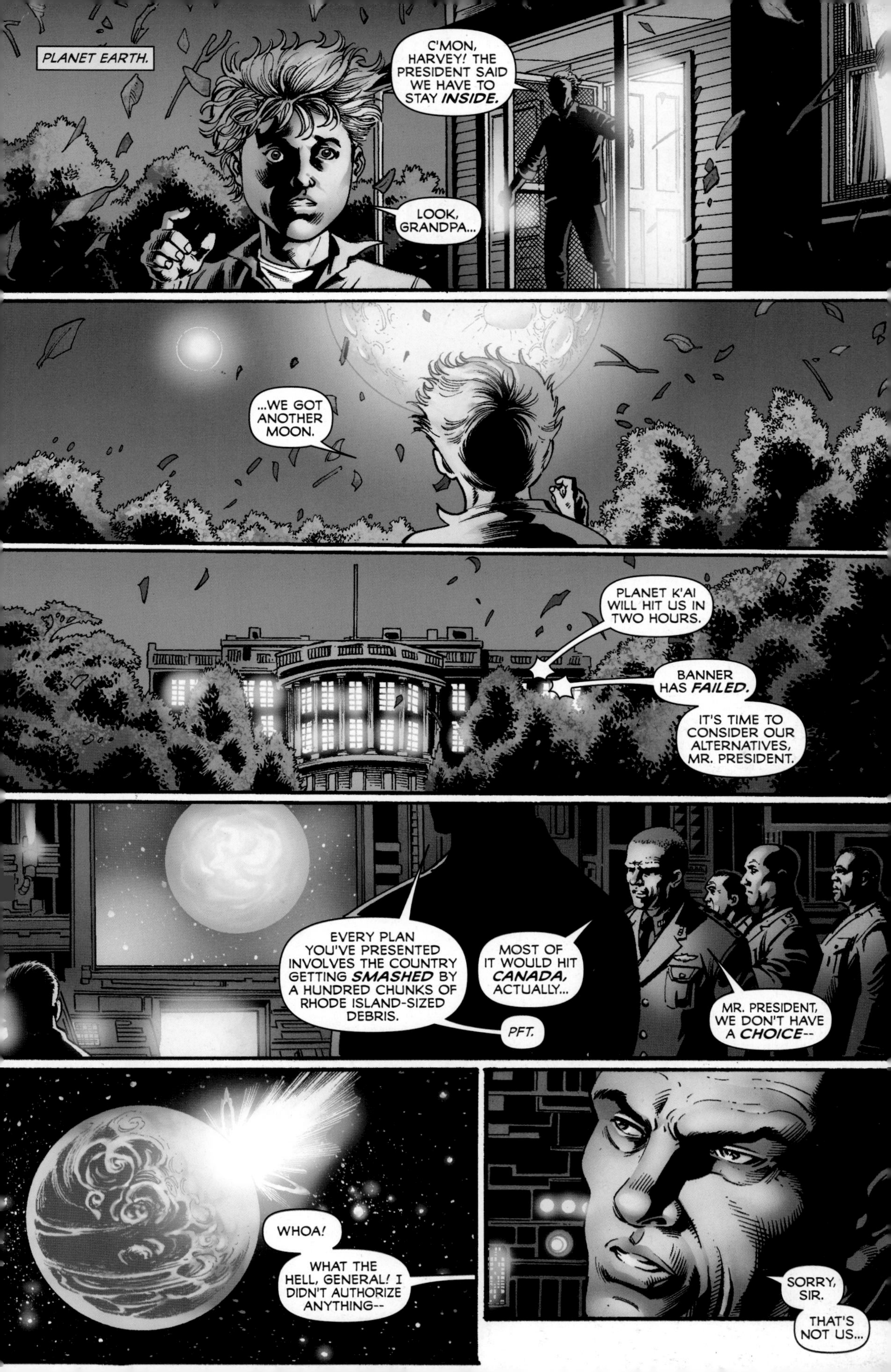
PLANET EARTH.
C'MON, HARVEY! THE PRESIDENT SAID WE HAVE TO STAY INSIDE.
LOOK, GRANDPA...
...WE GOT ANOTHER MOON.
PLANET K'AI WILL HIT US IN TWO HOURS.
BANNER HAS FAILED.
IT'S TIME TO CONSIDER OUR ALTERNATIVES, MR. PRESIDENT.
EVERY PLAN YOU'VE PRESENTED INVOLVES THE COUNTRY GETTING SMASHED BY A HUNDRED CHUNKS OF RHODE ISLAND-SIZED DEBRIS.
MOST OF IT WOULD HIT CANADA, ACTUALLY...
PFT.
MR. PRESIDENT, WE DON'T HAVE A CHOICE--
WHOA!
WHAT THE HELL, GENERAL! I DIDN'T AUTHORIZE ANYTHING--
SORRY, SIR.
THAT'S NOT US...

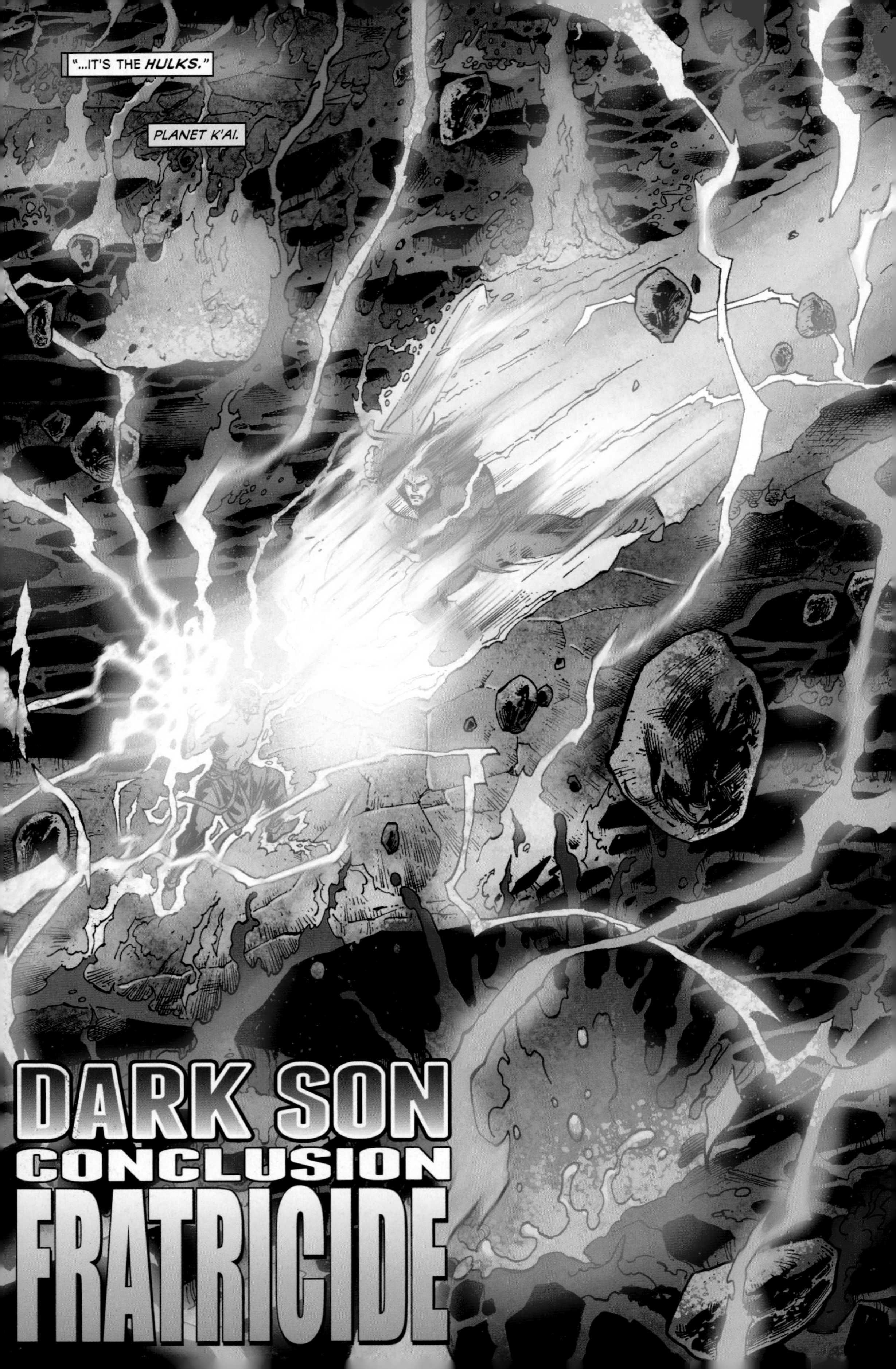
"...IT'S THE *HULKS.*"
PLANET K'AI.
DARK SON
CONCLUSION
FRATRICIDE

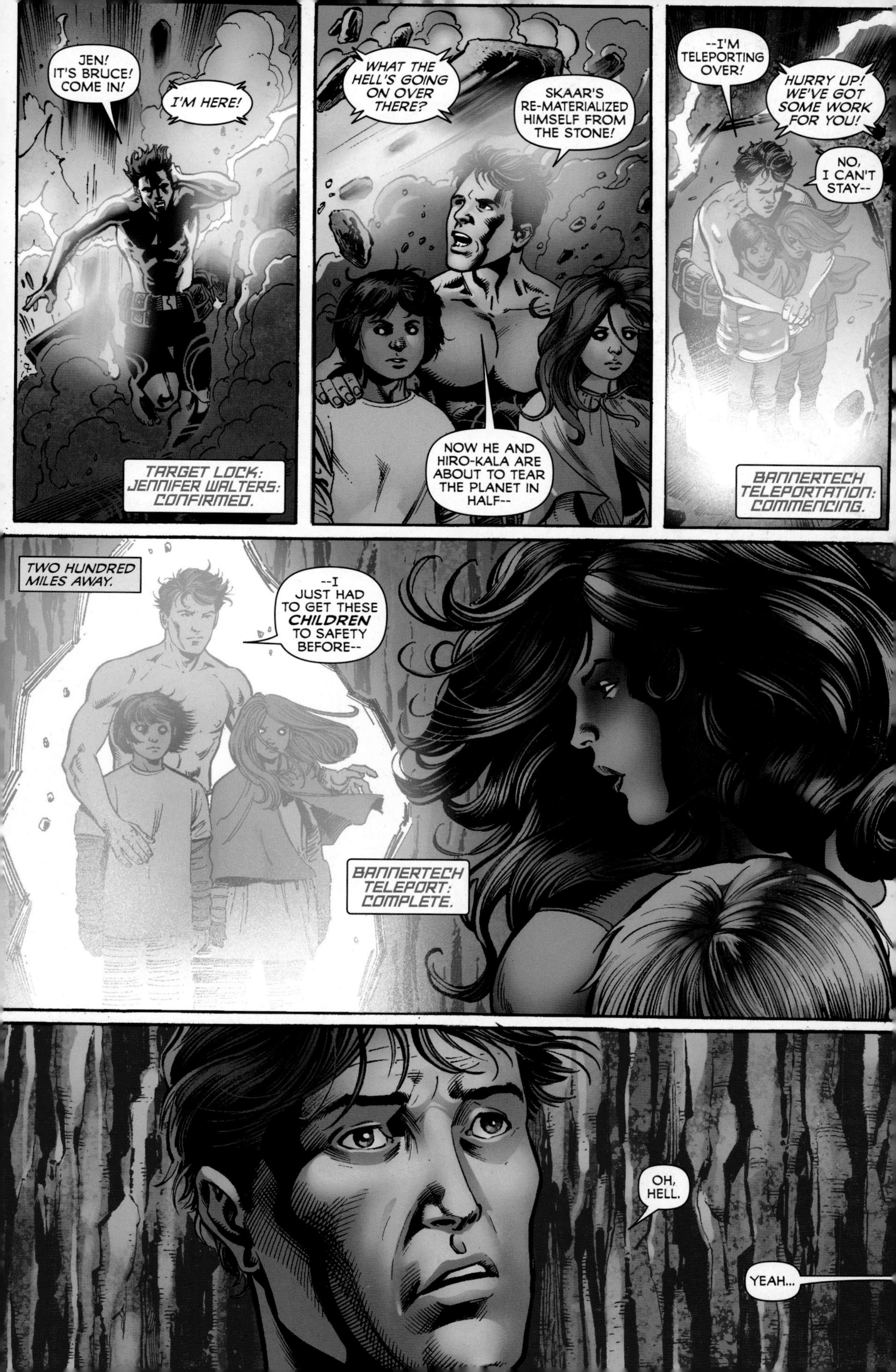
JEN! IT'S BRUCE! COME IN!
I'M HERE!
TARGET LOCK: JENNIFER WALTERS: CONFIRMED.
WHAT THE HELL'S GOING ON OVER THERE?
SKAAR'S RE-MATERIALIZED HIMSELF FROM THE STONE!
NOW HE AND HIRO-KALA ARE ABOUT TO TEAR THE PLANET IN HALF--
--I'M TELEPORTING OVER!
HURRY UP! WE'VE GOT SOME WORK FOR YOU!
NO, I CAN'T STAY--
BANNERTECH TELEPORTATION: COMMENCING.
TWO HUNDRED MILES AWAY.
--I JUST HAD TO GET THESE CHILDREN TO SAFETY BEFORE--
BANNERTECH TELEPORT: COMPLETE.
OH, HELL.
YEAH...

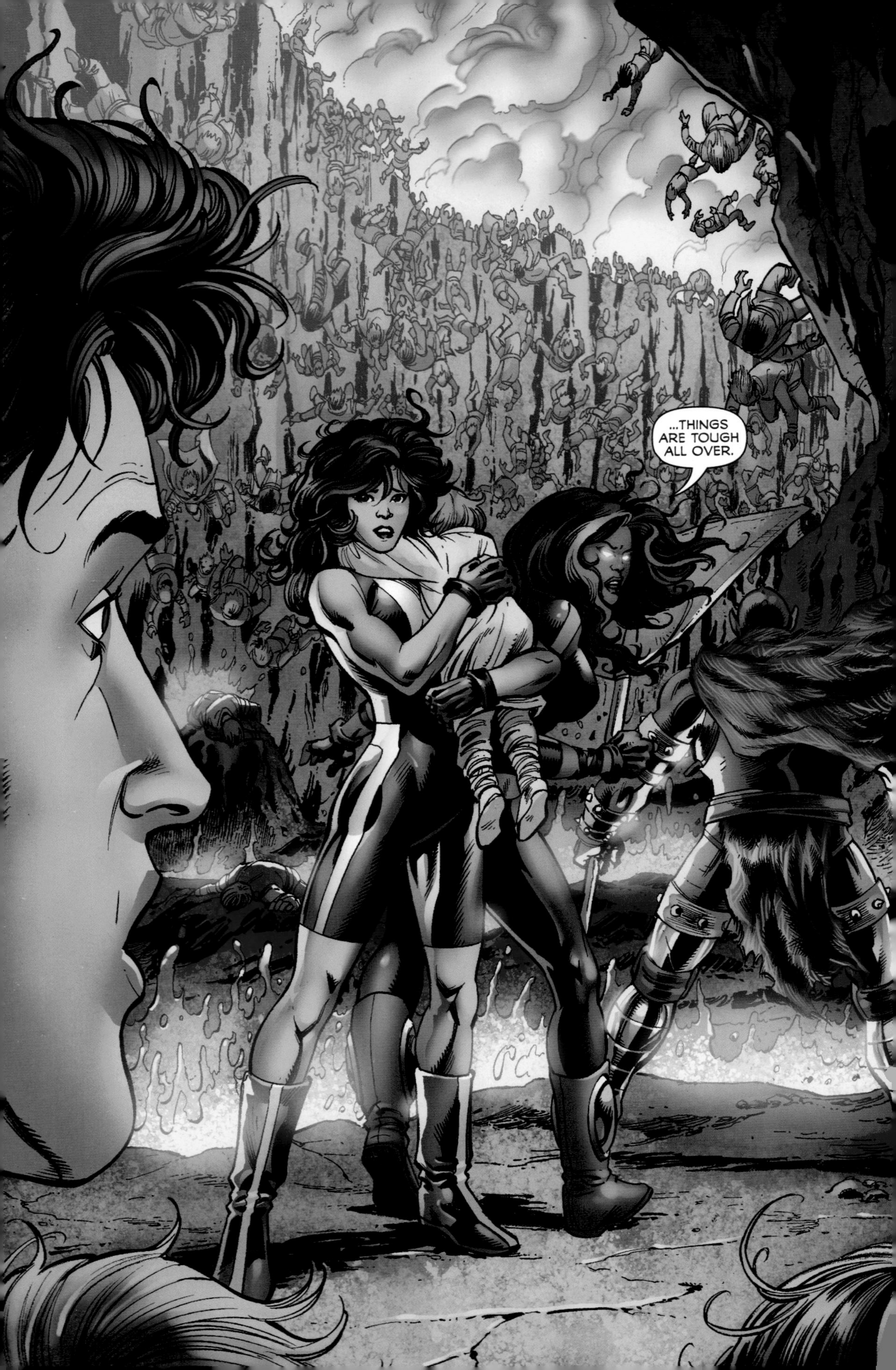
...THINGS ARE TOUGH ALL OVER.

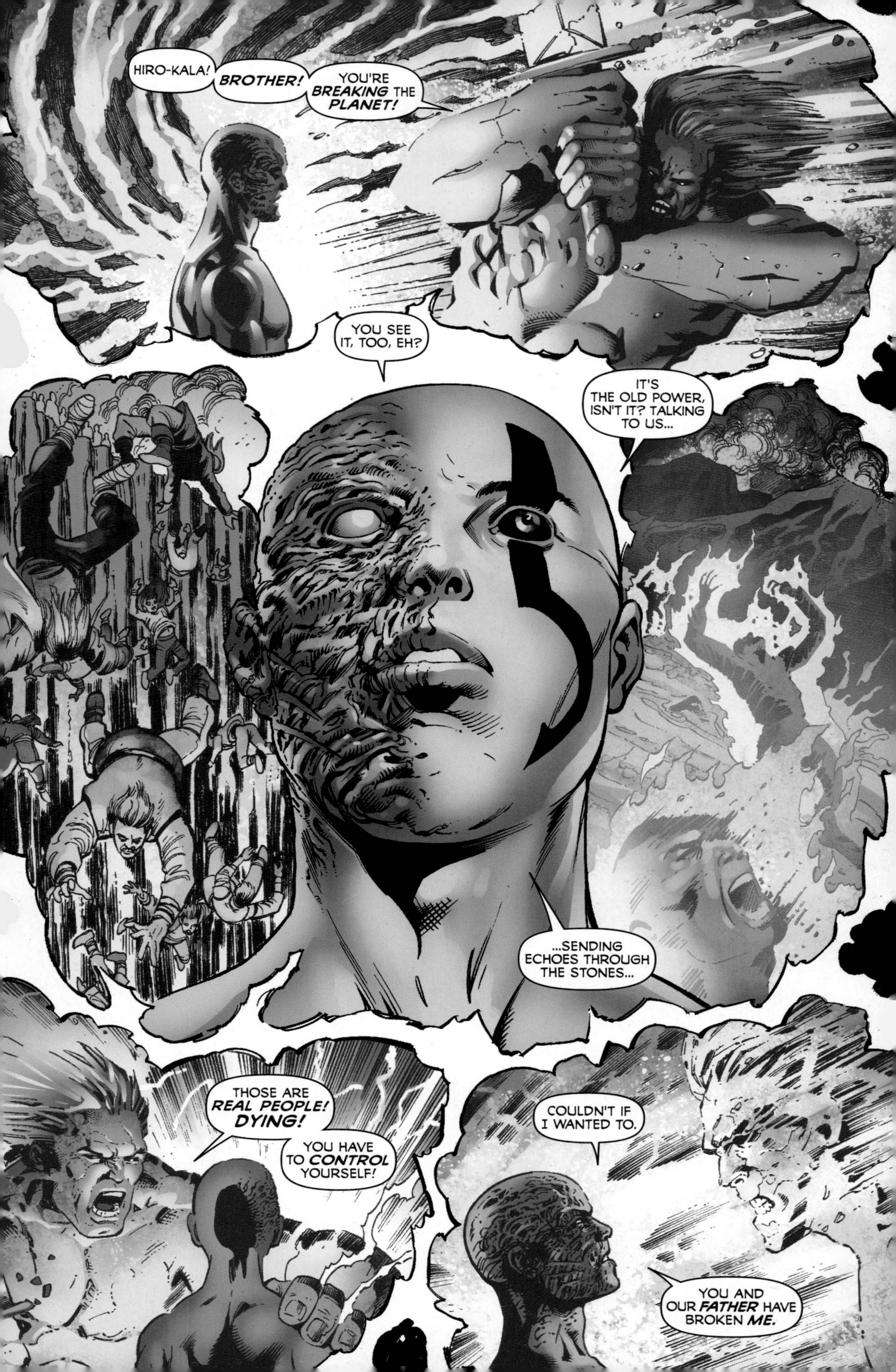
HIRO-KALA!
BROTHER!
YOU'RE BREAKING THE PLANET!
YOU SEE IT, TOO, EH?
IT'S THE OLD POWER, ISN'T IT? TALKING TO US...
...SENDING ECHOES THROUGH THE STONES...
THOSE ARE REAL PEOPLE! DYING!
YOU HAVE TO CONTROL YOURSELF!
COULDN'T IF I WANTED TO.
YOU AND OUR FATHER HAVE BROKEN ME.

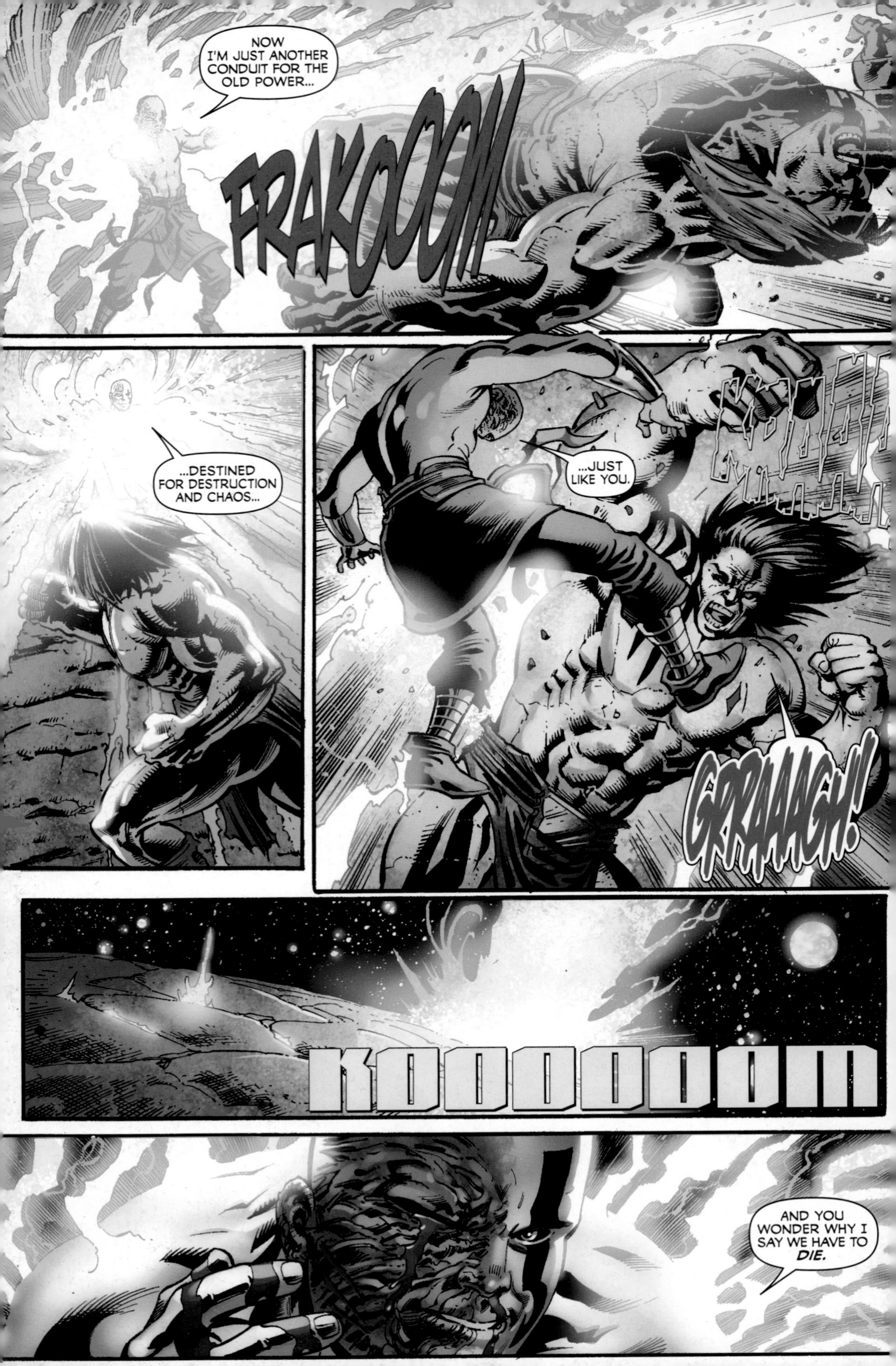
NOW I'M JUST ANOTHER CONDUIT FOR THE OLD POWER...
FRAKOOOM
...DESTINED FOR DESTRUCTION AND CHAOS...
...JUST LIKE YOU.
GRAAAGH!
KOOOOOOM
AND YOU WONDER WHY I SAY WE HAVE TO *DIE.*

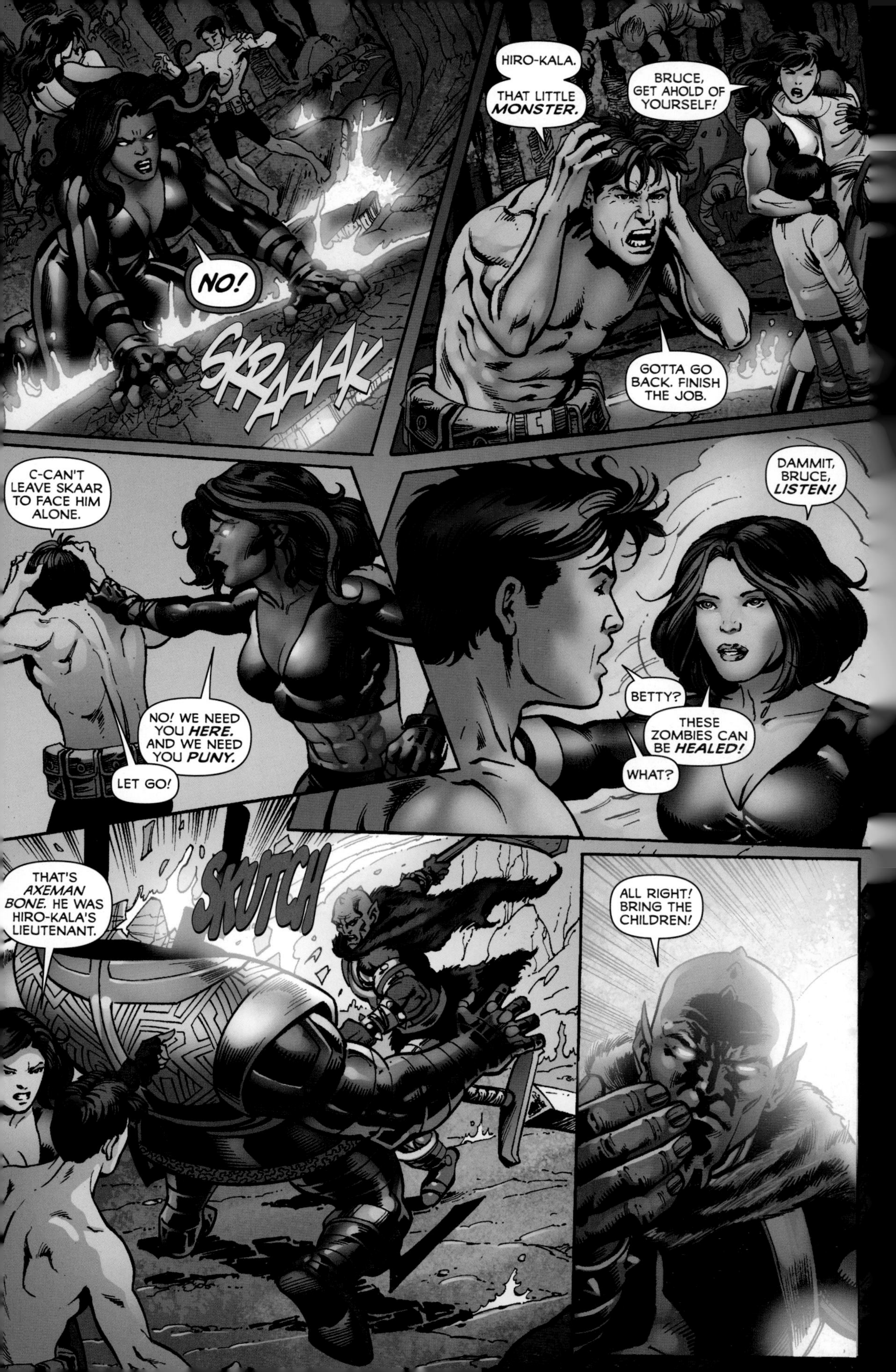
NO!
SKRAAAK
HIRO-KALA.
THAT LITTLE MONSTER.
BRUCE, GET AHOLD OF YOURSELF!
GOTTA GO BACK. FINISH THE JOB.
C-CAN'T LEAVE SKAAR TO FACE HIM ALONE.
NO! WE NEED YOU HERE. AND WE NEED YOU PUNY.
LET GO!
DAMMIT, BRUCE, LISTEN!
BETTY?
THESE ZOMBIES CAN BE HEALED!
WHAT?
THAT'S AXEMAN BONE. HE WAS HIRO-KALA'S LIEUTENANT.
SKUTCH
ALL RIGHT! BRING THE CHILDREN!

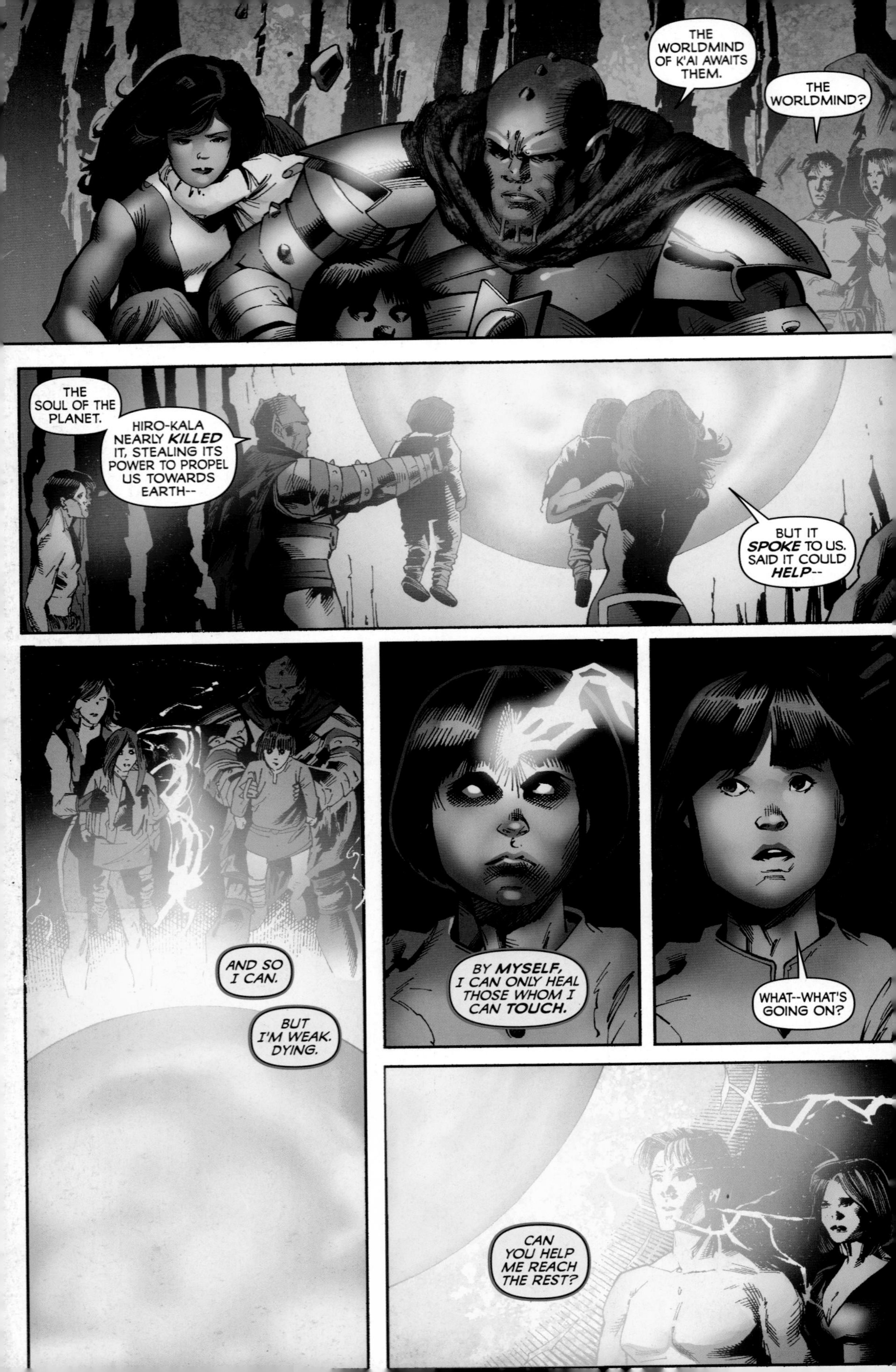
THE WORLDMIND OF K'AI AWAITS THEM.
THE WORLDMIND?
THE SOUL OF THE PLANET.
HIRO-KALA NEARLY KILLED IT, STEALING ITS POWER TO PROPEL US TOWARDS EARTH--
BUT IT SPOKE TO US. SAID IT COULD HELP--
AND SO I CAN.
BUT I'M WEAK. DYING.
BY MYSELF, I CAN ONLY HEAL THOSE WHOM I CAN TOUCH.
WHAT--WHAT'S GOING ON?
CAN YOU HELP ME REACH THE REST?

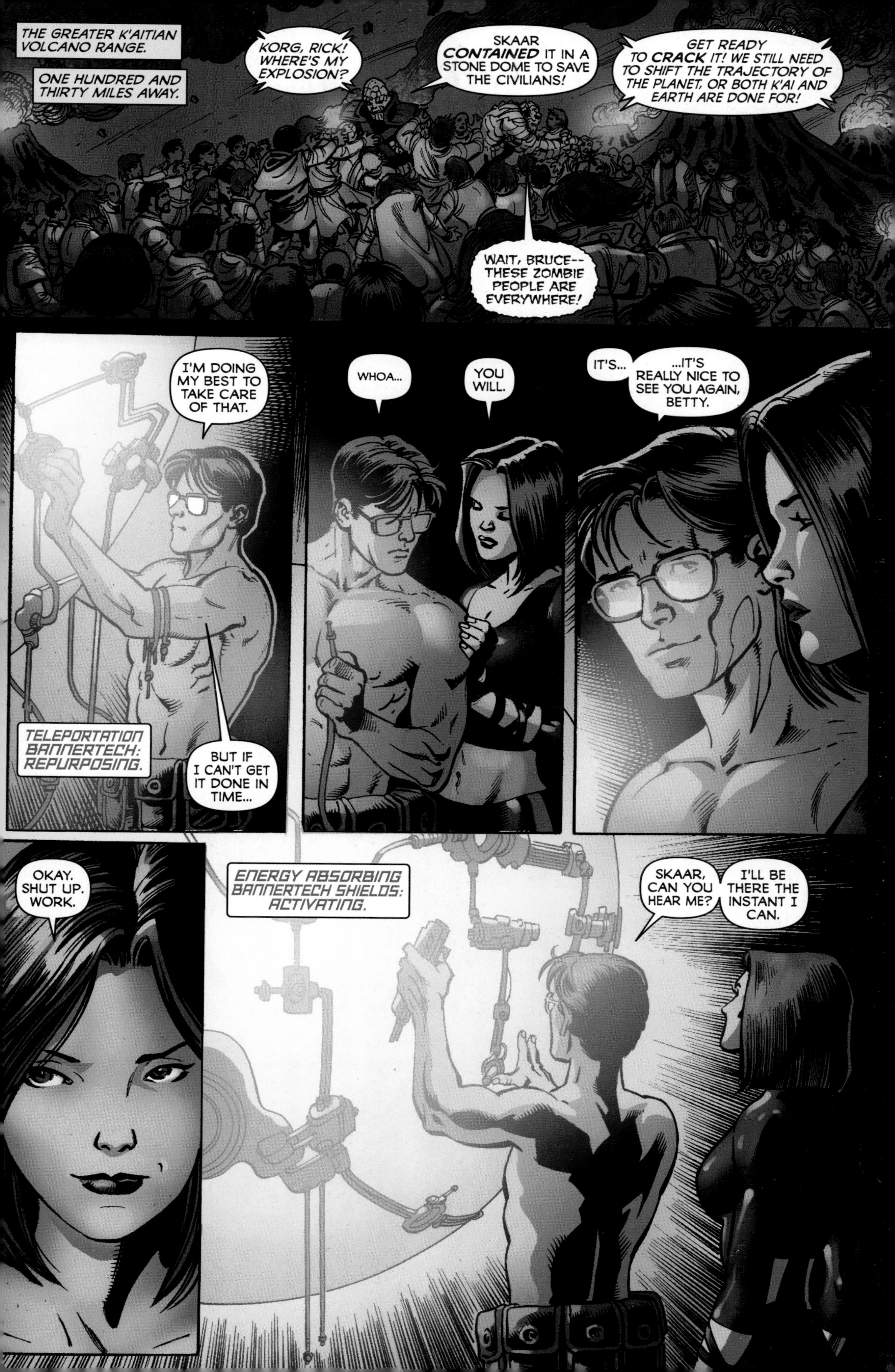
THE GREATER K'AITIAN VOLCANO RANGE.
ONE HUNDRED AND THIRTY MILES AWAY.
KORG, RICK! WHERE'S MY EXPLOSION?
SKAAR CONTAINED IT IN A STONE DOME TO SAVE THE CIVILIANS!
GET READY TO CRACK IT! WE STILL NEED TO SHIFT THE TRAJECTORY OF THE PLANET, OR BOTH K'AI AND EARTH ARE DONE FOR!
WAIT, BRUCE-- THESE ZOMBIE PEOPLE ARE EVERYWHERE!
I'M DOING MY BEST TO TAKE CARE OF THAT.
TELEPORTATION BANNERTECH: REPURPOSING.
BUT IF I CAN'T GET IT DONE IN TIME...
WHOA...
YOU WILL.
IT'S...
...IT'S REALLY NICE TO SEE YOU AGAIN, BETTY.
OKAY. SHUT UP. WORK.
ENERGY ABSORBING BANNERTECH SHIELDS: ACTIVATING.
SKAAR, CAN YOU HEAR ME?
I'LL BE THERE THE INSTANT I CAN.

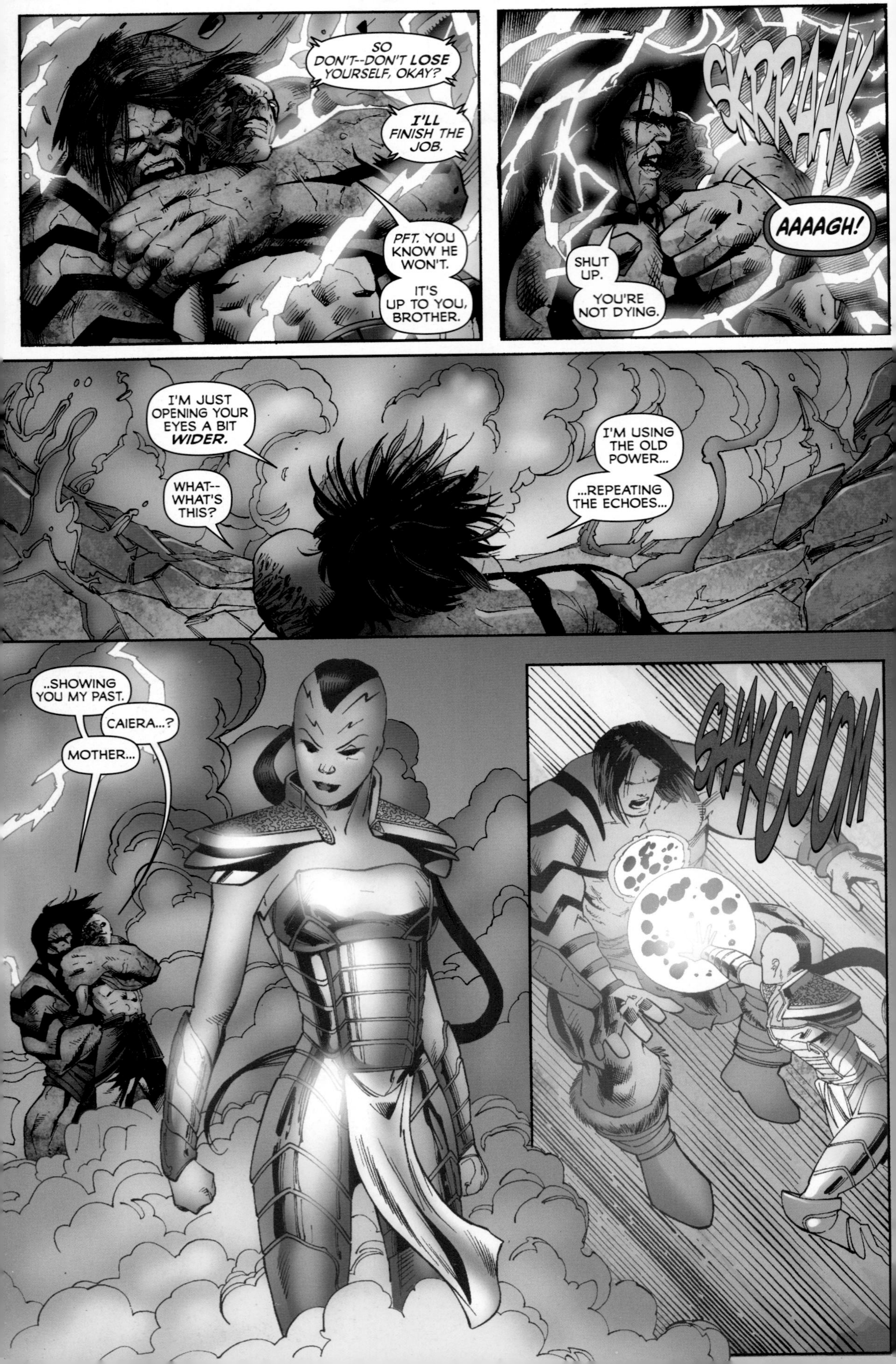

SO DON'T--DON'T LOSE YOURSELF, OKAY?
I'LL FINISH THE JOB.
PFT. YOU KNOW HE WON'T.
IT'S UP TO YOU, BROTHER.
SKRRAAK
AAAAGH!
SHUT UP.
YOU'RE NOT DYING.
I'M JUST OPENING YOUR EYES A BIT WIDER.
WHAT--WHAT'S THIS?
I'M USING THE OLD POWER...
...REPEATING THE ECHOES...
..SHOWING YOU MY PAST.
CAIERA...?
MOTHER...
SHKOOOM

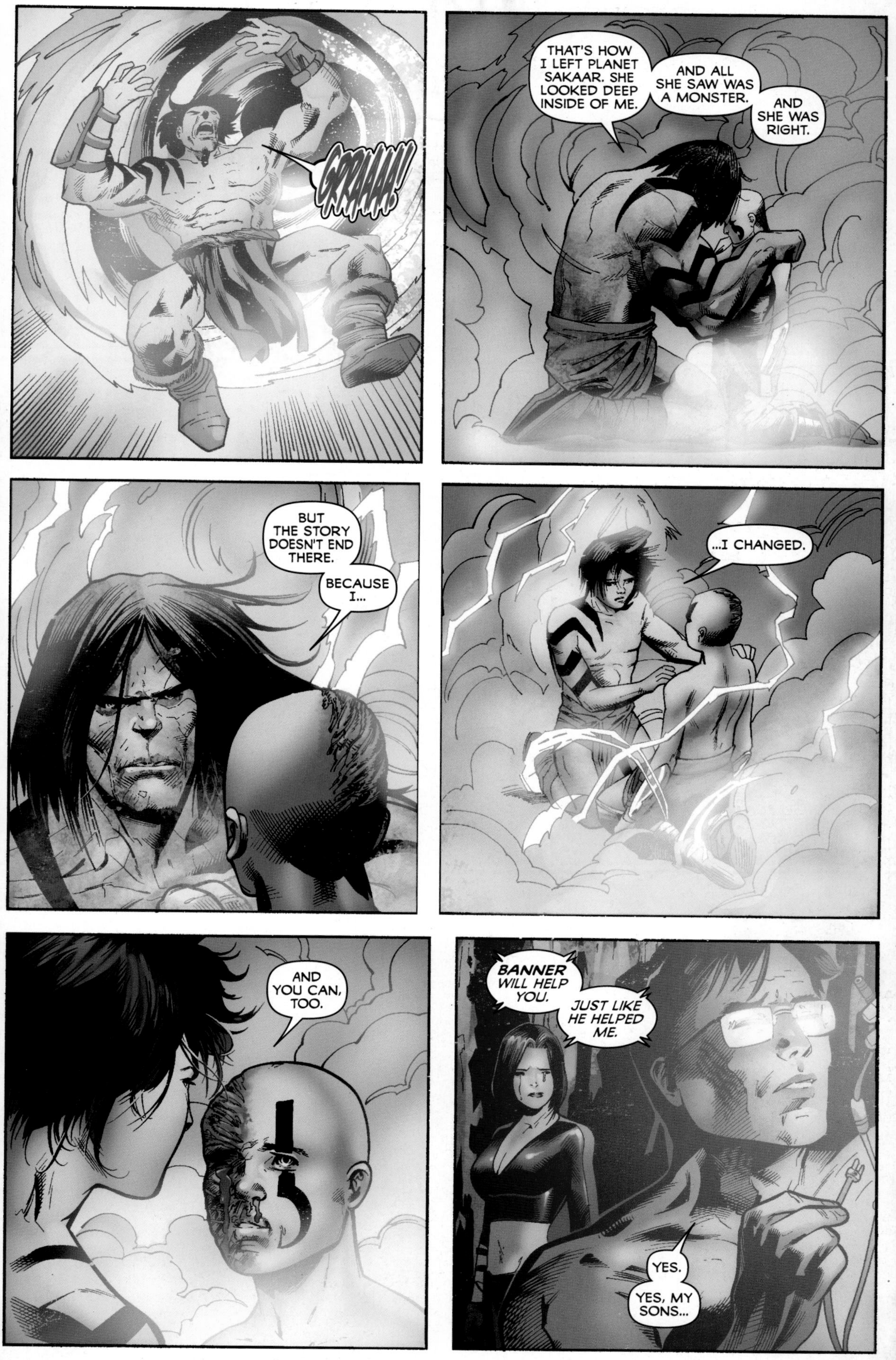
GRRAAAA!
THAT'S HOW I LEFT PLANET SAKAAR. SHE LOOKED DEEP INSIDE OF ME.
AND ALL SHE SAW WAS A MONSTER.
AND SHE WAS RIGHT.
BUT THE STORY DOESN'T END THERE.
BECAUSE I...
...I CHANGED.
AND YOU CAN, TOO.
BANNER WILL HELP YOU.
JUST LIKE HE HELPED ME.
YES.
YES, MY SONS...

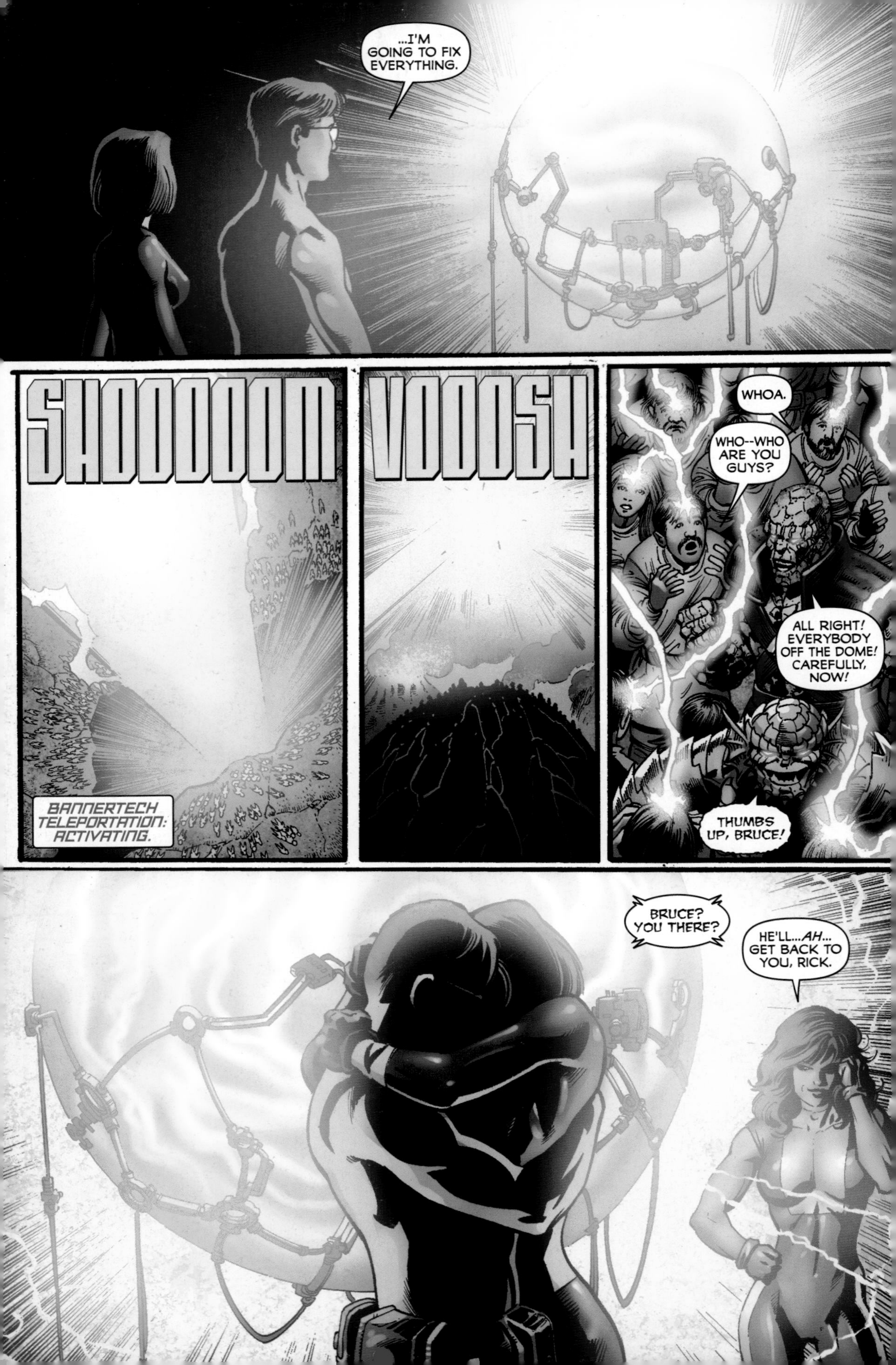
...I'M GOING TO FIX EVERYTHING.
SHOOOOOM
BANNERTECH TELEPORTATION: ACTIVATING.
VOOOSH
WHOA.
WHO--WHO ARE YOU GUYS?
ALL RIGHT! EVERYBODY OFF THE DOME! CAREFULLY, NOW!
THUMBS UP, BRUCE!
BRUCE? YOU THERE?
HE'LL...AH... GET BACK TO YOU, RICK.

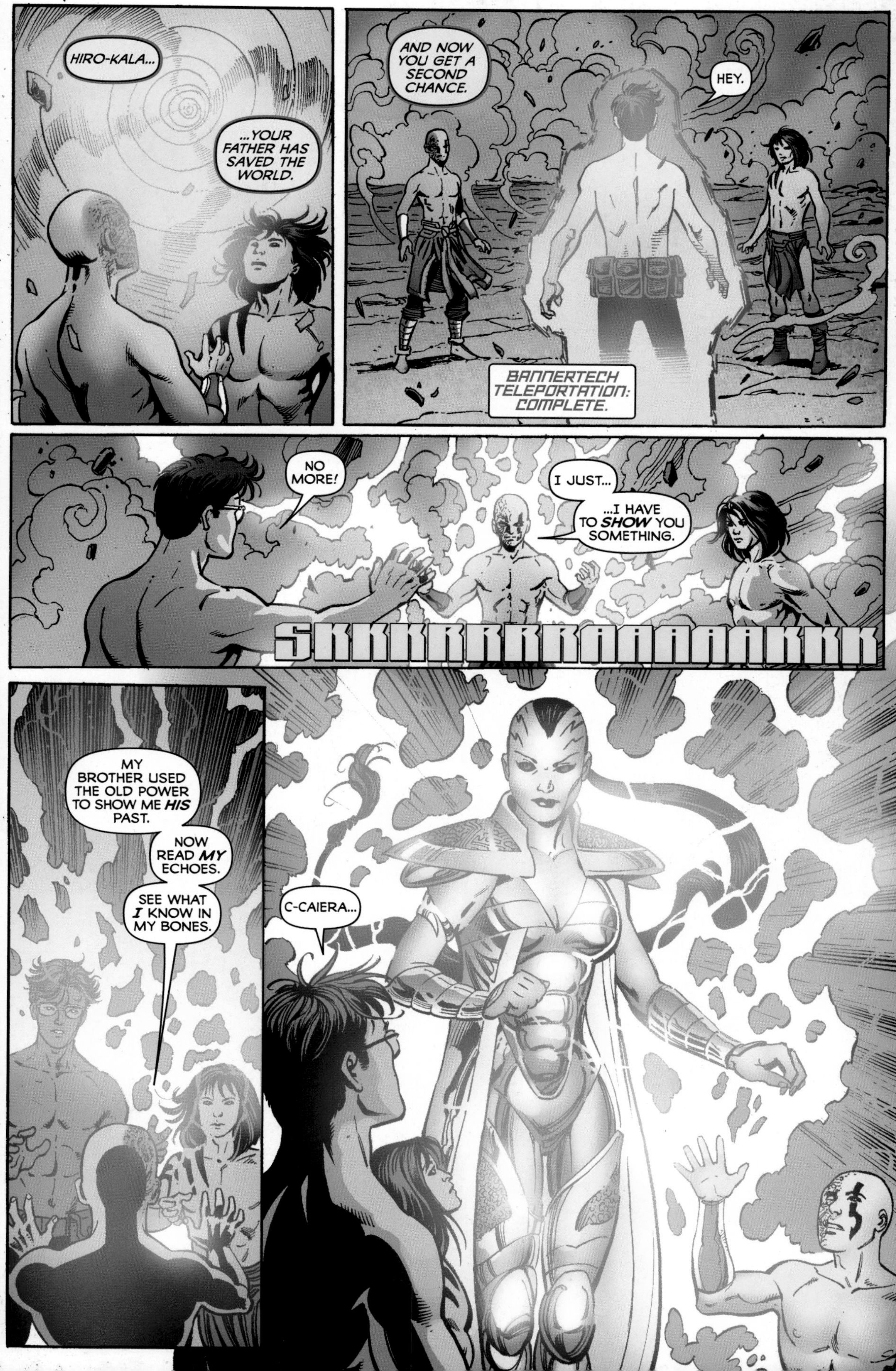
HIRO-KALA...
...YOUR FATHER HAS SAVED THE WORLD.
AND NOW YOU GET A SECOND CHANCE.
HEY.
BANNERTECH TELEPORTATION: COMPLETE.
NO MORE!
I JUST...
...I HAVE TO SHOW YOU SOMETHING.
SKKKRRRRRAAAAAKKK
MY BROTHER USED THE OLD POWER TO SHOW ME HIS PAST.
NOW READ MY ECHOES.
SEE WHAT I KNOW IN MY BONES.
C-CAIERA...

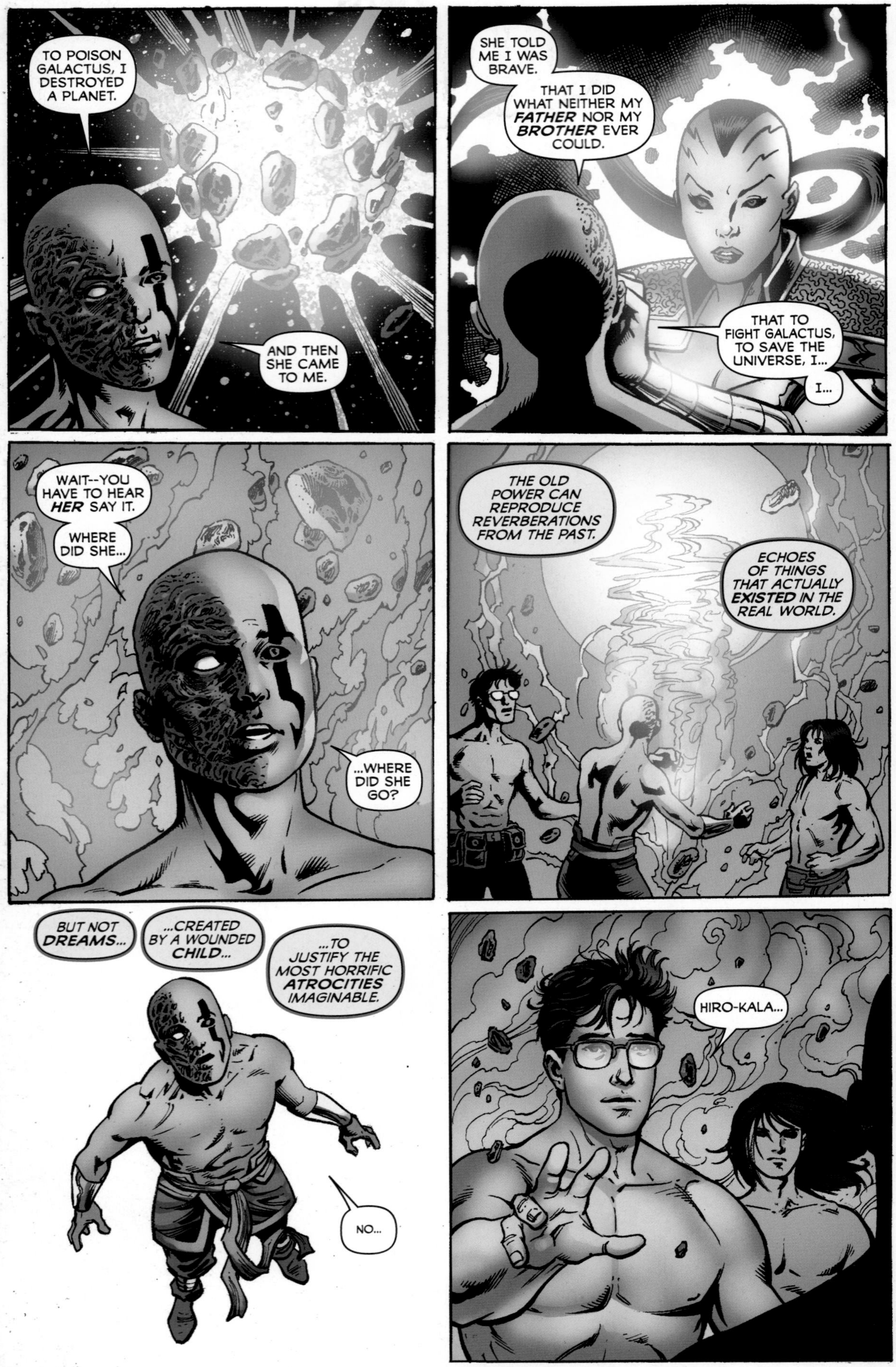
TO POISON GALACTUS, I DESTROYED A PLANET.
AND THEN SHE CAME TO ME.
SHE TOLD ME I WAS BRAVE.
THAT I DID WHAT NEITHER MY FATHER NOR MY BROTHER EVER COULD.
THAT TO FIGHT GALACTUS, TO SAVE THE UNIVERSE, I...
I...
WAIT--YOU HAVE TO HEAR HER SAY IT.
WHERE DID SHE...
...WHERE DID SHE GO?
THE OLD POWER CAN REPRODUCE REVERBERATIONS FROM THE PAST.
ECHOES OF THINGS THAT ACTUALLY EXISTED IN THE REAL WORLD.
BUT NOT DREAMS...
...CREATED BY A WOUNDED CHILD...
...TO JUSTIFY THE MOST HORRIFIC ATROCITIES IMAGINABLE.
NO...
HIRO-KALA...

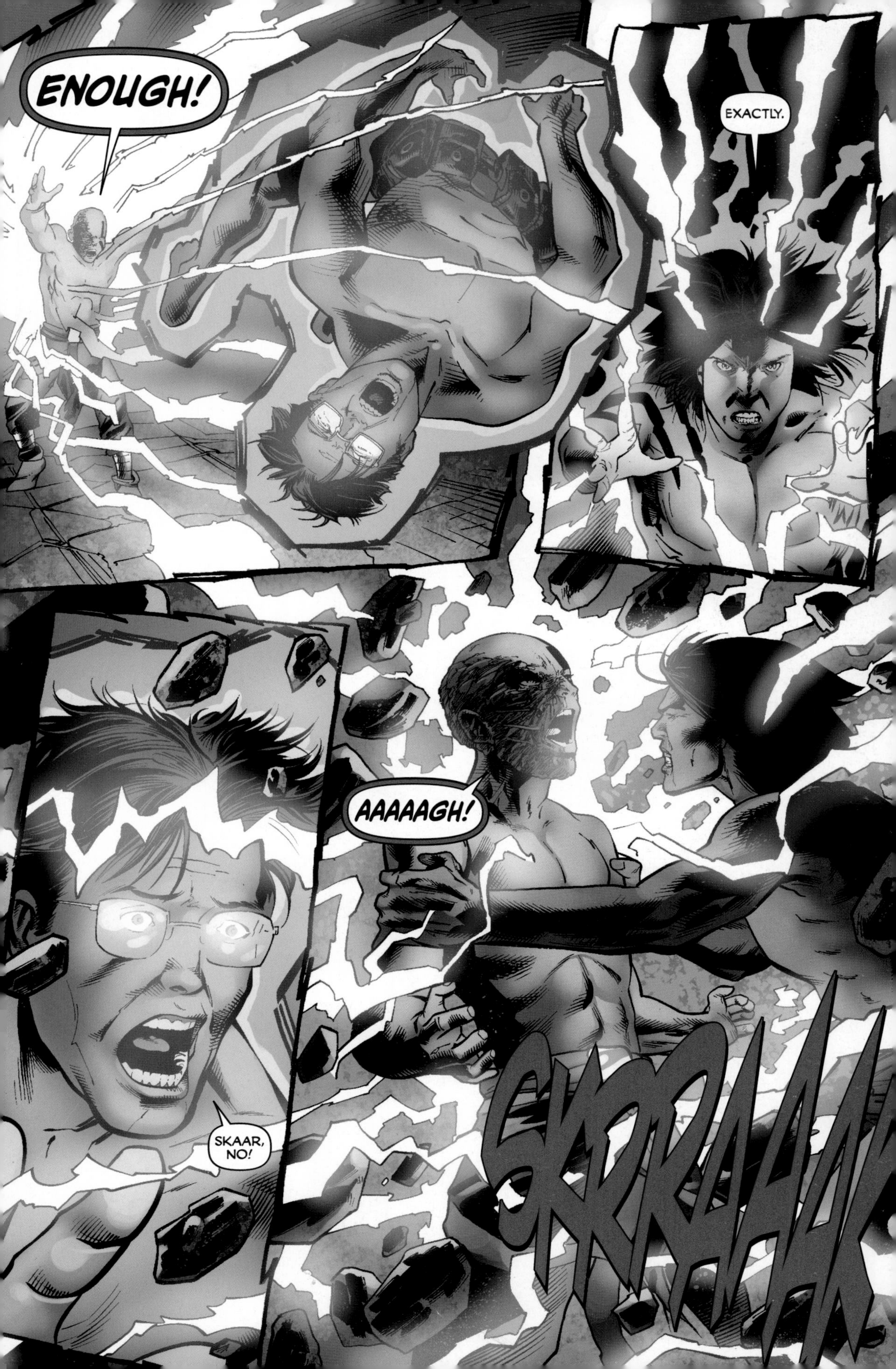
ENOUGH!
EXACTLY.
SKAAR, NO!
AAAAAGH!
SKRAAAAK

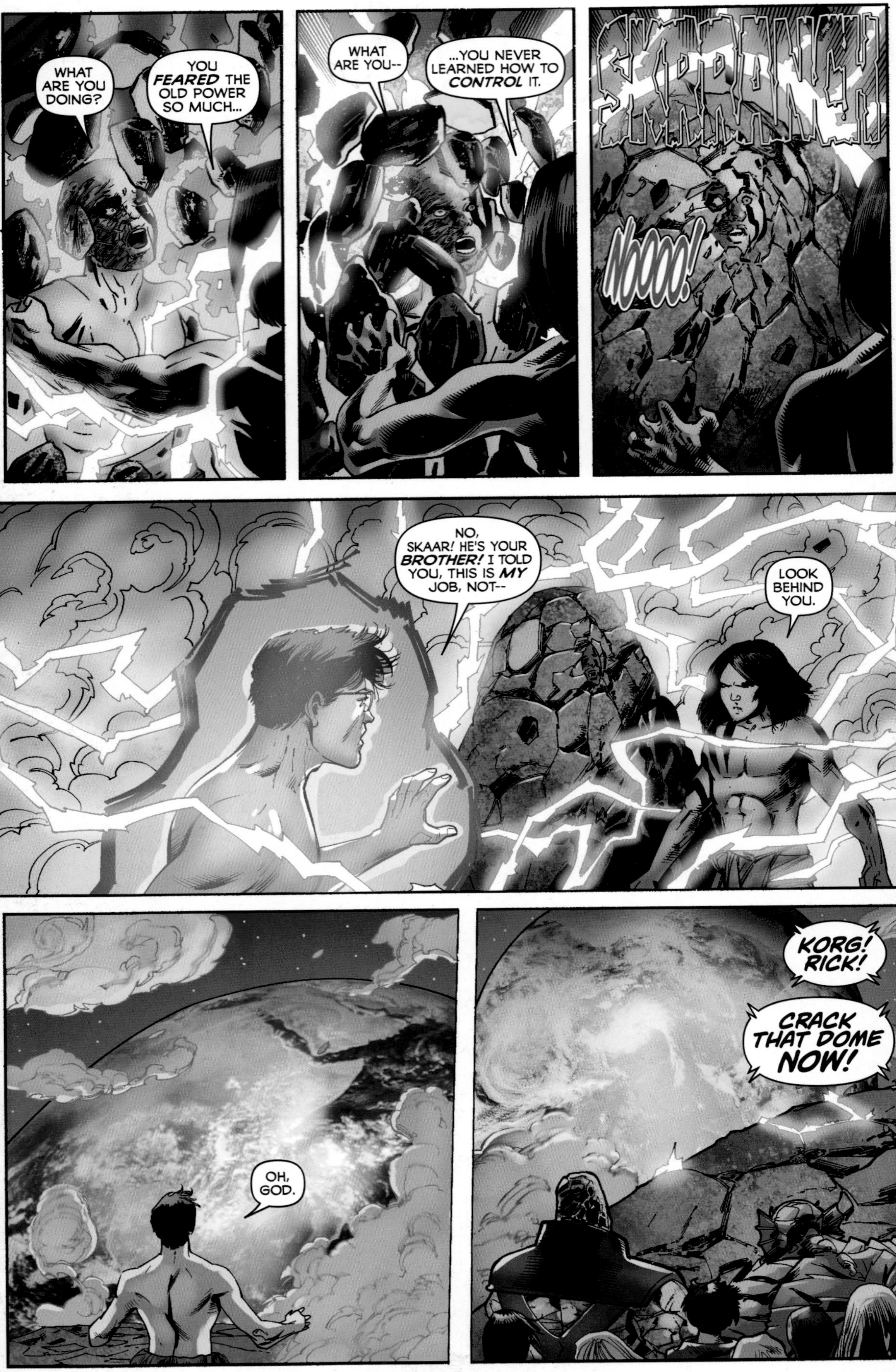
WHAT ARE YOU DOING?
YOU FEARED THE OLD POWER SO MUCH...
WHAT ARE YOU--
...YOU NEVER LEARNED HOW TO CONTROL IT.
SKRAKANCH
NOOOO!
NO, SKAAR! HE'S YOUR BROTHER! I TOLD YOU, THIS IS MY JOB, NOT--
LOOK BEHIND YOU.
OH, GOD.
KORG! RICK!
CRACK THAT DOME NOW!

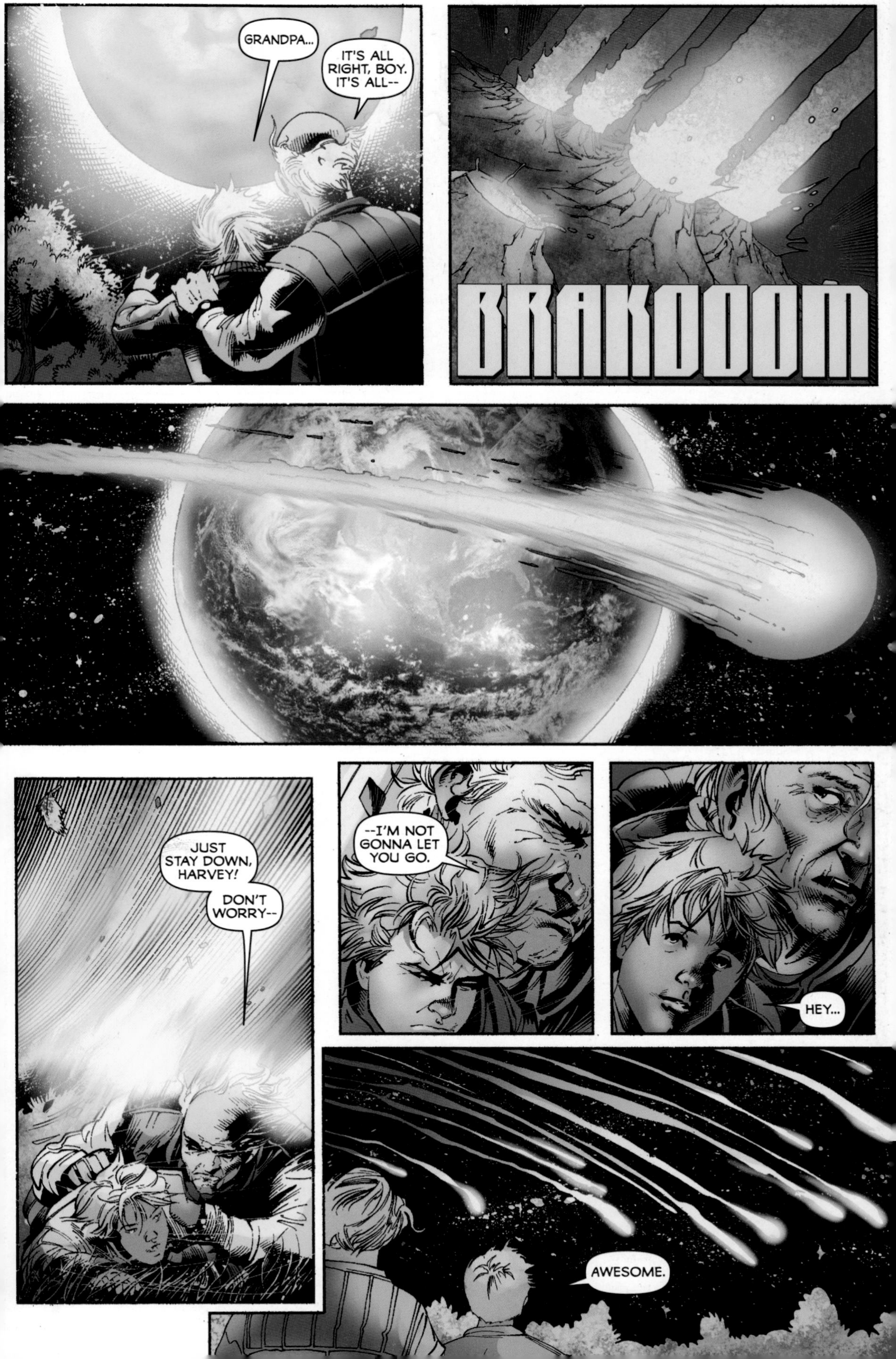
GRANDPA...
IT'S ALL RIGHT, BOY. IT'S ALL--
BRAKOOOM
JUST STAY DOWN, HARVEY!
DON'T WORRY--
--I'M NOT GONNA LET YOU GO.
HEY...
AWESOME.

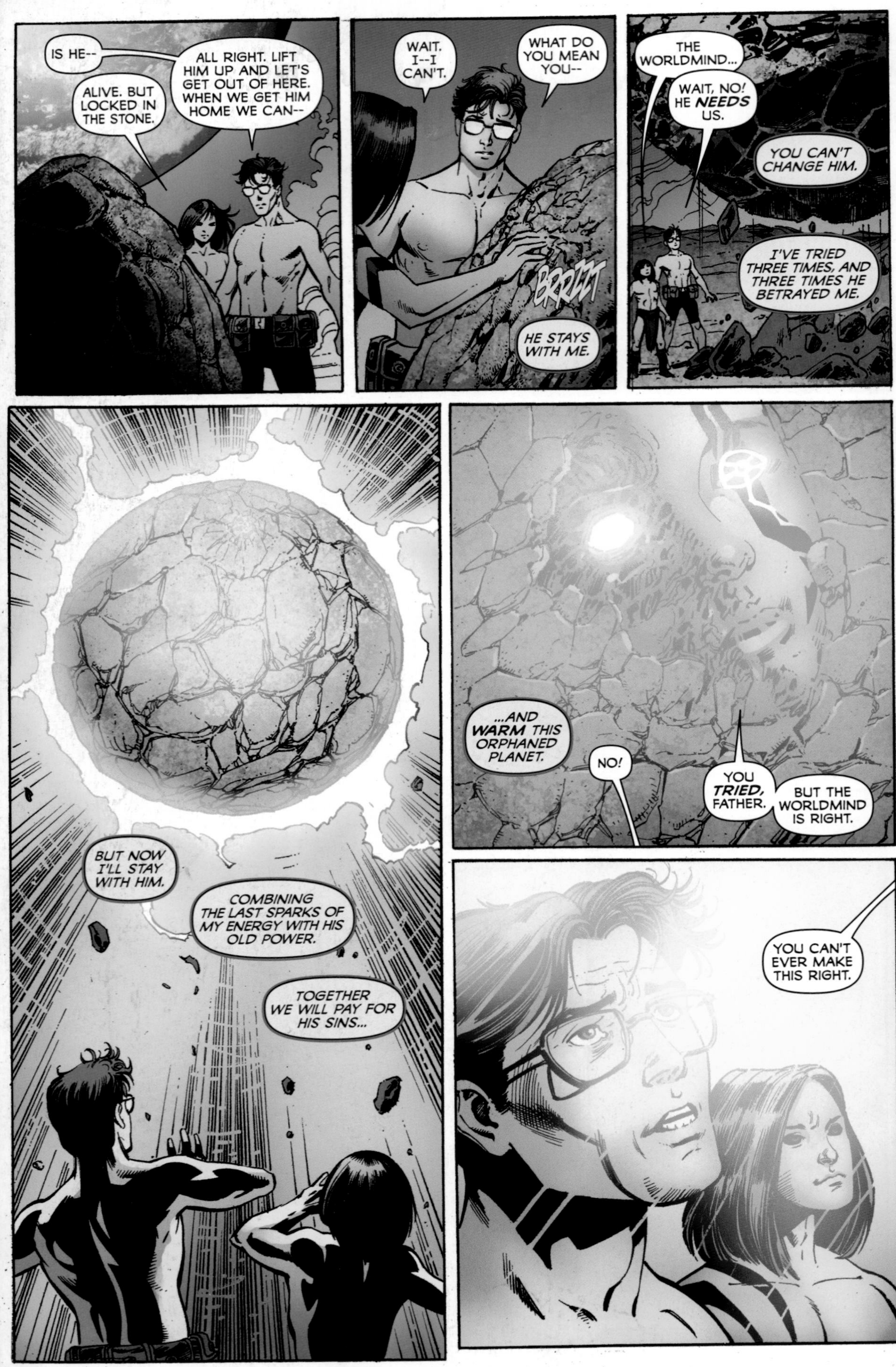
IS HE--
ALIVE. BUT LOCKED IN THE STONE.
ALL RIGHT. LIFT HIM UP AND LET'S GET OUT OF HERE. WHEN WE GET HIM HOME WE CAN--
WAIT. I--I CAN'T.
WHAT DO YOU MEAN YOU--
BRRZZT
HE STAYS WITH ME.
THE WORLDMIND...
WAIT, NO! HE NEEDS US.
YOU CAN'T CHANGE HIM.
I'VE TRIED THREE TIMES, AND THREE TIMES HE BETRAYED ME.
BUT NOW I'LL STAY WITH HIM.
COMBINING THE LAST SPARKS OF MY ENERGY WITH HIS OLD POWER.
TOGETHER WE WILL PAY FOR HIS SINS...
...AND WARM THIS ORPHANED PLANET.
NO!
YOU TRIED, FATHER.
BUT THE WORLDMIND IS RIGHT.
YOU CAN'T EVER MAKE THIS RIGHT.

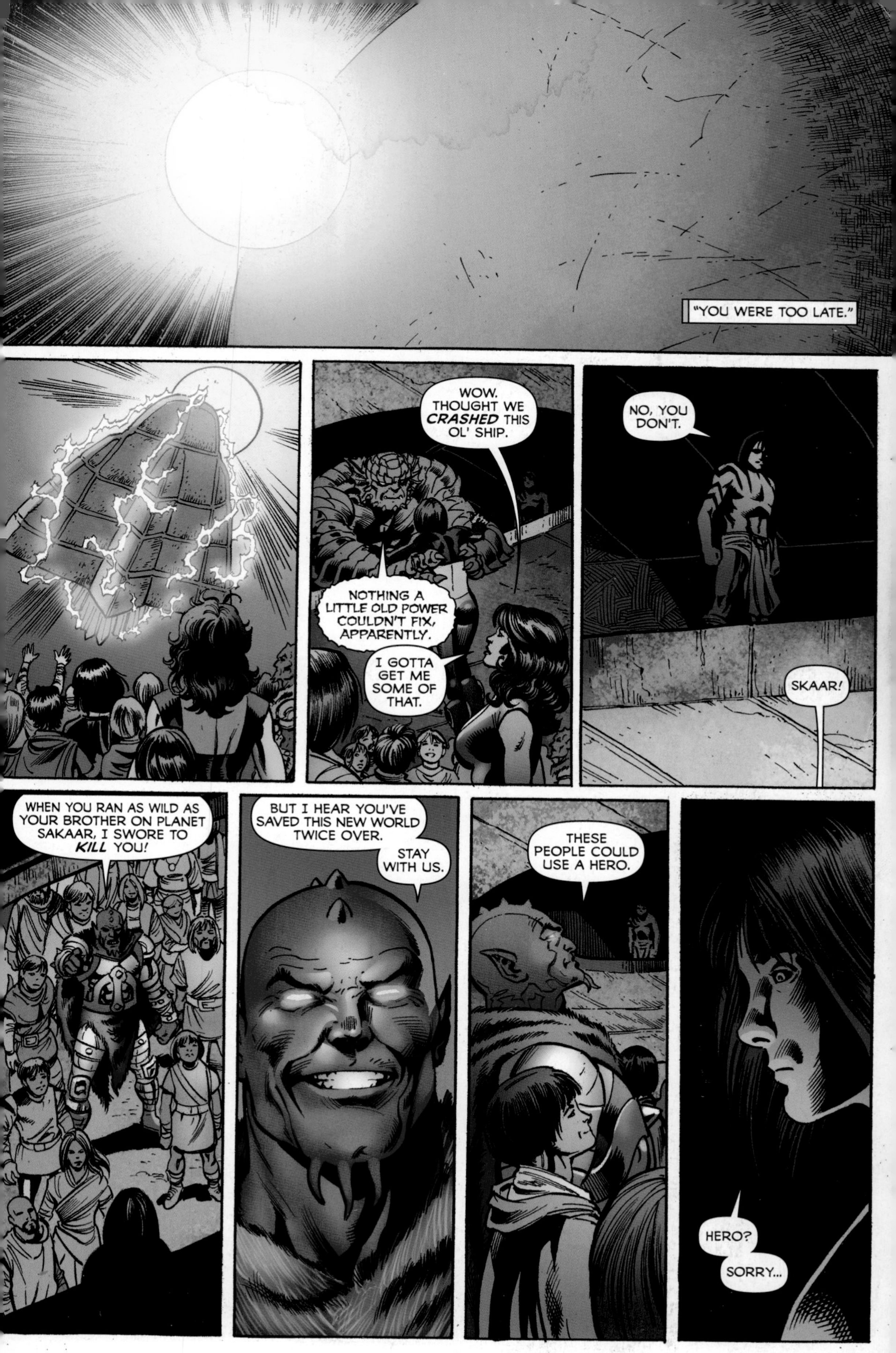
"YOU WERE TOO LATE."
WOW. THOUGHT WE *CRASHED* THIS OL' SHIP.
NOTHING A LITTLE OLD POWER COULDN'T FIX, APPARENTLY.
I GOTTA GET ME SOME OF THAT.
NO, YOU DON'T.
SKAAR!
WHEN YOU RAN AS WILD AS YOUR BROTHER ON PLANET SAKAAR, I SWORE TO *KILL* YOU!
BUT I HEAR YOU'VE SAVED THIS NEW WORLD TWICE OVER.
STAY WITH US.
THESE PEOPLE COULD USE A HERO.
HERO?
SORRY...

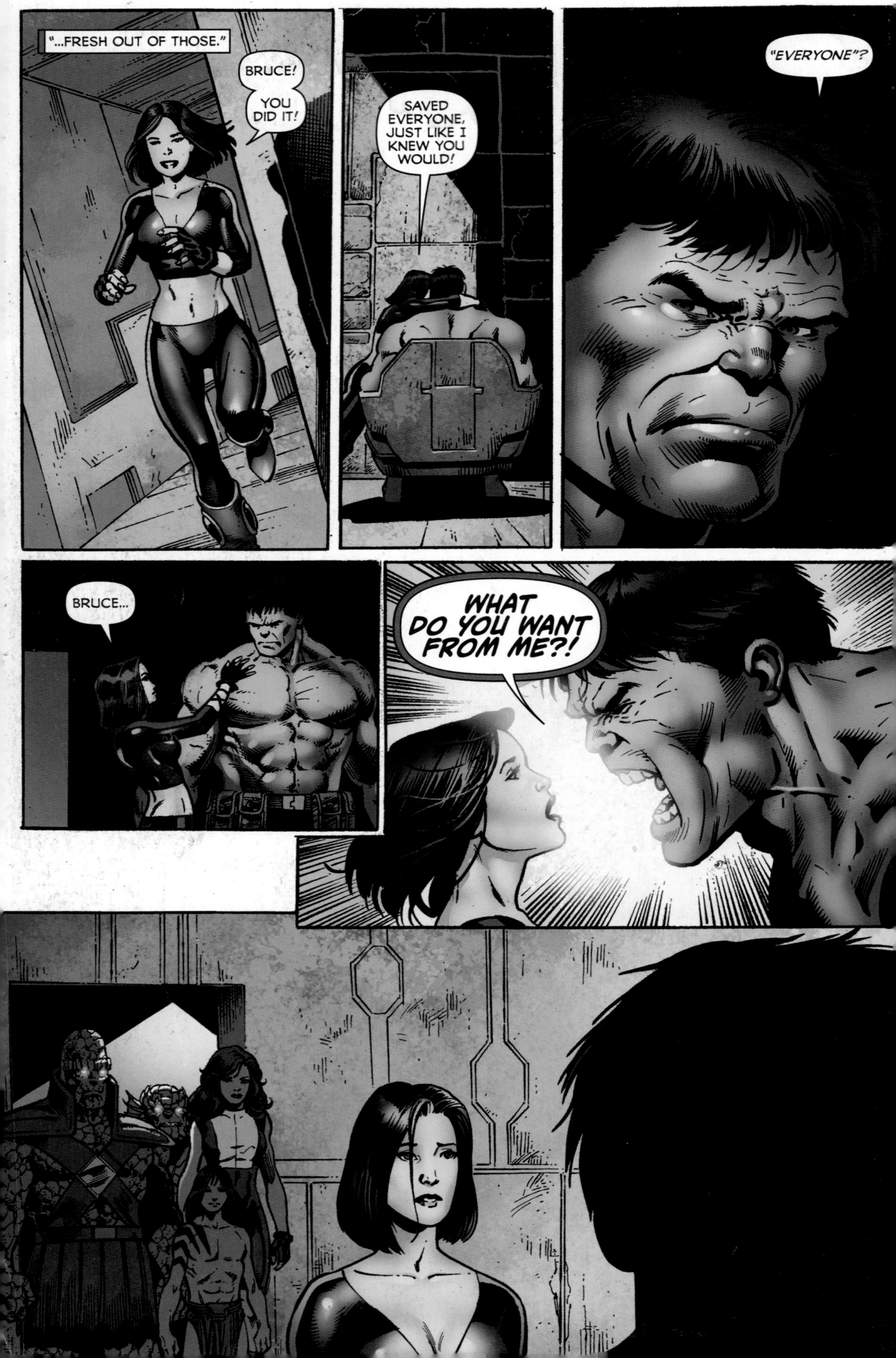
"...FRESH OUT OF THOSE."
BRUCE!
YOU DID IT!
SAVED EVERYONE, JUST LIKE I KNEW YOU WOULD!
"EVERYONE"?
BRUCE...
WHAT DO YOU WANT FROM ME?!

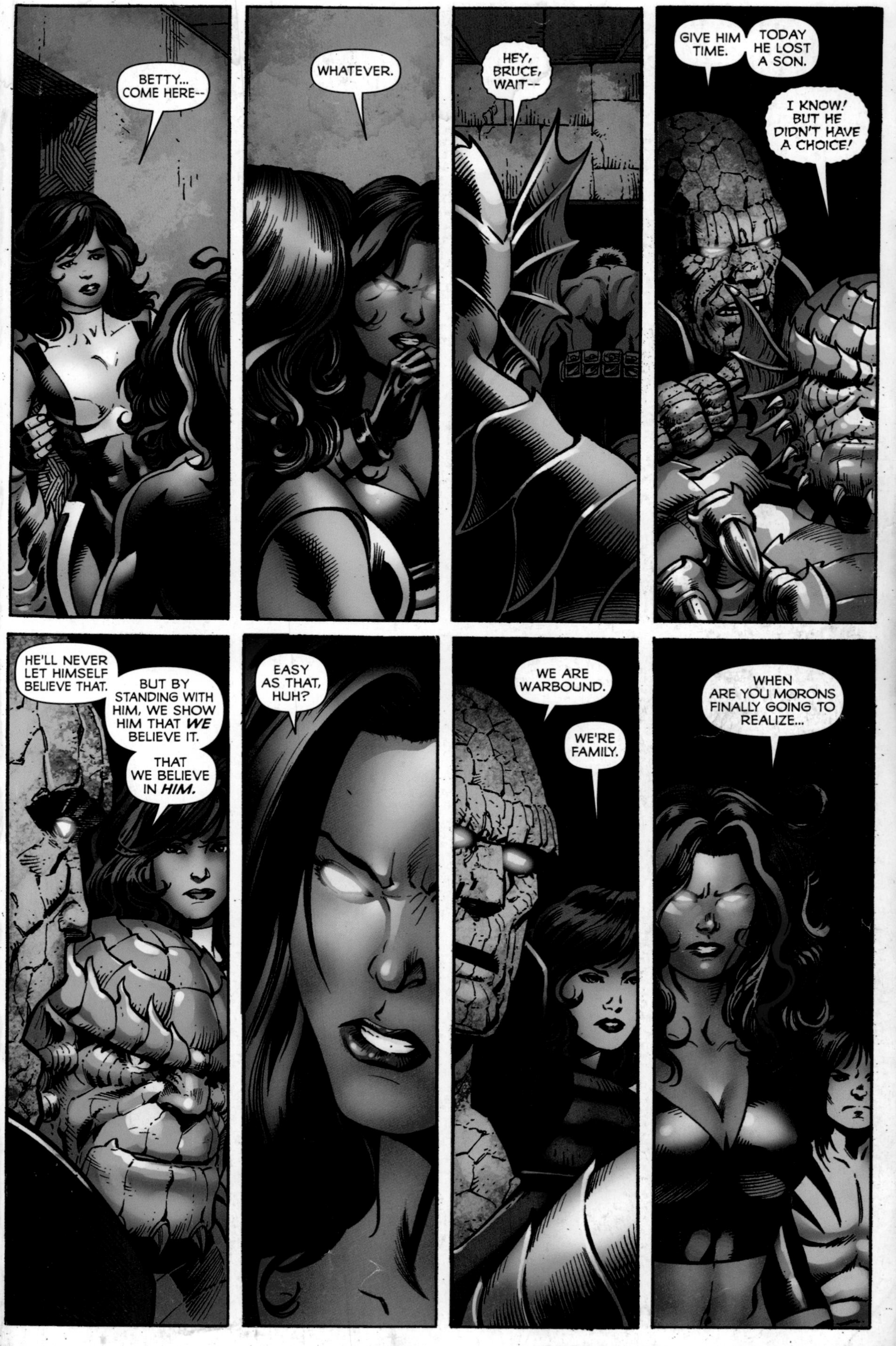
BETTY... COME HERE--
WHATEVER.
HEY, BRUCE, WAIT--
GIVE HIM TIME.
TODAY HE LOST A SON.
I KNOW! BUT HE DIDN'T HAVE A CHOICE!
HE'LL NEVER LET HIMSELF BELIEVE THAT.
BUT BY STANDING WITH HIM, WE SHOW HIM THAT WE BELIEVE IT.
THAT WE BELIEVE IN HIM.
EASY AS THAT, HUH?
WE ARE WARBOUND.
WE'RE FAMILY.
WHEN ARE YOU MORONS FINALLY GOING TO REALIZE...

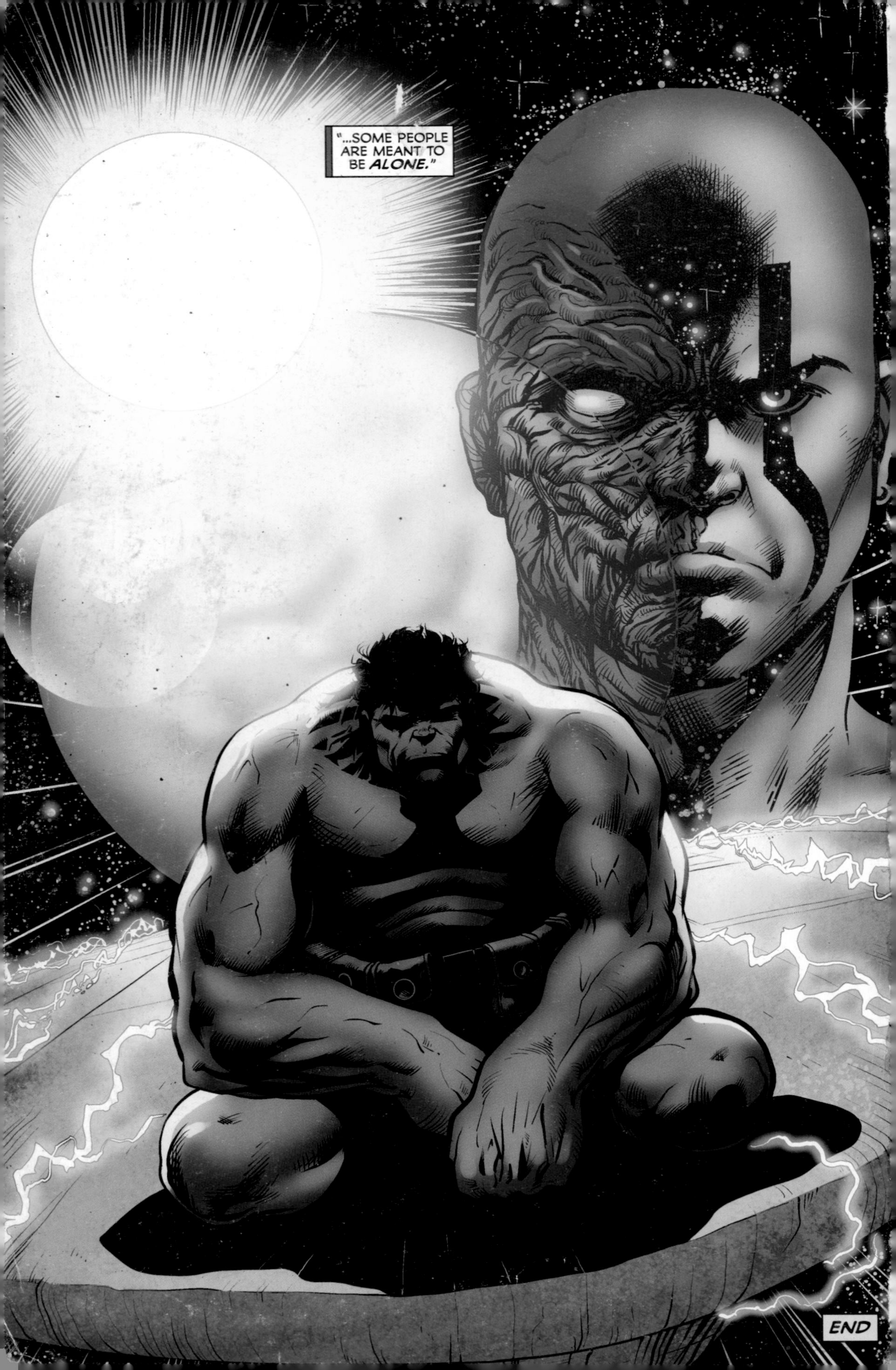
"...SOME PEOPLE ARE MEANT TO BE *ALONE.*"
END